# SPECIAL RESEARCH METHODS FOR GERONTOLOGY

**Editors:**
**M. Powell Lawton**
**A. Regula Herzog**

**Jon A. Hendricks, Series Editor**
***Society and Aging***

Baywood Publishing Company, Inc.
Amityville, New York

Printed in the United States of America.

Library of Congress Catalog Card Number: 88-33298
ISBN: 0-89503-053-5 (Paper)
ISBN: 0-89503-061-6 (Cloth)

**Library of Congress Cataloging-in-Publication Data**

**Main entry under title:**

Special research methods for gerontology.

(Society and aging)
Includes bibliographies.
1. Gerontology – Research – Methodology.
2. Gerontology – Longitudinal studies.
I. Lawton, M. Powell (Mortimer Powell),
1923- . II. Herzog, A. Regula (Anna
Regula), 1941- . II. Series.
[DNLM: 1. Geriatrics. 2. Longitudinal
Studies. 3. Research – methods. WT 29 S7406]
HQ1061.S678 1989 305.2'6'072 88-33298
ISBN 0-89503-061-6
ISBN 0-89503-053-5 (pbk.)

# Introduction

*M. Powell Lawton*
*A. Regula Herzog*

The growth of the over-sixty-five population and the recognition of the enormous implications of this growth for the well-being of our society has brought with it a national investment in research dealing with aging that would have seemed impossible two decades ago. In the early days of gerontology, methods used in research on younger age groups were often simply imported for use with the aged. However, experience quickly led to the recognition that studying older adults posed some special problems and that traditional methods had to be adjusted to take account of age-related differences. Such expertise, while accumulating, has been slow in finding its way into the research literature. To some extent then, every new investigator in gerontology must recapitulate the learning-by-doing process. Thus a need exists to assemble such expertise in a more easily accessible fashion.

It is also likely that the need for program evaluation within service and planning agencies has engaged many people not explicitly trained to perform research in tasks that demand such expertise. Again, bootstrap learning has not been easy. Standard works on research methodology may be rather forbidding for program people. For these settings, a compendium of relatively concrete discussions of how standard methodologies are relevant and may be applied to gerontological issues would be very useful.

At least two decades have passed since we began to replace the myths about aging that came about as a consequence of relying on cross-sectional research with findings based on longitudinal studies. At that time the Baltimore and Duke Longitudinal Studies were in place and the planning was beginning for the extension of the NIMH Human Aging investigation into a multiple-occasion longitudinal study.

One high point of the decade of the 1960s was the recognition of the methodological problems inherent in longitudinal research and the conceptualization of aging, cohort, and period as independent processes capable of affecting the person at a given time. The theory-based methodological work of Baltes, Riegel, Riegel, and Meyer, Schaie [1–3] and many others led to research designs that have become classic—the various sequential designs have aided in teasing out some of the confounds inherent in longitudinal data. While the confound problem has not been totally solved, the sequential design is now relatively commonplace and gerontological knowledge has become greatly enriched by the resulting research.

While the desirability of longitudinal investigations or sequential designs has been widely recognized, the challenges for the researcher remain formidable. For example, the investigator must keep track of study members over years, so that they can be recontacted for subsequent waves of data collection. With the degree of mobility in the United States this is not an easy task; it requires repeated contacts over the intervening time period with reports, thank you notes, and the like. Despite the researcher's efforts some respondents will be lost, requiring extensive tracking, and may possibly never be found. The investigator must deal with thorny measurement issues. Should questions be repeated, even if the early data from the study show them to be flawed? And even if questions are repeated in exactly the same form, the structure and meaning of concepts they indicate may have changed over time. What if new concepts emerge that seem germane to the original research objectives? The investigator faces complex data management tasks. Computer files of longitudinal investigations become very large. Organizing and documenting them can be extremely time consuming, requiring painstaking exactness. Yet, if file building and data management is not properly done, data analysis can become difficult to impossible. The investigator will have to wrestle with thorny data analysis issues. How is selective attrition to be dealt with, how should one handle auto-correlation, how is change to be conceptualized?

The increasing differentiation and refinement of research has also been evidenced by the recognized need to study older people in their great variety, as opposed to "the elderly," the sixty-five-plus-year-olds as a broad class. When one wishes to study subgroups with special needs or on whom knowledge is lacking, such people are often relatively rare in the population and difficult to locate for research purposes.

One of the methodological limitations of most existing longitudinal studies (including all of those mentioned above) is that they all began with purposive or convenience samples and are thereby limited in the degree to which they can represent any population subgroup. Often those older adults who are not represented are those who are particularly frail. In much gerontological research, comparison of a "case" group, treated group, or other unusual group with a control group is necessary. Sometimes the difficulty of establishing a representative control group leads to a decision not to use one at all. Scientific sampling methods provide procedures to draw representative samples of the population or its subgroups.

Some examples of universes that have not been studied in depth by means of representative samples are senile dementia, divorced or separated older people, men living alone, or three-generation families with cardiovascular illness in each generation. Not only are such people statistically rare, there may also be particular problems with this age group arising from the unwillingness of family members to identify or make asscessible their older members to the researcher.

The recently defined interest in the oldest-old (people 85 and over) has reminded us of the major biases in our knowledge about this group due to the unavailability of sufficiently large segments of this group in the standard household survey or in volunteer recruitment. Some exploration of the potential problems in this approach is required.

Because of the expense of drawing probability samples a substantial proportion of gerontological research and practically all research done by experimental psychologists, has been performed with convenience samples. We do not yet know fully the cost in erroneous inferences of using nonrepresentative samples. The most one can say is that the power of the representative sample is being increasingly recognized and a greater proportion of the major research projects are attempting to use such samples.

The major problem, of course, with both longitudinal research and representative samples is that they are extraordinarily expensive. Unfortunately this cost factor and the shortage of research funds may well have cancelled out the positive effects of the increased preference of researchers for these methods. The good old days of obtaining funding for beginning a frankly presented new longitudinal study are over. The large representative face-to-face interview sample is increasingly limited to occasional governmental endeavors or to questions added to all-purpose surveys: very rarely are large, investigator-initiated nongovernmental national surveys fielded.

The scarcity of funds for longitudinal research, drawing rare samples, and studying representative samples make more imperative the need to use existing resources to the best advantage. For example, how many researchers have gone to the expense of locating and studying a good sample of subjects, then gone on to other work, only later to recognize the need for knowledge that could come only from longitudinal study? We need to think of the possibility, at least, that every such sample constitutes a resource that should be preserved like any other resource. We should make provisions in every study that facilitate recontacting the respondent.

This book considers methodological questions that have been raised by both the changing circumstances under which gerontological research is being conducted and the kinds of substantive questions to which current research is addressed. It attempts to provide to researchers a collection of concrete treatments of both everyday research issues and of some unusual problems that may be more frequent in gerontological research. The content of the volume will deal with longitudinal studies and with a variety of other methodological areas. The methodology for dealing with the sequential aspects of longitudinal research are not the focus here. That work is reasonably well known and being regularly augmented in the literature. Neither are the textbook topics of research design, sampling methods and measurement issues our particular concern. The topics were assembled with that body of knowledge assumed. Rather, this book deals with specific methods and procedures that contribute to the soundness of the design and the research methods, yet that are rarely spelled out but must often be acquired in an "on-the-job" training fashion. The topics selected are those that are helpful enough to warrant being incorporated into everyday research practice but have not yet been formulated for this purpose in any organized manner. The keyword for this effort may well be *utility* for future research. The expertise of those who have successfully coped with both major and humdrum methodological problems needs to be milked and distributed to those who are only contemplating coping with the problems.

A number of the chapters were originally written for and discussed at a meeting on research methods held at the Philadelphia Geriatric Center on May 19–20, 1983. That conference was supported by a Teaching Nursing Home grant from the National Institute on Aging. In addition to this support, the Institute was very generous in allowing a number of its staff scientists to join the discussion. Special thanks are due the Philadelphia Geriatric Center staff members Laura Gitlin, Ph.D., Miriam Moss, and Bernice Albert for their assistance.

## REFERENCES

1. P. B. Baltes, Longitudinal and Cross-Sectional Sequences in the Study of Age and Generation Effects, *Human Development, 13*, pp. 258–268, 1968.
2. K. F. Riegel, R. M. Riegel, and G. Meyer, Socio-psychological Factors of Aging: A Cohort-Sequential Analysis, *Human Development, 10*, pp. 27–56, 1967.
3. K. W. Schaie, A General Model for the Study of Developmental Problems, *Psychological Bulletin, 64*, pp. 92–107, 1965.

# Table of Contents

## PART TWO
## LONGITUDINAL RESEARCH 191

# PART ONE
# General Research Methods in Gerontological Application

# SECTION 1
# Increasing the Efficiency and Reducing the Costs of Research on Representative Samples and Rare Universes of Older People

The three chapters in this section are addressed to the questions of approaching difficult problems with increased efficiency. Kalton and Anderson approach this task by proposing methods that preserve or at least maximize the representativeness of the sample while reducing the up-front costs of screening and the low yields of traditional household sampling methods. Liang and Lawrence suggest the better use of expensively-produced high-quality data sets that are very inexpensive to use for secondary data analysis. Herzog and Kulka choose methods whose original costs are intrinsically lower than in-person interviews, telephone and mail surveys; they review research-based knowledge about the strengths and weaknesses of the data, as a guide to people contemplating these alternatives to the face-to-face interview.

Gerontological research on humans—like much research in other fields such as psychology and medicine—is mostly based on persons whose participation in the research was obtained in a nonscientific way. Researchers sometimes use their personal connections of their professional contacts to recruit participants for their research. Neighbors, friends of parents, members of the senior citizen club, alumni, or undergraduates fall into the second. The careful study of memory research reported by Camp, West, and Poon in Chapter 7 illustrates the widespread reliance on such convenience samples.

Several problems plague such procedures of subject selection, and all have implications for how well the research participants can represent the target population, for example, persons over sixty. First, the group from which the respondents are drawn—e.g., alumni—does not include all persons over sixty. This is usually referred to a coverage problem. As a consequence, the research findings cannot be generalized to apply to all persons over sixty. Second, persons are typically not selected in a rigorous manner from the group—i.e., alumni. Third, selected persons are usually not pursued rigorously to obtain their participation. (Of course, ultimately participation is voluntary, and this fact must be so stated to the person when participation is solicited.) The consequences of the latter two problems are that the research findings may not even generalize to the population of alumni because in effect no probability sample of alumni was drawn and because nonresponse was not kept to a minimum. Both factors are likely to introduce bias into the findings from such a sample.

Scientific selection procedures employ probability sampling methods to draw samples of research subjects in a way that allows generalization from the sample to the target population with a known degree of precision. A wide variety of probability sampling methods have been developed. Indeed, sampling theory and techniques are probably the best developed part of survey research methods. Several good texts on survey sampling techniques are available, including Kish's classic textbook [1], Sudman's book on applied sampling [2], and Kalton's sample introduction [3]. Textbooks on survey research methods usually also contain chapters on sampling techniques that provide useful introductions. For an example, see Moser and Kalton's two excellent chapters in their book on survey methods [4].

An issue of importance when one considers drawing a sample of older Americans is the sampling of rare populations. Since the standard procedure for drawing a sample of geographically defined population for a face-to-face interview survey involves sampling households and selecting from within sampled households, but since only about 25 percent of all households contain at least one person over sixty years of age, sampling older persons amounts to sampling a somewhat rare population. As a consequence, several households may have to be contacted and screened before finding an older person to interview. This fact can add complexity to the procedures and costs of an already fairly costly methodology. Various alternative ways of sampling rare populations have been proposed. Kalton and Anderson's Chapter 1, reprinted with permission from *The Journal of the Royal Statistical Society*, surveys and evaluates various methods of sampling rare populations. An alternative treatment of the topic is provided in the paper by Sudman and Kalton [5].

Although the reprinted chapter by Kalton and Anderson provides a general description of sampling rare populations and defines "rare" as no more than 10 percent of the population (p. 7), many of the procedures are directly applicable to sampling older adults.

*Screening* often represents the first step in a household sample of older adults or in a household sample with a substantial oversample of older adults. Screening is particularly suitable (compared to other procedures discussed in Chapter 1) for sampling older adults because a relatively sizeable proportion of U.S. households contain a person over sixty. As pointed out in the chapter, screening costs may not be severe when the rare population constitutes a sizeable proportion of the total population. Of course, if adults eighty-five years old and older are to be sampled, screening becomes much more expensive because the population of those eighty-five and over is much rarer than the population sixty and over.

Screening questions for age should not present major problems because age is a fairly straightforward piece of information to obtain. Yet, we know that older adults do not always report their age accurately [6]. Moreover, screening information is often obtained from the person who opens the door when the interviewer contacts the household and not necessarily from the older person him- or herself, further compounding the screening error. Procedures that can be used to increase the accuracy of the screening procedures are discussed in the chapter.

*Disproportionate sampling* is clearly less relevant for sampling older adults. Despite the publicity for geographic areas to which older persons like to retire, the concentration of older adults in these areas is only minimally higher than in other areas of the country. In other words, residents tend not to be segregated by age, but by ethnicity or sociodemographic status. Therefore, disproportionate sampling provides no real advantages for sampling a general population of older adults. It may, however, be useful for sampling some specific older subpopulations, such as older Blacks.

*Multiplicity sampling* procedures present an interesting alternative for sampling older adults, particularly when older adults possessing specific characteristics are sought. Older Blacks or older diabetics might, for example, be obtained through referral by their children. As another example, Kalton and Anderson suggest the possibility of sampling nursing home residents—a difficult population to sample—through multiplicity sampling techniques. However despite its attractiveness multiplicity sampling is not without its difficulties. These difficulties are well spelled out in Chapter 1 and should be carefully examined by anybody who is considering using this form of sampling.

The ideal solution for sampling a rare population is to identify a separate sampling frame with complete coverage of that population. When no single frame with complete coverage exists, it may be possible to find several incomplete frames that, between them, give a good overall coverage of the rare population. In either situation, the techniques of *multiple frames* may be used. This technique is seldom likely to be relevant for sampling older adults because in the United States there are no frames of any significant portion of the older population available. Of course, for special groups of elderly like the Gray Panthers or members of senior citizen centers, multiple frames may be quite feasible.

The use of *sequential sampling* may be valuable when conducting a household sample of older adults. It is often difficult to estimate the exact proportion of older residents in the geographic area where the sample is to be drawn. Such an estimate is, however, a critical factor in estimating the number of households to be chosen in order to arrive at the prespecified sample size. If the estimate is incorrect, the final sample size will be too large or too small. The consequence of too small a sample size is that the survey estimates will have less precision than intended; the consequence of too large a sample size is the extra expenditure incurred in conducting the additional interviews. To deal with the problem, samples can be designed in replicates that can be included sequentially without distorting the final sample. By these means the investigator can observe the proportion of older persons detected in early replicates of the sample, and use this information to determine the number of replicates to be included in order to give the desired sample size.

It is clear that most researchers who contemplate using methods such as those discussed by Kalton and Anderson will require expert consultation. However, it may give heart to many users to note how one of these methods (network sampling) was actually applied in the study of the black aged, as in Jackson's discussion of ethnic studies (Chapter 6), in a later section of Part One.

Liang and Lawrence contribute Chapter 2. It may well be a gold mine to researchers who begin with the notion that the ore is there in other people's data archives but are uncertian how to proceed in mining it. One must begin by acknowledging an earlier useful contribution to the technology of using secondary data in gerontological research by George and Landerman [7]. Liang and Lawrence extend and amplify the base of knowledge in a comprehensive how-to treatment of the topic. A very useful portion of this chapter is their overview of some of the major data sets. The reader should note particularly the dynamic nature of this resource: The treasury of such data sets is being augmented constantly. Thus an active effort by the research will be required to keep up with such additions. Again, by referring to regular newsletters providing such information, Liang and Lawrence save the archive searcher a great deal of effort.

It is obvious that even the most-used large data sets, such as the Parnes survey [8] or the National Council on the Aging [9] or the 1976 and 1981 Harris Surveys, contain underutilized resources that will be the sources of new knowledge for a long time. It may be worthwhile to consider how the use of secondary data may figure in a long-term research strategy. Frequently, basic descriptive data or, more likely, cross-tabulations or correlational analysis may provide the research with a first cut showing how variables in a particular content area relate to basic background, health, social, or mental health variables. Or, the item data for a large number of subjects may be used to examine the measurement qualities of various scales. As Liang and Lawrence note, however, all the critical variables are seldom in an existing data set. The preliminary secondary analysis, however, may be an avenue toward a better choice of variables and modes of measurement when developing new research in which the"missing" critical variables will be included or in which the scales or items with the best measurement qualities will be included.

Frequently, such in-depth research using the additional critical variables will lead in turn to the ability to specify further relationships whose existence may be tested through secondary analyses. This, the secondary analysis may either lead to or follow from primary data studies.

The third chapter in this section, Herzog and Kulka's treatment of telephone and mail survey methods, succeeds for the first time in integrating a great deal of difficult to locate data to document the advantages and pitfalls of such methods. Particularly helpful are the findings from their own studies, which fill several notable earlier voids in knowledge. It is likely that the conclusions from this chapter will represent the state of the art for some time.

Careful attention to these conclusions will enhance the ability of researchers to make scientifically valid interpretations of their data. For example, a great contribution to our knowledge is contained in the dual findings, first, that older people are *not* selectively lacking in telephones, and, second, that they *are* selective telephone survey non-responders. This generalization replaces the earlier clouded conclusion that "telephone surveys are less valid with older people." Herzog and Kulka's concludsion points not toward an avoidance of the telephone method but toward the need to explore in-depth the reasons for nonresponse. For example, it is clear that specific research attention is required to elucidate a series of points at which nonresponse may occur: The "protection" of the older household resident by another; the assumptions or unrealistic conclusions drawn by the older person about the purpose of the survey; the physics and the perceptual processes involved in the cognitive task of telephone responding; the temporal curve of attentiveness and fatigue during the interview. Their review allows many similar questions regarding mail survey responding to be framed for future research.

Equally important is their observation that in terms of response quality both telephone and face-to-face methods appear to work equally well. Unlike the popular stereotype, older adults who agree to participate can be interviewed face-to-face or over the telephone.

## REFERENCES

1. Kish, L. *Survey Sampling,* John Wiley and Sons, New York, 1965.
2. Sudman, S. *Applied Sampling,* Academic Press, New York, 1976.
3. Kalton, G. *Introduction to Survey Sampling,* Sage Publications, Beverly Hills, California, 1983.
4. Moser, C. A. and G. Kalton, *Survey Methods in Social Investigations,* Basic Books, New York, 1972.
5. Sudman, S. and G. Kalton, in *Annual Review of Sociology,* R. H. Turner and J. F. Short (eds.), Annual Reviews, Palo Alto California, 1986.
6. Herzog, A. R. and L. Dielman, Age Differences in Response Accuracy for Factual Survey Questions, *Journal of Gerontology, 40,* pp. 350–357, 1985.
7. George, L. K. and R. Landerman, Health and Subjective Well-Being: A Replicated Secondary Data Analysis, *International Journal of Aging and Human Development, 19,* pp. 133–156, 1984.
8. Parnes, H. S. From the Middle to the Later Years, *Research on Aging, 3,* pp. 387–402, 1981.
9. National Council on the Aging, *The Myth and Reality of Aging in America,* National Council on Aging, Washington DC, 1975.

CHAPTER

# 1

# Sampling Rare Populations[1]

*Graham Kalton and Dallas W. Anderson*

## 1. INTRODUCTION

The design of an efficient sample for surveying a rare population is one of the most challenging tasks confronting the sampling statistician. This chapter reviews a variety of methods available for sampling rare populations. Although emphasis here is on health surveys, the methods are applicable more generally. For present purposes a rare population is taken to be a small subset of the total population. "Small" may be as large as one tenth or as small as one hundredth, one thousandth or even less.

The initial consideration in designing a sample for a rare population is whether there exists a separate frame for that population. If a separate frame exists, is available for sample selection, and is deemed adequate, the sample may be selected from it using standard methods and no special problems arise. That situation will not be discussed further. Frequently no single separate frame of adequate coverage is available; the methods discussed below have been developed for this situation.

Three purposes in surveying a rare population need to be distinguished:

(i) The estimation of the number of persons in the rare population, $M$, the prevalence of the rare population in the total population, $P = M/N$, where $N$ is the size of the total population, and the prevalence in various subgroups of the population. (Following Elandt-Johnson [1], prevalence is defined here as the ratio of the number of cases at a given time to the size of the population at that time.) An example is a survey conducted to estimate

[1]This chapter is reprinted from the *Journal of the Royal Statistical Society* A (1986), *149* (Part 1), pp.65–82, with permission from the publisher and the authors.

the number of persons with a hearing defect, the prevalence of the defect in the total population, and the prevalence in age, sex and other subgroups.

(ii) The estimation of means of certain variables for persons in the rare population, or proportions of the rare population with certain characteristics. These population parameters may be denoted by

$$\bar{Y} = \sum_{i}^{M} Y_i/M;$$

in the case of a proportion, $Y_i = 1$ if the $i$th person has the characteristic, and $Y_i = 0$ if not. An example is a survey to estimate the mean annual cost of treatment for hearing defects among persons with such defects, and the proportion of these persons with hearing aids.

(iii) As Kish points out [2,3], sometimes the mean or total of the $Y$-variable may also be needed for the entire population, with $Y_i = 0$ for all those who are not members of the rare population. The population parameters are then

$$\bar{Y}_t = \sum_{i}^{N} Y_i/N = P\bar{Y} \quad \text{and} \quad Y_t = N\bar{Y}_t = M\bar{Y}.$$

An example is a survey to estimate the mean cost of treatment for hearing defects in the entire population, where the rare population comprises all persons with hearing defects.

In practice, of course, surveys are often required to serve more than one of these purposes.

In many cases, the sample design for a rare population includes the selection of a large sample from a more general population and then the identification of members of the rare population within that sample. The ease and costs of screening a large sample depend on the prevalence of the rare population in the more general population, the ease with which members of the rare population can be identified, and the methods of data collection used for screening and for the main survey. Issues of screening are taken up in Section 2. Sometimes information is available on the concentration of the rare population in different sectors of the more general population. In this case, disproportionate sampling may be used to reduce screening costs, with the sectors as strata and sampling the sectors in which the rare population is highly concentrated at higher rates; this approach is discussed in Section 3. Screening costs may also be reduced by allowing more than one member of the more general population to report on a rare event. This fact has led to the development of multiplicity (or network) sampling methods, covered in Section 4. Even though no single complete sampling frame is available for a rare population, there are sometimes incomplete lists that can be used to sample parts of the population. In this case, a combination of incomplete lists and a "catch-all" frame may be used; this approach is discussed in Section 5. Another possibility is to compile a frame for the rare population. Snowballing, discussed in Section 6, is one method for constructing such a frame. Section 7 then briefly describes the use of sequential sampling and some other methods for sampling rare populations. The chapter concludes with a comment on the usefulness of combinations of the methods previously discussed.

## 2. SCREENING

A common feature of most samples of rare populations is the need to screen a large sample in order to identify members of the rare population. Sometimes most or all of the listings that do not represent members of the rare population can be identified as such from the information on the sampling frame. In this case, the sampling issues are reasonably straightforward: either the frame can be cleaned of those listings before the sample is selected, or a larger sample can be selected initially and those selections that are clearly not members of the rare population based on the information given in the sampling frame can be eliminated prior to the fieldwork. Any remaining nonmembers of the rare population found in the sample are then eliminated at the data collection stage. Usually, however, the sampling frame does not contain the information necessary to distinguish between members and nonmembers of the rare population. Then, all the nonmembers have to be identified and eliminated at the data collection stage. If the rare population constitutes a sizeable proportion of the frame population, the screening costs may not be too severe, but screening costs increase rapidly as the degree of rarity rises.

A number of techniques may be employed to reduce screening costs. The most important is the use of an economical data collection method to obtain the screening information. Telephone interviewing is widely used in the United States for this purpose. If screening is conducted by telephone, it is convenient if the main survey is conducted by the same mode. If, say, the telephone is used to identify members of the rare population, and the main survey data are then collected by face-to-face interviews, the telephone sample generally needs to be clustered geographically to control the travel costs of the interviewers working in the main survey. A serious concern in using telephone sampling for a rare population is the coverage of the telephone frame for that population. Although only about 7 percent of United States households are inaccessible by telephone, there is the risk that this rate may be much higher for the rare population. Telephone surveys underrepresent low-income households, households in the South, households with non-white heads, households with heads under thirty-five, and households with single, divorced or separated heads [4]. If the rare population is concentrated in such groups, telephone sampling will be open to the possibility of significant bias. A telephone sample obtained by random digit dialing has, for instance, been found to underrepresent the deaf population and those limited in activity because of chronic conditions [5].

An alternative data collection method for screening is the mail questionnaire. This method is widely used in the United Kingdom where telephone coverage is not as high as in the United States and where the Register of Electors provides a sampling frame of names and addresses. Harris, for instance, describes a survey of the handicapped and impaired for which 250,000 households were screened by mail questionnaires at the initial phase [6]; a response rate of 85.6 percent was obtained for this phase. Cartwright sent a mail questionnaire to 29,400 persons to identify those who had been in hospitals in the last six months, and obtained a response rate of 87 percent [7]. Hunt sent a screening questionnaire seeking basic demographic details about the members of 11,500 households to identify a sample of the elderly, and achieved a response rate of 80 percent [8]. Although these response rates are high for mail surveys, there is the risk that the non-respondents include a sizeable proportion of members of the rare population.

Most sample designs employ clustering for reasons of economy. In face-to-face interview surveys, clustering is used to reduce both sample selection costs and travel costs of interviewers, while in telephone surveys clustering is used to increase efficiency in locating working household numbers. As a rule, clustering leads to a loss of precision in the survey estimates as compared with an unclustered design of the same sample size. The design effect for the mean of a variable from a cluster sample can be represented by $[1 + (\bar{b} - 1)roh]$, where *roh* is a synthetic measure of the homogeneity of the variable in the clusters [2]. In surveys of the general population $\bar{b}$ is the average sample size per selected cluster; when dealing with a subclass that is fairly evenly spread across the clusters, however, $\bar{b}$ is replaced by $\bar{b}_0$, the average subclass sample size per cluster. For a rare population (i.e., subclass) evenly spread across the clusters, a sample with a large $\bar{b}$ value for the general population can be tolerated since it will result in a small $\bar{b}_0$, and hence small design effects for estimated means of the rare population. Thus an efficient sampling procedure for selecting a sample of a rare population is to screen large samples in selected clusters. In face-to-face interview surveys, complete screening of blocks or other units can be an effective design for some rare characteristics, giving good coverage as well as being efficient.

When a rare population is geographically clustered, it can be efficient to sample the clusters in which the rare population is more heavily concentrated at higher rates. The widely-used method for improving the efficiency of random digit dialing sampling in telephone surveys described by Waksberg [9] can be adapted for this purpose. The first step is to select a cluster with probability proportional to the size of its total population, and to select one element in that cluster. If the selected element is a member of the rare population, it is included in the sample and further screening interviews are taken in the cluster until a set number of additional members of the rare population ($K$) is selected. If the initially selected element is not a member of the rare population, the cluster is rejected. The process is repeated until the required number of clusters is accepted for the sample. This procedure in effect samples the clusters with probabilities proportional to their numbers of members of the rare population. It may be noted that clusters with no members of the rare population are always rejected at the first screening interviews. Sudman gives a formula for the optimum choice of $K$ and describes a variety of possible applications of this approach [10], and Blair and Czaja describe its use with random digit dialing sampling for sampling black and affluent households [11]. A problem that can occur with the procedure is that in some of the clusters accepted for the sample the number of members of the rare population may be less than $(K + 1)$, the number required for the sample; this creates the need for weighting which causes a loss in efficiency [12].

The screening information needed to identify members of the rare population is not always straightforward to collect. Moreover, even when the screening questions are fairly simple, due attention needs to be paid to response errors. As Sudman observes [13], if the rare population is defined by some combination of characteristics (e.g., Black, adult, employed males under 30 years of age), response errors can occur to each of the several screening questions, thus possibly leading to serious levels of misclassification in the combination.

Identification of members of the rare population is sometimes a costly operation, as for instance when a medical diagnosis requires a trained physician or expensive, perhaps not transportable, equipment. When this applies, a two-phase approach can sometimes be profitable: at the first phase a relatively cheap but imperfect screening is used to divide a large sample into two or more strata according to the likelihood of being in the rare population, and then a subsample is selected for the expensive measurement, sampling the strata with higher likelihoods at greater rates. In many applications, the first phase sample is divided into just two strata, those who may be members of the rare population and those who are not; then often all of those in the first stratum and none of those in the second stratum are included in the second phase of the survey. Anderson et al., for example, conducted a survey of the prevalence of major neurological disorders in a rural county in the United States using a two-phase design [14]. At the first phase, a screening questionnaire was administered in inhabited dwellings to collect certain demographic and medical information on the occupants. The medical information was used to identify persons who required the second-phase clinical examination by a neurologist because of their likelihood of having one or more of the disorders under study.

A two-phase approach is beneficial only when the first phase screening costs are much lower than the second phase costs. Deming suggests that the ratio of the second to first phase screening costs needs to be at least 6:1 and it should be preferably much larger, e.g. 40:1 or more [15]. With an initial screening into two strata, those classified as members and nonmembers of the rare population, the stratum of those classified as nonmembers should contain very few members of the rare population if the first phase screening is to be effective. In other words the screening needs to keep the number of "false negatives" to a very small proportion: the proportion of "false positives" is not so critical. Deming gives tables from which he concludes that for the first phase screening to be economical, the proportion of false negatives needs to be less than one quarter of the overall proportion that members of the rare population represent of the total population [15].

One way that can sometimes be used to keep the proportion of false negatives small, at the cost of an increase in the proportion of false positives, is to use less stringent criteria for defining the rare population at the first phase. Thus, for instance, Fry et al. used a lower level of hearing loss for defining significant deafness in a sample of children at the first phase, when their hearing was measured at home, than was used at the second phase which was conducted in a controlled laboratory setting [16]. Similarly, in a fertility study of women aged fifteen to forty-five, the initial screening may specify a wider age range to deal with minor misreporting of ages at the boundaries. When the screening criteria are set such that the proportion of false negatives is negligibly small, there is no need to subsample from the negative stratum at the second phase: however, the assumption that the proportion of false negatives is negligible needs to be made with due caution, for if the negative stratum is large even a small proportion of false negatives can constitute a sizeable proportion of the rare population.

## 3. DISPROPORTIONATE SAMPLING

It is sometimes possible to identify strata with higher concentrations of the rare population. Thus, for instance, the rare population may be concentrated in certain geographical areas, or it may be concentrated in a stratum comprising a list frame. In such situations, it may be efficient to sample the strata in which the rare population is concentrated at higher sampling fractions.

*Editors note:* An extended technical consideration of procedures involved in disproportionate sampling that appeared at this point in the original article is included as an appendix to this chapter.

In line with Kish [2, p. 406] and Waksberg [17] , the general conclusion from the results in the appendix is that the gains from disproportionate stratification will be sizeable only when two conditions apply: first, the strata to be oversampled need high concentrations of the rare population and, second, the strata need to contain a substantial proportion of the rare population. This conclusion applies both for estimating the prevalence of the rare population and for estimating characteristics of the rare population.

As Waksberg points out, the computations of optimum sampling rates for disproportionate stratification are usually based on past data such as the most recent Census [17]. Changes in the distribution of the rare population across the strata since the time those data were collected commonly lead to lower concentrations of the rare population in the strata to be oversampled. When this is so, the gains in precision will be smaller than indicated in the appendix. The sample size for the rare population will also be smaller than predicted based on the past data.

Ericksen provides an interesting illustration and analysis of the use of disproportionate stratification with area sampling in the selection of a sample of females aged fifteen to nineteen years old, with a higher sampling fraction for Blacks [18].

## 4. MULTIPLICITY SAMPLING

The essential problem with sampling a rare population is that many contacts are required to identify the sample members with the rare trait. Multiplicity, or network, sampling can sometimes be used to reduce the number of contacts needed.

It is generally desirable that a sampling frame provides a single listing for each population element; otherwise the frame problem of duplicate listings arises [2, Section 11.2]. However, instead of seeking to avoid duplicate listings, multiplicity sampling creates such duplicates and capitalizes on them for data collection.

In a conventional household survey, information on persons with a rare trait is collected in respect of members of the sampled households only. Thus each member of the population is included in the sample only if his or her household is selected. The information may be collected from each person individually, or one member of the household may report the information for all eligible household members. The latter procedure has benefits in terms of economy of data collection, but it requires that the informant can provide the requisite information accurately for other household members. With a multiplicity sample design, information is provided by a selected household not only about its own household members but also about other persons who are linked to that household in clearly defined ways. One common form of linkage, for instance, is to include all close relatives of household members—e.g., children, parents and siblings; linkages of this type have been used in methodological and pilot studies of diabetes [19], cancer [20, 21], births and deaths [22] and Vietnam era veterans [23]. Another form of linkage is to include addresses adjacent to the selected households. Such linkages have been used in surveys of ethnic minorities [24], and in a pilot survey of home vegetable gardeners using sewage sludge [25].

Linkages need to be clearly specified so that the selection probabilities of sample members can be determined. Thus, for instance, in an equal probability sample of households with all members of selected households being included and with a multiplicity linkage to siblings, the probability that a given individual is included in the sample is proportional to the number of different households in which he and his siblings are living. Weights inversely proportional to these selection probabilities are needed in the analysis. Note that an individual living in an institution has no chance of being selected in a conventional household survey, but he or she may have a chance of being selected for a multiplicity sample: this is another advantage of multiplicity sampling.

The critical consideration in the choice of linkages is the ability of informants to provide the necessary information. At the least, they need to be able to provide details on the linkages and to give accurate information on whether those linked to them have the rare trait. These data are the minimum required for estimating the prevalence of the rare trait, but even for prevalence surveys more details are needed: for instance, a prevalence survey of diabetics would also need information on the age and sex of each sampled person so that age- and sex-specific prevalences could be computed. In a survey of the characteristics of those with the rare trait, information needs to be collected on those characteristics (for instance, on the cost of medical care for cancer patients). It is frequently impossible for a sampled person to provide information on these characteristics for others linked to him. In this case, he has to be able to provide a means of locating persons with the rare trait who are linked to him so that direct contact can be made with them. When direct contact is needed, this factor needs to be taken into account in defining the linkages. With a face-to-face interview survey, it is economically advantageous to restrict the linkages to persons living in the same geographical area as the initial informant. With telephone surveys, the initial informants have to provide information to make contacting the linked persons possible. Bergsten and Pierson, for instance, found that the information they collected from initial informants was sufficient to enable only 70 percent of neighbors to be contacted in a telephone survey [25].

The preceding illustrations of linkages are ones that have been purposively introduced in household surveys to extend the range of data collected from each informant. Multiplicity also occurs naturally when rare populations are sampled by means of their contacts with certain establishments, as for instance when patients with a rare illness are sampled from hospital records or from pharmacy records of prescriptions for drugs that treat that illness [26]. The establishments may have several records for each patient (e.g., several prescriptions) and the patient may have records with several establishments. The establishment records rarely contain information on the multiplicity and they seldom contain the substantive information to be collected in the survey. Thus, follow-up surveys with the patients are generally needed. Often a major obstacle to the conduct of a follow-up survey is that many establishments will refuse to grant permission for contact to be made with the patients. Even when they grant permission, a problem can arise with obtaining accurate information from the sampled patients on their multiplicity. Lessler describes a method for reducing this problem [27]. Bryan et al. describe an application of this use of multiplicity sampling in a pilot study on epilepsy [28].

Since the ideas of multiplicity sampling were first propounded by Birnbaum and Sirken [29], there have been a number of theoretical and conceptual developments of the technique [e.g., 22, 30–34]. There has also been a variety of applications. While multiplicity sampling is a useful addition to the battery of techniques for sampling rare populations, it is no panacea. A number of factors need to be taken into account when choosing between a conventional sample and a multiplicity sample. The clear advantage of a multiplicity sample is that it needs a smaller sample to yield the required sample size of members of the rare population. However, the use of informants in multiplicity sampling is frequently likely to increase significantly the level of response error (although their use may on occasion lead to a reduction of certain types of response bias [35]), and the need for weights in the analysis of a multiplicity sample causes an increase in sampling error. Problems can arise in determining the linkages with a multiplicity design, and in any case additional questions need to be asked to identify the linkages; item nonresponse to these additional questions also creates difficulties [19]. When sampled members of the rare population need to be contacted in person, the costs of tracing and contacting them in a multiplicity design may be considerable. An ethical question with multiplicity sampling is whether it is appropriate to collect the survey data from an informant who is not even a member of the linked person's household. In some cases this question may not raise much concern. However, with private information (which could include health matters) there may be serious difficulties, and especially so if the survey design calls for a subsequent interview with persons identified as having a rare trait. Thus, for instance, in a survey of cancer patients, there could be serious ethical concerns about interviewing a person identified as having cancer by a sibling living in a different household. For these various reasons the choice between a multiplicity and a conventional sample is a complex one that requires a careful assessment of relative costs and relative quality of the resultant estimators.

## 5. MULTIPLE FRAMES

Even though a complete list of the rare population is not available, there may exist one or more partial lists. Thus, for instance, hospital records may provide a means of identifying a sizeable proportion of persons with a particular illness, but they may fail to cover an important minority who have different characteristics from hospital attenders. In such a case, the sample may be made up of two components: first, a sample from the partial list and second a sample from the total population to screen for persons with the illness. Since the screening sample is expensive, an economic design will sample the partial list at a higher sampling fraction than is used for the screening sample. Sometimes several partial lists are available, but a screening sample from the total population may still be needed to give representation to those on none of the lists.

When multiple frames are used, it is likely that some members of the rare population will be included on more than one frame: for instance, a person with a particular illness may attend one or more hospitals for that illness and should also be covered by the area frame. The representation of some population members on more than one frame gives rise to the frame problem of duplicates [2, Section 11.2]. There are two basic approaches for handling duplicates: one is to redefine the frames so that they are non-overlapping and the other is to make compensations in the analysis.

## ELIMINATING OVERLAPS

One way to eliminate overlaps is to collate the several list frames into a single list without duplicates, and to define the screening sample from the total population to be a sample of rare population members not on the combined list. The collation of a single list requires the matching of listings across frames, a process that is notoriously error-prone. Problems such as misspelt names and alternative versions of addresses can give rise to failures to match and mismatches, and the resultant biases need to be taken into account. In practice, it is often wiser to define the frames in a way that makes matching simpler, even if this is achieved at the cost of some loss of statistical efficiency in the sampling methods.

One example of this general approach is the sample of retail stores described by Hansen et al. [35, pp. 516–558]. Within selected primary sampling units, all retail stores on a combined list were included in the sample and an area sample was taken to give representation to stores not on the list. Another example is a study of the deaf population in Washington in the 1960s. For this study, as complete a list of deaf persons as possible was compiled from organizations for the deaf, schools for the deaf, deaf informants, social agencies, etc. All those on this list found to be eligible were then included in the survey. In addition, an area sample with an overall sampling fraction of 1 in 120 was taken to check on the completeness of this list and, if needed, to give representation to unlisted deaf persons [37]. It may be noted that when a complete enumeration is taken from the combined list, failures to match listings across the separate frames are not so serious a problem since they will be resolved during fieldwork.

An alternative procedure for eliminating overlaps is to use a unique identification to specify one of the listings as the real listing, with the other listings being treated as blanks. This may be illustrated by the earlier example of persons with a particular illness. The hospital lists could be ordered, with a person being identified with the first list on which he or she appears, and then his or her inclusions on the lists of later hospitals are treated as blank entries; the area frame could be defined to include only persons with the illness who were on none of the hospital lists. The procedure involves selecting a sample of listings throughout the several frames, and then for each sampled listing searching earlier frames to determine whether there is a prior listing. If there is a prior listing, the element is rejected for the sample; if not, the element is accepted. The procedure avoids the need to collate the several frames; the searches are made only for sampled listings and only in prior frames. Even in this case the searches for matching listings are not always easy to conduct. Sometimes the searching task can be simplified by choosing a suitable order for the frames. For instance, a frame not in alphabetical order may be best placed last and a well-organized long frame placed first in the frame order [2, Section 11.2D].

The choice between these two procedures depends on the ease and accuracy with which a combined list can be generated and on the purpose of the survey.

When the lists are not computerized and when they are long and not ordered in a systematic fashion (e.g., not in alphabetical order), merging can be a major undertaking. Merging is much more feasible when the lists are computerized, but even in this case failures to match and mismatches can pose severe problems.

The creation of a combined frame without duplicates can be especially useful when the purpose of the survey is to estimate the size of the rare population, $M$, and rare population totals like $Y = M\bar{Y}$. Indeed, when the combined frame is comprehensive and contains no blanks, $M$ is known exactly and $Y$ may be estimated by $M\bar{y}$. Without combining the frames, $M$ has to be estimated by $Fm$ and $Y$ by $Fy$, where $F$ is the inverse of the sampling fraction (assumed the same for all lists), $m$ is the rare population sample size and $y$ is the sample total for members of the rare population. For a given sample size, $M\bar{y}$ has smaller variance than $Fy$ [2, Section 11.8].

## COMPENSATING FOR OVERLAPS

When a sample is drawn from two or more overlapping frames, the chance of an element being selected depends on the number of frames on which it appears. Compensation for the varying inclusion probabilities of different population elements may be made by means of a weighting adjustment in the analysis. One widely-used adjustment method is to assign sample elements weights made inversely proportional either to their inclusion probabilities or to their expected number of selections. Assuming that no population element can appear in the sample more than once, the weights should be made inversely proportional to inclusion probabilities. With independent sampling between lists, the inclusion probability for the $i$th sample member is

$$\sum_{j} p_{ij} - \sum\sum_{j<k} p_{ij}p_{ik} + \sum\sum\sum_{j<k<l} p_{ij}p_{ik}p_{il} \cdot \cdot \cdot ,$$

where $p_{ij}$ is the probability that the $i$th sample member is selected from the $j$th list. If a sample element selected from more than one list is included in the sample once for each selection, the weight should be made inversely proportional to the expected number of selections, i.e., inversely proportional to $\sum_{j} p_{ij}$. This latter weighting scheme is easier to compute. When the inclusion probabilities are small for all lists, the overall inclusion probability may also be approximated by $\sum_{j} p_{ij}$. Application of these weighting schemes requires knowledge of the lists on which each sample element is to be found. Where possible, this information is best obtained from the lists; otherwise, it may be obtained from the sampled elements, but in this case the reports may be subject to response errors.

A general approach for dealing with overlapping frames is obtained from the multiple frame estimator introduced by Hartley [38,39]. Since a full treatment is not possible here, we will discuss only some aspects of the simple and common case with just two frames, labelled $A$ and $B$. The members of the population of interest then fall into one of three mutually exclusive subsets: members on frame $A$ only, members on frame $B$ only, and members on both frames. One or both of the frames may also include listings that do not refer to members of the population of interest. The essence of the procedure is to divide those population members on both frames between their two listings. Thus the survey variables $Y_i$ are divided into two parts, $pY_i$ being associated with the listing on frame $A$ and $qY_i$ being associated with the listing on frame $B$ $(p + q = 1)$. In the same way, the count variable $X_i = 1$ may be divided into parts, $p$ for frame $A$ and $q$ for frame $B$. When the numbers of members of the population of interest are known for the three subsets ($N_a$, $N_b$ and $N_{ab}$), then a population total $Y$ may be estimated by the poststratified estimator

$$\hat{Y}_1 = N_a\bar{y}_a + N_b\bar{y}_b + N_{ab}(p\bar{y}'_{ab} + q\bar{y}''_{ab}),$$

where $\bar{y}_a$ is the sample mean for those who are only on frame $A$, $\bar{y}_b$ is the corresponding quantity for frame $B$, $\bar{y}'_{ab}$ is the mean of those on both frames sampled from frame $A$ and $\bar{y}''_{ab}$ is the mean for those on both frames sampled from frame $B$. When $N_a$, $N_b$ and $N_{ab}$ are unknown, then $Y$ may be estimated by

$$\hat{Y}_2 = F_A(y_a + py'_{ab}) + F_B(y_b + qy''_{ab}),$$

where $F_A$ and $F_B$ are the inverses of the sampling fractions for the two frames and $y_a$, $y_b$, $y'_{ab}$ and $y''_{ab}$ are sample totals. An important special case occurs when frame $A$, say, provides complete coverage (e.g., a frame of the total population) while frame $B$ provides only partial coverage. In this case $N_b = 0$ and the terms $N_b\bar{y}_b$ in $\hat{Y}_1$ and $F_B y_b$ in $\hat{Y}_2$ drop out.

This approach provides a general framework for handling overlapping frames. The use of unique identification discussed in the previous subsection, for instance, can be viewed as a special case with $p = 1$. If $p$ is set equal to $F_B/(F_A + F_B)$, the estimator $\hat{Y}_2$ is equivalent to the one obtained by weighting sample members inversely to their expected numbers of selections. The approach has the attraction that it provides a means for determining the optimum sampling fractions and the optimum value of $p$ to be used. Thus, the values of the sampling fractions and of $p$ can be determined to minimize the variance of the sample estimator subject to some cost function for sampling from each of the frames. For further details, the reader is referred to the papers by Hartley [38,39], Cochran [40], Fuller and Burmeister [41], and the sizeable recent research on the use of dual frame estimation techniques to augment telephone surveys by face-to-face interviews [42–45].

## 6. SNOWBALLING

The techniques discussed so far can be valuable tools for sampling rare populations, but even with their use a survey of an extremely rare population can still remain prohibitively expensive. For extremely rare populations, researchers sometimes resort to what is generally known as snowball or reputational sampling.

A necessary condition for successful applications of snowballing is that members of a rare population know each other. This condition does not hold for all rare populations, but is may well hold for certain rare ethnic minorities, religious groups, persons with disabilities (e.g., deaf people), etc. One application of snowballing is to create a frame of members of the rare population. The approach is to identify a few members of that population, to ask each of them to identify other members, to contact those so identified and ask them to identify others, and so on. When the frame has been compiled, a probability sample can then be drawn from it. The critical issue with this use of snowballing is simply the completeness of the frame. Those missing from the frame are likely to be those socially isolated from other members of the rare population; the survey estimates will be biased if this factor is associated with the survey variables.

A more common application of snowballing avoids the construction of the frame by simply continuing the snowballing process until a sufficient number of members of the rare population has been found for the survey. Survey interviews can be conducted with the members of the rare population as they are identified, thus avoiding the recontacts that are needed with the frame construction approach. With this approach, those with many contacts with other members of the rare population are more likely to be included in the survey than those with few contacts (unless, as sometimes applies, the survey aims to take all the members of the rare population). However, since the sample is not a probability sample, objective weighting adjustments cannot be employed in the analysis to compensate for this factor. Steps may be taken to make the sample conform to known or hypothesized distributions for certain background variables, as in quota sampling, but this cannot ensure that the sample produces unbiased estimates for other variables. Moreover, distributions of important background variables are seldom known for a rare population; the use of hypothesized distributions in place of known distributions introduces its own potential biases. Given the likelihood of substantial bias with this use of snowball sampling, the results from a snowball sample need to be assessed with considerable caution. The technique seems more suited for exploratory and qualitative investigations, as with case finding in the initial stages of an epidemiological study, rather than for statistical surveys.

Biernacki and Waldorf review problems and techniques of snowball sampling [46], and Welch [47] and Snow et al. [48] describe applications of its use. A theoretical paper entitled "Snowball sampling" by Goodman is often improperly cited in discussions of this topic [49]; that paper does not deal with the type of snowball sampling discussed here.

## 7. SEQUENTIAL SAMPLING AND OTHER TECHNIQUES

For surveys estimating characteristics of a rare population, a reasonably accurate estimate of the prevalence of the rare population is required so that the sampling fraction needed to yield the desired sample size can be determined. In practice, however, often no good estimate of prevalence is available. This difficulty can be handled by some form of sequential sampling. One approach is to select an initial sample of size sufficient to give the desired sample size of members of the rare population ($n$) based on the highest estimate of prevalence. This sample will yield, say, $n'$ members of the rare population, and also an estimate of prevalence. If $n' < n$, a second sample is selected to produce the remaining $(n - n')$ members of the rare population based on the prevalence figure obtained from the initial sample. Another approach is to construct a large sample as a set of replicate samples, with the size of the large sample being sufficient to generate the desired number of members of the rare population based on the lowest estimate of prevalence. The replicates are then assigned for fieldwork in turn until the desired sample size is attained. These sequential approaches cause some inefficiencies in fieldwork for face-to-face interview surveys, but they can be fairly easily implemented with telephone surveys.

In addition to the techniques discussed here, three others should be mentioned [2]. One is the use of multipurpose surveys, where several investigators pool resources to conduct a single survey to study several rare traits simultaneously. Market researchers frequently use multipurpose surveys to study reactions of users to infrequently purchased products. The second technique is the cumulation of cases with the rare trait over several rounds of a continuous survey. The continuous survey may be used either simply to screen for members of the rare population or to collect the full details required for the survey of the rare population. Another possible way of cumulating cases is by secondary analysis of a set of surveys that have collected the necessary information to identify members of the rare population and that provide the required measures for them. However, problems of inconsistent definitions, classification errors and different populations sampled can present severe difficulties in pooling cases from diverse surveys [50]. The third additional technique for finding rare elements has a different purpose from the others. The method is batch testing, which is applicable when the rare trait is detected by means of material that is expensive to test. Samples of the material from several units may then be pooled and tested together. Thus, for instance, samples of drinking water from several households may be pooled and tested for contaminants.

## 8. CONCLUDING REMARKS

When a sample of a rare population is required, the first consideration is whether there is a special list (or a combination of lists) that gives complete, or almost complete, coverage of the population and that does not contain many foreign elements. If an adequate list is found, the sampling problems reduce to the usual ones encountered in surveying any population. If no such list is available, the techniques described above may often be used effectively to select a sample of a rare population. However, when the population is extremely rare or when the identification of members of the rare population is expensive, there may be no satisfactory solution to the sampling problem.

For convenience of exposition, the techniques discussed above have been treated separately, although in practice they are commonly used in combination. Thus, for instance, disproportionate sampling is frequently used with screening and can be used with multiplicity sampling; multiplicity sampling involves screening, so that the issues discussed under screening apply with multiplicity sampling also.

# APPENDIX
# DISPROPORTIONATE SAMPLING

## ESTIMATING PREVALENCE

Suppose that the purpose of the survey is to estimate the prevalence of the rare population, $P = M/N$. For simplicity, suppose that there are two strata, with stratum 1 having a high prevalence of the rare population ($P_1$) and stratum 2 a low prevalence ($P_2$), and assume that the selections are to be made by simple random sampling in each stratum. Then, by standard theory for optimum allocation, the sample sizes ($n_h$) in the two strata should be made proportional to $W_h S_h / \sqrt{c_h}$, where $W_h$ is the proportion of the overall population, $S_h \cong \sqrt{(P_h Q_h)}$ is the element standard deviation, $Q_h = 1 - P_h$, and $c_h$ is the cost per unit of sampling, all in stratum $h$ ($h = 1, 2$). Often the costs $c_h$ in the two strata are approximately equal, in which case the optimal allocation reduces to the Neyman allocation, $n_h \propto W_h \sqrt{(P_h Q_h)}$. Ignoring fpc's, the ratio of the variance of the sample estimate of prevalence with Neyman allocation to that with a proportionate allocation based on the same sample size is [51, p. 110]

$$R_0 = \{\Sigma\, W_h \sqrt{(P_h Q_h)}\}^2 / \Sigma\, W_h P_h Q_h.$$

To illustrate the magnitude of the gains from using Neyman allocation, consider a situation where the prevalence of the rare characteristic is $p = 0.05$ or 5 percent. Table 1 gives the values of $R_0$ for various combinations of $W_1$ and $P_1$. Also given in each cell of the table are the values of: $k_0 = \sqrt{(P_1 Q_1 / P_2 Q_2)}$, the value of the ratio of the optimum sampling rate in stratum 1 to that in stratum 2; $P_2 = (P - W_1 P_1)/(1 - W_1)$, the proportion of the second stratum with the rare trait; and $A = W_1 P_1 / P$, the proportion of the rare population in stratum 1. For convenience in Table 1 and subsequent tables $W_1$, $P_1$, $P_2$ and $A$ are expressed as percentages.

Table 1. Estimating Prevalence: Values of $R_0$, $k_0$, $P_2$ and $A$ for Combinations of $P_1$ and $W_1$, with $P$ = 5%

| Values of $P_1$ | | Values of $W_1$ 5% | 10% | 15% | 20% | 25% | 35% | 45% |
|---|---|---|---|---|---|---|---|---|
| 10% | $R_0$ | 0.99 | 0.98 | 0.97 | 0.96 | 0.94 | 0.89 | 0.77 |
| | $k_0$ | 1.4 | 1.5 | 1.5 | 1.6 | 1.7 | 2.0 | 3.2 |
| | $P_2$ | 4.7 | 4.4 | 4.1 | 3.8 | 3.3 | 2.3 | 0.9 |
| | $A$ | 10 | 20 | 30 | 40 | 50 | 70 | 90 |
| 20% | $R_0$ | 0.96 | 0.90 | 0.82 | 0.68 | 0.25 | — | — |
| | $k_0$ | 2.0 | 2.2 | 2.6 | 3.6 | ∞ | — | — |
| | $P_2$ | 4.2 | 3.3 | 2.4 | 1.3 | 0 | — | — |
| | $A$ | 20 | 40 | 60 | 80 | 100 | — | — |
| 30% | $R_0$ | 0.92 | 0.79 | 0.49 | — | — | — | — |
| | $k_0$ | 2.4 | 3.1 | 6.0 | — | — | — | — |
| | $P_2$ | 3.7 | 2.2 | 0.6 | — | — | — | — |
| | $A$ | 30 | 60 | 90 | — | — | — | — |
| 40% | $R_0$ | 0.89 | 0.61 | — | — | — | — | — |
| | $k_0$ | 2.8 | 4.7 | — | — | — | — | — |
| | $P_2$ | 3.2 | 1.1 | — | — | — | — | — |
| | $A$ | 40 | 80 | — | — | — | — | — |
| 50% | $R_0$ | 0.85 | 0.1 | — | — | — | — | — |
| | $k_0$ | 3.1 | ∞ | — | — | — | — | — |
| | $P_2$ | 2.6 | 0 | — | — | — | — | — |
| | $A$ | 50 | 100 | — | — | — | — | — |

The results in the table show that sizeable gains in precision in the estimation of $P$ (i.e., sizeable reductions in $R_0$ below 1) accrue only when $P_1$ is much larger than $P$ and when $W_1$ is large. For a given value of $P_1$, the minimum value of $R_0$ occurs when $P = W_1P_1$ so that $P_2 = 0$; in this case, no sampling is needed in stratum 2, and $R_0 = W_1 = P/P_1$. The minimum value of $R_0$ with $P_1/P = 2$ is thus $R_0 = 0.5$; with $P_1/P = 4$ it is $R_0 = 0.25$, etc. The values of $R_0$ increase rapidly above their minimum values when $W_1$ is less than its maximum value of $P/P_1$. Thus, for instance, with $P/P_1 = 2$, the minimum value of $R_0 = 0.5$ occurs when $W_1 = 50$ percent; as can be seen from the table, with $P = 5$ percent and $P_1 = 10$ percent, when $W_1 = 45$ percent, $R_0$ is substantially higher than

0.5 at 0.77; similarly it can be shown that with $P = 10$ percent and $P_1 = 20$ percent, when $W_1 = 45$ percent, $R_0 = 0.79$.

The above findings can be expressed in a variety of alternative ways. Large values of $P_1$ and $W_1$ imply small values of $P_2$ and large values of $A$, the proportion of the rare population in stratum 1. Thus substantial reductions in $R_0$ require a large value of $P_1$ and a small value of $P_2$, or large values of $P_1$ and $A$. Note also that a large value of $P_1$ is not sufficient to ensure a substantial reduction in $R_0$; a large value of $A$, or a small value of $P_2$, is also needed.

## ESTIMATING A MEAN FOR THE RARE POPULATION

Consider now the estimation of a mean $\bar{Y}$ for members of the rare population. As before, suppose that there are two strata, with stratum 1 having a high prevalence and stratum 2 a low prevalence of the rare trait. Suppose that simple random samples are selected from the two strata, with the sampling fraction in stratum 1 being $k$ times that in stratum 2, and assume that the strata are large so that fpc terms may be ignored. Let $A$ be the proportion of the rare population in stratum 1 and $(1 - A)$ be the proportion in stratum 2. We assume initially that $A$ is known, although in practice this will seldom be the case. With this assumption $\bar{Y} = A\bar{Y}_1 + (1 - A)\bar{Y}_2$ may be estimated by $\bar{y} = A\bar{y}_1 + (1 - A)\bar{y}_2$, where $\bar{y}_1$ and $\bar{y}_2$ are the means of sample members in the rare population in the two strata. For simplicity we assume that the element variances of the $y$ variable for members of the rare population are the same in the two strata. We also assume that the costs of data collection are the same for the two strata. However, we allow for a difference in the costs of sampling members of the rare and nonrare populations. This difference is needed to reflect the fact that when a member of the rare population is sampled a full interview is conducted, whereas when a member of the nonrare population is sampled the interview can be terminated at the end of the screening questions.

Letting $c$ be the ratio of the cost of sampling a member of the rare population to that of sampling a member of the nonrare population, the ratio of the variance of $\bar{y}$ under a disproportionate allocation to that under a proportionate allocation is approximately

$$R \cong \frac{[kp - (k - 1)W_1P_1][(c - 1)\{P + (k - 1)W_1P_1\} + (k - 1)W_1 + 1]}{kP[(c - 1)P + 1]} \qquad (1)$$

and the optimum choice for $k$, the ratio of the sampling fractions in the two strata, is given by

$$k_0^2 = \frac{P_1[(c - 1)(P - W_1P_1) + (1 - W_1)]}{(P - W_1P_1)[(c - 1)P_1 + 1]} \qquad (2)$$

The derivations of these results are given in the appendix to the original paper.

If the costs of sampling members of the rare and nonrare populations are assumed to be the same, i.e., $c = 1$, the above formulae simplify considerably, with $k_0$ reducing to $\sqrt{(P_1/P_2)}$. For this case, equivalent results—but expressed in terms of different parameters—are derived by Waksberg, who also gives a discussion of them [17]. Table 2 presents values of $R_0$ (the value of $R$ when $k = k_0$), $k_0$, $P_2$ and $A$ for various combinations of $P_1$ and $W_1$ when the overall population percentage with the rare trait is 5 percent and when $c = 1$. As with

Table 2. Estimating a Mean for the Rare Population: Values of $R_0$, $k_0$, $P_2$ and $A$ for Combinations of $P_1$ and $W_1$, with $P = 5\%$ and $c = 1$

| Values of $P_1$ | | Values of $W_1$: 5% | 10% | 15% | 20% | 25% | 35% | 45% |
|---|---|---|---|---|---|---|---|---|
| 10% | $R_0$ | 0.99 | 0.98 | 0.97 | 0.95 | 0.93 | 0.88 | 0.76 |
| | $k_0$ | 1.5 | 1.5 | 1.6 | 1.6 | 1.7 | 2.1 | 3.3 |
| | $P_2$ | 4.7 | 4.4 | 4.1 | 3.8 | 3.3 | 2.3 | 0.9 |
| | $A$ | 10 | 20 | 30 | 40 | 50 | 70 | 90 |
| 20% | $R_0$ | 0.94 | 0.87 | 0.78 | 0.64 | 0.25 | — | — |
| | $k_0$ | 2.2 | 2.4 | 2.9 | 4.0 | ∞ | — | — |
| | $P_2$ | 4.2 | 3.3 | 2.4 | 1.3 | 0 | — | — |
| | $A$ | 20 | 40 | 60 | 80 | 100 | — | — |
| 30% | $R_0$ | 0.88 | 0.71 | 0.43 | — | — | — | — |
| | $k_0$ | 2.9 | 3.7 | 7.1 | — | — | — | — |
| | $P_2$ | 3.7 | 2.2 | 0.6 | — | — | — | — |
| | $A$ | 30 | 60 | 90 | — | — | — | — |
| 40% | $R_0$ | 0.80 | 0.50 | — | — | — | — | — |
| | $k_0$ | 3.6 | 6.0 | — | — | — | — | — |
| | $P_2$ | 3.2 | 1.1 | — | — | — | — | — |
| | $A$ | 40 | 80 | — | — | — | — | — |
| 50% | $R_0$ | 0.72 | 0.10 | — | — | — | — | — |
| | $k_0$ | 4.4 | ∞ | — | — | — | — | — |
| | $P_2$ | 2.6 | 0 | — | — | — | — | — |
| | $A$ | 50 | 100 | — | — | — | — | — |

| $W_1 = 5\%$ | Values of $P_1$: 60% | 70% | 80% | 90% | 100% |
|---|---|---|---|---|---|
| $R_0$ | 0.62 | 0.52 | 0.40 | 0.27 | 0.05 |
| $k_0$ | 5.3 | 6.7 | 8.7 | 13.1 | ∞ |
| $P_2$ | 2.1 | 1.6 | 1.1 | 0.5 | 0 |
| $A$ | 60 | 70 | 80 | 90 | 100 |

Table 1, Table 2 shows that the reduction in variance from using the optimum disproportionate allocation over proportionate allocation is small unless $P_1$ and $A$ are large. For small values of $A$, even large values of $P_1$ are not adequate to cause $R_0$ to be small; for instance, when $P_1 = 50$ percent and $W_1 = 5$ percent (hence $P_2 = 2.6$ percent), $R_0$ is as high as 0.72. For a given value of $P_1$, the value of $R_0$ declines at a relatively slow rate as $A$ increases to about 80 percent, and then declines rapidly as $A$ increases from 80 percent to 100 percent. The maximum reduction occurs for a given value of $P_1$ when $A = 100$ percent in which case $R_0 = W_1$.

When $A = 100$ percent, $P_2 = 0$ and $k_0 = \infty$: no sampling is needed in stratum 2 since it contains no members of the rare population. When $A$ is close to 100 percent, $P_2$ is close to 0, so that a sample taken in stratum 2 will yield only a small number of members of the rare population. For this reason, it is common practice to confine the sample to stratum 1 when $(1 - A)$ is known to be sufficiently small. This practice leads to biased estimators, but provided $(1 - A)$ is sufficiently small and the members of the rare population in stratum 2 are not too different from those in stratum 1, the bias will be negligible compared with the standard error of the estimator. One application of this approach can arise when using area sampling to sample members of a minority population. If the minority is highly concentrated geographically, it may be possible to identify a small proportion of areas that contains a high proportion of the minority, and then restrict the sample to those areas [52]. A sufficiently high degree of concentration occurs seldom in practice, however. Moreover, considerable caution is needed in applying this cut-off method, since the data on which the exclusions are made are generally out-of-date: if the distribution of the minority has changed markedly in the interim, a serious bias can result.

Table 3 illustrates the effect of differential costs for including members of the rare and nonrare populations in the survey. The table gives values for $R_0$ and $k_0$ for varying values of $P_1$ and $c$, holding $P$ and $W_1$ fixed at 5 percent and 10 percent respectively. The results show that for a given value of $P_1$, the value of $R_0$ increases and the value of $k_0$ declines as $c$ increases. With $P_1 = 40\%$, for instance, $R_0 = 0.50$ if $c = 1$ but $R_0 = 0.76$ if $c = 10$. When $c$ is much greater than 1, as would often be the case in practice, the gains from optimum allocation are appreciably less than those given in Table 2.

A limitation to the preceding results is that they are based on the assumption that $A$, the proportion of the rare population that is in stratum 1, is known, whereas in practice this will rarely be the case. When $A$ is unknown, $\bar{Y}$ may be estimated by $\bar{y}' = a\bar{y}_1 + (1 - a)\bar{y}_2$, where $a = m_1 f_2(m_1 f_2 + m_2 f_1)$, with $m_1$ and $m_2$ being the sample sizes of members of the rare population and $f_1$ and $f_2$ being the sampling fractions in the two strata. When $\bar{y}'$ is used as the estimator, formulae (1) and (2) for $R_0$ and $k_0$ need modification to include terms involving the difference between the stratum means in the survey variable. However, if $\bar{Y}_1$ and $\bar{Y}_2$ are assumed equal, these additional terms disappear, and the preceding formulae hold

Table 3. Estimating a Mean for the Rare Population: Values of $R_0$ and $k_0$, for Various Values of $P_1$ and $c$, with $P$ = 5% and $W_1$ = 10%

| | $P_1$ | | | | | | | | | |
|---|---|---|---|---|---|---|---|---|---|---|
| | *10%* | | *20%* | | *30%* | | *40%* | | *50%* | |
| $c$ | $R_0$ | $k_0$ | $R_0$ | $k_0$ | $R_0$ | $k_0$ | $R_0$ | $k_0$ | $R_0$ | $k_0$ |
| 1 | 0.98 | 1.5 | 0.87 | 2.4 | 0.71 | 3.7 | 0.50 | 6.0 | 0.10 | $\infty$ |
| 2 | 0.98 | 1.5 | 0.89 | 2.3 | 0.75 | 3.3 | 0.55 | 5.1 | 0.14 | $\infty$ |
| 5 | 0.99 | 1.4 | 0.92 | 1.9 | 0.82 | 2.6 | 0.66 | 3.8 | 0.25 | $\infty$ |
| 10 | 0.99 | 1.3 | 0.95 | 1.7 | 0.88 | 2.1 | 0.76 | 2.9 | 0.38 | $\infty$ |

as approximations for this case also. Moreover, even if $\bar{Y}_1$ and $\bar{Y}_2$ are not equal, formulae (1) and (2) will still serve as good guides provided that the between stratum variance is small relative to the within stratum variance, as will often be the case in practice.

Finally, it should be noted that the values of $R_0$ reported in the above tables are the minimum values obtained with the optimum allocation. The value of the optimum ratio of the sampling fractions in the two strata, $k_0$, depends on the parameters $P_1$, $W_1$ and $c$. In practice, none of these will be known precisely, so that the optimum allocation will not be achieved exactly. Provided a value of $k$ close to $k_0$ is used, however, the associated value of $R$ will not be much greater than $R_0$.

## ACKNOWLEDGEMENTS

We wish to thank Joseph Waksberg for valuable comments on an earlier version of this chapter, and also a referee who made a number of helpful suggestions.

## REFERENCES

1. R. C. Elandt-Johnson, Definitions of Rates: Some Remarks on Their Use and Misuse, *American Journal of Epidemiology, 102,* pp. 267–271, 1975.
2. L. Kish, *Survey Sampling,* Wiley, New York, 1965.
3. ________,Selection Techniques for Rare Traits, in *Genetics and the Epidemiology of Chronic Diseases,* Public Health Service Publication No. 1163, U.S. Department of Health, Education, and Welfare, Washington, D.C., 1965.
4. O. T. Thornberry and J. T. Massey, Coverage and Response in Random Digit Dialed National Surveys, *Proceedings of the Section on Survey Research Methods, American Statistical Association,* pp. 654–659, 1983.
5. H. E. Freeman, K. J. Kiecolt, W. L. Nicholls, and J. M. Shanks, Telephone Sampling Bias in Surveying Disability, *Public Opinion Quarterly, 46,* pp. 392–407, 1982.
6. A. Harris, *Handicapped and Impaired in Great Britain.* H.M.S.O., London, 1971.
7. A. Cartwright, *Human Relations and Hospital Care,* Routledge and Kegan Paul, London, 1964.
8. A. Hunt, *The Elderly at Home,* H.M.S.O., London, 1978.
9. J. Waksberg, Sampling Methods for Random Digit Dialing, *Journal of the American Statistical Association, 73,* pp. 40–46, 1978.
10. S. Sudman, Efficient Screening Methods for the Sampling of Geographically Clustered Special Populations, *Journal of Marketing Research, 22,* pp. 20–29, 1985.
11. J. Blair and R. Czaja, Locating a Special Population Using Random Digit Dialing, *Public Opinion Quarterly, 46,* pp. 585–590, 1982.
12. J. Waksberg, A Note on "Locating a Special Population Using Random Digit Dialing," *Public Opinion Quarterly, 47,* pp. 576–579, 1983.
13. S. Sudman, On Sampling Very Rare Human Populations, *Journal of the American Statistical Association, 67,* pp. 335–339, 1972.

14. D. W. Anderson, B. S. Schoenberg, and A. F. Haerer, Racial Differentials in the Prevalence of Major Neurological Disorders: Background and Methods of the Copiah County Study, *Neuroepidemiology, 1,* pp. 17–30, 1982.
15. W. E. Deming, An Essay on Screening, or on Two-Phase Sampling, Applied to Surveys of a Community, *International Statistical Review, 45,* pp. 29–37, 1977.
16. J. Fry, J. B. Dillane, R. F. McNab Jones, G. Kalton, and E. Andrew, The Outcome of Acute Otitis Media (A Report to the Medical Research Council), *British Journal of Preventive and Social Medicine, 23,* pp. 205–209, 1969.
17. J. Waksberg, The Effect of Stratification with Differential Sampling Rates on Attributes of Subsets of the Population, *Proceedings of the Social Statistics Section, American Statistical Association,* pp. 429–434, 1973.
18. E. P. Ericksen, Sampling a Rare Population: A Case Study, *Journal of the American Statistical Association, 71,* pp. 816–822, 1976.
19. M. G. Sirken, B. I. Graubard, and M. J. McDaniel, National Network Surveys of Diabetes, *Proceedings of the Section on Survey Research Methods, American Statistical Association,* pp. 631-635, 1978.
20. M. G. Sirken, P. Royston, R. Warnecke, E. Eastman, R. Czaja, and D. Monsees, Pilot of the National Cost of Cancer Care Survey, *Proceedings of the Section on Survey Research Methods, American Statistical Association,* pp. 579–584, 1980.
21. R. Czaja, R. B. Warnecke, E. Eastman, P. Royston, M. Sirken, and D. Tutuer, Locating Patients with Rare Diseases Using Network Sampling: Frequency and Quality of Reporting, in *Health Survey Research Methods, 1982,* C. F. Cannell and R. M. Groves, (eds.), pp. 311-324. Publication No. (PHS) 84–3346. U.S. Department of Health and Human Services, Washington, D.C., 1984.
22. G. Nathan, An Empirical Study of Response and Sampling Errors for Multiplicity Estimates with Different Counting Rules, *Journal of the American Statistical Association, 71,* pp. 808–815, 1976.
23. G. S. Rothbart, M. Fine, and S. Sudman, On Finding and Interviewing the Needles in the Haystack: The Use of Multiplicity Sampling, *Public Opinion Quarterly, 46,* pp. 408–421, 1982.
24. C. Brown and J. Ritchie, *Focussed Enumeration. The Development of a Method for Sampling Ethnic Minority Groups,* Policy Studies Institute and Social and Community Planning Research, London, 1981.
25. J. W. Bergsten and S. A. Pierson, Telephone Screening for Rare Characteristics Using Multiplicity Counting Rules, *Proceedings of the Section on Survey Research Methods, American Statistical Association,* pp. 145–150, 1982.
26. M. G. Sirken, Discussion: Survey Methods for Rare Populations, in *Health Survey Research Methods, 1982,* C. F. Cannell and R. M. Groves, (eds.), pp. 347–349. Publication No. (PHS) 84–3346. U.S. Department of Health and Human Services, Washington, D.C., 1984.
27. J. Lessler, Multiplicity Estimators with Multiple Counting Rules for Multistage Sample Surveys, *Proceedings of the Social Statistics Section, American Statistical Association,* pp. 12–16, 1981.
28. F. A. Bryan, J. T. Lessler, M. F. Weeks, and N. N. Woodbury, Pilot Study for a National Survey of Epilepsy, in *Health Survey Research Methods, 1982,* C. F. Cannell and R. M. Groves, (eds.), pp. 329–334. Publication No. (PHS) 84–3346. U.S. Department of Health and Human Services, Washington, D.C., 1984.

29. Z. W. Birnbaum and M. G. Sirken, *Design of Sample Surveys to Estimate the Prevalence of Rare Diseases: Three Unbiased Estimates,* National Center for Health Statistics, Series 2, No. 11, U.S. Government Printing Office, Washington, D.C., 1965.
30. M. G. Sirken, Household Surveys with Multiplicity, *Journal of the American Statistical Association, 65,* pp. 257–266, 1970.
31. ________ Stratified Sample Surveys with Multiplicity, *Journal of the American Statistical Association, 67,* pp. 224–227, 1972.
32. ________ Variance Components of Multiplicity Estimators, *Biometrics, 28,* pp. 869–873, 1972.
33. M. G. Sirken and P. S. Levy, Multiplicity Estimation of Proportions Based on Ratios of Random Variables, *Journal of the American Statistical Association, 69,* pp. 68–73, 1974.
34. P. S. Levy, Optimum Allocation in Stratified Random Network Sampling for Estimating the Prevalence of Attributes in Rare Populations, *Journal of the American Statistical Association, 72,* pp. 758–763, 1977.
35. M. G. Sirken and P. N. Royston, Reasons Deaths Are Missed in Household Surveys of Population Change, *Proceedings of the Social Statistics Section, American Statistical Association,* pp. 361–364, 1970.
36. M. H. Hansen, W. N. Hurwitz, and W. G. Madow, *Sample Survey Methods and Theory, Vol. I,* Wiley, New York, 1953.
37. J. D. Schein, *The Deaf Community: Studies in the Social Psychology of Deafness,* Gallaudet College Press, Washington, D.C., 1968.
38. H. O. Hartley, Multiple Frame Surveys, *Proceedings of the Social Statistics Section, American Statistical Association,* pp. 203–206, 1962.
39. ________,Multiple Frame Methodology and Selected Applications, *Sankhya C, 36,* pp. 99–118, 1974.
40. R. S. Cochran, Multiple Frame Sample Surveys, *Proceedings of the Social Statistics Section, American Statistical Association,* pp. 16–19, 1964.
41. W. A. Fuller and L. F. Burmeister, Estimators for Samples Selected from Two Overlapping Frames, *Proceedings of the Social Statistics Section, American Statistical Association,* pp. 245–249, 1972.
42. R. E. Lund, Estimators in Multiple Frame Surveys, *Proceedings of the Social Statistics Section, American Statistical Association,* pp. 282–288, 1968.
43. R. J. Casady, C. B. Snowden, and M. G. Sirken, A Study of Dual Frame Estimators for the National Health Interview Survey, *Proceedings of the Section on Survey Research Methods, American Statistical Association,* pp. 444–447, 1981.
44. R. M. Groves and J. M. Lepkowski, Alternative Dual Frame Mixed Mode Survey Designs, *Proceedings of the Section on Survey Research Methods, American Statistical Association,* pp. 154–159, 1982.
45. J. M. Lepkowski and R. M. Groves, The Impact of Bias on Dual-Frame Survey Designs, *Proceedings of the Section on Survey Research Methods, American Statistical Association,* pp. 265–270, 1984.
46. P. Biernacki and D. Waldorf, Snowball Sampling, Problems and Techniques of Chain Referral Sampling, *Sociological Methods and Research, 10,* pp. 141–163, 1981.
47. S. Welch, Sampling by Referral in a Dispersed Population, *Public Opinion Quarterly, 39,* pp. 237–245, 1975.

48. R. E. Snow, J. D. Hutcheson, and J. E. Prather, Using Reputational Sampling to Identify Residential Clusters of Minorities Dispersed in a Large Urban Region: Hispanics in Atlanta, Georgia, *Proceedings of the Section on Survey Research Methods, American Statistical Association,* pp. 101–106, 1981.
49. L. A. Goodman, Snowball Sampling, *Annals of Mathematical Statistics, 32,* pp. 148–170, 1961.
50. J. S. Reed, Needles in Haystacks: Studying "Rare" Populations by Secondary Analysis of National Sample Surveys, *Public Opinion Quarterly, 39,* pp. 514–522, 1975.
51. W. G. Cochran, *Sampling Techniques.* 3rd Edition, Wiley, New York, 1977.
52. B. M. Hedges, Sampling Minority Populations, in *Social and Educational Research in Action,* M. J. Wilson (ed.), pp. 244–261, Longman, London, 1979.

CHAPTER
# 2

# Secondary Analysis of Sample Surveys in Gerontological Research

*Jersey Liang and Renée H. Lawrence*

## I. INTRODUCTION

Secondary data analysis refers to the analysis of existing data initially collected for another purpose. Thus, although the primary focus of the original research concerns has been addressed in the original analysis, the process of extracting knowledge need not cease. "Secondary" merely refers to the fact that the analysis was not originally planned, and certainly does not imply that it is of lower status or lesser importance when compared to primary analysis [1]. Indeed, secondary analysis provides valuable opportunities for increasing scientific knowledge and refining theoretical inquiry. Primary and secondary data analyses should not be viewed as competing strategies to each other but rather as complementary for advancing knowledge. The value of secondary data analysis is also illustrated by the fact that it has been a major mode of research in many disciplines including economics, demography, sociology, political science, and epidemiology.

Broadly speaking, secondary data analysis includes at least five distinct approaches. The first involves secondary analysis of sample surveys. To accomplish this, the researcher must have access to the survey data sets. The second approach is meta-analysis which entails counting statistically significant results and the averaging of quantitative outcome measures across studies [2]. The third approach involves the use of published data such as rates, crosstabulations, and in some cases, correlation or covariance matrices from census, vital registration, and sample surveys [3]. This method is often favored by economists, epidemiologists, and demographers in making estimations and projections. The fourth approach calls for the analysis of personal documents such as autobiographies, letters, diaries, and essays [4]. The fifth approach involves the examination or content analysis of mass communication documents which include literary productions, newspapers, magazines, motion pictures, and radio or television broadcasts [4]. Given that these five types of secondary analysis call for rather different methodologies, and a discussion of all five strategies is certainly not feasible at the present time, it is our intention to concentrate on secondary analysis of sample surveys.

## PRINCIPLES OF SECONDARY DATA ANALYSIS

As with primary data analysis, the decision to undertake secondary data analysis is predicated upon a clear specification of the research question and the basic research design. Nevertheless, this process is not always unidirectional. Oftentimes various design concerns as well as opportunities may lead to a redefinition of the research questions and design. Further, many of the procedures, notably multivariate statistical techniques, apply equally well to secondary as well as to primary data analysis. Accordingly, only principles somewhat unique to secondary data analysis will be covered in this chapter.

Hyman discussed the three distinctive features of secondary analysis [5] : 1) research design; 2) selection of indicators and index construction; and 3) problems of error. With reference to research design, the secondary analyst rearranges survey parts either from one survey or from several surveys. Besides designing by rearranging or combining parts, the secondary analyst also exercises design control by eliminating parts of the original survey or surveys that either would complicate the analysis or are not relevant to the analysis. Research design decisions entailing the elimination of complicating elements could include recognizing ambiguous or poor eliciting questions, and/or recognizing measurement or distribution concerns regarding the question and response to the question (e.g. missing data, lack of variation in responses). Attending to the quality and accuracy of the original research procedures in selecting surveys, eliminating error burdened sections or questions, and attenuating error by combining surveys are all research design strategies that the secondary analyst employs to reduce error.

Selection of indicators and index construction is another distinctive principle. A critical task for secondary analysts is searching and securing appropriate indicators to measure concepts of interest. To the extent the analyst is successful, and valid indicators are selected or constructed, measurement error is minimized. However, when stretching the definition of a construct and careless cultivating of variables to compose an index occur, the instrument does not measure what it is supposed to and the costly result is error in measurement [5].

Error in measurement is not uncommon in primary data, although difficult to quantify, and indeed the task of controlling error is central to primary as well as secondary data analysis. Nevertheless, the efforts and strategies to control error in secondary analysis are different and deserve emphasis. As already mentioned, control, appraisal, and reduction of error should be exercised when one selects surveys and, additionally, selects indicators. However, such efforts can be thwarted to the extent one lacks enough information about the original procedures to allow for sound appraisal of errors in the data [5]. Thus, for example, error can result when a survey procedure done by the original investigator for one purpose is translated by the secondary user as if it would serve another purpose, especially if done without clear appraisal of the original procedure and purpose. Appraisal of and concerns about errors are not necessarily removed even when the original procedures seem well documented. After all, evaluation of the impact of procedure upon conclusions is essential and should not be easily dismissed just because the procedures are of good quality, since that procedure may be useful only to the original purposes. For example, in longitudinal research one may find that the response format was changed over the course of research although the same question was asked. Similarly, in a series of multiple surveys question wording may vary as well as number of response options. Undoubtedly a major principle for performing good secondary analysis is appraising the original methods and exercising informed judgement on whether to accept the original investigator's judgements. In addition, it is helpful to have a thorough understanding of methods, procedures, and limitations associated with primary data.

Secondary data can be used in conjunction with primary data. This obviously depends on the nature of the research question and research design. Hence, secondary data analysis does not imply the exclusion of primary data collection. In fact, researchers often supplement and enhance secondary data with primary data. One such example is the follow-up of respondents involved in the original cross-sectional study. As a result, a two-wave panel data set can be assembled. Accordingly, it should be noted that the process involved in secondary data analysis is in fact quite similar to that in the primary data analysis with the exception that the data were gathered primarily by acquiring previously collected information.

## BENEFITS AND COSTS ASSOCIATED WITH SECONDARY ANALYSIS

Compared with primary data analysis, secondary analysis involves certain tradeoffs. One major benefit in undertaking secondary analysis is savings associated with cost, time, and personnel. For a fairly typical probability sample survey, involving 1,500 personal interviews of elderly respondents, it is not uncommon that the total cost of data collection exceeds $200,000. Frequently, primary data collection accounts for more than 40 percent of the total direct cost. This includes the design of an instrument, sampling, pilot study, field operation, coding, data cleaning, data management, and data processing. This process can easily take six months or longer and requires expertise and resources that many organizations and researches do not possess. In contrast, one can usually purchase a high quality survey data set for less than $200. Thus, secondary analysis can be utilized by a wide range of researchers not just those able to secure funds or those associated with well established research organizations.

As a point of reference it is useful to note that the annual budget for the National Health Interview Survey is $6.5 million. There is no easy way to duplicate such data for under $2-3 million given the cost of primary data collection for a survey with highly trained interviewers, high response rates, and quality control. In addition, collection of that data set took four years and provides a multipurpose survey that creates a good national profile. Data analysts can purchase the tapes for this data set for $260 (M.G. Kovar, personal communication, January 5, 1987). Clearly, as Kovar points out, this does not deny the role of supplemental specialized surveys which provide data in greater depth on a particular issue, particularly if the same questions, procedures for overall control, and response variables are used as in the national survey.

In addition to the direct savings, secondary data analysis also yields some indirect benefits. To the extent that research questions can be addressed by secondary analysis, resources can then be directed toward the collection of additional new data which do not duplicate existing data bases. Furthermore with secondary data, the researcher can afford to spend relatively more time and energy in data analysis than the primary data analyst who must make a substantial investment in data collection.

Aside from the above advantages, secondary analysis of sample surveys is a research strategy of great versatility. For instance, it is an excellent way of undertaking preliminary analysis prior to collecting primary data. One can examine issues related to measurement thus identifying indicators for further work. In addition, secondary data analysis provides certain options which are often unavailable to primary analysts without extensive resources. These options may include multiple sample replications, longitudinal analysis, and cohort analysis. Moreover, as mentioned, under many circumstances secondary data can be supplemented by primary data, thus presenting additional opportunities.

Despite its many advantages, secondary analysis of sample surveys does have certain limitations. There are two major limitations which are unique to secondary analysis. First, suitable data sets may not be available or accessible. Frequently, the selection of appropriate measures may be severely limited since the data used are often not generated with the purpose of specific secondary analyses in mind. Thus, a major challenge confronted by the secondary analyst is to obtain the data suitable for the research questions. To a certain extent, the difficulty of data acquisition can be overcome. More discussion of strategies of data acquisition will be presented later.

The second limitation lies in the fact that the analyst may not know enough about the original procedures to make a sound appraisal of errors in the data [5]. Frequently, the secondary analyst does not have access to collateral materials such as verbatim answers to open-ended questions, comments of respondents, interviewers' reports, etc. Sometimes the analyst may be faced with inadequate documentation regarding essential research operations like sample selection and coding conventions. However, these limitations can be avoided or minimized by careful selection of data sets and a vigorous search of information related to the data sets chosen. In addition, often one can obtain additional information by contacting the researcher, the manager of the data collection, or the organization which undertook the data collection originally. Strategies dealing with quality appraisal will be discussed in a later section (Data Acquisition and Appraisal).

By now it should be quite obvious that secondary data analysis is certainly no substitute for primary data analysis. Instead, there are often trade-offs involved. Under certain circumstances, secondary data analysis is quite appropriate and very useful. With the availability of high quality survey data sets, better access to computers, and more sophisticated analytical techniques, secondary analysis of sample surveys has increasingly become a viable and appealing option for gerontologists. Nevertheless, this option often remains unrecognized due to several obstacles. One has been a lack of awareness of the opportunities available. A related difficulty is not knowing where and how to acquire data. Yet another obstacle has been that researchers often are not skilled regarding the particulars of the procedures and principles associated with secondary analysis of survey data [5] and/or are not familiar with survey research methods in general [4, 6]. Even when secondary analysis has been undertaken, it may not be well executed, leaving the skeptical increasingly cautious and the naive confused, at best.

It is our intent in this chapter to acquaint the interested with the general strategies of secondary analysis of sample surveys as it relates to gerontological research. Following this general introduction, information and procedures unique to secondary analysis will be presented first. These include a brief description of major sources of data and the guiding principles of data acquisition and data appraisal. Second, major designs of secondary data analysis with illustrations of such applications will be described. Finally, some characteristics of successful secondary analysts will be defined. The topics discussed will be relevant not only for those planning or hoping to conduct secondary analysis, but for those who want to be informed in order to better evaluate presentations and publications based on secondary analysis.

## II. MAJOR SOURCES OF DATA

With the growing potentialities for secondary data analysis, it is important to know how to identify, obtain, and evaluate data sets. In the process of identifying relevant and potential data sources, three general resources are suggested: 1) published research, 2) data archives, and 3) major data programs. Of course, one should review and consider as many potential data sources as possible to ensure a good match between need and availability.

Published research may be helpful in two ways. First, one can identify public data sources used by other researchers. Second, published research may be helpful by identifying a primary researcher who may be willing to share data, particularly if proper credit is granted. Further, locating relevant surveys can be facilitated by other researchers through informal networks among researchers of a common interest area.

Thanks to the foresight and commitment of many social scientists and agencies providing financial support, archives were created to preserve and distribute machine-readable social data [7]. Accordingly, data archives can function as valuable resources in identifying relevant data sets. Data archives are organized and function much like libraries or other archives: they provide repositories for many collections of data sets which are made available to interested researchers. Among the goals of data archives are preparing, maintaining and organizing computer-readable data, compiling documentation, making such resources available, providing services to facilitate these goals (e.g., assistance and methodological training), and recently, acting as an intermediary for dissemination of federally collected data. Further, as Traugott notes, with availability increasing in amount and kind, archives will be challenged to explore and develop means for simplifying access to such increasing resources [8]. Archives provide directories or catalogues of holdings which are usually available upon request, although a small charge may be necessary. Such catalogues make it possible to review available data sets. In addition, data archivists can be of help by directly aiding in the process through their familiarity with their own holdings and through referrals to other archives.

Since several discussions are available regarding major data archives in the United States and abroad, we will provide only a brief overview before focusing on archives especially relevant to aging. Readers interested in more information and/or a broader presentation of the major data archives are directed to a recent Sage publication by Kiecolt and Nathan [7] which presents a nice review and summary of major public access social science data archives. For additional information on the archives briefly reviewed here, readers are encouraged to contact the archives (addresses of the archives discussed are provided in Appendix A).

## OVERVIEW OF MAJOR U.S. AND FOREIGN ARCHIVES

Within the United States there are several major archives of general interest and purpose. There are three archives of particular importance for our purposes: the Inter-University Consortium for Political and Social Research (ICPSR), the Roper Center for Public Research, and the Louis Harris Data Center.

ICPSR (a consortium including most of the major U.S. universities as members) is housed at the University of Michigan and is the world's largest repository and dissemination service center for machine-readable social science data. The contents housed represent contemporary and historical phenomena encompassing all social science disciplines: economic, sociological, historical, organizational, social, psychological, and political concerns. The archive receives, processes, and disseminates data on social phenomena occurring in over 130 countries.

Further, the archive is constantly expanding the breadth and variety of topics and resources available [9,10].

ICPSR publishes a catalogue of their data holdings known as the *Guide to Resources and Services* yearly. They also publish a bulletin which is sent quarterly to ICPSR Official Representatives and other interested parties. The bulletin provides an update of new collections acquired by the archive. The *Guide to Resources and Services* provides an extensive section outlining the holdings entitled *Archival Holdings*. This section contains a brief abstract of each data set maintained by the archive. This section is organized alphabetically by general subject area, of which there are seventeen (e.g., Education, Health Care and Health Facilities, Mass Political Behavior and Attitudes, and Social Indicators). Within each general subject area the description of the data sets are organized alphabetically by the name of the data collector(s) or principal investigator(s). The *Guide* also has four special indices to facilitate use: 1) ICPSR Study Number/Documentation Index (arranged numerically by ICPSR study number which serves as a point of reference for information contained in the *Archival Holdings* section and the Subject Index), 2) ICPSR Title/Documentation Index (contains identical information as the previous special index except the entries are arranged alphabetically by title), 3) Principal Investigator Index (data sets or studies are organized alphabetically by name or names of the principal investigators or original collectors), and 4) Subject Index (which alphabetically organizes data sets by detailed subject terms, including geographical area).

The Roper Center for Public Opinion Research and the Louis Harris Data Center are two major poll data archives in the United States. The Roper Center has become one of the largest public opinion archives in the world and is housed at the Institute for Social Inquiry at the University of Connecticut in cooperation with Williams College. The archive's holdings emphasize social values, social and political attitudes, policy preferences, and personal assessments. Surveys held by the Center include surveys ranging from 1930 through the present, foreign as well as domestic [11-13].

To facilitate access to the data holdings, the Center publishes *Data Acquisitions* in January and July to inform users of newly acquired data sets. Several other Roper Center publications are available, two of which are worth mentioning: *A Guide to Roper Center Resources for the Study of American Race Relations* [13] and *The Roper Center American Collection: Profiles of the Major Collections*, which surveys their major U.S. holdings. The *Profiles of the Major Collections* is published every six months (January and July). To keep users informed during the interim, The Roper Center also sporadically publishes *Data Set News* which provides summary descriptions of the newly acquired data sets and variables contained in the data sets. For additional information, the interested reader is referred to Kiecolt and Nathan [7] and/or the Roper Center [11-13].

The Louis Harris Center is part of the Social Science Data Library maintained at the University of North Carolina, Chapel Hill. The Center maintains polls conducted by Louis Harris and Associates which both Louis Harris and Associates and the University agreed were and are appropiate for the archive. Accordingly, various Harris surveys are available at the Center covering a variety of topics including elections and buying intentions.

The Institute for Research in Social Science (Chapel Hill) has available reference guides for holdings of the Louis Harris Center [14]. The Institute provides a volume of brief descriptions and a set of abstracts with indices for the Harris surveys. In addition, the *Directory of Louis Harris Public Opinion Machine-Readable Data* (1981) can be obtained from the Institute, as can the *Sourcebook of Harris National Surveys*: *Repeated Questions 1963-1976* [15]. The latter volume indexes social indicators found in questions which have appeared (in identical or slightly altered form) in two or more Harris polls.

There are two foreign archives for which we will provide a brief overview. These archives are located in Britain and Holland. It should be noted that these archives also administer their nations' memberships in the ICPSR.

The largest repository of social science data in Britain is the Social Science Research Council (SSRC) Data Archive housed by the University of Essex. The archive contains academic surveys, opinion polls, government studies, and market research projects, and it also maintains a current record of British social surveys. A complete data catalogue is published by the archive (the *Guide to the Survey Archive Social Science Data Holdings and Allied Services*)[16], as is an abbreviated guide for quick reference. In addition, the archives provide a triannual *Data Archive Bulletin* which includes discussions of new data file acquisitions.

In Holland there exists the Royal Netherlands Academy of Arts and Sciences Social Science Information and Documentation Centre, of which the Steinmetz Archives are part [17]. The available data sets are extensive, reflecting all of the social sciences. Among the numerous holdings are the weekly opinion polls conducted by the Netherlands Institute of Public Opinion and Marketing Research (NIPO). The archive prepares a *Catalogue and Guide* for distribution and also provides a monthly list of new acquisitions.

## ARCHIVES IN AGING

Two additional archives, both located in the United States, are especially relevant to aging. One is the National Archives of Computerized Data on Aging (NACDA) and the other is the Data Archive for Aging and Adult Development (DAAAD). Both archives have been established with the explicit purpose of making available to researchers resources relevant to the study of aging. It is worth noting that the December 1981 issue of *Research on Aging* (Volume 3, Number 4), edited by Patrick and Borgatta, was a special issue on available data bases for aging research [18]. Accordingly, it provides additional information regarding relevant data bases. It should also be emphasized that relevant data sets on the elderly and aging may also be carved from other surveys. That is, to the extent that the sampling procedure reflected efforts to obtain samples representative of the population, there will be a subsample, though often small, of respondents in the upper age cohort available for analysis.

The Inter-University Consortium of Political and Social Research in Ann Arbor Michigan houses the National Archives of Computerized Data on Aging (NACDA) and publishes a catalogue quarterly for these special holdings on topics related to aging [9]. The catalogue of Data Collections is free to ICPSR members and includes descriptions of the collections which are organized alphabetically by the name of the primary investigator. The descriptions provide a brief introduction to the substantive content, the number and length of records, and a designation regarding the level of processing done on the data set by ICPSR. (The designation relates to the amount of processing completed by ICPSR to enhance accessibility, not to the substantive quality of the data). The holdings of individual-level data from surveys can be organized into three major fields of interest: 1) social and economic status studies, 2) health and well-being studies, and 3) life-cycle studies. In addition, other services are provided, including customized data preparation. Customizing or special handling requests may include requests for data to be distributed as computer print-outs or on floppy disks rather than on magnetic tapes. Some customized data extracting is also available if the entire data set is not desired.

In addition to the catalogue listings of its collection, NACDA publishes a quarterly bulletin to provide current information on existing as well as newly acquired data sets and archive activities relevant to researchers in the area of aging. In a recent bulletin (Fall 1986, Volume 5, Number 1) readers were notified that the Variables Database (VDB) has been established by ICPSR providing researchers a means of rapidly sorting through various data collections for question texts or response wordings on topics of interest. Computer accessibility to VDB can be arranged for both local and remote users.

The Duke Center for the Study of Aging and Human Development established DAAAD (The Data Archive for Aging and Adult Development) in 1976. The Center Provides a *Reference Guide* [19] which describes current data holdings and explains how to obtain data from the archive. Surveys in the *Reference Guide* are described with regard to several relevant characteristics, including original investigator, survey date, design and purpose, sample information, and content areas of interest. The descriptions also indicate the quality of the documentation and data types as well as some major publications of interest related to the survey.

## OTHER SOURCES OF DATA

Non-academic sources should also be considered when trying to identify data sources [20-25]. Although often overlooked, there are many programs, governmental and nongovernmental, conducting surveys which can be valuable resources for social scientists. Again, more exhaustive discussions are available [7, 8], while our focus is on a few programs which may be of particular relevance to a wide range of researchers interested in gerontology.

Before discussing a few of the relevant programs, it is worth mentioning the National Technical Information Service (NTIS). NTIS archives and distributes all Federal surveys, the decennial censuses, and vital statistics. In addition, NTIS also archives and distributes all Federal reports, including reports that are never published. Many Federal agencies publish catalogues of public-use data tapes, and accordingly it is worth writing to agencies of interest.

The Bureau of the Census collects a tremendous amount of information which has been recognized by many as a rich resource for social scientists although the information was collected for governmental purposes [7]. Of particular relevance is the information obtained from the decennial census (representative samples drawn from the decennial census constitute the Public Use Microdata Samples), and information from the Current Population Survey (CPS) which is conducted monthly.

Before discussing information obtained from the decennial census and the Current Population Survey, it is worth mentioning that the Bureau of the Census has been conducting the national Annual Housing Survey (AHS) for the Department of Housing and Urban Development since 1973.(Now conducted biennially, it is called the American Housing Survey). The sampling design is longitudinal with respect to housing units. With samples of new housing units being added each time the goal of AHS is to track components of change in the housing inventory, particularly information about housing and neighborhood changes across the nation, as well as household characteristics [26].

The Public Use Microdata Samples (PUMS) from the decennial census of population and housing contain self-reported data on a variety of subjects such as basic demographic information, income, and poverty. Further, a sample of the population is administered an expanded version of the questionnaire which includes additional social indicator questions. As mentioned, the PUMS files are representative samples drawn from the decennial census records. The bureau and other organizations provide aids for using PUMS and the documentation which accompanies the files provides information about sampling procedures and data organization (dictionary), a glossary, and a description of the file.

The Current Population Survey (CPS) is a national survey funded by the Bureau of Labor Statistics of the civilian noninstitutionalized population and is designed primarily to monitor labor force activity. Supplemental information is also collected, some of which is on a regular basis and some of which represents one-time questions. For example, beyond collecting the standard monthly information, each March the CPS collects extensive sociodemographic information on every member of each sample household. Other regular supplemental information has included multiple job-holdings and adult education, educational topics, voting behavior, marital history, and immunization against disease data.

The Bureau publishes the *Bureau of the Census Catalogue* informing interested researchers about census products and services (available for purchase) and a *Directory of Data Files* summarizing available machine-readable data tapes. In addition, the bureau also publishes a monthly newsletter, *Data User News*, describing census products, services, reference materials, conferences, and workshops. The bureau also provides lists of various user services, fields of interest and specific topics, and the names and phone numbers of Census Bureau contacts including regional offices and satellite office telephone numbers.

The *Monthly Product Announcement* provides technical and price information about the latest census products and additional information on those data files can be obtained by requesting a *Data Developments Flyer* for files of interest. Both the monthly announcements and the flyers are free of charge from *Data User Services*. Data User Services also provide a *National Clearinghouse* list which identifies all public and private organizations that distribute census products. Copies of all census products for a given state are deposited in state data centers (of which there are 44). Data Centers are operated in conjunction with state governments and provide Census Bureau data as well as data from other federal agencies and state sources. It should be mentioned that dissemination of data from PUMS and CPS is available from some social science data archives including the ICPSR.

Another valuable data program is the National Center for Health Statistics (NCHS). NCHS conducts national surveys generating information on health and related topics. NCHS releases, free of charge, catalogues summarizing their holdings. The data files and accompanying documentation are sold through the National Technical Information Service. Three of NCHS's continuing and specialized general population surveys are the National Nursing Home Survey (NNHS) Systems, the National Health Interview Survey (NHIS) and the National Health and Nutrition Examination Survey (NHANES), all of which are of much promise to those interested in aging issues.

The National Nursing Home Surveys (NNHS) Systems of the NCHS produces national baseline data on the institutionalization of the aged, including data about both the recipient (for residents and discharges) of services and the provider. Data on samples of residents and discharges are collected by interviewing the nurse most familiar with the recipient and by referring to medical records. For residents only, the nurse supplements the report with working knowledge of the client. The NNHS System covers all types of nursing homes. Client data includes demographic, social activities, health status, services received, and method of payment for care. The Health status information includes data on chronic conditions, behavioral problems, and functional status. Information on the providers includes data about the facility, costs, and staff [27].

The NHIS is designed to collect data on a range of health-related topics, such as incidence of acute illnes, prevalence of chronic illness and impairment, extent of disability, and utilization of health care services. NHIS relies on weekly household interviews with all persons seventeen years of age and older (health information on children is obtained from an adult). It incorporates a repeated core set of items assessing health, socio-economic, and demographic information. Supplements, which are usually annual, emphasize current health topics (e.g., smoking and home health care). Data tapes for the supplements to the NHIS are released by the Division of Health Interview Statistics, NCHS. One supplement of particular interest for studies of aging was the 1984 Supplement on aging.

NHANES (begun in 1971 and expanding upon its forerunner the National Health Examination Survey) provides information about the health status of the population through physical and laboratory examinations and emphasizes nutrition as a health determinant. In addition interviews and questionnaires are included to assess household and individual background information, recall of dietary intake, food regulation and food program. The sampling overrepresents groups thought to be at high risk for malnutrition, of which the elderly are one. Data are available for two completed NHANES surveys (I and II) and are obtainable; both surveys had an upper age limit of seventy-four years. In addition, the 1961–1962 NHES survey (Wave I) concentrated on respondents aged eighteen through seventy-nine. The NHANES III now being designed will extend the age range beyond age seventy-four.

Another federal survey data collection agency of relevance is the Social Security Administration. For example, in 1969 this agency began the Longitudinal Retirement History Survey (LRHS). The LRHS is a ten–year longitudinal study of American retirement which concentrates on expenses, income, and retirement benefits [28,29]. It included interviews of a national sample of 11,000 persons, most of whom were still active in the labor force at the initiation of the study. The sample consisted of men between fifty-eight and sixty–three years of age and women of the same ages who had no husband present in the household. The design provides the opportunity for longitudinal studies of married couples and longitudinal studies of widowhood.

The National Opinion Research Center (NORC), at the University of Chicago, conducts the General Social Survey (GSS). The survey has been conducted yearly since 1972 (with the exception of 1979 and 1981). The purpose of the GSS is to obtain data on a wide variety of attitudes, beliefs, and behaviors including demographic data and pre- and early-adult background characteristics (e.g., job histories, religious background, childhood family composition, and age at first marriage). Some items are included in each survey while others follow a rotational scheme. In addition, the GSS design now allows for intensive one-time coverage of a given topic (e.g., the 1985 survey covered the topic of social networks). The design allows for the study of social change through trend and cohort analyses. The cumulative GSS data files and documentation are available from ICPSR or the Roper Center.

## III. DATA ACQUISITION AND APPRAISAL

Once appropriate data sets have been located, the process of obtaining data sets entails contacting the archive or organization regarding the data sets of interest. If the data collections are held at an archive, the attainment process is usually straightforward. For example, requests for data sets housed in the National Archive of Computerized Data on Aging should be addressed to the archive through the ICPSR official representative for those affiliated with colleges and universities holding membership in the ICPSR, or directly if there is no affiliation. Researchers at institutions which are not ICPSR members are assessed a charge for access based on the size of the data set requested. When requesting a data set one should provide the survey name, year, and ICPSR number as listed in the catalogue. For the majority of other archives, the procedure involves directly contacting the archives to obtain copies of the data set(s) and documentation. Again, the cost of the data sets varies.

If the data set is held by non-academic institutions or other researchers, the process of accessing data may vary, as may the terms. As Kiecolt and Nathan note [7], it is important for researchers to clarify that their goals will not interfere or conflict with the organization's objectives or with the primary investigator's objectives.

In addition to the data file, one should obtain all available documentation. Among the documentation to obtain are the codebook, interview schedule, final report, and previous research papers. Securing such documentation allows one to evaluate how the original study was conducted and to know as much as possible about the original procedures to make a sound appraisal of the errors involved in the data. Obtaining adequate documentation allows one to reduce the limitations which are associated with secondary analysis.

An additional critical step in the preliminary process of conducting secondary analysis is data appraisal. There are really two appraisal processes: 1) appraisal of the quality of the data and 2) appraisal of the obtained data files and records.

The first appraisal process usually begins prior to obtaining data sets and is part of evaluating and identifying data sources and sets. Specifically, this appraisal process relates to evaluating the quality of the data in terms of the original research design, methods, and procedures. This process continues as one examines all of the available documentation and examines the data with reference to distribution concerns (i.e. skewness, kurtosis) related to items of interest.

Further, once a data set has been selected and obtained, it is important to verify the accuracy of the archival data (appraisal of the obtained data files and records). Accuracy of the data can be established by conducting descriptive analyses of the relevant items and comparing them to those originally reported. In many instances the codebook or other documentation obtained provides frequencies for the data set. Another check of the data entails replicating a published analysis. Often catalogues or listings of the collections for many data sets include related publications against which one can verify the data set. To the extent one is able to obtain published research papers, they can be helpful for appraising the accuracy of the data. In addition, it is often helpful to speak to the original investigator and researchers who have used the data.

## IV. MAJOR APPLICATIONS OF SECONDARY DATA ANALYSIS IN GERONTOLOGICAL RESEARCH

In the following some basic designs of secondary analysis will be examined. These include designs involving the use of a single survey as well as multiple surveys. In addition to cross-sectional surveys, secondary analysis of longitudinal data will be discussed. Furthermore, the possibilities of supplementing secondary data with newly collected data will be reviewed. Gerontological examples will be used to illustrate all designs.

### ANALYSIS OF A SINGLE SURVEY

Hypothesis testing which requires extensive data can sometimes be best accommodated by the analysis of a single survey. This is particularly true given the increasing availability of high quality surveys of national probability samples of elderly people. These surveys often include widely used scales and an oversample of minority groups.

One such survey is the National Council on the Aging (NCOA)— Harris Survey, The Myth and Reality of Aging, conducted in 1974. Two questionnaires were used, one asking eighteen to sixty-four year olds their perceptions of how people sixty-five and over felt about aging, and the second asking people sixty-five and over how they actually felt. In addition, both groups were asked general questions on attitudes toward growing old, their interests, and demographic characteristics. There were four national samples : 1) a cross-section of approximately 1,500 adults eighteen years and older; 2) an oversample of approximately 2,400 adults aged sixty-five years and over; 3) an oversample of approximately 360 adults aged fifty-five to sixty-four; and 4) an oversample of approximately 200 blacks aged sixty-five and over.

A large number of studies were generated from the NCOA—Harris Survey. In the following, two such studies will be illustrated. The first is an analysis of intergenerational family support among black and white elderly undertaken by Mutran [30]. Mutran was concerned with the question whether family differences are due to culture or socio-economic factors. Commenting on the fact that earlier studies often used less representative samples, Mutran took advantage of large national samples in the NCOA—Harris Survey. Given that she was only interested in black and white respondents, sixty-five and over, who have adult children, Mutran obtained a subsample based on 194 Blacks and 1,120 Whites, still a quite respectable sample size by any standard. Using this data set, Mutran went on to show that black elderly parents give and receive more help than white elderly parents. The greater amount of help received by older blacks is due to socio-economic factors, while the greater amount of help they give is accounted for by a combination of socio-economic and cultural factors.

The second example is a study on self-conception and life satisfaction by McClelland [31]. This research seeks to integrate the activity theory explanation of adjustment to aging with the age subculture theory. A multiple indicators causal model was specified to delineate the differential importance of self-conception as an intervening variable between activity and life satisfaction. Again, capitalizing on the large sample size of the NCOA—Harris Survey, McClelland was able to undertake this analysis by comparing the elderly person who preferred to be with individuals of their own age (n = 1,324) and those who did not (n = 439).

Concerning the two examples above, it is obvious that the NCOA—Harris is a good data set for secondary analysis. Specifically, there is adequate documentation regarding the conduct of the original study. Hence the research design and quality of data can be evaluated. Another requirement is the inclusion of relevant variables needed for the proposed secondary analysis. As illustrated by the works of Mutran [30] and McClelland [31], this requirement can often be met by a careful choice of items in conjuction with scaling analysis. In particular, Mutran (1985) constructed measures of giving and receiving family help by performing principal component analysis of indicators of various support activities and computed Cronbach's alpha [30]. McClelland used a multiple indicators approach in measuring activity, self-concept, and life satisfaction, and adjusted for measurement error in estimating structural parameters [31]. Nevertheless, it is important to recognize when using the NCOA—Harris Survey that sample weights were used to reconstruct the U.S. population of eighteen years and older. The codebook provides documentation of the procedures.

In addition to being a free-standing analysis, secondary analysis of a single survey often serves as an excellent replication of previous studies. It has long been recognized that replication is a classic and powerful procedure in validating findings obtained from single or special samples [32]. It not only makes the findings less vulnerable to sampling error (as well as measurement and classification error) but also protects the study results from the accidental circumstances which impinge on the particular survey procedures [5]. Hence, by replicating the analysis on different samples, one is able to evaluate the generalizability more rigorously.

One such example is the study undertaken by Collette [33]. He was interested in evaluating the generalizability of the finding that there are few sex differences in the causal process determining life satisfaction. In contrast with the American data used by Liang, Collette used data from a survey of 1,050 respondents representative of the elderly population in Sydney, Australia. Whereas Collette's measures were not identical to those in Liang's research, conceptually they are similar. More importantly, Collette found few sex differences in the causal process determining life satisfaction, thus replicating and further extending the generalizability of the findings reported by Liang.

On the other hand, secondary analysis of a single survey also provides opportunities for internal replications, the examination of structural variations, and/or both. When the sample size is large enough, one may randomly split the sample into subsamples, thus enabling the researcher to replicate the analysis on all subsamples. One such example is the examination of the structure of the Philadelphia Geriatric Center (PGC) Morale Scale [35] undertaken by Liang and Bollen [36]. In this research, a multiple indicator structural equation model including three first-order factors and one second-order factor was proposed to delineate the dimensionality of the PGC Morale Scale. This formulation was empirically examined by using the 1968 National Senior Citizens Survey which involved 3,996 non-institutionalized elderly respondents. To minimize capitalization on chance, the sample was randomly divided into four samples. After excluding cases with missing data, the effective sample size ranged from 828 to 874. One subsample was first analyzed for developing a model with an acceptable fit. The analysis was further extended by using the other three subsamples.

Replication frequently can also lead to further specifications of the theoretical model under examination. A given relationship may vary depending on the particular context. By systematically replicating the analysis under different conditions or within different populations, one may identify contingent associations or interaction effects. Accordingly, further specifications of the model can be made.

The utility of secondary analysis in examining structural variations is illustrated by a series of studies undertaken by Liang and his associates [37–39]. In these studies, the structure of the PGC Morale Scale was analyzed in terms of sex, age, and race differences. These analyses were also replicated by using four random subsamples. Specifically, the hypothesized measurement model was applied to various sex, age, and race subgroups. Significance tests were performed on equivalence constraints placed on various parameter matrices. Whereas few sex and age differences were found, race differences were uncovered in the measurement error variances associated with two items.

## SECONDARY ANALYSIS OF MULTIPLE SURVEYS

The possibilities of secondary analysis can be greatly extended by involving multiple surveys. These possibilities include: 1) multiple replications, 2) pooling, 3) cohort analysis, and 4) cross-national studies. When multiple surveys are involved, comparability in terms of sampling design, measures, and the context becomes a critical issue. For instance, accurate description of differences between groups or individuals over time presupposes comparability of the procedures. Incomparabilities in research design can seriously confound analysis and interpretation of the data. Consequently, before presenting designs involving multiple surveys, the issue of comparability will be addressed.

A useful distinction has been made in the literature between empirical and conceptual replication [40]. Empirical replications involve research designs where the procedures are as identical as possible, particularly with regard to operationalization and instrumentation. Conceptual replications involve research designs where different operational definitions are used to evaluate the same hypotheses or relationships. Both empirical and conceptual replications are critical aspects of replicated secondary data analysis and, accordingly, for establishing the robustness of phenomena. That is, both are critical in examining generalizability of findings. However, it should be noted that given the nature of design for conceptual replications, incompatible results may represent differences across populations and/or instrumentation as well as complexities of the phenomenon.

When a secondary analysis calls for the comparison of equivalent items across multiple surveys, problems of item comparability need to be resolved. Roughly comparable items may have an unequal number of response categories or some of the response categories may differ. Seemingly identical questions on different surveys may also be noncomparable when some are contingency questions or filter questions. In addition, the context and sequence of the survey may influence the responses. A question may be placed differently with respect to other topics or the ordering of items may vary [5, 7, 41].

Another major source of noncomparability may be due to differences in sampling designs across surveys. For instance, the target population and methods of locating and selecting respondents may differ. The increasing use of telephone rather than face-to-face interviews does cause differences in population coverage and nonresponse [5,7,41].

These are difficult issues to address. Frequently, additional information or evidence needs to be provided in order to show that such differences do not invalidate the analysis. If such evidence is not available, the secondary analyst may redefine the research question such that only comparable items are included in the analysis. Furthermore, one should note that the degree of comparability required clearly varies depending on the research question. In general, multiple independent replications where direct comparison is not always necessary does not demand nearly as much comparability as designs like cohort analysis, time series, and cross-cultural comparisons.

In the following, major applications involving multiple surveys will be discussed. When several comparable data sets are available, they provide a good opportunity for undertaking replications as well as the examination of structural variations.

*Replications and/or the examination of structural variations* — George and Landerman used replicated secondary data analysis to explore the bivariate and net (multivariate) relationships between health and subjective well-being [40]. By using replicated secondary data analysis they were able to explore the stability of these relationships across different samples and operationalizations (empirical and conceptual replications). Seven data sets were used allowing for thirty-seven replications. Each data set had multiple indicators of subjective well-being and/or health along with indicators to evaluate, in varying degrees, ten classes of control variables. The control variables had been identified as theoretically relevant and statistically significant correlates of subjective well-being during later life.

The analyses supported a moderate and robust relationship between subjective health assessments and subjective well-being; physician-assessed health exhibited lower correlations which did not remain significant after including covariates. They found that the relationship between subjective health and subjective well-being is stronger for negative affect. In addition, the relationship between subjectively assessed health and well-being appeared larger in samples of older people than in samples of all adults. This observation was supported by further analysis using one of the surveys (Myth and Reality of Aging Harris Survey).

Liang illustrates a secondary analysis incorporating four surveys [34]. The purpose of this study was to determine whether the same causal mechanism accounting for life satisfaction is operating among elderly men as well as elderly women.

Data for this study came from one national survey and three state surveys. The national survey was the 1968 National Senior Citizens Survey (N = 3,996) conducted by Schooler [42]. The state surveys were: 1) the Social Indicator Survey done by the North Carolina Governor's Council on Aging in 1971 (N = 961) [43]; 2) the Survey of the Needs of Wisconsin's Older People by the Wisconsin Department of Health and Social Services in 1971 [44] (N = 2,000), and 3) the Survey of the Status and Needs of Minnesota's Older People conducted in 1971 [45] (N = 1,500).

With the exception of socio-economic status, all variables were measured by multiple items. These variables included health status, financial satisfaction, objective integration, subjective integration, and life satisfaction. Composite indexes were generated on the basis of item analysis. Since four different data sets were involved, in some instances different items were used to measure a given conceptual variable. This is viewed as a strength rather than a limitation in that replication across different populations and methods not only makes the findings less vulnerable to sampling error but also protects them from accidental circumstances operating on a particular procedure [5].

It should be noted that in Liang's study, the design involves both the replications of analysis and the examination of structural variations due to sex. The findings were replicated across four data sets: No systematic sex differences in structural parameters were found. Hence, Liang was able to conclude that the same causal mechanism is operating among the males and the females [34].

Using the same data sets, Liang and Warfel further examined the relationship between urbanism and the causal process determining life satisfaction [46]. To achieve a better approximation to the whole range of urbanism, five categories of place size were used instead of the more conventional urban-rural dichotomy. The categories were: 1) rural area with a population of less than 2,500, 2) small towns with a population between 2,500 and 49,999, 3) cities with a population between 50,000 and 249,000, 4) cities with a population between 250,000 and 999,999, and 5) metropolitan areas with a population of 1,000,000 or more. Given the nature of the data sets involved, only three categories (i.e., rural, small towns, and cities) applied to the North Carolina Survey, and only four categories applied to Minnesota and Wisconsin (i.e., all but 1,000,000 or more). Thus, the number of replications varied depending on the size of place.

The findings revealed that urbanism does not have a direct effect on life satisfaction. However, it exhibits both main and interaction effects indirectly. In particular, urbanism exerts a direct influence on the determinants of life satisfaction such as objective and subjective integration. Moreover, the effects of health and subjective social integration on life satisfaction vary depending on the size of place.

*Pooling of multiple surveys*— In secondary analysis, the opportunities for characterizing one or more social groups can be quite significant. A group that is often too small in any single survey for the findings to have stature can be expanded by a design which combines the data from multiple surveys [5]. This provides a way of studying rare groups and carrying their analysis to a more refined level. For instance, in their analysis of the relationship between aging and party identification, Glenn and Hefner pooled data from three to five surveys at six different dates in order to obtain enlarged samples [47]. This approach conceivably can be employed to study special groups in aging. These may include the oldest-old (aged 85 and over), the elderly Black, the elderly Asian Americans, and elderly widows and widowers. Of course it is necessary to note that the assumption of survey comparability underlying this strategy of combining different surveys may be questionable, as discussed above. That is, the potential noncomparability of different surveys (e.g., changing circumstances causing potential invalidity) needs to be considered carefully, particularly because it is difficult to evaluate the extent of the errors stemming from such an assumption.

Another illustration of pooling multiple surveys comes from a study of the health behaviors of Asian Americans by Liu and Yu [48]. In particular, NHIS data from several years were combined to yield a modicum of health estimates for Asian Americans and Asian American elderly. However, these efforts were possible only by treating Asian Americans and Pacific Islanders as if they were a homogeneous group since the NHIS program does not make any distinction between the two groups.

*Comparative studies*— Oftentimes secondary data analysis can be applied to cross-cultural comparative studies. An American-Japanese comparison of the factorial structure of the Philadelphia Geriatric Center (PGC) Morale Scale was undertaken by Liang, Asano, Bollen, Kahana and Maeda [49]. Assessment of the cross-cultural factorial invariance involved first evaluating the construct validity of the scale within each of the two societies and then proceeded by using the model which fit both cultures well. The appropriateness of a 15-item model developed by using U.S. data [36] was initially evaluated. Although it was found to fit the U.S. samples reasonably well, it did not fare as well with the Japanese samples. Four items were identified as responsible for the poor fit to the Japanese data: two items exhibited a factor complexity greater than one and two items displayed relatively low standardized factor loadings. The revised model of eleven items was found to fit the samples and it was then evaluated for factorial invariance. No major differences were found between the American and Japanese data sets. A closer look at some of the methodological issues and decisions made may be instructive.

The American sample came from the National Senior Citizens Survey [42] and consisted of a national sample of 3,996 elderly respondents. The Japanese data set came from a survey of a two-stage random sample of 345 Japanese aged persons in the Tokyo area [50]. Since the Tokyo sample was more restrictive than the American in terms of sampling, the American sample was limited to respondents who resided in metropolitan areas with a population greater than one million in order to make the samples more comparable.

Because the PGC Morale Scale was first translated into Japanese and subsequently administered to the Japanese respondents, the comparability in terms of the accuracy of translation was evaluated. Specifically, a back-translation procedure was used. In this process, the Japanese version of the PGC Morale Scale was translated back into English by four Americans and one Japanese who had no prior knowledge of this scale. According to the translations, the Japanese version seemed to be generally accurate. However, it differed from the English version in format. Whereas the original items were presented as statements, they were phrased as questions in the Japanese version.

Other differences between the two data sets needed to be acknowledged. In particular, the survey in Tokyo was conducted in 1983 whereas the U.S. study was undertaken in 1968. The consequences of such a difference are difficult to assess. However, for the immediate research purposes, it was assumed that the differences would not have a substantial effect on the factorial structure of the scale. Further, the authors explicitly acknowledged this consideration and recognized it as an empirical issue which could be examined when data were available.

Another difference between the samples was the age of the respondents. The U.S. sample included only persons aged sixty-five and over, while the Japanese sample included persons sixty years of age and older. Rather than reducing the sample size of the Japanese data set by excluding those aged sixty to sixty-four years, the difference was allowed to remain. That is, in view of the different cultural definitions of being old in these two societies, the difference may be entirely appropriate.

Once again, replications were undertaken. Both the American and Japanese samples were each randomly divided into two subsamples and the analysis was replicated by using both subsamples. As noted earlier, such a strategy allows one to minimize capitalization on chance.

*Cohort analysis*— A cohort analysis involves longitudinal data on more than one cohort and involves as well cross-sectional or intercohort comparisons [41]. In this context, cohort refers to a group of people who experienced a common significant life event. Cohort analysis is particularly useful in assessing change over time. More generally, it has great potential for providing insight into the effects of aging and into the nature of social change. Given the limitations of cross-sectional data for the study changes and the paucity of good longitudinal data, cohort analysis involving the use of existing survey data can yield much information to those who are adept at secondary analysis.

There have been numerous applications of cohort analysis in studies of the effects of aging on political attitudes and behavior. One such example is a study concerning aging and party identification undertaken by Glenn and Hefner [47]. This research covered a span of twenty-four years (1945-1969) and involved data for seven dates at four-year intervals. All of the surveys selected were conducted within a short period after a presidential election. For each date except 1945, data from three to five surveys were pooled in order to enlarge the sample size. Furthermore, data were corrected for underrepresentation of low-education people in the earlier Gallup samples.

This analysis did not support the belief that aging has been an important influence for Republicanism in the United States. Aging cohorts have become more Republican in a relative sense as a result of a secular trend away from Republicanism in the total adult population. This trend grew out of the dying off of the older, more Republican cohorts, which were the cohorts least affected by the massive defections from the Republican party during the Great Depression [47]. Hence, this study provides no direct evidence in favor of the effects of aging on political liberalism-conservatism.

Another example of cohort analysis is provided by Okraku [51]. Okraku used data from the General Social Surveys to explore trends and cohort changes in attitudes toward multigenerational residence (specifically, an aged parent sharing residence with an adult child). Six surveys (between 1973 and 1983) were examined which incorporated a single question on attitudes toward multigenerational residence. The response category permitted separate analyses of unconditional and conditional support for co-residence. Okraku found an increase (positive shift) in the proportion of all respondents indicating approval of multigenerational residence. In addition, all cohorts demonstrated the increase in approval between 1973 and 1983 although there was support for a strong inverse relationship between level of approval and age. Further, the rate and nature of the change varied among cohorts with the pattern being somewhat curvilinear: the lowest rate of change was in the middle cohort (1914-1923) with an upturn for the two oldest cohorts (1903 or before and 1904-1913) for conditional approval which was in contrast to the younger cohorts (1924-1933, 1934-1943, and 1944-1953) who expressed more unconditional support for co-residence. These basic patterns of change (cross-sectional and intracohort) remained intact even after controlling for sex, race, educational level, and marriage-work status. This suggested little influence for cohort effects but introduced the possibility of negative age effects masked by strong positive period effects.

## LONGITUDINAL ANALYSIS

The aforementioned designs can work equally well with longitudinal data sets. The differences between previously discussed designs and longitudinal applications lie in the definition of the research question and the availability of suitable data sets. In the following, secondary data analysis of both single as well as multiple longitudinal data sets are illustrated.

*One study* — With secondary analysis the opportunities to overcome the concerns with and limitations of cross-sectional data are significant and relatively inexpensive. Answers to many questions necessitate longitudinal designs. For example, one focus of Morgan's investigation of intergenerational economic support dealt with the limitations of cross-sectional data [52]: the conclusion that downward intergenerational support is interrupted by the death of the spouse rests upon the assumption, rather than empirical evidence, that there is a change from prewidowhood patterns of family support. Morgan used data from two waves of the Longitudinal Retirement History Survey (LRHS) (1969 and 1975). The subgroups selected for the analyses were continuously married men as controls ($n$ = 4,518) and both men ($n$ = 214) and women ($n$ = 825) who became widowed during the six-year span between the data points used. Although, as Morgan notes, the sampling strategy introduces some bias (favoring more advantaged respondents given employment status) and caution regarding generalizability (it is difficult to gauge the influence of widowhood on attrition), the strategy nevertheless allows one to assess true changes and still provides a large sample of both widowers and widows. Morgan found that widowhood *per se* is not the predictor of financial assistance patterns: the largest single effect of any variable considered on 1975 support was having provided this type of aid in 1969. Differences in the probabilities between married men and widowed women in terms of economic support given to offspring are the result of race and income characteristics, not directly the result of loss of spouse in the recent past.

*Multiple studies* — In order to examine sex differences in the antecedents and consequences of retirement, George, Fillenbaum, and Palmore used two longitudinal data bases [53]: the Longitudinal Retirement History Survey (LRHS) (waves 1969, 1971, 1973, and 1975 were used) and the Duke Second Longitudinal Study (four waves with the modal years of data collection corresponding to the LRHS interviews). Such a strategy permitted evaluation of the issue without being hindered by, in particular, two methodological problems: small and/or unrepresentative sampling in studies of women and retirement, and cross-sectional studies which conduct comparisons between retirees and workers without information about preretirement status. The data bases were chosen because they had sufficient numbers of women to allow for meaningful comparisons of sex differences. Respondents were selected in order to restrict the sample to those for whom longitudinal data were available and to compare those who became retired with those who did not. The resulting sample sizes were still sufficient to avoid previous methodological concerns: 456 women (377 from the LRHS and 79 from the Duke Second Longitudinal Survey) and 1624 men (1468 from the Retirement History Survey and 156 from the Duke Second Longitudinal Study). Variables suggested in previous research for the antecedents and consequences of retirement were used. Sex differences were found with reference to the variables that predict retirement: the variables that predict retirement for men did not predict retirement for women. In addition, retirement was found to relate to more outcomes for men than for women given the variables selected based on past research.

## SUPPLEMENTING SECONDARY DATA WITH PRIMARY DATA

Often the researcher may propose a design by merging secondary data with primary data. Supplementing existing data to pursue a new focus can take form in various creative designs, depending on the missing links. Thus one might use existing data as independent variables and collect new data to trace subsequent effects or supplement an old survey with a new survey making the new focus analysis of trends. Such strategies obviously could offer a powerful analysis and we shall attend to some possible applications of such strategies in gerontological research in the following.

*Creating panel studies (turning a cross-sectional study into a longitudinal study)* — One design of merging old and new data involves redefining a previous survey as the starting point for a panel study. By refocusing the original study into one of a two-wave panel study, one can reduce the practical and methodological problems associated with conducting long-term panels. That is, by using such a strategy, the costs and burdens of the first wave will have already been dealt with by the previous investigator.

Panel designs building upon earlier studies can pursue two basic types of opportunities: measurement of changes in dependent variables specifically measured originally, and/or measurement of a new phenomenon that developed in the interim. Assessment of these processes may be analyzed in relation to the original independent variables, although there are other possibilities reflecting the various strategies of merging old and new data.

It should be noted that although the advantages and opportunities to such strategies are numerous, so are the new obstacles which result from attempting to employ such strategies. Beyond the practical obstacles (assuming one can determine and identify respondents of the original sample) are ethical considerations. Obtaining the necessary information to relocate individuals requires access to confidential materials.

Hyman presented a design which attempted to minimize practical obstacles without jeopardizing informational value [5]. "Selective experimental empanelling," the label he gave to the general design and strategy, basically entails identifying and reinterviewing a smaller, general subsample, or restricting the panel to selected strata. The options of course are a function of the investigator's interests and research problem.

In the following, two such applications will be illustrated. The first is a study of non-sampling errors in survey research conducted by Rodgers and Herzog [54,55]. Face-to-face interviews were undertaken with 1,491 respondents in the Detroit metropolitan area in 1984. Independent validating information for many of the survey answers was sought from existing, publicly accessible records. Specific sources of error investigated were: 1) nonresponse; 2)"Don't know" responses; and 3) validity of responses, established by methods of comparison against external validation criteria and construct validity. Although initially not anticipated, it became apparent that the data base can be greatly enriched by incorporating further follow-up interviews. This is particularly true in view of the fact that little is known about the stability of such survey errors and their impact on data analysis. Consequently, a follow-up survey was proposed. In addition, persons who could not be interviewed in the original survey would also be contacted.

Sometimes, the collection of primary data can further extend a longitudinal study. Markides and his associates undertook a two-wave panel study of the health of older Mexican Americans and Anglos: 510 persons aged sixty and over in southwest San Antonio were interviewed in 1976 with a 1980 follow-up of these respondents. Four years later, Markides [56], was able to obtain a third wave of observations on 249 of the original participants. Given the additional wave of data, the potential usefulness of this data set is greatly enhanced. It should be noted that the third follow-up was not initially anticipated. Hence, the additional data collection did constitute an example of supplementing secondary data with new information.

*Creating cross-national studies* — Recently, Liang proposed a cross-cultural study of comparing the well-being of the American elderly and that of the Japanese elderly. In particular, this study involves an American-Japanese comparison of the factorial structures of some widely used measures of well-being. To undertake this analysis both secondary and primary data will be analyzed. Specifically, secondary data on the American elderly will come from three national surveys undertaken between 1968 and 1981. These include 1) the 1974 NCOA-Harris Survey of Myth and Reality of Aging in America, 2) NCOA-Harris Survey, Aging in the Eighties, and 3) the 1968 National Senior Citizens Survey. These surveys are further augmented by a recently initiated national study of the middle-aged and elderly people concerning productivity, stress, and health in middle and late life. This project consists of a national survey of about 3,400 Americans aged twenty-five and over. Blacks and persons over sixty are oversampled. These data on the American aged are to be merged with new primary data which will come from a national survey of 2,500 Japanese aged sixty and over. Given that there is an abundance of high quality data and that the principal investigator has access to all four American data sets, it seems quite sensible to analyze only secondary data on the well-being of the American aged. On the other hand, because of the lack of national data on the well-being of the Japanese aged, the collection of primary data with which to make the comparison to America is justified.

## V. CONCLUSIONS: SUCCESSFUL APPROACHES TO SECONDARY DATA ANALYSIS

At different points reference has been made to the unique aspects of conducting secondary analysis. As this chapter draws to a close it seems appropriate to conclude with an overview of the characteristics associated with the successsful secondary data analyst and a review of the limitations and strengths of secondary analysis of sample surveys.

Among the limitations and/or obstacles to successful secondary analysis are incomplete collateral materials and control over the design and indicators available. Certainly one of the necessary characteristics is the ability to cope with the obstacles standing in the way of adequate assessment of the data base and critical treatment of errors. Earlier we mentioned some techniques to alleviate the limitations of secondary analysis. For instance, efforts to obtain documentation relevant to the surveys may require commitment of time and energy more than a special characteristic or style. Nonetheless, the process can be frustrating and many may abandon secondary analyses prematurely because of the degree of frustration. In fact Hyman presents high frustration tolerance as a necessary ingredient and clearly persistence on the part of the prospective analyst is important [5].

Frustration is also encountered with attending to and treating errors, which is a central theme in secondary analysis [5, p. 82] as well as in primary data. Successful analysts attempt in various ways to estimate the magnitude of the errors and the effect of the errors on the conclusions. In dealing with the various sources and levels of frustration, there is no replacement for being sensitive to the deficiencies of and problems with the original data. Without this sensitivity, there is no realistically adequate way to take the deficiencies into account and/or compensate for them in order to effectively conduct secondary data analysis and produce meaningful results.

A critical element for success in secondary data analysis and in pursuing a new focus is the validity of the relation between the existing indicator(s) and the concept of interest [5]. Such linkages may be vague and translation can be difficult. Thus, a successful secondary analyst must have the power of abstraction and, once again, sensitivity: the ability to combine data, rethink issues, recognize availability — in general be able to perceive beyond preconceived notions about the perfect indicator (reconceptualizing), recognize opportunities, and be open to reworking the proposed design [5]. The investigator must thus possess a variety of interests and be flexible in approach. Both of these ingredients certainly benefit from a sound and comprehensive grasp of theory. Accordingly, alternatives are more readily available given a strong theoretical foundation, powers of abstraction, varied interests, and abilities to reorganize. Thus when frustration is encountered and efforts thwarted in one approach to the issue, the successful secondary analyst is able to define and pursue another approach.

As mentioned before, knowledge of major sources of data is critical to success in secondary analysis. Furthermore, the secondary analyst should always be alert to the emergence of new data which often provide good opportunities for exciting research. In addition, a secondary analyst must be reasonably proficient with the processing of computerized data sets since most of the data are not generated by the analyst. Hence, it is important to know various technical specifications of computerized data. This can be critical in the situation where the data set is not compatible with the technical requirements of the computing facilities at the analyst's institution.

Current and prospective secondary analysts should be aware of avenues for training. Several of the archives (e.g., DAAAD and ICPSR) offer consulting or training services on substantive and methodological aspects of secondary analysis. For example, the Inter-university Consortium for Political and Social Research offers summer training programs in quantitative methods. The objectives of the programs include providing training for individuals who expect to become practicing social methodologists and instruction for the development and improvement of quantitative skills. The offerings emphasize research design, statistics, data analysis, and social methodology. In addition, instruction is coordinated with active participatory data analytic experiences. Of course, another important consideration and option for training is to work with an experienced secondary data analyst.

In conclusion, the cautions and limitations associated with secondary data analysis of sample surveys includes obtaining suitable data sets for selecting appropriate measures and obtaining enough information about the original study to appraise the errors. Both of these limitations can clearly be overcome for many gerontological research undertakings. Indeed, it was one of our goals to demonstrate that despite the limitations, secondary data analysis is and has been a promising and powerful research strategy. Included among the major strengths of this technique are: 1) pursuing new research questions without the costs of primary data procedures, 2) obtaining sufficient sample sizes to evaluate relationships by using multivariate techniques, and 3) being able to conduct replication designs (both empirical and conceptual). In closing let us also reemphasize that secondary data analysis provides valuable opportunities for increasing knowledge and refining theory, and should be viewed as a complementary, not competing, strategy to primary data analysis for advancing knowledge.

## APPENDIX A:
## Social Science Data Archives

Archives Outside the United States

Social Science Research Council Data Archive (SSRC)
University of Essex
Wivenhoe Park
Colchester CO4 3SQ
Essex, England
(44)206-860570;206-862286

Steinmetz Archives
Herengracht 410-412
1017 BX Amsterdam
(020)225061

U.S. Archives

Data User Services Division
Customer Services Branch
Bureau of the Census
Washington, DC 20233
(202)763-4100

Data Archive for Aging and Adult Development
Survey Data Laboratory
Center for the Study of Aging and Human Development
Duke University
Box 3003
Duke University Medical Center
Durham, NC 27710
(919)684-3204

Inter-University Consortium for Political & Social Research (ICPSR)
Institute for Social Research
P.O. Box 1248
Ann Arbor, MI 48106
(313)763-5010;764-5199

Louis Harris Data Center (and) Social Science Data Library
Institute for Research in Social Science
Room 10 Manning Hall 026A
University of North Carolina
Chapel Hill, NC 27514
(919)966-3346

National Archive of Computerized Data on Aging
Inter-University Consortium for Political & Social Research (ICPSR)
Institute for Social Research
P.O. Box 1248
Ann Arbor, MI 48106
(313)763-5010;764-5199

National Center for Health Statistics
3700 East-West Highway
Hyattsville, MD 20782
(301)436-8500

National Opinion Research Center
University of Chicago
1155 E. 60th St.
Chicago, IL 60637
(312)962-1213

National Technical Information Service
5285 Port Royal Road
Springfield, VA 22161
(703)487-4763

The Roper Center for Public Opinion Research
User Services
The University of Connecticut
Box 440
Storrs, CT 06268
(203)486-4440

## ACKNOWLEDGMENTS

The assistance provided by Joan Bennett and Peggy White is gratefully acknowledged. Regula Herzog, Mary Grace Kovar, Powell Lawton, Ethel Shanas, and Wayne Usui contributed many useful comments to an earlier version of this chapter.

## REFERENCES


1. C. Hakim, *Secondary Analysis in Social Research: A Guide to Data Sources and Methods with Examples,* George Allen and Unwin, Boston, 1982.
2. J. E. Hunter, F. L. Schmidt, G. B. Jackson, *Meta-Analysis: Cumulating Research Findings Across Studies,* Sage Publications, Beverly Hills, 1982.
3. H. Jacob, *Using Published Data: Errors and Remedies*, Sage Publications, Beverly Hills, 1984.
4. C. Selltiz, L. S. Wrightsman, and S. W. Cook, *Research Methods in the Social Sciences,* Holt, Rinehart, and Winston, New York, 1976.
5. H. H. Hyman, *Secondary Analysis of Sample Surveys: Principles, Procedures, and Potentialities,* Wiley and Sons, New York, 1972.
6. P. H. Rossi, J. D. Wright, and A. B. Anderson (eds.), *Handbook of Survey Research,* Academic Press, New York, 1983.
7. K. J. Kiecolt and L. E. Nathan, *Secondary Analysis of Survey Data,* Sage Publications, Beverly Hills, 1985.
8. M. W. Traugott, Archival Data Resources, *Research on Aging* (Special Issue: Available Data Bases for Aging Research), *3, pp.* 487–501, 1981.
9. Inter-University Consortium for Political and Social Research. *Data Collections National Archive of Computerized Data on Aging,* University of Michigan, Ann Arbor, MI, 1985.
10. Inter-University Consortium for Political and Social Research, *Guide to Resources and Services, 1985–1986,*University of Michigan, Ann Arbor, MI, 1985.
11. The Roper Center. *Data Acquisitions* (Vol. 5, Issue 1), Roper Center, Storrs, CT, 1986.
12. The Roper Center, *The Roper Center American Collection: Profiles of the Major Collections* (Vol. 5), The Roper Center, Storrs, CT, 1987.
13. The Roper Center, *A Guide to Roper Center Resources for the Study of American Race Relations,* The Roper Center, Storrs, CT, 1982.
14. Institute for Research in Social Science, *A Directory of Louis Harris Public Opinion Polls: Machine Readable Data Files,* Louis Harris Data Center, University of North Carolina, Chapel Hill, North Carolina, 1985.
15. E. Martin, D. McDuffee, and S. Presser, *Sourcebook of Harris National Surveys: Repeated Questions 1961–1976,* Institute for Research in Social Science, Chapel Hill, NC, 1981.
16. Social Science Research Council Survey Archive, *Guide to the Survey Archives Social Science Data Holdings and Allied Services,* University of Essex, Essex, n.d.
17. Royal Netherlands Academy of Arts and Sciences Social Science Information and Documentation Centre, *Steinmetz Archives Catalogue and Guide,* Royal Netherlands Academy, Amsterdam, 1983.
18. C. H. Partick and E. F. Borgatta, Available Data Bases for Aging Research. *Research on Aging* (Special Issue: Available Data Bases for Aging Research), *3,* pp. 371–501, 1981.
19. B. M. Burchett and L. K. George, *Duke University Data Archive For Aging and Adult Development: Reference Guide,* Survey Data Laboratory Center for the Study of Aging and Human Development, Duke University, Durham, North Carolina, 1985.

20. U.S. Department of Commerce, *Census of Population and Housing 1980: Public Microdata Samples Technical Documentation,* Bureau of the Census, Washington, DC, 1983.
21. U.S. Department of Commerce, *Bureau of the Census Catalogue, 1980,* Bureau of the Census, Washington, DC, 1980.
22. U.S. Department of Commerce, *Directory of Data Files,* Bureau of the Census, Washington, DC, 1979.
23. U.S. Department of Commerce, Bureau of Census, Current Population Survey: Annual Demographic File, 1982 [Machine Readable Data File]. Data User Services Division, Washington DC, 1982.
24. U.S. Department of Commerce, Bureau of Census, Census of Population and Housing, 1980 [Machine Readable Data File]. Data User Services Division, Washington, DC, 1980.
25. U.S. Department of Health and Health Services, *Catalog of Public Use Data Tapes from the National Center for Health Statistics,* U.S. Department of Health and Health Services, Hyattsville, MD, 1980.
26. S. J. Newman, Exploring Housing Adjustments of Older People: The HUD-HEW Longitudinal Study, *Research on Aging* (Special Issue: Available Data Bases for Aging Research), *3,* pp. 417–428, 1981.
27. J. F. Van Nostrand, The Aged in Nursing Homes: Baseline Data, *Research on Aging* (Special Issue: Available Data Bases for Aging Research), *3,* pp. 403–416, 1981.
28. L. M. Irelan, Retirement History Study: Introduction, *Social Security Bulletin, 35,* pp. 24–33, 1972.
29. L. M. Irelan and K. Schwab, The Social Security Administration's Retirement History Study, *Research on Aging* (Special Issue: Available Data Bases for Aging Research), *3,* pp. 381–386, 1981.
30. E. Mutran, Intergenerational Family Support Among Blacks and Whites: Response to Culture or to Socioeconomic Differences, *Journal of Gerontology, 40,* pp. 382–389, 1985.
31. K. A. McClelland, Self-Conception and Life Satisfaction: Integrating Aged Subculture and Activity Theory, *Journal of Gerontology, 37,* pp. 723–732, 1982.
32. S. W., Huck, W. H. Cormier, and W. G. Bounds, *Reading Statistics and Research,* Harper and Row, New York, 1974.
33. J. Collette, Sex Differences in Life Satisfaction: Australian Data, *Journal of Gerontology, 39,* pp. 243–245, 1984.
34. J. Liang, Sex Differences in Life Satisfaction Among the Elderly, *Journal of Gerontology, 37,* pp. 100–108, 1982.
35. M. P. Lawton, The Philadelphia Geriatric Center Morale Scale: A Revision, *Journal of Gerontology, 30,* pp. 85–89, 1975.
36. J. Liang, and K. A. Bollen, The Structure of the Philadelphia Geriatric Center Morale Scale: A Reinterpretation, *Journal of Gerontology, 38,* pp. 181–189, 1983.
37. J. Liang and K. A. Bollen, Sex Differences in the Structure of the Philadelphia Geriatric Center Morale Scale, *Journal of Gerontology, 40,* pp. 468–477, 1985.
38. J. Liang, R. H. Lawrence, and K. A. Bollen, Age Differences in the Structure of the Philadelphia Geriatric Center Morale Scale, *Psychology and Aging, 1,* pp. 27–33, 1986.
39. J. Liang, R. H. Lawrence, and K. A. Bollen, Race Differences in Two Measures of Subjective Well-Being, *Journal of Gerontology.* (in press).

40. L. K. George, and R. Landerman, Health and Subjective Well-Being: A Replicated Secondary Data Analysis, *International Journal of Aging and Human Development, 19*, pp. 133–156, 1984.
41. N.D. Glenn, *Cohort Analysis,* Sage Publications, Beverly Hills, CA, 1977.
42. K. K. Schooler, Effect of Environment on Morale, *Gerontologist, 10,* pp. 194–197, 1970.
43. North Carolina State Department of Human Resources, Governor's Council on Aging, *Social Indicators for the Aged: A Report of the Survey of Needs,* Raleigh, NC, 1972.
44. Wisconsin State Department of Health and Social Services, The Division of Family Services, *The Needs of Wisconsin's Older People: An Assessment of the Social Status of Wisconsin's Elderly Through Social Indicator Methodology,* Vol. 1. Milwaukee, WI, 1971.
45. Minnesota State Governor's Citizens Council on Aging, *The Status and Needs of Minnesota's Older People,* Vol. 1. Minneapolis, MN, 1971.
46. J. Liang and B. L. Warfel, Urbanism and Life Satisfaction Among the Aged, *Journal of Gerontology, 38,* pp. 97–106, 1983.
47. N. D. Glenn and T. Hefner, Further Evidence on Aging and Party Identification, *Public Opinion Quarterly, 36,* pp. 31–47, 1972.
48. W. T. Liu and E. Yu, Asian/Pacific American Elderly: Mortality Differentials, Health Status, and Use of Health Services, *Journal of Applied Gerontology, 4,* pp. 35–64, 1986.
49. J. Liang, H. Asano, K. A. Bollen, E. F. Kahana, and D. Maeda, Cross-Cultural Comparability of the Philadelphia Geriatric Center Morale Scale: An American-Japanese Comparison, *Journal of Gerontology, 42,* pp. 37–43, 1987.
50. K. Yaguchi, D. Maeda, H. Asano, and A. Nishishita, Sex Differences in Morale of the Elderly Living in Community, *Shakai Ronen-Gaku* (Journal of Social Gerontology), No. 20, pp. 46–58, 1984.
51. I. O. Okraku, Age and Attitudes Toward Multigenerational Residence, 1973–1983, *Journal of Gerontology.* (in press).
52. L. A. Morgan, Intergenerational Economic Assistance to Children: The Case of Widows and Widowers, *Journal of Gerontology, 38,* pp. 725–731, 1983.
53. L. K. George, G. G. Fillenbaum, and E. Palmore, Sex Differences in the Antecedents and Consequences of Retirement, *Journal of Gerontology, 39,* pp. 364–371, 1984.
54. W. L. Rodgers, and A. R. Herzog, Interviewing Older Adults: The Accuracy of Factual Information, *Journal of Gerontology, 42*, pp. 387–394, 1987.
55. W. L. Rodgers, and A. R. Herzog, Covariances of Measurement Errors in Survey Responses, Unpublished Manuscript, Institute for Social Research, University of Michigan, Ann Arbor, MI, 1986.
56. K. S., Markides, H. W. Martin, and E. Gomez, *Older Mexican Americans: A Study in an Urban Barrio,* University of Texas Press, Austin, Texas: 1983.

CHAPTER

# 3

# Telephone and Mail Surveys with Older Populations: A Methodological Overview[1]

*A. Regula Herzog*
*Richard A. Kulka*

The principal methods of administering questions in survey research are personal or face-to-face interviews, telephone interviews, and self-administered questionnaires, the latter either delivered in person or by mail. Of these basic approaches, survey researchers have long regarded the personal, face-to-face interview as the best data collection technique. By contrast, the other two common tools for survey research contact, telephone and mail, have typically been viewed as inherently inferior substitutes for this much heralded standard, to be used only where there is no other choice [1–3]. In response to increasing difficulties associated with gathering survey information by face-to-face interviews—notably rising costs and declining response rates—researchers have started to turn to these alternative modes for the collection of survey data [1, 4].

Recent published estimates suggest that the cost of a telephone survey may be less than half that of a comparable interview conducted face-to-face [5–9], and that the costs of data collection by mail are generally even lower than those encountered for telephone interview surveys [1, 2, 6]. Moreover, although response rates for face-to-face surveys continue to be higher than those for telephone and mail surveys, the most recent literature suggests that the gap is less pronounced

[1]Preparation of this paper was partially supported by Grant No. R01 AG02038 from The National Institute on Aging. Earlier versions of the paper were presented at The Conference on Aged Research Populations, Philadelphia Geriatric Center, Philadelphia, May 1983 and at the 36th Annual Scientific Meeting of the Gerontological Society of America, San Francisco, November 1983.

than in past years [1, 2, 4]. In addition to such factors, which are making the traditional face-to-face technique less attractive to survey researchers (especially to those working within severe constraints on time and money), the rising popularity of surveys by telephone and mail is also a result of a number of *positive* factors. Those factors include the increased accessibility of the population via telephone, improvements in telephone technology and telephone interview techniques, and the rapid and continued development of innovative and effective methodologies for conducting both telephone and mail surveys [1, 2, 4, 10–15]. Hence, the continued and increased use of these alternatives to the face-to-face interview for the collection of survey data from various populations and subpopulations is virtually assured, and a substantial research literature has evolved to support these efforts.

Within this literature, however, surprisingly little attention has been focused on the relative suitability of these particular research strategies for certain subgroups in the population, such as the elderly [16, 17]. In the absence of such research, one encounters considerable speculation about the appropriateness of these approaches for surveying older people, based primarily on conventional wisdom or indirect evidence about the capabilities, attitudes and circumstances of the elderly. Such speculation generally takes one of two forms. First, some have suggested that, since the elderly are likely to be underrepresented as telephone subscribers, they are a particularly inappropriate subpopulation either for surveys by telephone or for mail surveys that depend on samples from telephone directories. For example, Horton and Duncan [18], otherwise unabashed advocates of the use of telephone interviewing, asserted that "the telephone should not be expected to be a viable technique for the very aged who have no access to telephones (in group or public accommodations)," further noting, however, that "most of these groups cannot be reached with any method" [18, p 262]. In his recent book on survey research by telephone, Frey has also raised the issue of sample coverage of older people in telephone surveys, suggesting that "for the study of some subpopulations, such as the poor and elderly, accounting for households without phones is very important" [4, p. 36]. Similarly, in her "letter to the editor" critique of a two-stage mail survey method for enumerating and surveying a sample of the elderly proposed by Lee and Finney [19], Blumenthal suggested that the percentage of people who do not have telephones "is disproportionately high among the elderly, particularly the poor elderly, so that to use households with telephones as the sampling base already introduces a substantial bias into the population being sampled" [20, p. 322].

Others have focused more directly on the willingness or capacity of older people actually to respond to mail and telephone surveys. For example, based on reports by interviewers of their experiences in the National Medical Care Expenditure Survey (NMCES), Fleishman and Berk concluded that "on complex health questionnaires, at least the elderly should not be interviewed by telephone . . . where the main respondent is sixty-five or older, all interviews must be conducted face-to-face" [21, p. 255]. Or, with respect to mail surveys, Dillman hypothesized that older persons seem likely to be underrepresented among those who return a mail questionnaire, "partly because of lower educational attainment, but also because of more difficulties with their seeing and writing capabilities" [1, p. 53]. In contrast, at least one gerontological researcher postulated that "a sample of the older population might be more amenable to answering mail questionnaires than the general public" [22, p. 281].

While observations such as these clearly merit the attention of researchers planning studies of the aged, the fact is that very little empirical evidence exists to support any of these contentions. The sparsity of information on telephone and mail survey methods with aged populations is all the more deplorable, since the costs of surveying aged populations are even greater than the already high costs associated with surveying a sample of the entire age range. The relatively high costs of surveying a sample of older persons are primarily a function of the screening for older persons that must be completed in a typical household probability sample. Only about one in five households in the community contains a person over sixty years of age; even fewer households contain a person over seventy-five or over eighty-five. Screening on the telephone or by mail is, of course, considerably cheaper than personal screening because no expenses for transportation and travel time of interviewers are required.[1]

In this chapter we will review some of the evidence that does exist about telephone and mail surveys and consider potential advantages and limitations of these two principal alternatives to the face-to-face interview for surveys of the aged. Specifically, we will address potential differences between modes in: 1) their ability to reach a representative sample of the older population; and 2) the quality of responses obtained.

## SAMPLE REPRESENTATIVENESS

In general, the representativeness of a sample may be jeopardized in two ways. First, the sample may be drawn inaccurately, and/or from a frame which systematically excludes certain members of the population. Second, persons who are identified by sampling procedures as respondents may not participate in the survey, thereby potentially introducing a systematic bias into the resulting data.

### RESPONDENT SELECTION

Face-to-face surveys typically draw area probability samples of households, thereby excluding persons living in institutions. This means that in those samples the approximately 5 percent of the elderly population who live in nursing homes and/or other institutional settings are omitted [23]. State-of-the-art sample surveys

[1]Screening by mail may, however, be less accurate because it cannot be as closely controlled.

conducted by telephone typically employ random digit dialing (RDD) procedures under which telephone numbers are dialed at random to avoid excluding unlisted telephone numbers or new numbers not yet included in directories. Such procedures provide probability samples of all persons living in households with a telephone. However, since RDD and other telephone designs also typically exclude individuals living in institutions, such designs are as deficient as face-to-face surveys with regard to the residents of institutions. Moreover, persons without a telephone are also systematically excluded from samples of telephone subscribers, thereby posing an additional threat to the representativeness of a sample drawn by RDD and other telephone methods.

Prior to the 1970s, the exclusion of households without telephones may indeed have been a problem when, for example, such homes constituted 26 percent of the 1959 University of Michigan Survey Research Center sample, and persons sixty-five and over were significantly underrepresented among telephone subscribers [24]. By 1981, however, about 92 percent of the population lived in a household with a telephone [25],[2] and, contrary to the conventional wisdom described earlier in this chapter, telephone coverage among older adults is actually more complete than for any other age group [27]. Based on data from the National Health Interview Survey in 1976, about 94 percent of persons aged sixty-five and over lived in a household with a telephone [28] and by 1981 (Table 1) this rate had increased to about 97 percent [25].[3] Moreover, these rates varied little either by region of the country or by family income level. Thus, although predicted increases in the costs of telephone services may reduce these coverage rates to some degree in the future, current evidence would suggest that "if level of coverage were the only consideration, it would be difficult to reject the use of random digit dialing in planning a survey of the elderly" [28, p. 225].

While face-to-face and telephone surveys can provide samples of the general population in the ways just described, accessing a representative sample of the population constitutes a major problem in mail surveys which typically depend on published lists for drawing a sample. For the general population there simply are no published lists.[4] Specific lists used for drawing samples in mail surveys include telephone directories, city directories, drivers' license files, and utility lists, all of which exhibit known shortcomings [1, 2, 30]. But as we have just discussed, telephone directories, the most commonly used sample source for general public surveys, systematically exclude nonsubscribers, new subscribers,

[2]Another source indicates that approximatley 96 percent of all households had telephone service by 1980 [26].

[3]Such is not necessarily the case in countries other than the U.S., of course. In Great Britain, for example, Hoinville recently estimated that telephone ownership among the elderly is probably less than 50 percent [29].

[4]It is worth pointing out that some attempts have been made at assembling household listings for geographical units by compiling information from several lists such as reversed telephone directories, drivers' license files, and the like.

Table 1. Telephone Coverage by Age

| *Age* | *Telephone* | *Non-Telephone* | *Total (percent)* |
|---|---|---|---|
| Under 25 years | 90.5 | 9.5 | 100.0 |
| 25–44 years | 93.7 | 6.3 | 100.0 |
| 45–64 years | 96.3 | 3.7 | 100.0 |
| 65–74 years | 96.8 | 3.2 | 100.0 |
| 75 years and over | 96.4 | 3.6 | 100.0 |
| All ages | 93.2 | 6.8 | 100.0 |

**Note**: Reprinted by permission from Thornberry [25].

and those with unlisted numbers (and addresses). Since telephone coverage among the elderly is relatively complete, and since the elderly tend to be less mobile than younger adults [31], such directories may actually be a more suitable sampling frame for the older subpopulation than for other subgroups or for the population as a whole, providing that the incidence of unlisted numbers among the elderly is relatively low [32] and that suitable methods of screening for age eligibility by mail can be derived [19, 29].

If a survey is to be conducted of a specific well-organized group of the aged, such as veterans or retired teachers, lists of the members of these organizations may well be a suitable sampling frame, although even these lists are not always complete or current, or are not readily available. For example, the Electoral Register, a main source for address sampling in Great Britain containing age relevant information, has been shown to have a significant social class bias [33]. To summarize, the difficulty of obtaining a representative sample is likely to be as significant a disadvantage in mail surveys of the aged as in mail surveys generally.

If households are sampled, then a respondent is usually selected at random from all members once the household has been selected. In surveys of the aged only persons of a certain age are eligible; in other words, screening for elderly is necessary. Sometimes additional random selection has to be conducted, for example, when more than one eligible older respondent per household is found. These selections are more easily conducted and reinforced face-to-face or on the telephone than by mail. However, they are much more costly in the face-to-face surveys—where higher transportation costs and travel time are involved—than on the telephone.

## NONRESPONSE

Once eligible respondents have been determined, they must be located and agree to participate in the interview. The outcome of this process determines the response rate.

Nonresponse tends to be higher in telephone surveys than in face-to-face surveys—i.e. the response rate is lower [5, 8, 34–36; but see [37] for lack of more differences], although the calculation of response rates in the telephone survey mode is not entirely straight-forward.[5] Mail surveys attain even higher proportions of nonresponse than telephone surveys [1, 3], although response rates in mail surveys vary so much that an average response rate is not a very informative measure [12, 13]. Also, there are several factors involved in improving response rates in mail surveys, such as the number of follow-up mailings, incentives for returning the questionnaire, and relevance of the topic of the survey for the respondent. These factors were highlighted in a number of reviews that should prove useful for investigators considering a mail survey [11–14].

Aside from the overall differences between modes, age-specific mode differences in response rates are possible. Older adults may be more reluctant to respond to telephone or mail surveys than to a face-to-face survey, since they are more likely to have hearing and/or visual problems [38, 39], less likely to be used to the telephone, and generally have less formal education. On the other hand, some older persons may be more likely to participate in a survey conducted by either mail or telephone, because many of them are concerned about being victimized [40], and neither of these alternative survey methods requires the admission of a stranger to one's home. Indeed, in a study reported by Rogers [41], older respondents (60 and over) were significantly more likely than younger respondents to prefer being interviewed by telephone than being contacted in person, and "reluctance to open the door to a stranger" was one of the most frequent reasons given for this preference.

With regard to telephone surveys, however, the preponderance of evidence suggests that, although older people are more likely than younger adults to have a telephone, they are less likely actually to participate in telephone surveys [42–45]. In a recently-published report [46], we were able to assess empirically the extent to which telephone and face-to-face surveys of the general population reach respondents of varying ages by comparing age distributions of survey respondents to three national RDD surveys and four national face-to-face surveys with age distributions of the target population, as represented by the Current Population Survey (CPS). As shown in Figure 1, older respondents are apparently underrepresented in both types of surveys, but the underrepresentation is substantially greater for the telephone than for the face-to-face surveys. While visually these differences may not appear all that large, we estimated that a telephone survey targeted only for persons over the age of sixty-five would miss almost half of those eligible for an interview. Consistent with this finding, estimates derived in studies conducted by the National Center for Health Statistics suggest telephone response rates of 57 and 63 percent among adults aged sixty-five and over, significantly lower than those for other age groups [25, 45].

[5]See Groves and Kahn [5, pp. 63–64] for a discussion of response rate calculations in telephone surveys.

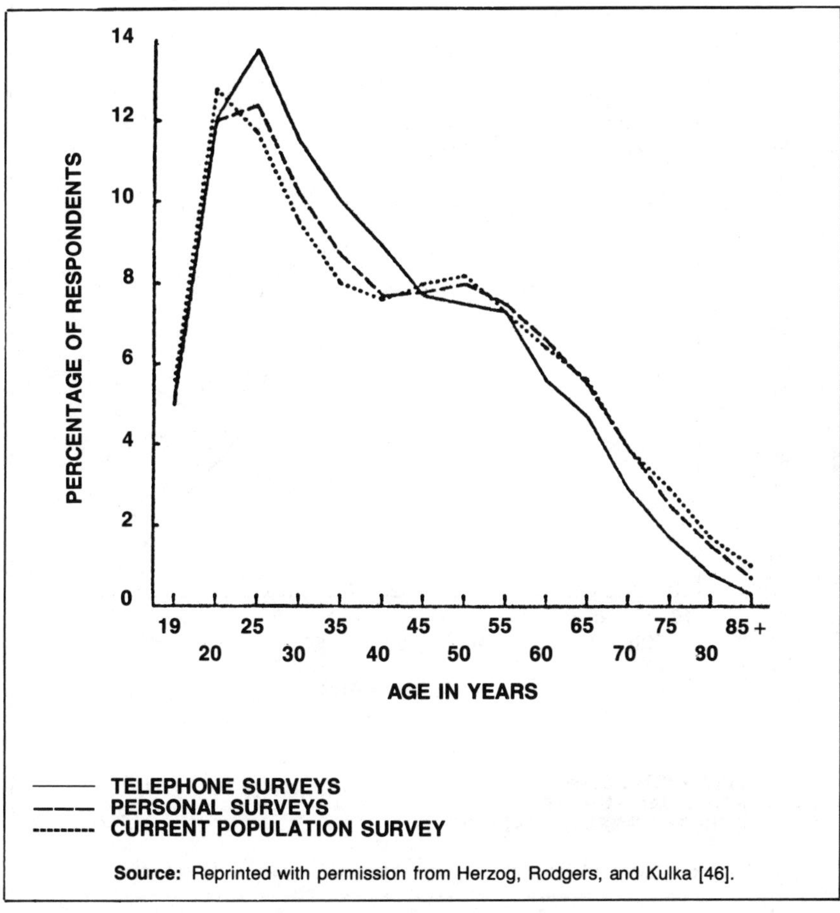


**Source:** Reprinted with permission from Herzog, Rodgers, and Kulka [46].

Figure 1. Age distribution of respondents interviewed by telephone, in person, and in CPS.

Moreover, as shown in Figure 2, the underrepresentation of older respondents in telephone surveys carries with it a potentially large source of bias. On average, older respondents to telephone surveys are substantially better educated than older people interviewed face-to-face. Corroborating these data from the nationwide surveys mentioned earlier, we were also recently able to replicate this statistical interaction between mode, age, and educational attainment in a local health survey conducted in Florida [36].

For mail surveys corresponding comparisons are rare, and we have not conducted any of our own investigations in this area. The evidence which is available,

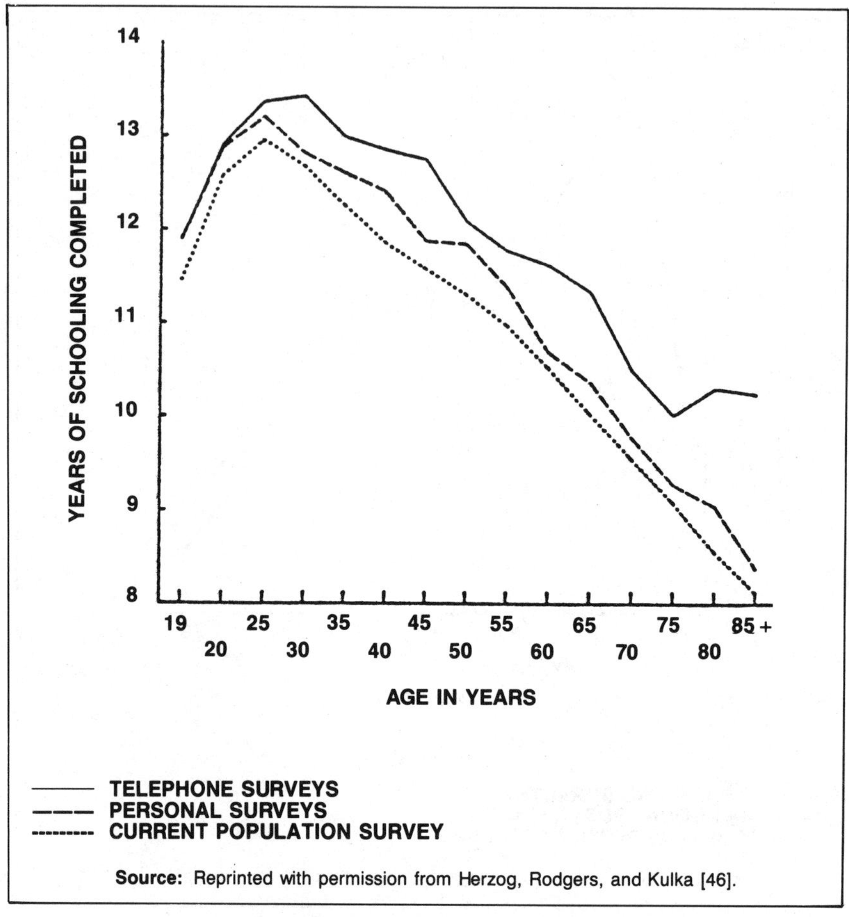


Figure 2. Education, by age distribution of respondents interviewed by telephone and in person.

however, does not necessarily imply some inherent tendency for older people to be less cooperative respondents to mail surveys, since the range of response rates to mail surveys conducted with aged samples generally parallels the wide range of response rates typically observed in mail surveys of other segments of the general population. For example, while Scott reported a response rate of only 43 percent for a mail survey of older women selected from poll-tax exemption lists [22], Atchley obtained a response rate of over 90 percent in a mail follow-up survey of respondents and nonrespondents to a previous face-to-face survey of retired women [48]. Similarly, Britton and Britton report a response rate of 78 percent for a mail survey of retired secretaries [49], but response rates of only 57 and 34 percent for a parallel survey of retired male and female teachers, respectively.

Using the Total Design Method (TDM), a standard set of mail survey procedures developed by Dillman [1], a 74 percent response rate was obtained in a statewide needs assessment survey of senior citizens in the state of Washington [50]. Although this study employed a somewhat controversial two-stage sampling procedure [19], under which the questionnaire was sent only to senior citizens in households responding to a previous screening inquiry also sent by mail, this result corresponds well with the average response rates achieved by the TDM—70 percent for general public surveys and 77 percent for specialized ones, as averaged by Dillman [1].

That elderly respondents manifest no inherent reluctance or incapacity to respond adequately to mail questionnaires is further suggested by the results of a drop-off/mail-back survey on long-term care insurance recently conducted among Medicare enrollees in six states by the Research Triangle Institute (RTI) [51]. Although for cost reasons the survey used only one follow-up procedure—a single "thank-you/reminder postcard" mailed seven days after the questionnaire was left at the conclusion of a face-to-face interview—the survey achieved a response rate of 65 percent, and RTI's experience with other mail surveys of this type suggests that, with adequate follow-up, this response rate could have been increased to 80 percent or more.

As in the case of telephone surveys, however, there is some evidence that mail surveys of more heterogenous populations may underrepresent older adults relative to other age groups, although the evidence with regard to mail surveys is less consistent. For example, a comparison of respondents to four statewide mail surveys of the general public to corresponding census estimates made by Dillman and his colleagues revealed an underrepresentation of persons sixty-five and older among mail survey respondents in all four states [52]. Similarly, some more specialized studies have suggested that older people are less likely to be respondents to mail surveys [53, 54], including the study cited earlier by Britton and Britton [49], who, even among a homogeneous sample of retired teachers, found older women (those over 75 years of age) less inclined to respond.

In contrast, a number of other studies have found little evidence of a relationship between nonresponse and age in mail surveys [47, 49 (for retired secretaries and retired male teachers), 55, 56]. Indeed, at least one recent study found a strong positive association between age and tendency to respond to a mail questionnaire [57] (Table 2). At work here may well be a question of *interest* rather than capacity. That is, older people may well manifest a high level of cooperativeness in mail surveys which are of direct interest to them, while being less cooperative than others in more general population surveys which are not especially of interest to them [29].

Table 2. Response to Postal Questionnaire by Age Group of Victim[a]

| | Age | | | | | | | | | | | | | | | |
|---|---|---|---|---|---|---|---|---|---|---|---|---|---|---|---|---|
| | *15–29* | | *30–39* | | *40–49* | | *50–59* | | *60–69* | | *70–79* | | *80+* | | *Total* | |
| | % | *N* | % | *N* | % | *N* | % | *N* | % | *N* | % | *N* | % | *N* | % | *N* |
| Non-respondents | 33.5 | 58 | 28.6 | 22 | 22.5 | 18 | 12.4 | 15 | 14.0 | 14 | 8.3 | 8 | 7.6 | 5 | 19.6 | 140 |
| Respondents | 66.5 | 115 | 71.4 | 55 | 77.5 | 62 | 87.6 | 106 | 86.0 | 86 | 91.7 | 88 | 92.4 | 61 | 80.4 | 573 |
| Total | 100.0 | 173 | 100.0 | 77 | 100.0 | 80 | 100.0 | 121 | 100.0 | 100 | 100.0 | 96 | 100.0 | 66 | 100.0 | 713 |

$x^2 = 45.40$, $d.f. = 6$, $p < 0.001$.

[a]Excludes age group 0–14 for whom parents were responding (143 non-respondents, 298 respondents).

**Note**: Reprinted with permission from Maclean and Genn [57].

## DATA QUALITY

Another major criterion for evaluating telephone and mail surveys of the elderly relative to those conducted face-to-face is the quality of data obtained using these various modes. Several aspects of data quality may be distinguished: the level of missing data, the amount of information obtained to open-ended questions, and, above all, the validity of responses. Unfortunately, the types of objective information required to permit a direct evaluation of the validity of responses by mode is seldom available. In the absence of such external validating information, evaluations of the quality of data generated by alternative survey modes generally involve comparisons of response distributions by mode on identical items.[6] Where differences by mode are observed, a "mode effect" is indicated, but it cannot be determined which mode represents more valid reporting. For some specific questions the assumption is sometimes made that higher percentages reflect better reporting. Examples of responses where such an assumption may be justified are generally underreported events such as number of sick days or number of illness conditions, or undesirable behaviors and attitudes such as drug use or deviant behaviors. Moreover, even where no mode difference in response distributions are observed, one mode may still conceivably provide more accurate data than the other [9].

Overall, while most such mode comparisons in the literature find at least a few differences between response distributions obtained by a telephone survey and those gathered in face-to-face interviews, most recent reviews of the literature conclude that these differences are neither large enough nor systematic enough to suggest that one of these two modes of data collection is consistently superior to the other [3, 5, 6, 8, 9, 35, 37, 58–60]. As noted recently by Bradburn, "there is general consensus that telephone interviewing yields results as valid as face-to-face interviews and that for most items one can move freely from face-to-face to telephone interviewing and back again if one wishes" [61, p. 295]. On the other hand, some suggestions of lower data quality on the telephone come from a few studies that found a higher level of missing data in telephone surveys [5, 35], a higher level of response set [35], and less numerous responses to open-ended questions [5]; and the controversy over the best mode to obtain sensitive information continues [61, 62].

In spite of the overall comparability of these two modes, there is ample reason to suspect that one or the other may produce higher quality data for older people in particular. Differences in nonresponse have already been noted. In addition, the telephone interview process might be conceived as more stressful and demanding than the face-to-face interview, because the former relies solely on

[6]Of course, alternative explanations such as compositional differences between the respondents reached by the two modes (e.g., educational attainment, income level) must be excluded for differences in response distributions to be attributed to data quality.

auditory cues and provides less opportunity for the establishment of rapport between the interviewer and respondent [62]. These two features may be especially critical in interviews with older people due to their failing sensory capacities [63], their concerns about their performance, and their needs for feedback and support in order to perform well. Accordingly, 97 percent of the interviewers surveyed by Fleishman and Berk [21] felt that face-to-face interviewing was more suitable for interviewing the elderly, although, as noted previously, evidence reported by Rogers [41] indicated that older people were significantly more likely than younger respondents to *prefer* being interviewed by telephone.

In addition, although recent experimentation with telephone interview methodology has attempted to slow down the interview process on the telephone, telephone interviews often proceed at a more rapid pace than face-to-face interviews [5, 64], and there is some evidence that the time differential between these interview types may be greater for older people [41]. Yet, high speed is another factor that may be particularly detrimental to the cognitive performance of older respondents [65]. Consistent with such speculations, our own recent research [46] indicates that older respondents interviewed by telephone are significantly more sensitive than younger respondents to the length or pace of interviews: Although telephone interviews were on average shorter than personal interviews, older people interviewed by telephone were significantly more likely than younger respondents to ask how much longer the interview would last (Figure 3) and rate the interview as lengthy (Figure 4), whereas in interviews conducted face-to-face concerns about interview length were not related to age.

Despite lower response rates and such theoretical predictions for specific difficulties in telephone surveys of the aged, however, in our own research we have found very little evidence for age-specific differences in the quality of responses obtained by the two survey modes. Using the data collected by Groves and Kahn [5] and a more recent methodological study based on the Health Interview Survey [34], our analyses revealed "no differential response effects attributable to interviewing mode that appear to be specifically associated with surveying older respondents" [46, p. 415]. Our analyses were based on responses to open-ended questions and levels of missing data, as well as responses to sixty-five different questions.

Similarly, a set of experiments conducted by the Census Bureau, in which a procedure that maximizes personal visit interviewing was compared to one that maximizes telephone interviewing, revealed little evidence that the elderly are more vulnerable to differences in mode of interview than other age groups. In one experiment, conducted with aged and disabled persons using the Current Medicare Survey protocol [67], no significant differences between telephone and face-to-face interviewing were found for twenty-one different measures. In a parallel study, conducted in connection with the National Crime Survey (see Table 3), a significant interaction between interview mode and age was found in reports of victimization rates for personal crimes (in particular, crimes of theft),

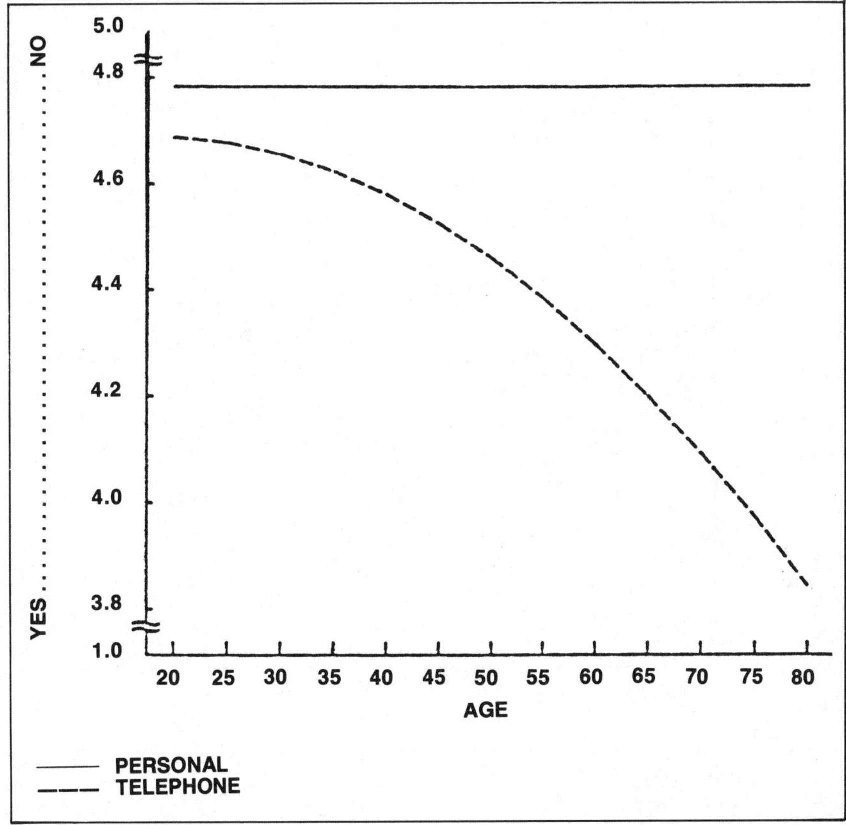


Figure 3. Did respondent ever ask how much longer interview would take?

with persons aged twenty–forty-nine reporting higher rates of victimization in person than by telephone, but no significant difference by mode for those aged fifty and older [66].

In contrast, Aneshensel and her colleagues [37, 58] report a few instances in which older adults show slightly stronger mode differences on health-related questions than adults of other age groups. In addition, in a recent health survey conducted in Florida by RTI using a split telephone-personal interview sample [36], we found a few differences by mode in preventive behaviors, which were more substantial among the aged than other age groups (see Table 4). However, in the same study no major differences of this type were found for various health conditions (see Table 5). Similarly, in the large-scale experiment recently conducted by Cannell and his colleagues for the National Center for Health Statistics [34], telephone respondents were consistent (across sex, age, and education groups)

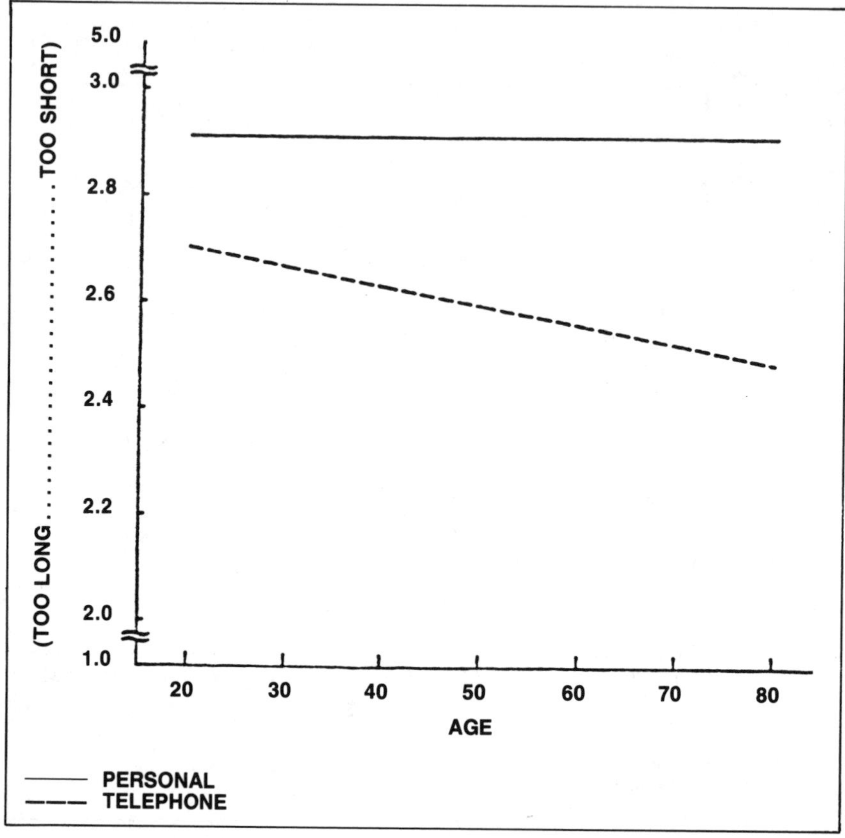


Figure 4. Perceived length of interview.

in reporting more health events than respondents in the interviews conducted face-to-face, *except among the elderly*, who reported somewhat more such events in face-to-face interviews [25].

Studies of potential data quality differences between mail and either of the other two survey modes are even less common than those comparing telephone and face-to-face surveys. In perhaps the most innovative study to date, Siemiatycki compared telephone, mail and home interview strategies using the same sampling frame [8]. His findings indicated that responses by mail were at least of equal quality to those obtained by telephone, and that both of these modes yielded data equivalent to those obtained in face-to-face interviews. His findings are of particular interest because for a few questions external validating information was available from health insurance records. In these comparisons, validity of response

Table 3. Comparison of Victimization Rates for Personal Crimes by Interview Procedure

| | *Victimization Rates per 1,000 Persons 12+* | | | *Differences Between Procedures per 1,000 Persons 12+* | | | |
|---|---|---|---|---|---|---|---|
| *Type of Crime* | *Current NCS* | *Maximum Personal Visit* | *Maximum Telephone* | *Current NCS Minus Maximum Personal Visit*[a] | *Estimated Standard Error* | *Current NCS Minus Maximum Telephone*[a] | *Estimated Standard Error* |
| (a) *Total Persons 12+* | | | | | | | |
| Total Personal Crimes | 129 | 130 | 119 | −1 | 4 | 10 | 4 |
| Crimes of Theft | 97 | 96 | 87 | 1 | 3 | 10 | 3 |
| Crimes of Violence | 32 | 34 | 32 | −2 | 2 | 0 | 2 |
| Assault | 25 | 26 | 25 | −1 | 2 | 0 | 2 |
| Robbery | 6 | 7 | 7 | −1 | 1 | −1 | 1 |
| (b) *Males 12+* | | | | | | | |
| Total Personal Crimes | 151 | 147 | 133 | 4 | 6 | 18 | 6 |
| Crimes of Theft | 109 | 104 | 91 | 5 | 5 | 18 | 5 |
| Crimes of Violence | 42 | 43 | 42 | −1 | 3 | 0 | 3 |
| Assault | 34 | 35 | 31 | −1 | 3 | 3 | 3 |
| Robbery | 8 | 8 | 10 | 0 | 1 | −2 | 2 |
| (c) *Females 12+* | | | | | | | |
| Total Personal Crimes | 109 | 115 | 106 | −6 | 5 | 3 | 5 |
| Crimes of Theft | 87 | 89 | 84 | −2 | 5 | 3 | 4 |
| Crimes of Violence | 22 | 26 | 22 | −4 | 2 | 0 | 2 |
| Assault | 17 | 18 | 18 | −1 | 2 | −1 | 2 |
| Robbery | 4 | 6 | 3 | −2 | 1 | 1 | 1 |

*(continued)*

Table 3. *(continued)*

| Type of Crime | *Victimization Rates per 1,000 Persons 12+* | | | *Differences Between Procedures per 1,000 Persons 12+* | | | |
|---|---|---|---|---|---|---|---|
| | *Current NCS* | *Maximum Personal Visit* | *Maximum Telephone* | *Current NCS Minus Maximum Personal Visit*[a] | *Estimated Standard Error* | *Current NCS Minus Maximum Telephone*[a] | *Estimated Standard Error* |
| (d) *12–24 Years Old* | | | | | | | |
| Total Personal Crimes | 207 | 205 | 197 | 2 | 8 | 10 | 8 |
| Crimes of Theft | 148 | 140 | 140 | 8 | 7 | 8 | 7 |
| Crimes of Violence | 59 | 65 | 57 | −6 | 5 | 2 | 5 |
| Assault | 48 | 60 | 47 | −12 | 5 | 1 | 4 |
| Robbery | 9 | 12 | 9 | −3 | 2 | 0 | 2 |
| (e) *25–49 Years Old* | | | | | | | |
| Total Personal Crimes | 128 | 131 | 114 | −3 | 6 | 14 | 6 |
| Crimes of Theft | 99 | 103 | 83 | −4 | 6 | 16 | 5 |
| Crimes of Violence | 29 | 28 | 31 | 1 | 3 | −2 | 3 |
| Assault | 23 | 22 | 23 | 1 | 3 | 0 | 3 |
| Robbery | 5 | 6 | 7 | −1 | 1 | −2 | 1 |
| (f) *50 or More Years Old* | | | | | | | |
| Total Personal Crimes | 56 | 57 | 51 | −1 | 5 | 5 | 5 |
| Crimes of Theft | 46 | 46 | 42 | 0 | 4 | 4 | 4 |
| Crimes of Violence | 10 | 11 | 10 | −1 | 2 | 0 | 2 |
| Assault | 6 | 7 | 5 | −1 | 2 | 1 | 2 |
| Robbery | 4 | 4 | 4 | 0 | 1 | 0 | 1 |

[a] Differences are obtained from rounded victimization rates.

**Note**: Reprinted with permission from Woltman, Turner, and Bushery [66].

Table 4. Utilization of Health Care Resources for Telephone and Area Sample Surveys

| | *Telephone* | | | *In-Person* | | |
|---|---|---|---|---|---|---|
| *Utilization Characteristic* | *17–44* | *45–64* | *65+* | *17–44* | *45–64* | *65+* |
| *Usual Source of Care* | | | | | | |
| None | 25.0 | 26.2 | 25.9 | 24.8 | 28.0 | 15.3 |
| Private Physician | 60.5 | 65.9 | 68.8 | 60.2 | 56.8 | 74.3 |
| Public Health Clinic | 2.5 | 1.4 | 1.7 | 3.6 | 0.6 | 0.9 |
| Outpatient Clinic | 1.4 | 3.2 | 2.9 | 1.0 | 5.0 | 4.1 |
| Emergency Room | 1.4 | 0 | 0.2 | 1.3 | 1.2 | 0.4 |
| Other | 9.9 | 3.3 | 0.5 | 9.2 | 8.4 | 4.9 |
| *Problems Obtaining Health Care* | | | | | | |
| None | 88.0 | 95.2 | 91.2 | 86.3 | 88.5 | 93.9 |
| Not available when needed | 3.8 | 0 | 0 | 3.1 | 2.8 | 1.2 |
| Cost of Care | 2.8 | 0.7 | 0.0 | 3.0 | 2.9 | 0.1 |
| Did not know where to go | 8.8 | 4.2 | 8.0 | 9.9 | 7.6 | 4.2 |
| No way to get there | 2.3 | 0 | 0 | 0.8 | 2.6 | 2.0 |
| Hours inconvenient | 1.1 | 0.7 | 0.9 | 0.4 | 0.2 | 3.3 |
| *Use of Diagnostic Procedures by Females* | | | | | | |
| Pap Smear | 54.8 | 19.0 | 26.1 | 57.2 | 31.5 | 26.6 |
| Breast Exam by Physician | 67.4 | 57.6 | 65.6 | 60.9 | 39.3 | 40.0 |
| Breast Self Exam | 73.01 | 71.1 | 70.3 | 75.5 | 70.4 | 44.4 |

*(continued)*

Table 4. *(continued)*

| | *Telephone* | | | *In-Person* | | |
|---|---|---|---|---|---|---|
| *Utilization Characteristic* | *17–44* | *45–64* | *65 +* | *17–44* | *45–64* | *65 +* |
| *Use of General Diagnostic Procedures* | | | | | | |
| Blood Pressure Exam | 65.4 | 71.7 | 85.7 | 60.6 | 64.6 | 79.0 |
| Eye Exam for Glasses | 20.6 | 38.1 | 50.7 | 21.6 | 36.1 | 43.4 |
| Glaucoma Test | 15.4 | 40.3 | 53.4 | 14.4 | 36.0 | 41.7 |
| Hearing Test | 12.6 | 14.7 | 26.6 | 9.3 | 9.2 | 6.2 |
| Urine Test for Diabetes | 32.5 | 43.7 | 53.1 | 25.4 | 28.1 | 36.1 |
| Blood Test for Anemia | 35.6 | 40.4 | 43.9 | 25.8 | 30.1 | 33.6 |
| Rectal Exam | 19.4 | 31.8 | 34.3 | 15.7 | 23.9 | 22.4 |
| Percent of persons with one or more health problems who had one or more service utilizations | 74.2 | 82.6 | 87.2 | 72.4 | 75.9 | 84.0 |
| Number of Physician Visits per person per year | 2.5 | 3.5 | 4.2 | 1.9 | 4.8 | 3.5 |
| Number of Ambulatory Care Visits per person per year | 2.8 | 3.1 | 3.6 | 3.1 | 3.4 | 5.0 |
| Number of Hospital Stays per 100 persons per year | 12.2 | 14.1 | 22.5 | 13.5 | 21.1 | 31.7 |

**Source:** Reprinted from Lessler and Kulka [36].

Table 5. Measures of Health Status for Telephone and Area Sample Surveys

| | *Telephone* | | | *In-Person* | | |
|---|---|---|---|---|---|---|
| *Health Status Characteristic* | *17–44* | *45–64* | *65+* | *17–44* | *45–64* | *65+* |
| Percent with one or more chronic conditions | 49.6 | 69.8 | 85.5 | 36.7 | 65.8 | 85.1 |
| Percent with one or more self care impairments that affect activities of daily living (walking, going outside, using toilet, bathing, dressing, eating) | 1.5 | 4.6 | 12.7 | 2.2 | 9.4 | 22.7 |
| Percent with one or more instrumental impairments that affect activities of daily living (preparing meals, shopping, doing chores, handling money) | 2.0 | 3.0 | 8.2 | 1.5 | 5.3 | 11.7 |
| Percent of persons with one or more health problems | 53.3 | 70.1 | 87.1 | 42.2 | 70.1 | 86.9 |
| Disability days per person per year | 15.1 | 19.0 | 25.2 | 12.0 | 31.2 | 26.8 |

*(continued)*

Table 5. *(continued)*

| | *Telephone* | | | *In-Person* | | |
|---|---|---|---|---|---|---|
| *Health Status Characteristic* | *17–44* | *45–64* | *65+* | *17–44* | *45–64* | *65+* |
| Percent of persons with selected chronic conditions | | | | | | |
| Digestive Condition | 5.7 | 9.5 | 7.1 | 7.1 | 8.8 | 13.8 |
| Muscle-Skeletal | 13.8 | 35.2 | 49.6 | 10.6 | 27.4 | 44.1 |
| Endocrine/Blood | 1.3 | 6.4 | 11.3 | 3.1 | 6.6 | 9.8 |
| Migraine | 3.5 | 0.3 | 0.0 | 1.9 | 2.8 | 0.0 |
| Skin Conditions | 6.9 | 4.4 | 8.6 | 4.5 | 4.3 | 13.2 |
| Eye, Ear, Speech | 6.2 | 15.2 | 29.4 | 7.2 | 16.1 | 40.0 |
| Genito-Urinary | 4.5 | 10.5 | 10.3 | 1.7 | 3.0 | 8.0 |
| Circulatory System | 8.4 | 28.8 | 44.6 | 8.9 | 29.7 | 54.6 |
| Respiratory | 19.0 | 23.0 | 20.0 | 15.6 | 20.1 | 17.4 |
| Malignant Neoplasms | 2.2 | 4.0 | 9.4 | 1.2 | 6.0 | 13.7 |
| Number of Chronic Conditions | | | | | | |
| 0 | 50.4 | 30.2 | 14.5 | 63.3 | 34.2 | 14.9 |
| 1 | 31.6 | 29.0 | 24.3 | 18.3 | 26.3 | 17.1 |
| 2 | 10.9 | 18.4 | 24.8 | 9.6 | 15.1 | 20.2 |
| 3 or more | 7.1 | 22.5 | 36.4 | 8.8 | 24.5 | 47.8 |

**Source:** Reprinted from Lessler and Kulka [36].

and willingness to answer sensitive questions were actually greatest in the mail survey mode. With regard to the latter, Hochstim also found a greater tendency for respondents to report sensitive information about themselves in mail questionnaires or telephone interviews than in face-to-face interviews [6], a tendency which has gained a certain degree of consensus in the research literature [61, 68]. Overall, data from these and other studies [6, 47, 60, 69] provide little evidence for the assumption of decreased quality of responses in mail surveys compared with those conducted face-to-face, other than a somewhat higher level of missing data sometimes encountered in mail surveys compared with face-to-face interviews [1, 6, 47].[7]

Once again, of course, for the reasons specified by Dillman [1]—lower educational attainment and difficulties with seeing and writing—it is possible that while overall differences in data quality between mail surveys and the other two modes are small, such mode effects might be considerably greater among older persons. Unfortunately, we were able to locate very little information on potential age-specific differences in data quality between mail surveys and either of the other two modes. Scott [47] presents evidence that questionnaires mailed to persons fifty or over are more likely to be returned by someone other than the addressee, suggesting a higher level of "proxy" response, with a possible corresponding decrement in accuracy of reporting. In addition, some other studies suggest that item nonresponse is higher among older respondents to mail surveys than among younger respondents [70, 71], but this differential may not be any greater in mail surveys than one might find in surveys conducted by telephone or in person [72, 73]. In one of the very few direct studies of this issue, Leinbach reported that mail—as well as telephone—survey procedures used for needs assessment among the elderly in a Pennsylvania county yielded results equivalent to a face-to-face interview [74]. However, he also encountered more missing data in the mail survey than under either of the other two modes. Since his brief report lacks certain details with regard to design and sampling procedures and presents only an aggregate analysis of the data, these results, while encouraging, are difficult to evaluate properly.

## CONCLUSION

Contrary to popular beliefs favoring face-to-face interviews, there is no clearly superior method that yields the best results for all populations, circumstances, and types of questions [61]. Rather, telephone, mail, and face-to-face surveys all have certain strengths and certain limitations, and this obvious truism is apparently as applicable to surveys of the aged as it is to any other population. On balance, research evidence available to date, though clearly inadequate, generally supports the viability of conducting mail and telephone surveys with the elderly

[7]Dillman reports average item nonresponse for TDM mail surveys at 3.5 to 4.6 percent [1].

either as an adjunct to or as a reasonable substitute for face-to-face interviews. Although substantial additional research is needed to clarify further the advantages and disadvantages of conducting telephone and mail surveys with older people, surveys using either mode which are carefully designed with *known* limitations in mind appear just as feasible for studies of the elderly as for studies of the general population.

With regard to telephone surveys the research agenda is clear. Despite continuing protestations to the contrary, coverage is more complete in random digit dialed surveys of the elderly than for any other age group. This assurance is of little solace, however, when we subsequently discover that elderly respondents tend to have lower response rates than other groups to telephone surveys. And, since we know next to nothing concrete about what factors underlie this nonresponse, research focusing on the reasons for older adults' reluctance to participate in telephone surveys should receive top research priority. To the extent that we can establish why older adults may be more reluctant to participate in a telephone interview, we will be better able to design modifications of standard survey procedures to increase participation among the aged. To the extent that this is not possible, we will be forced to live with this known deficiency in our analyses and interpretation of survey data on the elderly, to derive post-survey adjustments to account for this nonresponse, or to evolve dual sampling frame/dual mode approaches for surveying this particular population. Several investigations have demonstrated that among a general population such "mixed-mode" approaches—such as the use of face-to-face interviews to survey persons who cannot be interviewed by telephone—are able to achieve relatively high response rates while keeping costs within reasonable bounds [6, 8, 75, 76].

Given the lack of evidence for large-scale differences in data quality between telephone and face-to-face modes, the telephone appears well suited for follow-up interviews. In follow-up surveys the sample has been drawn and the respondents' cooperation enlisted using the face-to-face mode. Thus, those shortcomings of the telephone survey are avoided. Recent experience in a regional six-week re-interview in Michigan yielded a response rate of 90 percent for the entire sample and a response rate of 84 percent for persons over sixty [77]. Similarly, a resurvey of a national sample of older adults one year after the initial survey [78] found a response rate of 76 percent to the re-survey if only respondents were included, and a response rate of 93 percent if respondents and proxies were included.

Since evidence available on mail surveys of the elderly is considerably more limited than that on telephone and face-to-face interviews, firm conclusions with regard to the past and future of mail surveys are more difficult to formulate. However, from what we have been able to gather and synthesize, we feel that the mail survey mode has perhaps been underestimated and deserves more serious consideration by gerontological researchers. This mode also needs some further systematic research addressed specifically to its use with the aged. While obtaining an adequate sample of the elderly from a general population frame clearly represents a serious problem, with persistent and innovative research this problem might be overcome. In contrast to telephone surveys, where substantial evidence of this sort is already available, we clearly need further comparisons of mail surveys to the other two modes that permit an assessment of potential interactions by age in order to assess both response rates and data quality. In particular, reflecting the major concern with nonresponse in this area of research, future research on mail surveys of the elderly should carefully examine potential differences by age in the effectiveness of various response inducement techniques—such as the use of personalization, alternative follow-up procedures, and incentives—for improving both the quality and quantity of response to such surveys.

Clearly, those who rely on surveys to obtain data on the elderly can no longer afford to be provincial about their choice of survey mode. The cost advantages of telephone and mail surveys in conjunction with lack of evidence for serious problems in data quality and a potential for improving response rates virtually mandate a more serious look at these alternatives.

## ACKNOWLEDGMENT

The authors thank their colleague Willard Rodgers for a critical reading of the manuscript.

## REFERENCES

1. D. A. Dillman, *Mail and Telephone Surveys: The Total Design Method,* John Wiley, New York, 1978.
2. D. A. Dillman, Mail and Other Self-Administered Questionnaires: In *Handbook of Survey Research*, P. H. Rossi, J. D. Wright, and A. B. Anderson (Eds.), Academic Press, New York, 1983.
3. R. P. Quinn, B. A. Gutek, and J. T. Walsh, Telephone Interviewing: A Reappraisal and a Field Experiment, *Basic and Applied Social Psychology, 1,* pp. 127–153, 1980.
4. J. H. Frey, *Survey Research by Telephone,* Sage Publications, Beverly Hills, CA, 1983.
5. R. M. Groves and R. L. Kahn, *Surveys by Telephone: A National Comparison with Personal Interviews*, Academic Press, New York, 1979.
6. J. R. Hochstim, A Critical Comparison of Three Stategies of Collecting Data from Households, *Journal of the American Statistical Association, 62*, pp. 976–989, 1967.
7. W. A. Lucas and W. C. Adams, *An Assessment of Telephone Survey Methods*, The Rand Corporation, Santa Monica, CA, 1977.
8. J. Siemiatycki, A Comparison of Mail, Telephone, and Home Interview Strategies for Household Health Surveys, *American Journal of Public Health, 69*, pp. 238–245, 1979.
9. M. F. Weeks, R. A. Kulka, J. T. Lessler, and R. W. Whitmore, Personal versus Telephone Surveys for Collecting Household Health Data at the Local Level, *American Journal of Public Health, 73*, pp. 1389–1394, 1983.

10. A. B. Blankenship, *Professional Telephone Surveys*, McGraw-Hill, New York, 1977.
11. W. J. Duncan, Mail Questionnaires in Survey Research: A Review of Response Inducement Techniques, *Journal of Management, 5*, pp. 39–55, 1979.
12. T. A. Heberlein and R. Baumgartner, Factors Affecting Response Rates to Mailed Questionnaires: A Quantitative Analysis of the Published Literature, *American Sociological Review, 43*, pp. 447–462, 1978.
13. L. Kanuk and C. Berensen, Mail Surveys and Response Rates: A Literature Review, *Journal of Marketing Research, 12*, pp. 440–453, 1975.
14. A. S. Linsky, Stimulating Responses to Mailed Questionnaires: A Review, *Public Opinion Quarterly, 39*, pp. 82–101, 1975.
15. T. T. Tyebjee, Telephone Survey Methods: The State of the Art, *Journal of Marketing, 43*, pp. 68–78, 1979.
16. F. M. Carp, Maximizing Data Quality in Community Studies of Older People, In *Special Research Methods for Gerontology*, M. P. Lawton and A. R. Herzog (Eds.), Baywood Press, Amityville, NY.
17. D. M. Gibson and W. Aitkenhead, The Elderly Respondent: Experiences from a Large-Scale Survey of the Aged, *Research on Aging, 5*, pp. 283–296, 1983.
18. R. L. Horton and D. J. Duncan, A New Look at Telephone Interviewing Methodology, *Pacific Sociological Review, 21*, pp. 259–274, 1978.
19. G. R. Lee and J. M. Finney, Sampling in Social Gerontology: A Method of Locating Specialized Populations, *Journal of Gerontology, 32*, pp. 689–693, 1977.
20. M. D. Blumenthal, Letter to the Editor, *Journal of Gerontology, 33*, p. 322, 1978.
21. E. Fleishman and M. Berk, Survey of Interviewer Attitudes toward Selected Methodological Issues in the National Medical Care Expenditure Survey. In National Center for Health Services Research, Public Health Service, U.S. Department of Health and Human Services. *Health Survey Research Methods,* Research Proceedings Series 1979. DHHS Publication No (PHS) 81-3268.
22. F. G. Scott, Mail Questionnaires Used in a Study of Older Women, *Sociology and Social Research, 41*, pp. 281–284, 1957.
23. Chartbook on Aging in America. Prepared for the 1981 White House Conference on Aging, 1981.
24. J. W. Schmiedeskamp, Reinterviews by Telephone, *Journal of Marketing, 26*, pp. 28–34, 1962.
25. O. T. Thornberry, Methodological Issues in Random Digit Dialed Surveys of the Elderly. Paper presented at the Annual Meetings of the American Public Health Association, Montreal, November 1982.
26. U.S. Bureau of the Census, *Statistical Abstract of the United States: 1982–83* (103rd ed.), Department of Commerce, Washington, DC, 1983.
27. L. M. Wolfle, Characteristics of Persons With and Without Home Telephones, *Journal of Marketing Research, 16*, pp. 421–425, 1979.
28. O. T Thornberry and J. T. Massey, Correcting for Undercoverage Bias in Random Digit Dialed National Health Surveys. Proceedings of the Section on Survey Research Methods, American Statistical Association, 1978.
29. G. Hoinville, Carrying Out Surveys Among the Elderly: Some Problems of Sampling and Interviewing, *Journal of the Market Research Society, 25*, pp. 223–237, 1983.
30. S. Sudman, Sample Surveys, *Annual Review of Sociology, 2*, pp. 107–120, 1976.

31. N. E. Cutler and R. A. Harootyan, Demography of the Aged, In *Aging*, D. S. Woodruff and J. E. Birren (Eds.), Van Nostrand, New York, 1975.
32. J. A. Brunner and G. A. Brunner, Are Voluntary Unlisted Telephone Subscribers Really Different? *Journal of Marketing Research, 8*, pp. 121–124, 1971.
33. J. Grimley Evans, M. Brewis, and D. Prudham, Electors Not Liable for Jury Service as a Sampling Frame for the Elderly, *Age and Ageing, 5*, p. 228, 1976.
34. C. F. Cannell, R. M. Groves, L. J. Magilavy, N. A. Mathiowetz, and P. V. Miller, An Experimental Comparison of Telephone and Personal Health Surveys. Final report to the National Center for Health Statistics, Institute for Social Research, Ann Arbor, MI, 1982.
35. L. A. Jordan,, A. C. Marcus, and L. G. Reeder, Response Styles in Telephone and Household Interviewing: A Field Experiment, *Public Opinion Quarterly, 44*, p. 210–222, 1980.
36. J. T. Lessler and R. A. Kulka, The Effect of Differences in Survey Interview Mode on Policy Decisions for the Aged. Paper presented at the Annual Meeting of the American Public Health Association, Montreal, November 1982.
37. C. S. Aneshensel, R. R. Frerichs, V. A. Clark, and P. A. Yokopenic, Telephone versus In-Person Surveys of Community Health Status, *American Journal of Public Health, 72*, pp. 1017–1021, 1982.
38. J. F. Corso, Auditory Perception and Communication, In *Handbook of the Psychology of Aging*, J. E. Birren and K. W. Schaie (Eds.), Van Nostrand Reinhold, New York, 1977.
39. C. S. Kart, E. S. Metress, and J. F. Metress, *Aging and Health*, Addison-Wesley, Menlo Park, CA, 1978.
40. F. Clemente and M. B. Kleiman, Fear of Crime among the Aged, *The Gerontologist, 16*, pp 207–210, 1976.
41. T. F. Rogers, Interviews by Telephone and In Person: Quality of Responses and Field Performance, *Public Opinion Quarterly, 40*, pp. 51–65, 1976.
42. M. Friedman and I. M. Wasserman, Characteristics of Respondents and Non-Respondents in a Telephone Survey Study of Elderly Consumers, *Psychological Reports, 42*, p. 714, 1978.
43. C. N. Weaver, S. L. Holmes, and N. D. Glenn, Some Characteristics of Inaccessible Respondents in a Telephone Survey, *Journal of Applied Psychology, 60*, pp. 260–262, 1975.
44. M. L. Monsees and J. T. Massey, Application of Personal Interview Survey Definitions to a Telephone Survey. Proceedings of the Social Statistics Section, American Statistical Association, pp. 7–14, 1979.
45. J. T. Massey, P. R. Barker, and S. Hsiung, An Investigation of Response in a Telephone Survey. Proceedings of the Section on Survey Research Methods, American Statistical Association, pp. 426–431, 1981.
46. A. R. Herzog, W. L. Rodgers, and R. A. Kulka, Interviewing Older Adults: A Comparison of Telephone and Face-To-Face Modalities, *Public Opinion Quarterly, 47*, pp. 405–418, 1983.
47. C. Scott, Research on Mail Surveys, *Journal of the Royal Statistical Society, 124*, Series A, pp. 143–195, 1961.
48. R. C. Atchley, Respondents vs. Refusers in an Interview Study of Retired Women: An Analysis of Selected Characteristics, *Journal of Gerontology, 24*, pp. 42–47, 1969.

49. J. H. Britton and J. O. Britton, Factors in the Return of Questionnaires Mailed to Older Persons, *Journal of Applied Psychology, 35*, pp. 57–60, 1951.
50. J. M. Finney, G. R. Lee, and M. Zeglen, Survey Research on the Elderly. Paper presented at the Annual Meeting of the Pacific Sociological Association, San Diego, 1976.
51. D. S. DeWitt and J. T. Lynch, The Long-Term Care Insurance Survey. Final report to the Health Care Financing Administration and National Center for Health Services Research, Research Triangle Institute, Research Triangle Park, NC, 1982.
52. D. A. Dillman, J. A. Christenson, E. H. Carpenter, and R. M. Brooks, Increasing Mail Questionnaire Response: A Four-State Comparison, *American Sociological Review, 39*, pp. 744–756, 1974.
53. J. E. Kivlin, Contributions to the Study of Mail-Back Bias, *Rural Sociology, 30*, pp. 323–326, 1965.
54. J. R. Hochstim and D. A. Athanasopoulos, Personal Follow-Up in a Mail Survey: Its Contribution and Its Cost, *Public Opinion Quarterly, 34*, pp. 69–81, 1970.
55. E. J. Baur, Response Bias in a Mail Survey, *Public Opinion Quarterly, 11*, pp. 594–600, 1947.
56. W. M. Phillips, Jr., Weaknesses of the Mail Questionnaire, *Sociology and Social Research, 35*, pp. 260–267, 1951.
57. M. Maclean and H. Genn, *Methodological Issues in Social Surveys*, Humanities Press, Atlantic Highlands, NJ, 1979.
58. C. S. Aneshensel, R. R. Frerichs, V. A. Clark, and P. A. Yokopenic, Measuring Depression in the Community: A Comparison of Telephone and Personal Interviews, *Public Opinion Quarterly, 46*, pp. 110–121, 1982.
59. W. R. Klecka and A. J. Tuchfarber, Random Digit Dialing: A Comparison to Personal Surveys, *Public Opinion Quarterly, 42*, pp. 105–114, 1978.
60. W. Locander, S. Sudman, and N. Bradburn, An Investigation of Interview Method, Threat and Response Distortion, *Journal of the American Statistical Association, 71*, pp. 269–275, 1976.
61. N. M. Bradburn, Response Effects, In *Handbook of Survey Research*, P. H. Rossi, James D. Wright, and A. B. Anderson (Eds.), Academic Press, New York, 1983.
62. E. Singer, Telephone Interviewing as a Black Box, In *Health Survey Research Methods*, National Center for Health Services Research, Public Health Service, U.S. Department of Health and Human Services, Research Proceedings Series 1979, DHHS Publication No. (PHS) 81-3268, 1981.
63. L. W. Olsho, S. W. Harkins, and M. L. Lenhardt, Aging and the Auditory System, In *Handbook of the Psychology of Aging*, 2nd ed., J. E. Birren and K. W. Schaie (Eds.), Van Nostrand Reinhold, New York, 1985.
64. R. Groves, On the Mode of Administering a Questionnaire and Responses to Open-Ended Items, *Social Science Research, 7*, pp. 257–271, 1978.
65. T. A. Salthouse, Speed of Behavior and Its Implications for Cognition, In *Handbook of the Psychology of Aging*, 2nd ed., J. E. Birren and K. W. Schaie (Eds.), Van Nostrand Reinhold, New York, 1985.
66. H. F. Woltman, A. G. Turner, and J. M. Bushery, A Comparison of Three Mixed-Mode Interviewing Procedures in the National Crime Survey, *Journal of the American Statistical Association, 75*, pp. 534–543, 1980.

67. J. M. Bushery, C. D. Cowan, and L. R. Murphy, Experiments in Telephone-Personal Visit Surveys. Proceedings of the Survey Research Methods Section, American Statistical Association, pp. 564–567, 1978.
68. S. Sudman and N. M. Bradburn, *Response Effects in Surveys: A Review and Synthesis*, Aldine, Chicago, 1974.
69. C. F. Cannell and F. Fowler, Comparison of Hospitalization Reporting in Three Survey Procedures, Vital and Health Statistics, PHS Publication No. 1000, Series 2, No. 8, Government Printing Office, Washington, DC, 1965.
70. R. Ferber, Item Nonresponse in a Consumer Survey, *Public Opinion Quarterly, 30*, pp. 399–415, 1966.
71. C. S. Craig and J. M. McCann, Item Nonresponse in Mail Surveys: Extent and Correlates, *Journal of Marketing Research, 15,* pp. 285–289, 1978.
72. K. J. Gergen and K. W. Back, Communication in the Interview and the Disengaged Respondent, *Public Opinion Quarterly, 30*, pp. 385–398, 1966.
73. N. D. Glenn, Aging, Disengagement, and Opinionation, *Public Opinion Quarterly, 33*, pp. 17–33, 1969.
74. R. M. Leinbach, Alternatives to the Face-To-Face Interview for Collecting Gerontological Needs Assessment Data, *The Gerontologist, 22*, pp. 78–82, 1982.
75. J. Herrman, Mixed Mode Data Collection: Telephone and Personal Interviewing, *Journal of Applied Psychology, 62,* pp. 399–404, 1977.
76. O. T. Thornberry, An Evaluation of Three Strategies for the Collection of Data for Households. Unpublished doctoral dissertation, Brown University, 1976.
77. A. R. Herzog and W. L. Rodgers, Interviewing Older Adults: Mode Comparison Using Data from a Face-To-Face Survey and a Telephone Re-Survey, *Public Opinion Quarterly, 52*, pp. 84–99, 1988.
78. M. G. Kovar and J. E. Fitti, A Linked Follow-Up Study of Older People. Proceedings of the Section on Survey Research Methods, Annual Meeting of the American Statistical Association, Las Vegas, Nevada, 1985.

# SECTION 2
# How to Obtain Good Data from Older Subjects

The following chapter by Carp constitutes a section of its own because it constitutes the most general guide to good practice in the interviewing and testing of normal older people living in the community. While certainly not the first contribution of this kind (for example, Carp cites earlier important contributions by Gibson and Aitkenhead [1], and Hoinville [2]), Carp's treatment is the most comprehensive and has the great advantage of being able to cite firsthand experience gained in many studies of her own, as well as empirical findings from research specifically designed to answer methodological questions.

Particularly helpful are Carp's presentations of the critical issue of the validity of older people's responses to questions that presume an evaluative response. She deals separately, for example, with the polarity question ("is satisfaction the opposite of dissatisfaction?"), positive response bias ("do older people give the 'rosy' response?") and frame of reference ("satisfaction by what criterion?").

Carp's discussion of the research sample overlaps hardly at all with the concerns of the authors of the first-section chapters. She offers a very rich discussion, with both qualitative and quantitative back-up data, of the hazards that might cause the designated sample member to be unsuccessfully recruited. Awareness of these potential barriers then leads naturally to useful suggestions for maximizing the yield.

The core of the process is the data collection itself. Both motivational and procedural suggestions are made. One section of Carp's explication deals with sample maintenance as a problem in longitudinal research. This section of her discussion is a complement to two chapters explicitly concerned about this issue in Part Two (Reisberg et al., Chapter 8, and Sharma, Tobin, and Brant, Chapter 9). The specific experiences reported by Carp are operationally related to the other methodological issues discussed earlier.

Viewing the Carp chapter as a whole it may be worth asking whether her analysis has demonstrated that special methods are indicated for older subjects. In several instances she implies that such a conclusion is not warranted. In fact, it is very important to note that the automatic use of such an assumption may in itself be "ageistic." On the other hand, a strong conceptual basis exists for examining age differences in response style or the frames of references underlying differences in response style. The interested reader might wish to investigate an age-cohort-period interpretation of apparent cohort or period changes in life-satisfaction [3]. Given that such changes have been shown to occur, does it follow that interviewing techniques should also be adjusted across time? At the very least it is clearly hazardous to view required differences in procedure as being demanded by the age of the subjects, rather than because of health, cultural differences, or interviewer effects such as ageism or incomplete training.

## REFERENCES

1. D. M. Gibson and W. Aitkenhead, The Elderly Respondent: Experiences from a Large-Scale Survey of the Aged, *Journal of the Market Research Society, 25*, pp. 283-296, 1983.
2. G. Hoinville, Camping Out Surveys among the Elderly: Some Problems of Sampling and Interviewing, *Journal of the Market Research Society, 25*, pp. 223-237, 1983.
3. B. J. Felton and P. Shaver, Cohort Variations in Adults' Reported Feelings, in *Emotion in Adult Development*, C. Z. Malatesta and C. E. Izards (eds.), pp. 103-124, Sage Publications, Beverly Hills CA, 1984.

CHAPTER
4

# Maximizing Data Quality in Community Studies of Older People

*Frances M. Carp*

This chapter covers methodological issues other than formal sampling techniques. It deals with knitty-gritty problems in instrument selection and development, following a sampling design, and collecting data from older community residents, with emphasis on longitudinal studies. Attention is directed to factors that may affect data quality: Biasing effects in instruments, forces that impede adherence to the sampling plan and sample maintenance, and data collection procedures that affect response rate or distribution. When possible, suggestions for ameliorating these influences are offered. My experience inevitably affects the suggestions. In light of their own experience, other investigators may disagree with them. No approach is equally appropriate across studies. Some require only attention on the part of the researcher; others add time and effort. Each researcher will judge the merit of any suggestion in relation to a particular study purpose, and assess the cost/benefit ratio.

The chapter is organized around instrument selection and preparation, adherence to the sample plan, data collection, and sample maintenance. The diminishing length of chapter sections, from first to last, may be attributed to fatigue effect, but it reflects the extent of overlap in content. In each section, issues are raised with regard to variables that might influence data quality. This is not a literature review, and the citations are illustrative only. For the sake of parsimony in the reference list, the same sources are cited for several issues, when possible. This is not meant to imply that they are the sole or best sources.

Research reports usually are focused on the final data, their analysis, and the conclusions they support. Due partly to space limitations, journal articles and book chapters may not include mundane details about some decisions and procedures that may have influenced the quality of the data that were collected. For example, there is a voluminous literature based on data from the three longitudinal studies at the Institute for Human Development (formerly the Institute of Child Welfare) of the University of California, Berkeley. The Guidance Study (GS) was begun in 1928 by Jean Walker Macfarlane, Ph.D. to study behavior problems among pre-school children. The Berkeley Growth Study (BGS) was initiated in 1929 by Nancy Bayley, Ph.D., to trace normal development during the first year of life. The Oakland Study (OGS) was undertaken in 1931 by Harold E. Jones, Ph.D., Mary Cover Jones, Ph.D., and Herbert R. Stolz, M.D., to study normal adolescence. Each investigation widened in scope and continued well beyond its originally anticipated termination. Despite differences among the studies in purpose, samples, and methodologies, they shared considerable common data. In 1967, plans were made to coordinate the three as the Intergenerational Studies (IGS) under the direction of Dorothy H. Eichorn, Ph.D., and the first IGS data were collected in 1969-1972. Subsequent analyses pooled data or pointed to differences between or among the three data sets, as appropriate. The major volume reporting longitudinal analyses involving the 1969-72 IGS data and the data collected by the three component studies at various previous intervals focused on the period of the life course between adolescence and middle-age. With the collection of another wave of data in 1981-83, the OGS clearly entered the domain of gerontology because its participants were then aged sixty-one to sixty-three, about eight years older than the other panels.

Throughout the extensive literature on this triumvirate of investigations, the purposes, measures, data collection procedures, and analytic approaches have been carefully described and documented. However, the mundane details of day-to-day and year-to-year strategies for sample maintenance, which have been remarkably successful over a period of fifty years and more, are not readily discernible. Obviously these strategies varied from study to study. OGS is the most gerontologically relevant, and Mary Cover Jones is the ideal source of practical information on its procedures for sample maintenance. She was one of the initiators of the study and remained with it beyond the 1981-83 data collection. From the first, one of her responsibilities was respondent interest, and during the adult follow-up years this was her primary role. Dr. Jones very kindly provided information on the practical aspects of sample maintenance of OGS for the last section of this chapter.

## INSTRUMENT SELECTION AND DEVELOPMENT

### AGEISM

"It is important to study at-risk populations. . . . However, reading the social gerontological literature, with its frequent focus on age related declines and pathologies, one sometimes walks away feeling that elderly individuals are in some ways 'victims' of their own age" [1, p. 1]. A common investigator "set" is expressed by Hoinville: "Design an interview in the expectation that respondents' comprehension and concentration will be low" [2, p. 231]. This despite documentation that cognitive decline is not inevitable or sizeable among the well elderly [3] and reports of high levels of cooperation from elderly respondents by Hoinville [2] himself as well as by others [4]. For samples of community-resident older persons, an investigator's expectation of low comprehension and concentration levels and poor cooperation will limit the types of data that are collected and therefore the issues that can be addressed.

Much of the research in social gerontology has dealt with frail older persons and those that require special assistance such as low-cost housing or other services for the elderly. Societal concern and consequent availability of research funds have channeled research along these lines, and studies of dependent groups are facilitated by the prior identification of participants; recently the need for information regarding the large majority of community-resident older persons has been stressed [5]. In responding to this need, investigators who have worked with the more dependent elderly may generalize inappropriately from that earlier experience when planning studies of the well elderly.

As a result they may, for example, limit cognitive instruments to measures of intellectual impairment, and they may not consider the relevance of differentiations within the normal range of intellectual functioning to the study purpose and design. Selection of an appropriate measure of competence in any domain depends upon the purpose: To assess variations within the normal range or to identify the impaired. With regard to mental competence, the ethical consideration of prior informed consent requires that each participant in any research must understand the consent statement, which includes a study description and explanation of any potentially deleterious effects on him. Various studies have carried out screening for such a level of mental competence using interviewer or staff judgements, or formal measures such as the Short Portable Mental Status Questionnaire (SPMSQ) [6]. Individuals with low ratings or scores are considered incapable of providing informed consent and are not interviewed. For some study purposes, procedures are established to avoid contaminating effects of intellectual deficiency or deterioration by eliminating the institutionalized [4] or candidates who score below a specified cut-off on a standard instrument [7].

In an early study of applicants to public housing for the elderly [8], when views on aging and competence were more negative than are current views [3], consultants scoffed at inclusion of such instruments as the Wechsler [9] Adult Intelligence Scale (WAIS), Thematic Apperception Test (TAT) [10], and Minnesota Multiphasic Personality Inventory (MMPI) [11] because they thought old people were unable to deal with the task. However, the tests were administered without difficulty, at baseline (when average respondent age was over 72) and again at eighteen-month and ten-year intervals, and inclusion of the standard intelligence and personality measures greatly enriched the data set.

Indicators of mental status, concentration level, and cooperativeness are sometimes used to assess the influence of such variables on outcomes [4, 8]. Some investigators prepare an abbreviated version of their instrument, containing core questions, for use with respondents who might prove to have difficulty with the regular protocol or collect data from proxy respondents in such instances [2, 4]. Collection of partial data on some subjects poses problems in data analysis and interpretation of results. Use of proxy data for frail subjects may involve bias due to the difference in data source according to level of competence or cooperativeness.

The point is that investigators need to be sensitive to characteristics of the target group for any study and to avoid unwarranted generalizations from one population to another; and to define the roles of such variables as mental status, concentration and cooperation levels in relation to ethical standards and the study purpose when specifying variables and selecting instruments.

## INSTRUMENT FORMAT EFFECTS

Neither simple closed-end nor open-end questions seem to pose difficulties for older persons [2, 4]. In a review of several studies, Hoinville suggested that interviews be as unstructured as possible [4] even to the extreme of total lack of structure, citing a study [12] in which unstructured interviews elicited "very coherent and full" material from fourteen confused elderly individuals. In a five-month program of testing different closed-end structures and subsequent completion of a large-scale survey of the elderly, Gibson and Aitkenhead used a variety of formats successfully, "the proviso being that care should be given to explain clearly the answering options available in a multiple-choice format" [4, p. 296]. This requires that the response options be suitable indexes of the variables being measured, and that they be meaningful to and manageable by respondents. To maintain awareness of response options, Gibson and Aitkenhead suggested imbedding them within questions and the use of prompt cards [4].

In a two-year period of pretesting formats and the consequent study [13], it was found useful also to have practice questions when introducing an unfamiliar response scale or question format. The interviewer read the instructions aloud, read while pointing to the response options on a card held by the respondent, and did a sample question herself. Then she read another sample question and provided any assistance the respondent needed in deciding how to use the response options to answer it. Enough samples were provided to allow several repetitions of practice, if necessary, before data collection began.

Hoinville perceived a limitation in the utility of showcards because some respondents cannot read them [2]. In some studies this was ameliorated by preparing two sets of cards, one in ordinary type and the other in extra large, clear type; and letting the respondent select which to use [8, 13, 14]. Hoinville perceived a source of bias in that some respondents cannot hear spoken questions and are able to hide this from the interviewer. It seems unlikely that a sensitive and well-trained interviewer would not pick up cues and adjust his voice level and speech speed to optimums for the respondent, and be sure to have her attention before stating a question. Preparation of material in both written and oral form is sometimes appropriate, making it available through two senses and casting the respondent in a more active role by allowing him to choose to have presentation orally, in written form, or both [8, 13, 14]. This provision of options is not the same as requiring the use of both sense modalities at the same time or building into the instrument the necessity to switch back and forth between them at rapid intervals, either of which may confuse respondents.

Obviously a stone-deaf person who cannot read lips is unable to respond to oral instructions, a blind individual cannot read a questionnaire, and one badly crippled by arthritis cannot perform certain paper-and-pencil tasks—though use of a writing instrument thrust through a soft rubber ball enables some to do so [13]. Common sense must guide data treatment in these instances. For example, an intelligence estimate should not include scores on subtests that are sensorially inaccessible to the respondent. Inability to see the block designs or hear the one-per-second numbers is not an index of cognitive competence. On the other hand, if motor competence is the issue, inability to stand alone, walk unaided, lift arms above shoulder level, or grasp a standard object is a legitimate score component [13].

People in the elderly cohort today are less familiar with structured, multiple choice questions than are those from later-born cohorts. Evidence suggests that such questions need not be abandoned on this account, but rather that efforts should be taken to clarify and maintain focus on the task. Careful attention should be paid to response-option labels [15]. Different labels elicit different response distributions. The question-and-answer procedure should be clearly explained. What seems obvious to the investigator or interviewer may not be so to the respondent. The use of sample questions when introducing complex or unfamiliar procedures not only has instructional value but also provides evidence to the interviewer that the respondent understands and is able to perform the task before data are collected. Response options can be maintained and reinforced by imbedding them within questions and by use of prompt cards.

Unstructured interviews are appropriate to certain investigations and may be easy to administer because a lonely or garrulous person can ramble on at will. They are not suitable to all studies and they require special competence on the part of the investigator in dealing with the mass of resulting data. Yes-no items are simple to administer; but the either-or forced choice may not provide a respondent adequate opportunity to express her view, and the restricted response range tends to weaken the power of a dichotomous item in correlational analyses that include items with larger variances.

During a two-year instrument-development period for a study [13] respondents acted as co-developers and they were asked for opinions and suggestions. Dichotomous items were consistently disliked. Older men and women objected to the response option as too restrictive. Dichotomous formats also elicited many "no answer" and "don't know" responses, which is consistent with the respondent criticism. They simply could not describe their views in terms of the options available. Five-point scales were best liked, elicited the smallest amount of missing data (no response and cannot say), and the best response distributions (little skewness, good variance). Longer response scales were not preferred, elicited more "don't know" answers and failures to respond, and had more skewed distributions. For some purposes and populations, a larger number of categories have the advantage of increasing variance [15]. However, this advantage accrues only if respondents can work effectively with the greater number of options. Considering the trade-off between the difficulty experienced by the current cohort of elderly in dealing with larger numbers of categories and the possible loss of variance with smaller numbers, five response options seems to be a good compromise.

This may be true not only for interview questions but also for items in some standard measures. A dichotomous format is often used in gerontological instruments as appropriate in terms of ease for older persons. In a two-year period of instrument development, items in existing instruments were administered with various response formats. Some items had so little variance, with any format, that they did not contribute to scale scores. A 5-point response scale showed the same advantages as for interview items. In the main study of eighty-eight older women [13] outcome instruments were Uselessnesss, Happiness, and Senility [16]; Bradburn Affect Balance [17]; Philadelphia Geriatric Center (PGC) Morale [18]; Campbell et al. Well-Being [19]; CES-Depression [20]; and new tests for Alienation/Anomie, Apprehensiveness, and Attitude to Aging. The 5-point scale was used and, to avoid the position or "set" effect of presenting all items from one instrument together, items from the several instruments were randomly mixed for presentation. Whenever an alteration is made in an existing instrument, there is the possibility of damaging its structural properties and validity. Alphas were acceptable except for PGC Morale total and each factor score; and interrelationships among instruments and results of factor analysis at scale-score level indicted that validities remained intact.

In an effort to identify the structure underlying several measures of well-being, factor analysis at the item level was appropriate [21]. To avoid effects of differences in variance, it was advisable to use the same response format for all source instruments. The preferred 5-point scale was used, and items from source instruments were randomly mixed. They were Well-Being [19], Bradburn [17] Affect Balance, PGC Morale [18], Happiness [16], Life Satisfaction-A (LSI-A) [22] and Well-Being [23]. For two large samples aged twenty five and older, alphas for responses using the 5-point scale were satisfactory (though that for PCG Morale Factor 2 was a marginal .60); and intercorrelations among source scales indicated that validities were not destroyed. In the study of older women and the study of men and women ages twenty-five to ninety-eight, scale properties determined from use of their originally more limited response options remained intact when the 5-point format was used.

Question and answer format for some instruments is fixed. For example, the validity of standardized cognitive measures would be unknown if the procedure was altered. If several instruments are used, their temporal ordering can be manipulated. Cognitive competence was a predictor in a study of residential satisfaction and psychological well-being among older women who lived alone in the community [13]. An extensive battery of cognitive instruments was selected to differentiate among respondents within the normal range of intellectual functioning that was expected. To identify any respondents with serious cognitive impairment, the Short Portable Mental Status Questionnaire (SPMSQ) [6] was included. In pretests the data collectors found it awkward to ask SPMSQ questions of independently living men and women. Therefore in the main study testing began with the WAIS [9] Comprehension subtest, on the basis of which there was a decision rule about whether to complete testing with the SPMSQ or to administer the other instruments. They were ordered for presentation according to suggestions of pretest subjects to maintain interest and distribute the most taxing and "test-like" tasks. This strategy makes the battery useful for a broader range of persons, but the SPMSQ never had to be used in the study. The expectation that there might be serious cognitive impairments among persons capable of living alone in the community were inappropriate. It would not enter an investigator's mind when planning a study of younger community residents.

Even with standardized cognitive measures, modifications in procedure that do not affect scoring may be acceptable. Decrements in performance on timed tests and aversion of older persons to them are widely acknowledged [3]. In some studies [8, 13] testers were trained to record when the time interval was up, but to allow the respondent to continue beyond it. Only responses given within the time limit were scored, but respondent sense of failure was reduced. Perhaps as a consequence, nonresponse to timed items and drop-out from the longitudinal study attributed to unwillingness to perform the tasks at later intervals were infrequent.

## AMBIGUITY AND SENSITIVITY

Non-response and "don't know" answers create problems in data analysis because they require such strategies as arbitrary assignment to the value of the mean of the group or subgroup (men or women, experimental or control) or to some other value that the investigator deems appropriate such as one extreme of the scale (e.g., no response on a frequency scale = never); or computation of variable scores on the basis of whatever items a respondent answered, which means that the instrument varies in content from respondent to respondent.

Sometimes failure to respond is attributable to ambiguity in the question. For example, a respondent may be unable to say how satisfied he is when the question referent is, in his view, multidimensional, and his evaluation of its various dimensions are not similar. Inability to respond may be due to unclarity about the response options or forgetting them because they were not imbedded in the question or available on a prompt card. Another cause may be the sensitivity of the question content. Opinion differs regarding the sensitivity of older persons as compared to others. Hoinville included among "special characteristics of interviews with the elderly that distinguish them from interviews with the rest of the population" [2, p. 230] the assertion that older persons are more likely to become emotional and distressed, and to regard more questions as sensitive or threatening, increasing failure to answer. By contrast, according to Gibson and Aitkenhead : "Any concern about over-emotional or oversensitive respondents being disproportionately represented in older age groups is misplaced" [4, p. 293].

Whether or not older people are unusually sensitive, threatening questions should be identified and dealt with in pretests. Gibson and Aitkenhead [4] found that upsetting issues occurred at points that the investigators found "unexpected and unprecedented," demonstrating the need for trials with persons similar to those to be in the study, prior to its conduct. Some items may have to be eliminated. For example, for a study of mobility among retired persons, a set of stimulus cards was prepared showing various pedestrian and vehicular situations. One depicted an elderly person at the top of a long flight of poorly-lit stairs, apparently beginning to descend. Aversion to this picture in pretests, often shown by immediately returning the card to the interviewer or turning it to the blank side, indicated that the stimulus card would elicit little useful response. More important, the threat it imposed seemed unethical. The card was not used in the study [24].

The decision may be to retain a high non-response item that does not seem unduly upsetting to respondents. In a study that covered the most sensitive and personal areas of people's lives, pretest refusal rate was low except for the seemingly innocuous: "How often does someone from your church/synagogue come to visit you?" Pretest respondents did not perceive the question as threatening when a "don't know" response was immediately accepted and the interviewer moved on to the next question in matter-of-fact fashion. The item was relevant to respondent self-concept and well-being. Therefore it was retained, without probes, and was treated as a dichotomous variable (no answer, "don't know," and "never" = 0; all other options = 1) [8].

Many investigators [4] report that responses regarding income are not forthcoming from some elderly persons (as is true for some younger ones). This information usually is important as a predictor or control variable; and arbitrary assignment of values is problematic. One strategy that seems to increase response rate for income data is to ask for it (along with other factual items to avoid emphasis on income) in the last step, when rapport is good and the respondent may be relieved to hear that "this is the last page" [8, 13, 14, 25].

In addition to the usefulness of "no answer" and "don't know" responses for revising instruments prior to their use, the incidence and distribution of these responses are commonly monitored by data collectors throughout the study to alert the investigator to interviewer effects on the data. A respondent's overall rate of "don't know" responses may be a meaningful personal descriptor. Missing data, summed across the data set, correlated with the Disengagement Index [16], suggesting that rate of failure to respond in terms of proffered options may be a useful indicator of social involvement [24].

Ambiguity of question wording, failure to grasp or maintain the response options, or sensitivity of the topical area may also reduce variance in response. If most respondents select the scale mid-point, the results may reflect the fact that most have a definitive opinion on the matter (that it is, for example, neither satisfactory nor unsatisfactory). On the other hand, such a distribution may reflect general respondent inability to state a positive or negative opinion because the question implicitly includes both negative and positive aspects that tend to balance each other, or inaccessibility of the response scale; or it may seem a safe way to avoid probing in a sensitive area by immediately providing a noncommittal answer. Therefore the reasons for such distributions should be sought during pretests in order to ascertain whether appropriate revision requires elimination of ambiguity in questions and instructions, whether the area is a sensitive one, or whether the true opinions cluster closely at the midpoint. Finally, item retention depends upon the study purpose. For descriptive studies it may be important to identify areas in which the sample members show a high degree of agreement and items yielding such distributions should be retained. For correlational analyses, such items tend to have low power and thus may be deleted.

Skewness should also be assessed in pretest data. Highly skewed distributions may provide useful information for descriptive purposes. For other analyses they curtail the statistical advantages of using a non-dichotomous response format. For some items that evoke highly skewed response distributions, substitution of different response labels may spread out the answers and bring their central tendency closer to the scale mid-point [15]. If this is not possible, such items are likely to have little power in correlational analyses. Such items in a multi-item measure may not make a useful contribution to scores, or they may drop out in alpha [26] scaling due to skewness and limited variance rather than content relevance [27].

## ISSUES OF SCALE POLARITY

The degree of observed independence between such variables as satisfaction and dissatisfaction, or Positive Affect and Negative Affect, depends to some extent upon the response format. Using dichotomous options, Bradburn found "little or no" correlation between Positive Affect and Negative Affect [17], and developed separate scales. In response to Mettee's [28] criticism of the Bradburn format, Chiriboga [29] developed a 4-point scale based on frequency. Using this scale, Prothero and Herriott found a correlation between positive affect and negative affect of −.32 with ninety-six respondents aged sixty to ninety-two [30]. With the 5-point scale shown in pretests to be preferred by older people, and to reduce missing data and provide adequate response distributions, the correlations between Positive Affect and Negative Affect were −.37 and −.38 for two samples (*N*s = 1039 and 1571) aged twenty-five to ninety-eight, and −.39 for a sample of eighty-eight elderly women [31].

Such alterations might destroy Bradburn scale properties. However, using the 4-point frequency scale, Prothero and Herriott found that scale validity was intact, as indicated by correlations with other measures of happiness, life satisfaction, and morale [31]. With the same format, Chiriboga obtained two factors, [29] one positive and one negative, and the correlations of Affect Balance with other variables supported its validity. Using the 5-point scale with two large samples aged twenty-five and older, alphas for the three Bradburn scales were consistently above .80 and their correlations with other variables suggested that validities remained intact. Further, the items from Positive Affect and Negative Affect entered separate factors in the analysis with items from other instruments, suggesting that the structural properties had not been damaged [21]. For the small sample, Bradburn scale alphas were satisfactory, correlations with other variables supported the validities of Bradburn scales, and Positive Affect and Negative Affect entered separate factors in the scale-score analysis [31].

These findings do not negate but do moderate Bradburn's conclusion. Ability to account for variance in Positive or Negative Affect using the other as predictor is limited. The findings do point to the influence of response format on the observed degree of independence between them.

Scales to measure degree of satisfaction with a domain of life experience or with life in general often implicitly assume that satisfaction and dissatisfaction are polar opposites that define one psychological dimension. The .50 correlation between 5-point scales of satisfaction and of dissatisfaction with housing suggests that there is some degree of independence between these seeming opposites [25]. Further investigation is needed into the relationship between satisfaction and dissatisfaction because of the prevalent use of these variables. The finding calls into question the assumption of mirror-imagery between them and raises the possibility that forcing them into a single scale may confound two variables. Investigators should be alert to the need to check the psychological relationship between scale poles rather than to rely on semantic antonyms in scale construction.

## POSITION EFFECTS

Older people may be just like younger people in susceptibility to position effects on response, and gerontological instrument developers should not leave their psychometric training at home [32]. In one study for attitudinal but not factual items, one type of primacy effect was found to be significant: Either the positive or the negative end of the scale drew responses when that pole was presented first, for four samples of the California population aged sixty and older [33]. No differences were observed for either attitudinal or factual items in regard to a different primacy effect, that is, presentation of items early or late in the interview. These findings suggest that, for either type of item, response is not influenced by location within the interview, at least when fatigue effect is avoided; and they suggest that, for factual items, it does not matter which pole of the response scale is presented first (in oral presentation and at the top or left margin of the prompt card). On the other hand, they suggest that the order of presentation of scale poles does affect response to attitudinal items.

This has important implications for score reliability and validity. It means that, to obtain valid group or subgroup values for attitudinal items, these items should be administered to a random, equal number of respondents with the response scale in the positive-negative order and in the negative-positive order, and the results should be averaged. This is similar to computation of a sensory threshold by averaging responses to the stimulus presented in ascending order (increasing stimulus intensity from below the level of perception until the limen is reached) and descending order (decreasing stimulus intensity from well above the limen level until it is no longer perceived). To obtain individual respondent values for use in subgroup comparisons or other statistical manipulations, standard scores for the order-of-presentation group should be used, to remove this type of primacy effect. Some divergences between conclusions of various studies may stem partly from the happenstance of difference in the order in which response options were presented.

## POSITIVE RESPONSE BIAS

Older persons are notorious for giving "rosy" reports of themselves and their living conditions. This tendency has been attributed to age [19], although most studies did not use "age unbiased" scales so that this attribution was not clearly documented. Sex differences have been of less interest, but they may affect response and might influence age relationships because of the differences in proportions of men and women in the general population at various age levels. A study of two large samples of the California population aged twenty-five and older, using scales constructed to be "age fair" and "sex fair" in the psychometric sense [34, 35] showed positive linear relationships between age and the favorability of responses about characteristics of their housing and neighborhoods [23]. This study supports the relationship of positive response bias to age, though not the idea that this is a gerontological phenomenon. It may be a cohort effect, reflecting differences in circumstances and expectations of persons born at different times. It probably does not reflect objective status, because the older persons lived in less adequate conditions of housing and neighborhood.

The rosy bias may reflect ego defense or reduction of cognitive dissonance among persons trapped in undesirable situations. When qualified applicants for public housing for the elderly were interviewed before Housing Authority decisions regarding admission were made, ratings of present housing clustered at the scale mid-point ("all right, OK"). Fortuitously, a reliability check with selected items that included the housing rating was conducted immediately after the Housing Authority mailed out admission decisions. In reliability-check data, persons who had received acceptance notices rated their housing (which had not changed) toward the negative pole, while the non-admitted continued to rate their housing as "OK" [36]. Probably this is a human rather than aging phenomenon. Submariners would answer both negative and positive sociometric questions about crew mates when they were on surface cruises, but refused to answer negative items when they were on extended cruises under the ice-cap [31]. Campbell et al. found the rosy bias among the poor and the poorly educated, regardless of age [19].

Strategies of questioning can modify the positive response bias. Diminution of bias from global to specific items has been observed by many investigators [19]. Residents of elderly housing gave it high and highly skewed satisfaction ratings [38]. The most favorable and most skewed responses were to global questions. Ratings of specific characteristics of the building, tenant group, and administrative procedures had lower means and better distributions. Changing the context of the questioning resulted in a remarkable difference in the positive skew. When asked how future facilities could be even better, negative opinions about their current housing were forthcoming. Tenants were aware of design flaws, disliked some administrative practices, and experienced problems with group living. Criticism was inhibited by overall appreciation. ("Anyone who wouldn't be pleased with this would just be hard to please.") However, when motivation was to improve future facilities, and residents' experience was sought as a basis for guidance, the negative as well as the positive aspects were discussed freely.

In quality-of-life research a much-used question format involves the extent to which "______ is a problem to you" [39]. Responses tend to be positively skewed. This mode of questioning probably points as much toward the coping ability of the respondent as toward the factual circumstance purportedly to be evaluated. To test the hypothesis that degree of ego involvement implicit in the wording of a question is directly related to the favorability of response, two large samples of older persons were asked to give a *description* of their current situations in various domains (e.g., housing, income): "Setting aside how you feel about it, or are satisfied with it, please rate your ______ in a completely factual way"; to rate their *satisfaction* with it: "Considering only your own feelings about your current ______, please rate your satisfaction with it"; and to rate their own *coping* in respect to it: "Some people have trouble getting along even with good ______ while others get along fine with very poor ______. Please rate your situation." Means for coping were most favorable and those for description, least. The "problem to you" format was also included, and it elicited responses most similar to those for coping [25]. The results suggest that positive response bias is related to the degree of personal involvement implied in the question, and that results of surveys that use a "problem to you" format may be based on psychologically defensive rather than reality-descriptive data. The use of such data in describing the circumstances of older persons or for policy guidance is questionable.

## FRAMES-OF-REFERENCE FOR PREDICTORS OF SATISFACTION AND WELL-BEING

Differences between ratings of current situation and ratings of various reference frames have been used to predict domain satisfactions and overall well-being: For example, Campbell et al. [19] found that, among the frames of reference for responding to survey questions aspiration, expectation, most liked, typical American, close relatives, close friends, least liked, inmediately preceding, and five years ago, the aspiration frame provided the best predictors of domain satisfactions. These authors also found that when domain predictors were summed across domains aspiration was the best predictor of overall well-being, for persons under age fifty-five. Therefore aspiration level was the central reference frame in their conceptual model. The relative inefficiency of the model in accounting for outcomes with persons fifty-five and older was attributed to an accommodation process in which aspiration levels become lower among persons "trapped more or less permanently in a bleak situation." The poorness of fit between conceptual models based on younger people and data from older people is often a problem in gerontological research. To understand aging, there is need for models that are explanatory throughout the adult age-span.

Older persons cannot reasonably aspire to improvements in some conditions of their lives. Their satisfaction and well-being may depend more heavily upon the perceived equity of those conditions than upon the prospect for improvement. For three samples of Californians sixty and older, ratings of current status relative to what they "deserve and ought to have if everything was fair" accounted for significantly more variance in domain satisfactions and overall well-being than did discrepancies between aspiration level and current situation [40]. For a sample of Californians twenty five and older, the equity frame was used along with the frames Campbell et al. [19] found most potent (aspiration, typical American, best preceding) [33]. The consideration of equity was powerful in accounting for domain satisfactions throughout the age range; and discrepancies between current status and three different reference frames (equity, typical American, best previous), summed across domains, accounted for significant independent variance in psychometrically age-unbiased measures of psychological well-being. Equity was important at all ages; aspiration tended to be less important for older persons than for younger ones. The aspiration-current discrepancy was the only predictor that showed a significant interaction with age.

## TRADE-OFFS, PROXIMITY, AND MEANINGS OF FAILURE TO RESPOND

Ratings or rankings of the importance of variables is one frequently used strategy for determining preference. This format may not provide adequate opportunity for people to express their opinions, because many choices are made on the basis of a trade-off between positive and negative aspects. Regnier provided both positive (wish to have) and negative (wish not to have) response options to residents of middle- and upper-income elderly housing with regard to additional services [41]. The "negative preference" for some services was related to cost. The issue to respondents was not the desirability of the service but whether it was wanted in view of increased costs entailed. A similar trade-off option was offered by Smit and Joseph [42] who determined preferences for services by having people reallocate funds among the different services available in their municipalities and counties.

Trade-offs are not limited to service relative to cost but may involve positive and negative needs-meeting values of a service or facility. Proximity has been shown to positively affect service utilization [43]. Too great a distance between home and a service deters its use. However, a service facility too close to home may draw strangers into the neighborhood, increasing fear of crime, and decrease the esthetic quality of the immediate area. To look at two levels of proximity, elderly women living alone were asked, separately for "within easy walking distance" and "within a block of home," whether they would include or exclude each of a list of services and facilities in an "ideal" situation [44].

With their Delighted-Terrible scale, Andrews and Withey used "off scale" response categories that probably captured meaningful answers to questions that, without the off-scale options, would not have been answered by many subjects [15]. The investigators found off-scale categories useful in identifying concerns that were irrelevant or difficult. They included: "Does not apply to me" "I never thought about it," and "Neutral—neither satisfied nor dissatisfied" (although the scale mid-point was "Mixed—about equally satisfied and dissatisfied").

In the ideal neighborhood study, to clarify the meanings of some failures to respond in terms of "would include" and "would not include," there were two additional options: "It wouldn't matter one way or the other" and "I have no opinion, I don't know." This strategy allowed each respondent to deal separately with two components of neighborhood based on proximity to her own home and, for each component, to include an item in her ideal environment, exclude it, state that the item was irrelevant to her perception of the ideal situation, or say she had no opinion.

For the area within walking distance, incidence of "it wouldn't matter" was high, while "don't know" was rare. That area should be rich in the facilities and services the respondent wanted to use; others were irrelevant. With regard to one's block, responses were strikingly different. "It wouldn't matter" practically disappeared. For most items the majority response was that the service or facility should *not* be included. The only item the majority would place within a block of home was a stop for the bus that took them where they wanted to go.

The trade-off was clear. Positive needs-meeting resource value was weighed against negative concomitants, and the balance was influenced by proximity. Police and fire stations were viewed favorably for meeting specific safety needs, but danger from vehicles and noxious effects of noise dictated that they not be too near. Meal sites and senior centers had positive valences in provision of needed services and desired activities, but they had strong negative valences because of the attraction of (poor, old) strangers and the "nonresidential appearance" of such facilities. Concepts such as neighborhood are broad and nebulous. Responses regarding the same facilities were markedly different for "within walking distance" and "within a block of home." This points to the need to specify referents. Perceived irrelevance was quite different from lack of opinion, which suggests that the common "no answer" category includes important information that can be elicited by provision of suitable response options.

## THE SAMPLE: PLANNED AND ACHIEVED

Once the instruments are ready and a sampling plan has been established, the next step is acquisition of the sample. A variety of influences may impede adherence to the plan that has been adopted. Some may not be anticipated.

### SOCIAL FORCES

In a 1970 study of older San Franciscans, difficulty was immediately encountered in recruiting Black and Mexican-American (though not Chinese-American) persons selected according to the predetermined sample plan [14]. Such resistance had not been encountered a year earlier, when similar data were collected in San Antonio. Through discussion with data collectors who had been selected as appropriate to the ethnic minorities, it became apparent that activitist groups of young Blacks and Chicanos were working to persuade members of their communities of all ages not to participate—in the United States Census. Fortunately, activist leaders were willing, at first very tentatively, to meet with researchers. To our surprise, many groups included persons educated in the social sciences and already organized into research committees. If they did not, they recruited such persons to meet with us for explanation and discussion of the project. Once satisfied about the study purpose, data collection instruments and procedures, and means of maintaining confidentiality of data, they inevitably turned to another issue: The probability that at some point the data would become available to others, whose motives they could not assess. Individual respondents could not be identified, but ethnic groups could be. Was it possible that future analyses, beyond our control, could produce results detrimental to or derogatory of those groups?

Once the research team had made it clear that virtually the only possible negative product was evidence of inferior living conditions and transportation facilities, the community research groups gave their approval. This conclusion was passed along to and through the activists, and it quickly became possible to follow the sampling plan. Activists even volunteered to explain that we were not attached to the Census, if this would be helpful. These community leaders raised an important ethical consideration: In other hands, could one's data be used to support conclusions that might be detrimental to or derogatory of any group?

## INSTITUTIONAL GATEKEEPERS

Hoinville provided a good discussion of the "gatekeeper" and how this person could cause difficulties in gaining access to institutions selected for inclusion [2]. These considerations apply equally to community studies that involve people in elderly housing or those who use other service programs. For various reasons, administrators may be reluctant or unwilling to open the doors to investigators. There is the possibility of further bias due to the differential protectiveness or cooperativeness of lower-level staff after institutional approval has been obtained.

When staff of service programs play the gatekeeper role for some or all of the persons identified according to the sample plan, the solution seems to lie in early recognition of the differences in motivation between investigators and staff. Service personnel deserve to know the value of the study and to have sufficient information about its procedures that they can judge its harmlessness to participants. An additional problem lies in the fact that staff, whose function is to provide service to certain older individuals, and who have not seen any practical utility in previous research findings, often feel that money spent for additional studies would be invested better in support of their own work. Ideally, to ease this resistance, money for research would be accompanied by money directly for service provision. Such was the case in a study of public housing for the elderly [8]. The original funding agency also paid the salary of a director of social work and her staff for the facility. This was a rare situation.

Unfortunately, service-delivery staff often imagine that research funds can be made available to provide direct service. Another approved and funded study (that obviously cannot be identified) was not acceptable to the service institution through which the application was filed when the principal investigator refused to allow the institutional director to take over the research funds allocated to clerical positions. An institutional goal was development of a research branch that would be visible in both the research and local communities, and that would bring in money; the investigators supported these goals by locating the study within the service institution (though only about half of the participants were to receive its services) and by making it the recipient of any normal institutional benefits from the grant. Perceptions of the legitimate use of research funds were different between investigators and management. The dilemma was resolved by transfer of fiscal responsibility and the research site away from the service agency to a research institute, and revision of the sampling plan because the service agency denied access to its clients under the new arrangement. This divisive result might have been avoided by earlier and clearer recognition of the differences in roles and motivations of service providers and researchers. Neither is right or wrong; they are simply different. Such differences should be faced at the outset of planning rather than becoming issues of contention between service and research communities when funding is offered.

## FAMILY GATEKEEPERS

When family members are gatekeepers, motivations for interference with sampling plans range from protectiveness by daughters, to apprehensions of spouses about revelation of traits of their own, to irrational fear that the interview might end household income contributions from the old person. Interviewers for Gibson and Aitkenhead [4], for example, reported unexpected difficulty in isolating the selected person from coresidents of the dwelling during the interview, and the undesirable effects of coresident interference or mere presence upon data quality. Such isolation may be important during the attempt to gain cooperation from an older person in order to follow the sample design. Recruiters should be sensitive to the advisability of explaining the study to the selected subject in greater privacy than is sometimes achievable in the home, to minimize interference by others in the agreement to take part. From the first, it should be made clear that no one else is to be present during data-collection sessions.

The role of family gatekeepers with respect to the participation of older household members in research is perhaps more easily observed and minimized in studies for which the sampling plan is based on some record such as Housing Authority application files [8, 45] or birthdates in the Registrar of Voters' public record [27] than in the more usual procedure in which participants are identified in visits at the household that permit identification of which person from all persons in the household will be selected. With the first type of sampling plan, each individual is identified prior to the first contact with him, and efforts can be taken to make that contact a private and individual one. This may minimize noncompliance with sample plan due to the presence or more active interference by other household members, and may reveal some reasons for such interference in the more typical sampling situation in which coresidents are present during the individual selection step.

For example, one applicant to public housing for the elderly lived in a small servant's room of the home she had signed over to her daughter and son-in-law, and she performed the duties of maid to them—which they wanted to keep [8]. She was one of the several applicants who did not inform any members of their households about the application for different housing. She and several other women and men agreed to participate in the study only upon assurance that the research procedures would in no way suggest to family members the existence of the housing application. Other members of their households first heard of the application only after the old person had moved to the new housing. It is questionable whether the younger household gatekeepers would have allowed these persons to participate in a study that used the household selection procedure suitable to most studies, where younger coresidents would be present during the process of identifying the selected person and attempting to recruit him as a study participant.

## APPROACH TO THE SELECTED RESPONDENT

Once past the gatekeeper, if any, how is an older person best approached in order to arouse the levels of interest and of security that will lead to participation in accordance with the sampling plan? Most investigators find older people to be cooperative [2, 4], but the manner of approach may affect participation decisions. After trying a variety of strategies, the following seems best, in my experience. First, send a letter on institutional stationary to the selected household or individual (if previously identified) that explains 1) the institution's interest in the research, and the study purpose and potential utility that justify this interest; 2) the procedures (what a respondent will be expected to do, for about how many sessions of aproximately what duration), 3) confidentiality of all information; and 4) "what's in it" for the participant—money, if any, a report of findings in group form, and reference back to the study's purpose and potential utility to other older persons.

The letter should include the name and describe the identification material carried by the person who will phone or make a visit to provide additional information and answer any questions. The letter should be signed by the person responsible for the study (principal investigator); and it should include the name, address, and phone number of some outside person with whom people can check the study's credentials (e.g., an administrative officer if the research is conducted in a well-known university or institute, a municipal or other officer known to and trusted by citizens). Material must be pruned to essentials or many letters will be filed immediately in wastebaskets. Purpose and procedures can be very brief, with reference to the person who will phone or come to the home to provide details and answer questions.

The phoning step is often skipped when selection is to be from among members of the household. Phoning seems useful if participants have been identified previously. Older persons, and especially women alone (who are in great numbers), fear intruders [46]. In some areas (e.g., San Francisco) locked gates keep unexpected visitors from approaching the front door, even at single-family dwellings. Many older persons seem to be reassured by a phone conversation with the person who is to come to the home and may be more likely to respond to the doorbell when the visit is anticipated. This may reduce the bias of sex-linked apprehensiveness upon the sample that is obtained. When the phoning step is included, the (first) data collector should make the call, to begin a personal relationship favorable to establishment of rapport. The letter content should be reviewed (some recipients will not have read or fully understood it) and opportunity provided for questions. The goal is to set a time for a face-to-face visit to make explanations and answer questions in detail. Hopefully, agreement will be reached, a statement to that effect signed, and data collection begun on the first visit.

If participation is not elicited in the first visit, a period of cogitation and checking should be accepted as natural, and a date set for a second visit. Some persons want to make further inquiry with the investigator or institution, or to discuss the situation with a friend or relative before committing themselves.This provides opportunity to stress that "you" are the person selected to provide information, and to reiterate the one-on-one session format and the confidentiality of data from all others. The initial contact person should be alert to signs of potential personality clashes between herself and the subject, and immediately discuss with the supervisor the advisability of assigning a different person to the follow-up. If this is done, the principal investigator (whose signature is on the letter) should inform the prospective respondent and provide the name of the new person who will come.

## SOME REASONS FOR NON-COMPLIANCE WITH THE SAMPLE DESIGN

*Informed consent* — The ethical requirement of informed consent prior to participation and the need to prepare clear and informative consent statements have been mentioned, as have some procedures that are used to screen out candidates selected by the sampling procedure who are incapable of providing it. Loss from this cause is a fact of life that must be accepted by all investigators. The incidence of such cases may be, in itself, an important datum. Loss of participation on the part of these individuals is not an instance of non-compliance, because investigators are morally enjoined from designing studies that include data from such persons. Attrition due to incompetence does not occur in studies that use information *about* legally incompetent individuals (e.g., hospital and nursing-home records).

Some older persons who are able to give informed consent do not do so because they feel that they are too frail or ill to meet the study's demands, or that the study procedures would invade their privacy. A few who are willing to take part in the study are unwilling to sign the consent form. In my experience this occurs most often among women in this age cohort who have been admonished by husbands or sons that they are not to sign anything. Sometimes it is an issue, for either a man or woman, when financial reimbursement is offered, which requires recording of their Social Security numbers and payment by check in accordance with institutional responsibility. Some individuals do not want to complicate their income tax reports; others fear the loss of essential benefits at the slightest increase in their incomes. Recruiters should attempt to determine and record reasons for failure to obtain the consent signature in order that effects on adherence to the sample design can be assessed and reported.

*Confidentiality* — Presentation of the consent form often occasions further discussion of data management to insure confidentiality. The gatekeeper problem is, of course, closely allied to that of confidentiality. When explaining the study purpose and procedure it should be explained that *no one* else is to be present during interviews or to have any access to the material. There may be some refusals on this account, but the data that would be obtained in sessions with other persons present would be of questionable validity [4]. In my experience, people are more likely to express relief than chagrin. Some agree to participate only when they feel reassured that they can speak freely in sessions with only the interviewer present, and that everything they say will remain confidential, even with respect to that friend or relative who would most want to be present.

If the spouse or another coresident is also to be interviewed, assurance must be given that there will be no exchange of information by the data collector [4]. To insure confidentiality, some persons would prefer to have interviews conducted outside their homes [8]. This option should be offered in describing the study procedures: "Here at home or some other place your prefer." Gibson and Aitkenhead emphasized the need for especially strict attention to confidentiality in studies of older persons when surveys may include neighbors, on the grounds that older people are more likely to know their neighbors because their smaller social networks and geographic ranges of activity [4].

Confidentiality is particularly important in situations that involve service institutions [2]. Subjects who are organization clients may be most concerned about leakage to staff and it is imperative to establish procedures that insure the promise to respondents that nothing will be revealed to agency personnel. Service providers may feel that certain information would help them deal more effectively with a client. Being human, they also tend to be curious, especially about clients' reactions to them. In studies that require multiple sessions, and particularly in longitudinal research where cooperative relationships between staff and data gatherers must be maintained over long periods, this matter should be addressed in straightforward fashion at the outset. Staff at all levels need to know the study purpose and procedures, including what will be expected of them. They should be promised, and receive, relevant results in group form as soon as they become available. In early explanatory and question sessions with staff the matter of confidentiality should be raised, and it should be discussed as long and as often as necessary. When given an orientation similar to that of clients in regard to confidentiality, staff members put themselves into the respondent role and empathize with the client's need for anonymity. Often staff members too, provide data, sometimes including impressions of clients and even of one another. Wanting confidentiality for themselves, they find it easier to accept it for clients.

Reassurance about the measures that will be taken to insure confidentiality from *all* other persons is essential to unbiased recruitment of participants, and inadequacy of those procedures or of their explanation may cause deviance from the sample plan. Failure to enforce them is likely to cause attrition during the study period, especially in longitudinal research.

*Loneliness and activity* — Ready agreement to be interviewed because of loneliness has been mentioned [3] but my studies have included many elders who lived such full lives that they had to be assured of flexibility in scheduling sessions to acommodate their calendars, before they would agree to participate. Obtaining cooperation from a disproportionate number of lonely people biases the sample obtained as compared to the sample plan. Recruitment of both the lonely and the very active is necessary in order to conform to most community sampling plans.

*Personal gain* — Candidates may be offered money for participation in a study. Many older persons can well use the small sums. Perhaps more important, the offer can be supportive of their self-worth when it is made in recognition of their commitment of time and effort, and the value of their experience. Sometimes funds are not available for financial reimbursement. In one longitudinal study that required many sessions over an extended time period, small gifts seemed to be much appreciated by recipients and may have contributed to continued participation [41].

*Potential utility of the study findings* — In my experience the most effective motivator for most older persons to take part in research is the opportunity it affords to provide information that may prove useful to other aging persons. It is imperative that the recruiting person have this value firmly in mind and be able to explain it clearly but without exaggeration. Some individuals refuse to take part because they do not see such value, thereby hindering adherence to the sampling plan in a fashion that probably introduces a bias.

## DATA COLLECTION

At this point, the instruments are ready, the actual sample has been obtained, and it is time for collecting data. The quality of those data is highly dependent upon characteristics of the instruments that were selected and/or developed. If instruments are inappropriate, unreliable, or invalid, so the data will be despite the best efforts of interviewers. Pretesting should have led to revisions in instruments or instructions that will avoid unexpected difficulties on the part of data collectors, and to use of formats that facilitate tasks for them and for study participants. Adequate preparation of the data collectors for dealing effectively with the materials for the study is assumed. It is assumed also that the study plan includes strategies for monitoring data as they come in throughout the study in order to assure that pre-training standards are maintained and to rule out contamination by interviewer effect. Any deviations of the sample achieved from the sample planned have already occurred. Data collectors can only affect the degree and type of attrition from the achieved sample.Therefore, with regard to many issues regarding instruments and sample bias, reference is made to previous sections of the chapter. The following section is concerned with some procedural issues that may be troublesome during collection and that may not be covered by instructions in the instruments, and some issues of selection and assignment of data collectors that were not covered in an earlier section.

## MAINTAINING CONFIDENTIALITY AND NON-INTERFERENCE BY OTHERS

Data may be contaminated by the interference or mere presence of a third person, especially with attitudinal items [2, 4]. This undesirable situation can be minimized by agreeing during recruitment that no one else is to be present during sessions, but data collectors must enforce the policy. Some coresidents may try to be in the same room or locate themselves in a place from which they can observe or overhear. Relatives who live elsewhere may drop in just in time for a session. Some service providers persist in seeking knowledge of what clients said. Interviewers must be alert to allow no deviation from the rules agreed upon at the outset, in order to eliminate this source of contamination in data quality. Only after data collection has begun, some respondents may for the first time perceive the need to have sessions conducted outside their homes. From a letter to an interviewer:

> I couldn't talk very freely here yesterday as both the man and his wife are in and out of my kitchen frequently through the day for ice water, etc., and it is very easy to hear conversations there, as there is so much open space under and around the door. When you come next Wednesday, would it be asking too much for you to take me out some place we can have privacy?

Such requests should, of course, be followed. The most important principle underlying the advantages of interviews in the respondent's home is that data should be collected in a situation of maximum comfort and ease for the data provider. This situation may be at home, or it may be a coffee shop, the interviewer's automobile, or any other place that is private, comfortable, and convenient.

The value of maintaining confidentiality but excluding others from data sessions is often apparent in responses that are given. For example, in the context of a sociometric questionnaire that was administered to tenants of elderly housing, one woman volunteered about her husband (who had absented himself from their apartment according to previous agreement): "I wouldn't suggest him for dog catcher" [8].

Confidentiality may be breached by respondents. Often sharing responses between already interviewed and not yet interviewed people occurs unknown to data collectors and investigators. The effects of this breach upon data cannot be assessed. Sometimes the breach can be controlled, at least long enough to protect data from this source of contamination. For example, in collecting sociometric data in public housing for elderly, the researchers felt that it was necessary to carry out the task simultaneously within each corridor of every floor, and to have monitors stationed at each end of every corridor, to prevent discussion among residents about their responses to the items before the task was completed. Fortunately, by that time data collectors had become familiar and well liked people who could impose the discipline in good-natured fashion. The wisdom of the control was immediately apparent. As soon as all sociometric data had been collected in the building, and the monitors left their stations, residents thronged into the halls and into each others' apartments: "Who did you nominate for ______?" "Did you nominate ______ for anything?" "I said your were my best friend. Did you say I was yours?" [8, 48]. Breach of confidentiality by respondents cannot be eliminated, but in some instances its effects on the equality of the data can be controlled.

## FATIGUE EFFECTS

The advisability of ordering tasks within a session to maintain interest and reduce fatigue by distributing the most taxing and test-like tasks has been discussed. Effects of fatigue on data quality have generally focused on respondent weariness. This was perceived to be a factor with only five percent of the respondents in an interview that averaged eighty-nine minutes [4]; however, both the length of interview time and the incidence of fatigue were greater among the oldest groups (75-79 and 80+). The result was use of an abbreviated form or proxy data with more of the oldest respondents, which entailed a possible bias in the data. An alternative is to break the material into two or more sessions in order to obtain full information from more respondents, with less bias from use of partial and proxy information. I have used the rule-of-thumb of one-hour- maximum, with instructions to interviewers and testers to terminate any session when they perceive fatigue or flagging interest on the part of the respondent or themselves. Interestingly, Gibson and Aitkenhead found *interviewer* fatigue to be an unexpected problem [4]. It influenced the decision about administration of the full or abbreviated instrument, may have affected data quality in later parts of many interviews because of the necessity to complete them in one session, and probably affected the decision to use proxy informants for slow responders.

## DATA COLLECTORS

The most carefully prepared instrument is invalid unless its items are properly presented and answers are faithfully recorded. The finest sampling design is useless unless the predetermined rules for selection of individuals are followed and identified individuals are recruited to participate; and the degree of adherence to the sampling plan in sample acquisition may be demolished by attrition before all data are collected. Community studies often require massive amounts of data, and only data collectors can estimate and try to counteract the effects of fatigue and lagging interest on their own part or that of the respondent. The selection, training, monitoring, and moral support of data collectors are vital to data quality.

*Interviewer-interviewee compatibility* — The importance of the degree of similarity between interviewer and interviewed has long been acknowledged [49]. It is common practice to match them according to characteristics such as age group, ethnic background, and language fluency. For the San Francisco Bay Area, for example, materials have been prepared and interviewers recruited for a variety of ethnic groups and languages (two Chinese dialects, Tagalog, Portugese, Japanese, Spanish) as well as English. With the recent influx of Southeast Asians, their various languages would now have to be included. Back-translation can handle the written word (except for some standardized instruments), but only the interviewer can discern whether the appropriate language or dialect is being used and whether there is a culture gap between him and a respondent. (Not all elderly Mexican-Americans feel comfortable with Chicanos or Chicanas, and vice versa, though they speak the same language.) The interviewer must not be reluctant to perceive the problem, acknowledge to the respondent that the difficulty is due to his own deficiency, and arrange with his supervisor for a different data collector and/or set of materials.

Some interesting situations arise. In a study of San Francisco's Chinatown, the plan was to have interviewers from the same cultural, age, and sex groups as the respondents [50]. However, restrictions on federally-funded projects did not allow hiring persons over sixty five. Fortunately, a sufficient number of Chinese individuals suitable as data collectors were born in China, and there was no official record of their birthdates. It is more difficult now than it used to be to assess effects of interviewer-respondent similarity in some characteristics (e.g., ethnicity, marital status) because employers are enjoined from asking for such information from interviewers.

*Interviewer-instrument compatibility and independence among variables* — For certain types of data, validity depends upon word-for-word presentation of stimulus material and strict adherence to rules regarding repetition or restatement (e.g., psychometric tests). In collecting other types of data, sensitive probing is essential. Obviously, training and experience backgrounds of data collectors will guide their selection and assignment to appropriate tasks, and training sessions for data collectors who are to use the two types of instrument will be different.

Some study designs require that different persons collect various types of data in order to maintain independence among variables. For example, in an investigation into environmental and personal-competence characteristics that affect residential satisfaction and psychological well-being, environmental measures were taken by environmental observers, personal-competence data by psychometricians, and outcome data by interviewers [27, 51]. Each type of data collector was selected and trained separately from the others, and there was no exchange of information about the study during training or data collection. The interviewer, who made the contact, explained the strategy in describing the study prior to obtaining informed consent. On her last visit, she left with the respondent the name of the psychometrician, who would come next, and reiterated the role of the environmental observer. In turn, the psychometrician, in her last session, left the name of the environmental observer and reminded the respondent that his role was to take objective measures of physical characteristics of her living unit and that, after letting him in, she could best help by staying out of his way.

The strategy worked well. Independence was maintained between the two types of predictors, and between each of them and the criteria. No one refused to participate or dropped out because of the change in data collectors. The interview was the ice-breaker because it was the least unfamiliar. The psychometrician's task may have been eased by the preparation for her appearance. Rapport was not an issue for the environmental observer. His tasks did not involve a personal relationship, and his admission to the home had been obtained during recruiting and reinforced by both interviewer and psychometrician. It is doubtful whether he would have been admitted without such preparation to the homes of these elderly women who lived alone. After completion of their participation, several of the women entertained the interviewer and psychometrician in a party at home or in a restaurant and a few included the environmental observer.

## SAMPLE MAINTENANCE IN LONGITUDINAL STUDIES

Attrition from studies over time is occasioned by death and the increasing frailty of persons as they age. It may be influenced by issues that were raised in the sections on instruments and data collection. New gatekeepers may appear and existing gatekeepers may become more influential or more insistent as remaining sample members become more dependent. Rapport between data collector and respondent is basic to sample maintenance and to data quality at each interval. When data are voluminous, endless patience, skill and sensitivity are required to lead respondents through thoughtful consideration of the materials. These requirements may become greater through the years.

In a study of applicants for public housing for the elderly, interviewers provided transportation for shopping, fed puppies with hand-held bottles, trapped escaped parakeets, and unplugged drains to provide time for the respondents to give undivided attention to the research tasks [8]. Funds were not available for payment so, to express appreciation for the significant contributions of time and effort and experience, token gifts were colorfully wrapped and given at the close of each round of data collection. The gifts were appreciated, and the situation provided additional data [33, 47]. All of the respondents agreed to participate in follow-ups, though some insisted that they wanted the same interviewer. Attrition over an eighteen-month period was limited to death except for one inmover (experimental group member) who moved out for undisclosed reasons.

For the study of long-term (10 year) effects of rehousing, reliance was placed on the Relocation Agency to keep track of control respondents. An unfortunate decision! The agency had information on one of the 105 when it was needed. Many members of the original sample of applicants who had not moved into the facility had continued to be in touch with their interviewers, however. For the remainder, old addresses were checked and changes of address were sought at the post office. The Housing Authority provided names and addresses of relatives in their files. However, address changes are not kept for long, and the Housing Authority maintained records only for the few who were still trying to get into public housing. Morgue records were searched for the past ten years. Former neighbors and local store keepers often had the facts. Hospitals and nursing homes were asked to search files. By such methods the date and place of death or the present address of every one of the 105 was determined [52]. In anticipation of such long time intervals, strategies to keep track of respondents should be implemented as the study begins.

The Oakland Growth Study (OGS) has done an enviable job of maintaining respondent interest and sample composition. At the time of first data collection in 1932, the 212 participants were ten-twelve years old (mean age = 11). For the third adult follow-up in 1981-83, about 60 percent of the original panelists (mean age =62) returned to Berkeley [53]. Primary reasons for nonparticipation were death, illness, and living at too great a distance. Research funds did not cover travel expenses. Nevertheless, people came from several states and one from Canada. Selectivity of attrition is an important issue in longitudinal research. Attrition from OGS was not selective by age, which is not surprising in view of the narrow age range; nor was it selective by sex [54]. Intellectual functioning has always been a central issue for OGS, and in other data investigators have observed that respondents who discontinued participation tended to have performed less well on cognitive tasks [55]. To test this potentially biasing effect, Stanford-Binet Intelligence Test [56] scores at age 17 were compared between participants in the 1981-1983 follow-up and all drop-outs since 1932. Neither the total nor either sex group showed a difference that even approached statistical significance [54].

The success in panel maintenance over a period of fifty years may be due partly to the fact that the youngsters were volunteers recruited from five schools whose parents agreed to cooperate and who planned to attend junior and senior high schools that had University affiliation. However, the study team provided inducements that varied with the life stages of participants. When the elementary school children came to the Institute, the full day schedule included time for play on attractive equipment and supplementation of brown bag lunches with ice cream bars and fruit drinks. During junior high school years, the Institute rented a residence next door to the school where study members and their friends could drop in, bring lunch, play games, stay after school, and have chaperoned evening parties. Lessons in automobile driving (not then available at school) were offered under the auspices of the Institute. In senior high school, probably due to high school fraternities and sororities and other social events, a house across from the school no longer appealed to study participants. Therefore the Institute provided excursions such as snow trips to the mountains, weekends at camp, and boat trips around the bay.

Adult follow-ups required several strenuous day-long sessions. However, staff members such as Dr. Jones were available to greet each participant as a familiar person, and to meet with them in small groups for informal, relaxed lunches with no agenda except catching up on personal experiences. Between the less frequent adult follow-ups, there is a steady flow of formal and informal correspondence. Staff members phone or send cards with personal notes at such events as birthdays, anniversaries, and Christmas. The Institute organizes get-togethers similar to high school class reunions and sends out newsletters with items contributed by study members. Results of data analyses are disseminated to panelists. The latter often write spontaneously about their lives. Institute records are kept up-to-date not only for addresses but also for names of wives and childeren, important events such as divorces or separations, illnesses, weddings in the family, acquisition of grandchildren and great grandchildren, actual or anticipated job changes, and application for Social Security and other retirement benefits (many are now 65 or older), as well as moves since the last contact. At a party celebrating completion of the most recent adult follow-up (1981-83), panelists credited their continued participation to the personal relationships that had developed as well as to their belief in the value of the study. On her birthday in 1986, Dr. Jones received phone calls or written messages from about half of the remaining study members.

## CONCLUSION

The goal in writing this chapter was to alert investigators to some potentially biasing effects in instrument preparation, adherence to the sampling plan that was adopted, data collection, and attrition. These influences may lie at the root of some differences in conclusions among studies and may misguide theory development. It is apparent that, in many cases, procedures to protect data quality add greatly to effort and cost. In such cases consideration might be given to use of a smaller sample, with more attention being paid to adherence to the sampling plan, and investment of proportionately more time in development and pre-testing of instruments, and training and monitoring of data collectors, relative to time spent in data collection [13]. The hard decision involves a trade-off with the statistical limitations imposed by a smaller sample. Elimination of some contaminating or biasing effects requires attention during planning stages. The effects may themselves be targets of inquiry and be purposefully included in study designs [25]. The adoption or rejection of any suggestion depends upon the study purpose and the investigator's preception of its value. The chapter's purpose was only to raise these issues for consideration.

## ACKNOWLEDGEMENT

I am most grateful to Mary Cover Jones, Ph.D., for making available the information on the Oakland Growth Study. Dr. Jones has been an integral part of the study since the planning stages and is ideally suited to describing the various strategies for maintaining the panel as its members moved from childhood to adolescence to adult status and on to retirement.

## REFERENCES

1. J. Karuza, Psycho-Social Issues in Successful Aging: A Change in Focus, *Adult Development and Aging News: Newsletter of Division 20 - American Psychological Association 13*: 3, pp. 1–2, 1986.
2. G. Hoinville, Carrying Out Surveys Among the Elderly: Some Problems of Sampling and Interviewing, *Journal of the Market Research Society, 25*, pp. 223–237, 1983.
3. W. Schaie, Primary Mental Abilities, In *Life-span Development and Behavior*, Vol. 2, P. Baltes, H. Reese, and J. Nesselroade (eds.), Academic Press, New York, 1979.
4. D. M. Gibson and W. Aitkenhead, The Elderly Respondent: Experiences from a Large-scale Survey of the Aged, *Journal of the Market Research Society, 25*, pp. 283–296, 1983.
5. F. M. Carp, Environment and Aging, In *Handbook of Environmental Psychology*, D. Stokols and I. Altman (eds.), Wiley, New York, 1986.
6. E. Pfeiffer, A Short Portable Mental Status Questionnaire. *Journal of the American Geriatrics Society, 23*, pp. 433–441, 1975.
7. G. Winocur and M. Moscovitch, Paired-associate Learning in Institutionalized and Noninstitutionalized Old People: An Analysis of Interference and Context Effects, *Journal of Gerontology, 38*, pp. 455–464, 1983.
8. F. M. Carp, *A Future for the Aged: The Residents of Victoria Plaza*, University of Texas Press, Austin, 1966.
9. D. Wechsler, *The Measurement and Appraisal of Adult Intelligence*, Williams and Wilkins, Baltimore, MD, 1958.
10. H. A Murray, *Thematic Apperception Test: Pictures and Manual*, Harvard University Press, Cambridge, 1943.
11. S. R. Hathaway and J. S McKinley, *Minnesota Multiphasic Personality Inventory: Revised*, Psychological Corporation, New York, 1951.
12. B. Clifford, J. Jeffcoate, and K. Janzon, *The Care of the Elderly: Summary of Research Findings and Issues*, Directorate of Social Services, London Borough of Lambeth, 1981.
13. F. M. Carp and A. Carp, A Complementary/Congruence Model of Well-Being or Mental Health for the Community Elderly, In *Elderly People and the Environment: Human Behavior and Environment: Advances in Theory and Research*, Vol. 7, I. Altman, M. P. Lawton, and J. F. Wohlwill (eds.), Plenum, New York, 1984.
14. F. M. Carp, The Mobility of Retired People, In *Transportation and Aging*, E. Cantilli and J. Shmelzer (eds.), United States Government Printing Office (USGPO), Washington, DC, 1971.
15. F. M. Andrews and S. B. Withey, *Social Indicators of Well-Being: Americans' Perceptions of Life Qual:ty*, Plenum, New York, 1976.
16. R. S. Cavan, E. W. Burgess, R. J. Havighurst, and H. Goldhamer, *Personal Adjustment in Old Age,* Science Research Associates, Chicago, 1949.
17. N. M. Bradburn, *The Structure of Psychological Well-Being*, Aldine, Chicago, 1969.

18. M. P. Lawton, The Philadelphia Geriatric Center Moral Scale: A Revision, *Journal of Gerontology, 30*, pp. 85–89, 1975.
19. A. Campbell, P. E. Converse, and W. L. Rodgers, *The Quality of American Life: Perceptions, Evaluations, and Satisfactions*, Russell Sage, New York, 1976.
20. L. S. Radloff, The CES-D Scale: A Self-Report Depression Scale for Research in the General Population, *Applied Psychological Measurement, 1*, pp. 385–401, 1977.
21. F. M. Carp and A. Carp, Structural Stability of Well-Being Factors Across Age and Gender, and Development of Scales of Well-Being Unbiased for Age and Gender, *Journal of Gerontology, 38*, pp. 572–581, 1983.
22. B. L. Neugarten, R. J. Havighurst, and S. S. Tobin, The Measurement of Life Satisfaction, *Journal of Gerontology, 2*, pp. 134–143, 1961.
23. F. M. Carp and A. Carp, Perceived Environmental Quality Assessment Scales and Their Relation to Age and Gender, *Journal of Environmental Psychology, 2*, pp. 295–312, 1982.
24. F. M. Carp, Effects of the Living Environment on Activity and Use of Time, *International Journal of Aging & Human Development, 9*, pp. 75–91, 1978.
25. F. M. Carp and A. Carp, It May Not Be the Answer, It May Be the Question, *Research on Aging, 3*, pp. 85–100, 1981.
26. L. J. Cronbach, Coefficient Alpha and the Internal Structure of Tests, *Psychometrika, 16*, pp. 297–334, 1951.
27. F. M. Carp and D. L. Christensen, Technical Environmental Assessment Predictors of Residential Satisfaction: A Study of Elderly Women Living Alone, *Research on Aging, 8*, pp. 269–287, 1986.
28. D. R. Mettee, Happiness is a Mystery Still, *Contemporary Psychology, 16*, pp. 245–246, 1971.
29. D. Chiriboga, Perceptions of Well-Being. In *Four Stages of Life*, M. F. Lowenthal, M. Thurnher, D. Chiriboga and Associates, Jossey-Bass, San Francisco, 1977.
30. J. Prothero and M. Herriott, Subjective Well-Being in the Old-Old. Paper presented at the 33rd Annual Meeting of the Gerontological Society, San Diego, CA, 1980.
31. F. M. Carp, Effects of Response Format on the Relationship Between Positive and Negative Affect, *International Journal of Aging & Human Development*, in press.
32. F. M. Carp, Position Effects on Interview Response, *Journal of Gerontology, 29*, pp. 581–587, 1974.
33. F. M. Carp and A. Carp, Test of a Model of Domain Satisfactions and Well-Being: Equity Considerations, *Research on Aging, 4*, pp. 503–522, 1982.
34. N. S. Cole, Bias in Testing, *American Psychologist, 36*, pp. 1067–1077, 1981.
35. N. S. Peterson and M. R. Novick, An Evaluation of Some Models for Culture-fair Selection, *Journal of Educational Measurement, 13*, pp. 3–29, 1976.
36. F. M. Carp, Ego Defense and Cognitive Consistency in Evaluations of Living Environments, *Journal of Gerontology, 30*, pp. 707–711, 1975.
37. S. B. Sells, Dimensions of Stimulus Situation which Account for Behavior Variance, In *Stimulus Determinants of Behavior*, S. B. Sells (ed.), Ronald, New York, 1963.
38. F. M. Carp, Long-Range Satisfaction with Housing, *Gerontologist, 15*, pp. 68–72, 1975.
39. L. Harris and Associates, Inc. *The Myth and Reality of Aging in America*, National Council on the Aging, Washington, DC, 1975.

40. F. M. Carp, A. Carp, and R. Millsap, Equity and Satisfaction Among the Elderly, *International Journal of Aging & Human Development, 15*, pp. 151–166, 1982.
41. V. Regnier, Preferred Services, Amenities and Design Features in Housing for the Middle to Higher Income Elderly. In *Housing for the Elderly: Preferences and Satisfaction*, V. Regnier and J. Pynoos (eds.), Elsevier, New York, 1987.
42. B. Smit and A. Joseph, Trade-off Analysis of Preferences for Public Service, *Environment and Behavior, 14*, pp. 238–258, 1982.
43. R. J. Newcomer, An Evaluation of Neighborhood Service Convenience for Elderly Housing Project Residents. In *The Behavioral Basis of Design*, Vol. 1, P. Suedfeld and J. A. Russell (eds.), Dowden, Hutchinson & Ross, Stroudsburg, PA, 1976.
44. F. M. Carp and A. Carp, The Ideal Residential Area, *Research on Aging, 4*, pp. 411–439, 1982.
45. M. P. Lawton and J. Cohen, The Generality of Housing Impact on the Well-Being of Older People, *Journal of Gerontology, 29*, pp. 194–204, 1974.
46. J. Goldsmith and S. S. Goldsmith, *Crime and the Elderly*, Lexington, Lexington, MA, 1976.
47. F. M. Carp, Reactions to Gifts as Indicators of Personality-Behavior Traits in the Elderly, International Journal of Aging & Human Development, 5, pp. 265–280, 1974.
48. F. M. Carp and A. Carp, Person-Environment Congruence and Sociability, *Research on Aging, 2*, pp. 395–415, 1980.
49. W. Donahue, Relationship of Age of Perceivers to Their Social Perception, *Gerontologist, 5*, pp. 241–246, 1965.
50. F. M. Carp, Attitudes of Old Persons Toward Themselves and Toward Others, *Journal of Gerontology, 22*, pp. 308–312, 1976.
51. F. M. Carp and D. L. Christensen, Older Women Living Alone: Technical Environmental Assessment Predictors of Psychological Well-Being, *Research on Aging, 8*, pp. 407–425, 1986.
52. F. M. Carp, Impact of Improved Living Environment on Health and Life Expectancy, *Gerontologist, 17*, pp. 242–249, 1977.
53. M. C. Jones, Personal communication, November, 1986.
54. L. P. Sands, Health and Cognitive Functioning in Midlife. Doctoral dissertation, University of California, Berkeley, 1986.
55. I. Siegler and J. Botwinick, A Long-term Longitudinal Study of Intellectual Ability of Older Adults: The Matter of Selective Attrition, *Journal of Gerontology, 34*, pp. 242–245, 1979.
56. L. M. Terman and M. A. Merrill, *Measuring Intelligence*, Houghton Mifflin, Boston, 1937.

# SECTION 3
# Methodological Issues in Specific Content Area

The last three chapters in Part One concentrate on substantive research areas as a focus for consideration of methodological issues. Palmore continues the theme of efficient substitutes for ideal respresentative-sample face-to-face interview methods. In a sense, medical records represent one of the classes of sample frames discussed by Kalton and Anderson earlier under the general heading, "multiple frames." To Palmore, medical records are rarely the perfect frame, but when the focus of the research is related to health, such records are more complete than any other lists. Using some of the multiple-frame approaches suggested by Kalton and Anderson it is very likely that a local area's list of people with medical records in different locations could approach completeness for some specified purposes.

There are also instances where medical records are, in fact, complete or representative and they can be treated as secondary data sets for analysis in their own right. In special instances, given adequate official clearance and compliance with confidentiality requirements, such representative data may be linked with primary data gathered by an investigator on a subset of the universe or representative sample (see, however, Lebowitz's discussion of the changing research environment around human-subjects considerations, Chapter 13).

Palmore is properly cautious about the quality of data to be found in medical records. He presents some data of his own regarding the completeness of information of a very basic type. While the results were encouraging regarding such background information, when one goes to more complex data one's expectations need to be moderated. Anyone who has worked with progress notes, with diagnoses, or even something as apparently objectifiable as the cause of death on death certificates, will recognize that such records should probably be used as a last resort, in the absence of better sources. In any case, the cautions offered by Palmore need to be taken seriously by every user of health records information.

Jackson's commentary on "Methodological Issues in Survey Research on Older Minority Adults" may well be the only in-depth inquiry into this vitally important issue. However, important experience from earlier attempts to study specific ethnic populations is surveyed by Jackson, one of the best being the three ethnic group research reported by Bengtson et al. [1]. Jackson also speaks from intensive personal experience, having fielded the first nationally representative sample study of the black aged. His review is encyclopedic in culling relevant material from many smaller-scale investigators.

Jackson begins by making an effective case for the utility of studying such differences for the understanding of aging as a total process. One thinks of Maddox's concept "aging differently" [2] as a theoretical structure in which ethnic differences may fit.

Especially important is Jackson's display of the way that conclusions based on methodologically suspect research may contribute to informational disarray or even simply wrong assumptions about the aging process or a particular subgroup. While large secondary data sets such as those discussed by Liang and Lawrence are appealing in offering ethnic subsamples of acceptably large size, every investigator needs to take very seriously the sometimes glossed-over inadequacies identified by Jackson. The moral is not that we should avoid these resources but that reports based on them should warn the reader about possible implications of their sampling bias and other potential problems.

The other substantive example provided in this section is the study of cognitive aspects of aging by Camp, West, and Poon. The usual approach in experimental psychology has been to identify the independent variables hypothesized to affect outcome and construct a pool of subjects so as to make subgroups that contrast in the critical independent variable. Where that variable is manipulated experimentally, random assignment is critical and can be achieved relatively easily in most cases. Where other independent variables are included, they are typically operationalized so as to be uncorrelated with one another. Thus research is created whereby the experimental condition can exert its effect, if any, with other background factors held constant.

In the real world however important factors are often not orthogonal to another. The case of education and measured IQ is an example of essentially confounded variables. Another problem is that variables neglected for matching or control may vary in such a way as to affect outcome through their sometimes unknown correlation with both independent and dependent variables. The outstanding example is early research in cognitive aging that compared age groups cross-sectionally by recruiting college students (young subjects) and residents of homes for the aged (old subjects). Differences in educational background and health status were frequently ignored in this research.

When population norms are required, the history of intelligence testing has shown a slow realization of the importance of representative sampling. The development of the successive versions of Wechsler's intelligence measures illustrates this process well. The original Wechsler-Bellevue used old age home residents as the main source of standardization group subjects [3], the next Wechsler Adult Intelligence Scale [4] mixed less healthy subjects with a basic core of healthy community residents from tha Kansas City study of normal aging. The later WAIS-R [5] finally attempted to approach a representative sample of older people, though we have yet to assemble a nationally representative sample out of which to construct such norms.

Camp, West and Poon first provide a major service for the psychologist whose training may not included sensitization to the tradeoffs between representative sample, matched sample, idiographic, and less well controlled experimental designs. They also provide a literature survey that demonstrates how frequently important research procedures are considered in terms of their effects on outcomes. For example, the small literature on volunteer versus paid subjects is summarized. They surveyed how frequently basic characteristics such as sex, education, verbal intelligence, and health were clearly reported or controlled for in published research.

A substantial contribution is their report on a survey of 250 researchers in cognitive aging regarding their research and choice of subjects. Finally they have assembled a bibliography of research publications in cognition and aging whose articles speak to the recruitment and design issues dealt with in their chapter.

One would hope that the publication of this chapter would alert every investigator to the desirability of full disclosure on recruitment and concomitant factors that may affect outcome. Its authors discuss, for example, the place of recruitment (viz., older employees, senior center participants, or nursing home residents) as an aspect of a study that requires full specification. In fact, place of recruitment may be a proxy for income, educational, or health level. It is probable that health is the most neglected variable in much published research. Frequently the phrase "older people in good health" is all that appears in a report. The day may come soon when a basic requirement for a publishable research report is an explicit measure of health and evidence about its effect on outcome. While there are many sources of error in every measure of health, the use of a simple self-rating of health ("Would you say your health is excellent, good, fair, or poor") is enough to add an increment to prediction (see [6], for evidence of the strong predictive power of self-rated health). Fortifying this rating with any of many serviceable health condition checklists (for example, that in the Philadelphia Geriatric Center Multilevel Assessment Instrument [1], is simple.

Of course, health records, ethnicity, and cognition are only a small number of content areas in gerontological research for which special methodological treatments would be desirable. Such a treatment on methods in the study of environment and aging appeared elsewhere [8]. Other very active areas deserving such methodological attention might be life-events stress, caregiving stress, social supports and conflicts, or gender and aging.

## REFERENCES

1. V. L. Bengtson, E. Grigsby, E. N. Corry, and M. Hruby. Relating Academic Research to Community Concerns, *Journal of Social Issues, 33*, pp. 75-92, 1977.
2. G. Maddox, Aging Differently, *The Gerontologist*, (in press).
3. D. Wechsler, *The Measurement of Adult Intelligence,* Williams and Wilkins, Baltimore, 1945.
4. D. Wechsler, *The Wechsler Adult Intelligence Scale: Manual,* The Psychological Corporation, New York, 1958.

5. D. Wechsler, *WAIS-R Manual: Wechsler Adult Intelligence-Revised*, Psychological Corporation, New York, 1981.
6. J. M. Mossey and E. Shapiro, Self-Rated Health: A Predictor of Mortality Among the Elderly, *American Journal of Public Health, 22,* pp. 800–808, 1982.
7. M. P. Lawton, M. Moss, M. Fulcomer, and M. H. Kleban, A Research and Service-Oriented Multilevel Assessment Instrument, *Journal of Gerontology, 37,* pp. 91–99, 1982.
8. M. P. Lawton, Methods in Environmental Research with Older People, in *Behavioral Research Methods in Environmental Design,* W. Michelson, R. Bechtel, and R. Marans Eds., Van Nostrand Reinhold, New York, 1987.

CHAPTER

# 5

# Medical Records as Sampling Frames and Data Sources

*Erdman B. Palmore*

It is becoming increasingly important to develop and use more efficient ways of sampling and data collection as the cost of these operations escalate and the funds available shrink. This is especially true of longitudinal research, because it is necessarily more expensive per unit than cross-sectional research. Yet prospective longitudinal research is the only way to accurately measure most change over time and, short of experiments, the best way to test cause and effect relationships.

This chapter will discuss how medical records can be highly efficient sampling frames, especially for rare populations and longitudinal studies, and efficient sources of data. It will also discuss the completeness and reliability of these records, as well as other problems.

## SAMPLING FOR RARE POPULATIONS

Suppose one wanted to study some rare type of person such as those with senile dementia, or any other serious illness, or those recently institutionalized, or aged men living alone, or persons over seventy-five. The usual household sampling methods would be extremely expensive and inefficient. Sampling from known groups of aged such as senior centers would be more efficient, but extremely biased since only about 5 percent of the population participate in such centers. Snowball sampling methods, in which a few persons in a category refer the investigator to others in that category, are subject to many unmeasurable biases, and many potential informants are unwilling to refer the investigator to others (see Chapter 1 in this volume by Kalton and Anderson). Churches and synagogues can usually identify their older members and the majority of older people do belong to a church or synagogue; but one would have to sample from all or most of the churches and synagogues in a community to get a broadly representative sample. This would be expensive and time consuming in most communities.

Medical records can be efficient sampling frames for developing representative samples of these rare populations. These health records may be hospital records, clinic records, personal care institution records, private physician records, or health insurance association records. At a minimum, these records usually contain the age, sex, race, and address of the patient. Some records have much more information such as education, occupation, marital status, living arrangement, diagnosis, mobility status, mental status, etc. This information often allows precise samples of very rare types, for example, aged black men, older people with a specific chronic disease, or those living alone.

An example of such a use of medical records was the Duke Second Longitudinal Study of Aging [1]. The membership records of the Durham Blue Cross/Blue Shield Association were used to sample Durham residents in eight specific age/sex cohorts. This was done at almost no expense to Duke University. The resulting sample proved to be fairly representative of the broad middle class of Durham in this age range, with some representation of the lower and higher socioeconomic groups.

Another example is the 1967 Social Security Administration's National Survey of Institutionalized Adults [2]. This was a multistage sample which resulted in a nationally representative sample of all adults in long-term medical care institutions. Epidemiological studies often use medical records for sampling frames.

## SAMPLING FOR A BEFORE AND AFTER STUDY OF AN EVENT

Suppose one wished to study the antecedents and consequences of some relatively rare event such as institutionalization, hospitalization, surgery, or widowhood. The problem here is to identify persons with a high risk of experiencing the event within the next few years so that they can be interviewed before the event (to establish base-line measures) and reinterview them after the event to measure change (experimental group), and to compare this change with similar high risk persons who did not experience the event (control group). The differences in the changes between the experimental and control group would be the effects of the event. The initial characteristics of those who later experienced the event would be the antecendents or predictors of the event.

It would be impractical to take a random sample of the total population for such a study because only a small percentage of the population would experience such an event in one or two years. It would be prohibitively expensive to examine a sample of the total population that was large enough to result in substantial numbers experiencing the event in the immediate future. It is essential to identify persons at high risk for the event, before examinations.

Some before and after studies of an event such as institutionalization have used waiting lists as their sampling frames [3]. This procedure has two disadvantages. Most of those on waiting lists for institutionalization are soon institutionalized, so no control group can be obtained for these lists. Tobin and Lieberman attempted to obtain a control group from participants at a Senior Center and their friends in the community. However, they found that this group was not really comparable to those on the waiting list because the Senior Center participants were much healthier, more socially active, and had higher morale than those on the waiting list. This disadvantage is related to a second one: the waiting list persons are not representative of the other persons at risk, because those on the waiting list have already decided to go into institutions and have begun to experience the effects of this decision. Some of the effects of institutionalization as a process probably occur while persons are still on the waiting lists. Most such effects would be missed in a longitudinal study of persons already on the waiting lists. The advantage of using medical records is that a sample of high risk persons can be drawn before they get on waiting lists.

The key to using medical records to identify such high risk persons is to do a preliminary study to develop a risk scale, based on information in the health records. Then the risk scale can be used to draw a sample from the records of persons at high risk for the event.

For example, we have proposed a study of the effects of institutionalization of the aged based on sampling from the records of the three major hospitals in Durham (Duke Hospital, the Veterans Administration Hospital, and the Community General Hospital ). In the preliminary stage, we would draw a random sample of in-patients over age seventy discharged during the two years before the study. Then we would find out (from records, physicians, or patients) which patients had become institutionalized during the two years since discharge. The medical records of all those institutionalized and an equal sample of those not institutionalized would be abstracted to develop a risk of institutionalization scale based on key demographic, socioeconomic, social, and medical variables. Stepwise logistic regression analysis would be used to develop the most efficient prediction equation.

We would then use this scale to select a new sample of recent discharges with high risk of institutionalization during the next two years. They would be given comprehensive physical, mental, and social functioning assessments in their homes. Two years after the initial assessments we would do comparable reassessments on both those who have become institutionalized and an equal sample of those who remained in the community (see Figure 1). Differences in changes between the institutionalized and the non-institutionalized groups would indicate the effects of institutionalization.

## MEDICAL RECORDS AS A SOURCE OF DATA

Medical records are a gold mine of relatively accurate and reliable information: not only health and medical information, but also demographic and social

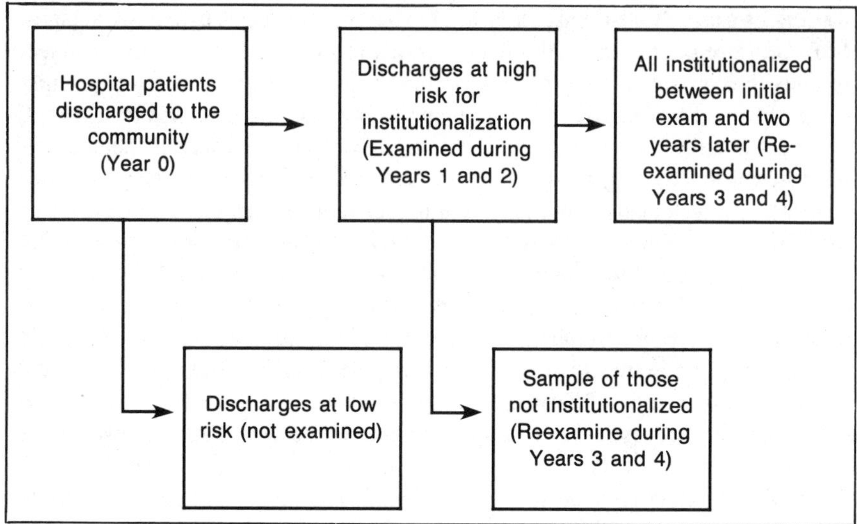


Figure 1. Model of effects of institutionalization study.

information. For example, the hospital records that we have been examining usually contain the age, sex, race, marital status, living arrangements, and education of the patients. They also usually contain the admission and discharge dates, diagnosis, mobility status, mobility aids required, activities of daily living, percent disability, mental status, competence to handle own affairs, and treatments prescribed. Of course, like real gold mines, there is a lot of ore that must be sifted and it may take some digging to find the desired piece of information, but it is usually there. Other medical records, such as health insurance association or private physician records, may be less informative, but nearly all contain much useful information for many research purposes.

If one is interested in medical care received, medical records are usually the most accurate source. Various studies have shown that most patients do not remember accurately what treatments they got from whom and when. Medical records are by far the most complete and accurate source for such detailed information. Numerous studies have used medical records as the primary source for such medical information.

## THE USE OF GOVERNMENT HEALTH SERVICES RECORDS

The Manitoba Longitudinal study is an outstanding example of the use of health service claims records to measure the amounts and kinds of health services receive in a longitudinal study [4]. Since health services (including nursing homes and home care services) are fully financed and administered by the Manitoba provincial government, the records of claims paid provide accurate and complete data on most health care received in the province. Furthermore, the master registry file for the population of Manitoba contains basic demographic and personal identification information for over 99 percent of the population. This file was used to draw a representative sample of all residents sixty-five years and older, stratified by residence status (community or residential facility) and region of residence. This sample appears to be free of most forms of selection bias.

An example of the use of government health services records in the United States is the National Institute on Aging's project titled "The Establishment of Populations for Epidemiologic Studies of the Elderly" (EPESE) [5]. The EPESE has now established four sites: East Boston, Massachusetts; Iowa and Washington Counties, Iowa; New Haven, Connecticut; and five Piedmont counties in North Carolina. In all of these sites hospitalization experience is determined using Health Care Financing Administration records supplemented by records of local hospitals. Admissions to nursing homes and other long-term care facilities are verified through abstraction of information from the facilities records from third-party payers (Medicare and Medicaid). These procedures are expected to produce highly accurate and complete data on hospitalization and institutionalization.

## COMPLETENESS AND ACCURACY OF HEALTH RECORDS

There are two main sources of information in medical records. One source is the forms that are supposed to be filled out for each patient which contain basic demographic data and minimal information for billing and reimbursement purposes. Sometimes these forms also have blanks for basic medical data as well. There are two problems with such forms. Sometimes they are not completely filled out and sometimes they are incorrectly filled out.

The other source is the narrative accounts or incidental comments on the patient ("Progress Notes," "Discharge Summary,"etc.). This source is more time consuming to use because it is less systematic than the forms and it is harder to locate the desired information, even if it is there. And, again, even if it is there, the information may be inaccurate.

In order to estimate the completeness and accuracy of information desired for our study to develop a risk of institutionalization scale, we examined the records of a random sample of patients over age seventy discharged from two of the hospitals. Table 1 presents the categories of information we desired and the percentage of records that had the information, for each hospital.

At the Duke Hospital most of the demographic and social information was recorded, except for education which was recorded only half the time. Also the education of some of those listed as having education recorded was actually estimated on the basis of occupation. All of the medical and disability information was recorded for nearly all of the patients. Overall, 92 percent of the information was recorded.

Table 1. Percent of Records with Information by Hospital

| *Information (Number of Records)* | *Duke (20)* | *VA (23)* |
|---|---|---|
| Patient address | 100 | 100 |
| Age | 100 | 100 |
| Sex | 100 | 100 |
| Race | 100 | 100 |
| Marital status | 100 | 100 |
| Living arrangement | 95 | 100 |
| Education | 50 | 70 |
| Admission date | 100 | 100 |
| Discharge date | 100 | 100 |
| Diagnosis | 100 | 100 |
| Mobility | 100 | 74 |
| Mobility aids | 100 | 96 |
| Activities of daily living | 100 | 91 |
| Mental status | 95 | 96 |
| Treatment prescribed | 100 | 100 |
| Total | 92 | 95 |

At the Veteran's Hospital most of the demographic information was recorded 100 percent of the time, except for education (70 percent recorded). The medical and health information was recorded most of the time except for mobility status. We believe that when nothing was noted in the mobility blank on the forms and there was no other notation of mobility limitation, there probably was no mobility limitation. Considering all the categories of information for all patients, over 95 percent of the Veteran's Hospital information was recorded.

As for the accuracy of the information recorded, we attempted to verify the information by checking for consistency between various forms and with other information derived from interviews with some of the patients. Nearly all the demographic data was found to be accurate with the exception of some inconsistency in age recorded for four patients. Health and medical information also appeared to be highly consistent, although coding on some dimensions needs to be fairly simple and use gross categories (see below).

For a further discussion of the accuracy of records of health expenditures and services see the proceedings of the two conferences on Health Survey Research Methods sponsored by the National Center on Health Services Research [6,7].

## PREDICTING PATIENT CARE

We are currently testing information from the nursing assessments of a skilled nursing home to determine how accurate they may be as predictors of care actually received by the patients. Fifty items from the assessments (including age, sex, length of prior hospitalization, primary diagnosis, and various symptoms) will be factor analyzed to determine if the number of independent variables can be reduced. Then the factors will be analyzed in a series of step-wise multiple regressions with each type of service as the dependent variables (such as skilled nursing hours, practical nursing hours, physician hours, amount of medications, etc.).

The prediction equations derived from the analysis of the first 100 patients will then be cross-validated on another 100 patients. The next step in the project is to try adding other information from interviews or observations to improve the prediction equations. The goal is to develop an intake instrument which is both brief and accurate in predicting the amounts and kinds of care the patients will actually receive.

## PROBLEMS WITH MEDICAL RECORDS

The first problem with using medical records is getting access to them. If one wishes only to abstract information without contacting the patient, it is relatively easy to get permission to use the health records. In hospitals for example, there is usually a medical records committee to whom one may apply for permission to examine their records. If the research appears to be worthwhile, they will grant permission. Of course the records must be examined at the hospital, and the records must be examined within a period of two weeks or so before they will be returned to storage.

If, however, one wishes to contact the patient for further information or to do a longitudinal study, it is more difficult to get permission. At the hospitals in Durham for example, not only must the research be thoroughly justified and approved by the research committee, but permission from the attending physician must also be secured for each patient to be contacted. Then the research must be explained to the patient and the patient must sign a consent form before any other information is requested or any interview is conducted. Usually, most physicians are cooperative, but there are always a few patients who refuse to cooperate with the study. Information on these refusals must be examined or estimate how they may bias the sample of those who do cooperate. One advantage of using medical records is that one can get considerable information from the records on which to base estimates of the similarly or differences between the refusers and participants. These estimates are important for questions regarding how representative the participants are of the target universe.

The representativeness of a sample selected from medical records is another problem. This of course depends on the target universe and the type of health records used. If the target universe is the total population or an age category within the total population, the hospital records would not provide a very representative sample. Only about 15 to 25 percent of the population are hospitalized in a given year, depending on age category [8]. Physician and clinic records would provide a more representative sample, since over three-fourths of the population have one or more physician visits per year. Members of the major local health insurance association may also provide a fairly representative sampling frame [1].

If however, the target universe is a population defined by, or associated with, some illness or disability, then hospital records may provide a fairly representative sample. If the universe is persons with senile dementia or severe cardiovascular disease, for example, hospital and nursing home records might provide and adequately representative sample. In our proposed study of the effects of institutionalization among the aged, we plan to sample from hospital records, because we have determined that the majority of aged admissions to long-term institutions have been in a hospital within the past two years.

A final problem is the coding of information. In our pilot study of hospital records, we found that the coding of demographic information such as age, sex, race, and marital status could be fairly precise, but the coding of much health and disability information had to be fairly gross because of variations between forms and between nurses and physicians in terms used. For example, in rating impairments in mental status, activities of daily living, and mobility, the simplest and most reliable code would be a dichotomy: some impairment vs. no impairment. However, we hope to develop a reliable trichotomy in these dimensions, such as no impairment, mild impairment, and severe impairment. Also the coder may have to assume that when a blank on a form labeled "Limitations in ADL," for example, is left blank, then there are no limitations in ADL. To some extent this can be verified by reading the narrative portion of the discharge summary on other portions of the record.

## SUMMARY

Medical records can be efficient sampling frames for developing representative samples of rare populations. They can also be efficient sampling frames for longitudinal studies of persons at high risk for experiencing some event such as institutionalization or hospitalization within the near future. In order to do this, a preliminary study must first be done to establish a risk scale based on the medical records. Medical records are also an inexpensive source of relatively accurate and reliable information of both demographic characteristics and medical history. The completeness and accuracy of information varies with the type of information desired, the type of record, and the type of patient. However, a preliminary study of hospital records in Durham found that most information on most dimensions examined was complete and fairly accurate. Our current study is testing the accuracy of intake information in predicting actual care received.

There are three problems with using medical records: access, representativeness, and coding. Access is easiest if the patient is not to be contacted. Permission to contact the patient usually requires approval by a research committee and by the attending physician. The representativeness of a sample drawn from medical records depends on the target universe and the type record used. Physician and clinic records, as well as health insurance associations records, are more representative of the total population than are hospital records. Hospital records can provide a representative sample of persons with some illness or disability. Coding of demographic information can be fairly precise, but coding of health and disability information usually must be fairly gross.

In summary medical records can provide a solution to the dual problems of increasing costs in research and shrinking funds for research.

## REFERENCES

1. E. Palmore (ed.), *Normal Aging II*, Duke University Press, Durham, NC, 1984.
2. P. Frohlich, Social Security Survey of Institutionalized Adults: 1967, Report No. 2, Publication No.(SSA) 72-11 714 Washington DC: U.S. Department of Health, Education and Welfare, 1972.
3. S. Tobin and M. Lieberman, *Last Home for the Aged*, Jossey-Bass, San Francisco, 1976.
4. J. Mossey, N. Ross, and E. Shapiro, The Manitoba Longitudinal Study on Aging, *The Gerontologist, 21*: pp. 551-558, 1981.
5. J. Cornoni-Huntley, D. Foley, L. White, et al., Epidemiology of Disability in the Oldest Old, *Health and Society, 63*(2), pp. 350-376, 1985.
6. National Center for Health Services Research, *Health Survey Research Methods Conference, 1979*, DHHS Publication #PHS 81-3268, U.S.G.P.O., Washington, DC, 1981.
7. National Center for Health Services Research, *Health Survey Research Methods Conference, 1982,* DHHS Publication # PHS 84-3356, U.S.G.P.O., Washington DC, 1984.
8. National Health Interview Survey,Current Estimates for 1980, National Center for Health Statistics, Series 10, Number 139, U.S.G.P.O., Washington, DC, 1981.

CHAPTER

6

# Methodological Issues in Survey Research on Older Minority Adults[1]

*James S. Jackson*

## INTRODUCTION

The purpose of this chapter is to examine methodological problems in survey research on black and other ethnic and racial older adult populations. Methodological issues in conducting survey research in these groups have not been the explicit focus of previous study. The survey research method, however, is probably the most commonly used social science data collection technique in the study of minority adults and the elderly, particularly in certain disciplines [1–5]. The focus in this chapter on survey research procedures does not denigrate the value and importance of other research approaches to the study of aging and human development [6, 7]. Its growing use, however, as a data collection technique in research on aging and human development [2], especially in ethnic and racial populations [1, 3] makes the survey approach an important topic of methodological inquiry.

The present chapter focuses on the more systematic applications of survey procedures generally associated with large research organizations or universities. The basic survey process, however, regardless of the quality of its institutional base, is susceptible to potential errors consequent to ignoring the role of cultural and racial factors [8]. The potential for error in sample surveys of black and minority elderly is magnified by the separate effects of aging, cultural and cohort factors [9], both between and within different racial groups [10]. The disentanglement of these factors is extremely difficult.

The methodological problem of interviewing older adults is of long-standing

[1]This chapter was written while the author was a Ford Foundation Senior Postdoctoral Fellow at the Groupe d'Etudes et Recherches Sur la Science, Ecole Des Hautes Etudes en Sciences Sociales, Paris, France.

scientific interest [11, 12]. Herzog and Rodgers recently have conducted the most systematic and detailed empirical methodological work on problems in surveying older persons [13]. This chapter owes a debt to their ongoing research program. In general, Herzog and Rodgers reported few age differences in their methodological investigations [13]. Overall, their analysis of secondary data sources suggested that older, in comparison to younger, respondents tend to: 1) have higher non-response rate, particulary in telephone sampling; 2) give more "don't know" responses; 3) be less productive than younger respondents in open-ended questions; 4) use stereotypic response styles, yielding more measurement and random error; 5) the interviewers behavior show stronger effects upon their responding. Herzog and Rodgers' were hampered in the conjoint study of age and minority status for many of the same reasons that will be discussed in the present chapter [13]—small sample sizes of Blacks and other minorities and the lack of attention to race and cultural differences when the surveys were originally conducted.

The problems that challenge social scientists, however, in conducting research on minority and black aging populations have not received the same scrutiny as that provided by Herzog and Rodgers' investigation of the general elderly population [13]. A basic purpose of this chapter is to consider how previously identified sources of error, as well as sources of error unique to racial and ethnic minorities, in planning and conducting survey research, may contribute to difficulties in research in these groups. This chapter draws heavily upon my own survey research experiences in directing the National Survey of Black Americans [3], the Three Generation Family Study [14] and the National Black Election Study [15]. The focus of these national surveys was largely nonmethodological. Because of the paucity of previous research on black populations, however, many methodological problems were encountered and addressed during the course of these studies.

It is hoped that the material reviewed here will sensitize researchers to problems that can be addressed in the design, execution, analysis and interpretation stages of sample surveys that include black and other minority elderly respondents. For the most part data reported in the present chapter will draw upon research experiences with black adult and aging populations. It is within these groups that the largest amount of a relatively restricted pool of research has been conducted [16–18]. The comparatively smaller body of research on Hispanics [1, 19, 21], Asian-Americans [22, 23] and other groups [24, 25] will also be included.

## CULTURALLY PLURALISTIC APPROACHES TO SURVEY RESEARCH ON OLDER MINORITY ADULTS

The importance of cross-national research in aging is growing [7, 10, 26, 27]. Prior research has not, however, considered the importance of race and class within national boundaries as deserving similar treatment [10, 28]. Some work suggests that black and other racial minority Americans may experience a very different process of development and aging within this society [10, 29, 33], and that the study of these groups should be conducted within a culturally pluralistic framework [3, 7, 8,26, 32, 34–36]. Ample empirical evidence does exist indicating that black Americans respond differently than whites to research situations and that these differences might be best viewed within a cross-cultural context [3, 32].

The cultural differentiation among ethnic and racial subgroups is considered by some researchers to contribute sufficient variability in the survey process to warrant serious attention [4, 32, 37]. This perspective has been noticeably absent in the empirical research literature [10]. Jacquelyne Johnson Jackson proposed a similar argument, calling for the scientific study of aging within a "ethnogerontology model" [10]. Martin makes a related point in her chapter on the general problem of comparing sub-groups in national survey studies [8]. Word and others [1, 17, 38, 39] demonstrated that modified cross-cultural research techniques were necessary and effective in eliciting accurate responding from black and other ethnic racial groups.

Some survey researchers [1, 39, 40], have suggested that value differences among cultural groups can greatly influence the responses to standard survey questions (see Schuman and Kalton [28], for an alternate view). The emphasis on measurement equivalence among Western oriented social sciences may have come at the expense of masking legitimate differences among groups [3]. This same point has been argued in much of the research literature on other ethnic and racial groups as well [1, 29, 39, 41]. If recognized and systematically understood, such differences among older adults could be modeled and studied [32, 37, 42].

For example, previous research on language has indicated that blacks have a well developed language form that is distinctly different from that of white Americans [43]. In the highly language dependent methodology of survey research, race related language differences will be magnified. This is particularly true for an older cohort of blacks reared or born in the South, having distinctive language patterns that differ from those of other black Americans. Perhaps even more apparent are language problems in the study of Hispanics [19] or Asian-American groups [16, 25]. Similarly, a great deal of research also points to cultural differences in style [44] and expression (both behavioral and verbal) that can affect responding in an interview situation [45]. Again such style differences are heavily influenced by the nature of the life experiences of older blacks and other ethnic and racial group members [30].

Our work [46] has demonstrated that consideration of cross-cultural methodological issues [34, 47] can contribute substantially to improving the quality of research and the accuracy of responding [3]. Finifter labels this general orientation to research on race and ethnicity as "agnostic," since it seeks to determine the existence of cross-cultural differences without making errors of a Type I (specifist) or Type II (universalist) nature [35]. Levine suggests the need to consider such characteristics as race as more than mere sources of error and essential aspects of aging and human development:

> Gender, socio-economic class, and ethnicity/race are more than sociological characteristics of the population of older people. ... they afford different life experiences and condition different psychological realities that cannot be disregarded. Furthermore, any paradigm that singles out one set of life experiences and its concomitant psychological reality as normative is unethical. It can only lead to inaccurate assessment of, and inappropriate conclusions about, the preferred life-styles, abilities, and needs of older adults [32, p. 139].

## SOURCES OF ERROR IN SURVEY RESEARCH ON OLDER MINORITY ADULTS

### NATURE OF SURVEY RESEARCH ON MINORITY POPULATIONS

There is no explicitly agreed upon single definition of a sample survey. One recent definition indicates that a sample survey is: ". . . a method of gathering information from a number of individuals, a sample, in order to learn something about the larger population from which the sample has been drawn" [48]. It is the development of population probability sampling methods that distinguishes the modern sample survey from other modes of data collection in the social sciences [28, 49, 50].

Surveys can be addressed to a wide variety of topics and concerns. Often these issues are imprecisely divided into those of a subjective versus objective nature [28, 51, 52]. Subjective phenomena usually refer to areas or topics for which there are no readily available, objectively verifiable, validity criteria. Attitudes and values are normally thought of in this manner. Objective data, on the other hand, usually refer to information which, at least in principle, can be externally verified, e.g., date of birth or possession of a drivers license. As indicated by Turner and Martin, however, this distinction is more often than not blurred in practice [53]. What has been proposed in recent years is that both types of phenomena are affected greatly by the types of survey errors discussed in the present chapter [13, 28, 51]. In principle, the general definition of a sample survey does not preclude the collection of either subjective or objective phenomena. Generally in the social sciences, however, attention has focused largely on the collection of subjective material, e.g., attitudes, values and preferences.

In sum, a sample survey can be defined as a rigorous data collection procedure that systematically applies common stimuli (questions), assesses categorical responses (answers) and is conducted on a sample rigorously drawn from a known population. Thus a sample survey does not differ in intent from any other data collection procedure in the physical, natural, behavioral or social sciences. The differences arise in the nature of the degree of control that can be exerted over the situation and the extent of causality that can be assumed. A molecular physicist has much greater control over the substance of his/her investigation than does a laboratory social psychologist. The survey researcher has concern with the same fundamental scientific processes as any other empirical scientist, i. e. the rigorous collection of data in response to some carefully presented set of environmental manipulations (questions) that can be unambiguously replicated. Elements of the rigorous sample survey, then, include: 1) a known population; 2) a sample drawn in a systematic and statistically appropriate manner; 3) a well designed questionnaire that is administered by; 4) well trained competent interviewers (or self-administered); 5) responses that are coded in a standard and replicable manner; and 6) analyses and interpretations of the data that are conducted appropriately with sensitivity to the nuances of the population and topic under investigation.

In practice, however, much of what transpires as survey research lacks the systematic and replicable features noted above as part of the survey process. The inattention to the systematic nature of survey research has been particularly observable in research on minority adult and elderly populations [1]. This nonsystematic approach has characterized work conducted by highly respected survey research organizations as well as research conducted, for example, as part of class projects in the university. In the wide variety of research settings investigators have paid little or no attention to basic issues regarding the reliability and validity of methodological approaches to research in black and other minority group aging populations.

Even in many surveys performed by large respected survey organizations, poor samples and lack of attention to differences among subgroups raise questions about much of the research to date [18]. National samples of minority elderly have been small and often non-representative of their respective populations. In non-national samples, the basis for the bulk of information on minority elderly, accepted guidelines are frequently violated, including lack of defined populations, non-systematic samples, poorly constructed stimulus materials, conceptual and coding difficulties, and problems with analysis and interpretation. Examples of such problems are rife in the literature on minority aging and human development [10]. It is these facts that make the interpretation of existing data on the effects of race and age on the survey research process extremely difficult. To the extent that the sample survey has become the major data collection procedure in many of the social science disciplines [5], and of increasing importance in the study of aging [2, 26] designing and executing reliable and valid surveys of black and other minority older adult populations is particularly important [10].

## ERRORS IN SURVEYS

The survey research process contains several distinct structural and process components: the formulation and nature of the research objectives, population and samples, concepts and questions, administration mode (face to face, telephone, mail, mixed), editing-coding, data processing, analysis and interpretation [28, 54]. The potential for error resides in any and all of these different aspects of the survey process. It is this error, often referred to as total response error, that concerns all survey researchers and is the source of reliability and accuracy problems in survey results:

> ....the conclusions we reach may be subject to serious errors due to faults in the method of measurement or observation. These response errors may arise from the questionnaire, from the execution of the fieldwork or from the nature of the data collection process. The form, extent, sources and effect of these errors are the concern not only of survey design but also of survey analysis [55, p. 193].

Bradburn [51] and his colleagues [52] have contributed a great deal to our knowledge in their conceptualization of sources of error in the total survey situation [52]. In their model errors in surveys can and do arise in two fundamental manners—errors in sampling and errors in non-response and other factors endemic to the survey interview process. Both sources of error are of central importance in the study of human development and aging among black elderly.

Errors of sampling and non-response have long been thought primarily to affect estimates of population values [28, 51]. Recent work, however, suggests that these types of errors have significant effects in analysis and interpretation of data [56, 57]. Sampling and non-response effects have received the greatest attention in the literature [49, 58, 62]. Less well attended to, however, has been the problem of sampling rare populations such as the elderly [63] or black and ethnic and racial minority elderly which present special problems of distribution and identification [64–66].

The second large group of errors has also received considerable attention, although not necessarily concentrated on particular problems of blacks or other ethnic and racial minorities and the elderly. Research in this area has focused on issues of question wording and context, administration mode (face to face, telephone, self), editing and coding, data processing and analysis and interpretation. From a role perspective the entire area of non-sampling errors can be construed as difficulties having to do with the task, interviewer, and respondent [52, 62].

In the next two sections of this chapter a brief, focused review of potential approaches to these sources of error in surveys of ethnic and racial minorities, with particular attention to black Americans, is presented. The state of knowledge regarding these sources of error in aging and race research is summarized. Particular emphasis is placed upon what is known or can be inferred about survey research on black and other minority group elderly. These include errors of: 1) sampling nonresponse; 2) errors related to the nature of the survey task; and 3) errors related to interviewer and respondent factors. The final section presents a general summary with suggestions for future methodological research on the types of surveys errors reviewed in this chapter in black and other minority group aging populations.

# SAMPLING AND NON-RESPONSE IN OLDER MINORITY ADULTS

## TRADITIONAL APPROACHES TO SAMPLING OLDER MINORITY ADULTS

Over the last few years renewed efforts has been devoted to examining the nature of and methods for sampling rare populations [65, 70]. Historically, sampling black and other racial minority populations either has been done haphazardly or conducted under assumptions only appropriate for general population sampling. Among the more rigorous sampling approaches have been those employed by large centers. One technique has been to include blacks and other rare population groups in the full sample as they are distributed in the population [18]. Obviously in even relatively large sample surveys of 1,500 respondents, for example, blacks would constitute only about 150 of the completed sample (assuming no differences in non-response rates by racial subgroups) [64]. Hispanics and other racial/ethnic group members would be even less well represented using these same procedures [1, 16, 19].

Samples of such small size are not sufficient for the type of subgroup multivariate procedures needed to analyze complex social science phenomena [18, 31, 71, 72]. As discussed later, because the black population is not distributed as the general population, the sampling characteristics of these small subsamples of elderly blacks and other ethnic and racial minorities are not known. Obviously, the sizes of the subgroups within these samples do not permit even the most basic types of within-group analyses.

The most common method developed to address this problem of small subgroup samples has been to over-sample blacks and other groups in areas of their high geographical concentration as a supplement to general population sampling [18, 70, 73]. Although effecting a cost and effort saving, this type of approach does not address the issue in ethnic and racial populations of their differential geographical distribution from that of the general population.

An examination of previous national surveys that had utilized large supplemental samples of blacks revealed unacceptably large clustering effects for black subsamples when blacks were over-sampled from areas of high geographical concentration [31]. This supplemental sampling process, thus, has not permitted a complete and full representation of blacks or any other ethnic and racial minority group in geographical areas of interest. The diversity which exists in minority communities has not been adequately sampled using this procedure because of the tendency of geographically proximate individuals to share socio-economic and attitudinal characteristics. This supplement approach to sampling becomes even more problematic when the intent is to sample a rarer subgroup like the black elderly.

As indicated earlier, one of the major problems in previous research has been the failure to generate representative and adequate sized samples of black and other minority elderly in social science research. Although there have been some notable exceptions ([74], for example), for the most part knowledge about minority elderly has come either from subsamples of large national studies [75] or from small haphazardly obtained samples of conveniently available respondents [1]. Both procedures raise the types of sampling issues presented earlier. While this problem has long been thought to affect largely external validity or generalizability, recent work suggests that biased samples have important influences on the nature of observed relationships in multivariate analyses [56, 57, 65]. While most of the work in this area has been done on face-to-face surveys, some recent work suggests that the problems may be more exaggerated in telephone sampling and other modes of survey data collection [13, 64, 76].

In their review of sampling issues, Gibson and Herzog suggested that major approaches to the probability sampling of black elderly have not addressed a combination of substantive and cost effectiveness problems [64].Their proposed telephone sampling procedure addresses the cost-effectiveness issue and points to a major developing problem in the sampling of black elderly and other racial ethnic minorities. Just as in area probability procedures, the distribution of the black population and telephone ownership patterns are different from those of the general population [68]. In addition, because the black population also has a significantly lower home telephone ownership rate [11], particularly exaggerated in poorer households, obtaining national probability samples of black households may be difficult using standard procedures.

Since the telephone has become the predominant mode of data collection in survey research [50], this is a serious problem for future studies of black and other racial and ethnic populations. The differential in telephone ownership and findings in the literature [13] of lower response rates than whites in the black elderly (as is found in older people generally) raise serious questions about the potential of the telephone for research on black and other ethnic and racial elderly [76].

## METHODS FOR ADEQUATELY SAMPLING OLDER MINORITY ADULTS

A major impediment in previous attempts to conduct national research on representative samples of black Americans has been the unacceptable costs associated with scientifically locating blacks in geographical areas of high proportion white [14, 65]. In reponse to the problems of geographical distribution and clustering in national probability surveys, Jackson, et al. [3] proposed two procedures designed to screen for blacks in both high and low density white geographical areas in the area probability NSBA survey [65, 78]. The sample design was similar in number of Primary Sampling Units (PSU) to most samples of the total population but had other features (e.g., probabilities of selection of areas, stratification) tailored to the black population. This was accomplished through the creation and implementation of two novel screening procedures [78].

The multi-stage, national probability NSBA sample frame was based upon the 1970 Census (and subsequent updates) distribution of the black population. The selection of the seventy-six certainty and non-certainty PSU's was done in order to maximize the utilization of the University of Michigan Survey Research Center's (SRC) sample areas that attained minimum size requirements for black households. The overall rate of selection was 1:2,300. Approximately 58 percent of the black sample areas were also in the 1970 SRC national sample. The sample was self-weighting and every black American household in the continental United States had the same probability of being selected. The sampling of housing units within primary areas was done in an effort to yield approximately the same level of clustering and precision of estimates as SRC household samples of comparable size. This outcome was accomplished through extensive work in the Institute for Social Research Sampling Section and the development of the Standard Listing and Screening Procedure (SLASP) and the Wide Area Screening Procedure (WASP).

The SLASP approach was applied in both mixed and mostly black areas and provides a unique method of identifying black households by using reference housing units within clusters. Clusters are blocks or groups or blocks within Census Tracts or Enumeration Districts that are the smallest geographic unit in the multi-stage procedure prior to the selection of housing units (HU) and individuals within these housing units. Reference housing units were systematically designated prior to the interviewer's entering the area and individuals within these units were asked about the racial composition of their own unit and the racial composition of other units within the cluster.

The WASP approach was developed for use in areas with suspected few or no black occupied households. This procedure employed the reference housing unit approach but in a less systematic manner than SLASP. The number or location of these reference HUs depend on the interviewers' assessment of the number and distribution of HUs in the area. Only white interviewers were used in the WASP clusters. Whereas the SLASP interviewers listed and classified each HU in a cluster, the WASP interviewers asked the reference HUs about blacks in the area and listed only the black HUs. This procedural difference minimized the cost of screening in geographical areas of low density black and was highly effective in reducing the cost and time in locating and listing black housing units. Within sample households one person was randomly chosen from the list of eligible respondents (18 years of age, self-identified black and U.S. citizens) using the Kish selection procedure [49].

Twenty percent of the WASP clusters were selected for intensive screening of households to estimate the extent of undercoverage, if any. Analyses indicated that the procedure was far more effective than originally anticipated. Only eight black households in the sampled WASP clusters were missed, the majority of these in one particular cluster. Because of the selection procedures, none of the overlooked black housing units would have been selected for the study. The WASP procedure permitted the NSBA sample to be obtained with clustering and precision comparable to SRC household samples of comparable size for a fraction of the cost. It also appears to be an effective and generally useful screening method for future sample surveys of blacks and other rare population groups [78].

Overall, the national NSBA sample is fairly representative of the black population as reported by the 1980 Census. There is, however, a disparity in the proportion of women to men and a slight tendency to underrepresent younger people of both sexes and to overrepresent older women. Analyses reveal no sex differences between respondents and indentified non-respondents. The sex disparity may be due to the disproportionate representation of black female headed households in the United States. In 1980 approximately 40 percent of all black households were female headed. For the most part these household contain few eligible males (18 years of older). The comparable male headed households where the opposite composition holds was ten times smaller (4.0%) in 1980 [79]. Thus, the selection of a female in a female headed household, even using a random selection procedure [49], is almost guaranteed (as is a male in a male headed household). Since the probability of selection of females is approximately 50 percent in the remaining 56 percent of husband and wife households, females have a greater overall opportunity to be selected in any national sample of blacks based upon the distribution of black households (the rough Census figures presented here yield a 62% to 38% proportion of females to males— exactly the numbers found in the NSBA sample). Because of increased female headed households among black and other minority groups with increasing age, this greater proportion of female interviews will be even more exaggerated in samples of the elderly. There has also been a slight increase in the representation of females in national samples of the general population. It may be due, as argued here for blacks, not so much to the greater cooperativeness of females in comparison to males, but instead to the increasing proportion of female headed households in the general population over the last twenty years [79].

Finally, there is a slight tendency in the NSBA sample to overrepresent low income groups and for a slightly higher proportion of individuals to come from the South than their distribution in the population would indicate. These differences from expected Census distributions are relatively slight (particularly if undercount and enumeration problems in the black population are considered) in comparison with other large studies of the black population.

These methodological innovations generate adequate sized and representative samples of the black population at reduced costs. In addition procedures for generating probability samples of older blacks and families (multiplicity sampling) have also been developed [66, 69, 78]. (See Chapter 1 by Kalton in this volume.) These methods were adapted to provide a methodology for obtaining new samples of blacks from traditional cross-section samples. In the Three Generation Family Study (TGFS) of black three-generation lineage family members [65], special procedures were used to obtain the relevant information from the original cross-section respondents in the NSBA cross-section sample. A final section of the questionnaire permitted interviewers to determine with a few simple questions whether the respondent was a member of an existing multiple generation lineage family or not. If not, the cross-section interview was terminated. If the respondent was a member of a three-generation family, then the interviewer used a specially developed sampling booklet to ascertain which two family members were to be randomly selected. Given the nature of the three-generation lineage family type (Parent/Child, Grandparent/Parent or Child/Grandchild), respondents were asked questions regarding the eligible numbers of these individuals in the adjacent generations. Once this information was ascertained, a random selection table was used to obtain the appropriate family members. Respondents then were requested to supply names and addresses (if the family member did not live in the household). A letter explaining the study and requesting an appointment, countersigned by the respondent, was prepared and mailed by the interviewer or respondent immediately following the interview.

During the course of the study, many respondents also telephoned relatives to inform them of the impending interview. If the family member lived within a fifty mile radius, then the original interviewer conducted the interview. If the three-generation family member was outside of this radius, then the identifying information (coversheet) was mailed to Ann Arbor and reassigned to the nearest interviewer. In the case of three-generation family members selected who were less than eighteen years of age, signed consent forms were obtained from parents or legal guardians. Finally, the original interviewer made an appointment with the respondent to complete the re-interview. Because of the unanticipated costs of conducting this complicated study, and the dispersion of three generation respondents across the country, both within and outside the seventy-six major sampling areas (primary sampling units) of the NSBA, many of the potential three generation interviews could not be efficiently conducted by interviewers in the field. Based upon scientific and financial considerations, it was decided to complete these interviews using telephone interviewing procedures.

These field procedures were used successfully in obtaining three-generation interviews. Few refusals to divulge three-generation family members' names and addresses were experienced and almost uniform cooperation was the rule. An analysis of the three generation sampling outcomes was extremely encouraging [65]. Adequate sized and representative samples of three generation lineages and supplemental samples of black elderly were generated and interviewed [80].

Gibson and Herzog proposed a variant of this procedure for telephone sampling [64]. Additionally, Jackson, Hatchett and Gurin contributed to the development of a new disproportionate sampling scheme that permits the generation of random digit dial black samples based upon the geographical distribution of black households [15]. Analysis of the outcome of this method used in the National Black Election Study [68] shows it to be an effective and generally useful procedure. It has been replicated on two subsequent occasions with similar positive results.

## PROBLEMS OF NON-RESPONSE IN OLDER MINORITY ADULTS

As indicated earlier, Herzog and Rodgers reported that older adults are somewhat more likely than middle-aged adults to become non-respondents [13]. They found, however, few remaining differences that distinguish respondents from non-respondents. Their analyses on dropouts from short-term panels suggested that age plays a minor role and that across all ages these individuals tend to be disproportionately male, black, not presently married and of lower educational background. Markides, Dickson and Pappas reported in a four-year panel study of people sixty years and older that dropouts were male, significantly older, less healthy and less active than those remaining in the sample [21]. Additionally, dropouts were more likely to be Anglo rather than Hispanic. These findings are consistent with those of Herzog and Rodgers who found significant substantive differences between dropouts and panel continuers [13]. Markides et al. also reported that dropouts who were deceased or could not be located were socioeconomically disadvantaged while refusers tended to be disproportionately advantaged [21].

One of the most extensive examinations of non-response was completed by Hawkins [59, 60]. His secondary analysis of ten Detroit Area Study surveys spanned an approximately twenty-year period. Consistent with Herzog and Rodgers [13] and Markides et al. [21], Hawkins reported that terminal non-respondents over this twenty-year period tended to be older than respondents [59]. His findings indicated, however, period or cohort effects during this interval; in earlier years (1950s) non-respondents were the older, retired segment of the population while during the 1970s non-respondents were drawn from middle-aged groups. With regard to race, Hawkins' analysis revealed a set of mixed findings [59]. In early years blacks appeared to be overrepresented in the respondent categories and in more recent years in the non-respondent categories. This change to greater representation in non-response categories appeared to be due primarily to an increase in unavailability rather than refusals. Overall, Hawkins proposed that firm conclusions regarding race could not be drawn from his analysis:

> Overall, however, the trends regarding the response of blacks in these surveys are not clear. While there is some evidence of the effects of differential callback policies on their non-response, other evidence supports the idea of a varying pattern of non-response for blacks and whites that is influenced perhaps by other, unexamined factors [59, p. 95].

The lack of multivariate analyses in these studies of non-response makes difficult the drawing of definitive conclusions. The fact that blacks tend to be disproportionately socio-economically and educationally disadvantaged may play a significant role in their response patterns. Similary, our research has shown large regional variation in rates of cooperation and timing of response—southern blacks being more cooperative. Similarly, Hawkins' analysis raises the question of secular and cohort trends in the data [59], suggesting that different factors may operate at different points in time for different age cohorts. For example, if non-response is a cohort phenomenon then Hawkins' findings of increased proclivity for middle-aged individuals to be non-respondents indicate future problems and increasing non-response in studies of older populations [59]. The lack of multivariate analyses, however, and the simultaneous examination of the factors that may underlie non-response in older respondents of different racial and ethnic backgrounds makes an interpretation of the available data extremely difficult [13].

## SUMMARY

In summary, while it is not always necessary to use full probability samples (pilot and exploratory efforts, for example [1]), both the area and telephone probability methods described here can be implemented for acceptable costs. The continued use of powerful parametric statistics on haphazardly drawn samples of minority elderly is becoming less and less justifiable [56]. The procedures proposed and developed, for example, by Jackson and Hatchett [65] and Gibson and Herzog [64] now make it possible to generate adequate sized and representative samples of black American adults and families. This work has also lead to improvements in the methods by which supplemental samples of black older Americans are drawn [18, 70]. An example is the ongoing national study of 3,600 Americans twenty years of age and older, Americans' Changing Lives, at the Institute for Social Research [81]. The new approaches do not completely solve the problem of sampling black populations. When combined with other advances in sampling rare populations [66], however, and statistical procedures for addressing errors introduced by sampling difficulties [55, 58, 63, 82], future samples of blacks as well as other ethnic and racial group elderly in both national and regional survey studies should demonstrate vast improvements over previous efforts [65].

## NATURE OF THE SURVEY TASK AND OLDER MINORITY ADULTS

The remaining classes of errors, as described by Bradburn [51], Sudman and Bradburn [52], Tanur, [62], Schuman and Kalton [28], and Turner and Martin [53], relate to the execution of the sample, the nature of the survey interview and subsequent data manipulation. Based upon the Sudman and Bradburn model, these classes of errors refer to problems in research objectives and conceptualization, the nature of concepts, question wording, mode of survey administration, editing and coding errors and errors that enter during data processing, analysis and interpretation. Besides sparse reports on issues of community involvement [16, 39, 83, 84], interviewer matching [1], and language [19], little systematic research has been conducted in this area on minority populations.

Hardly any work has focused on the nature of problem conceptualization and research objectives in the study of ethnic racial groups (10,46). Errors in these domains are of a fundamental nature but as of yet have not received the same type of scrutiny as other more procedural and statistical errors. These are areas, however, where potential for large errors has been identified [3]. Analysis and interpretation are also points where large errors are possible because of poor or inappropriate conceptualization of research problems and the failure to comprehend and empirically investigate the possible substantive role of race and ethnicity [1, 4, 10, 17–19, 32, 40, 41, 46].

Major research emphasis has been directed to errors due to interviewer and respondent roles and to the nature of the survey task in the general population [28, 62]. In our work on blacks, we have attempted to address task issues in the nature of survey instruments, question presentation and data collection modes. As Sudman and Bradburn suggest:

> The task variables are primarily determined by the interview schedule or questionnaire. The questionnaire content, independent of the formulation of the questions, will have some influence, particularly on the variables of saliency and self-presentation. The formulation of the questions, however, plays an important role because they determine the degree of structure in the questionnaire, can radically affect the perceived saliency of the requested information and can exacerbate or modify problems of self-presentation. Thus we believe that questionnaire construction and question formulation lie at the heart of the problem of response effects [52, p. 13].

We have concentrated attention on the conceptualization of constructs and the creation of questionnaires that are responsive to the cultural idiosyncracies of black adult behavior [3]. In recent reviews of the response effects literature Bradburn [51] and Schuman and Kalton [28] both point to the relative lack of good methodological research on variables related to the survey task. They conclude with regard to race issues that only the saliency of the questions themselves has a clearly demonstrated effect on the quality of survey responses and that this occurs largely through interaction with interviewer and respondent characteristics.

In general, the available research shows that increasing the length and detail of questions about health can result in more detailed and better reports of health conditions [85]. In our own work with black elderly we have found that long questions tend to lead to respondent restlessness and inattention to the interviewers' questions. Similarly, research on question specifity has shown that a small change in wording can have profound effects on the distribution of responses. Schuman and Kalton, however, concluded that these effects are often not substantial [28].

Schuman and Kalton reported that issues of question sensitivity are often considered to be more important than has been demonstrated in empirical research. When attention is focused on various subgroups of the population, however, it may be that certain questions will be of a more sensitive nature for these groups than others. For example, we found it very difficult during the pre-test of the NSBA to ask questions of a sexual nature; euphemisms had to be substituted, particularly with the oldest respondents. This same level of aversion was not noted in younger respondents. Similarly, the very nature of racial identity had to be addressed in the questionnaire. For example, we gave black respondents the opportunity to racially self-designate by any label they desired (colored, Negro, nigra, black, Afro-American). Not surprisingly many of the older blacks in our sample preferred to be called colored or Negro. Again lack of attention to this and other seemingly "small" issues could lead to respondent resentment and non-cooperation.

With regard to research on open and closed question responding, Herzog and Rodgers reported that older respondents give a significant greater proportion of " don't know's " in response to close-ended questions [13]. Similarly they also reported that older individuals tend to be less productive in response to open ended probes and finally that they tend to use stereotypic responses more often than younger respondents. Besides the finding that older blacks tended to show a disproportionately high non-response rate, Herzog and Rodgers reported few age by race effects [13]. These possible interactions, however, were not systematically explored in their research.

Schuman and Kalton reported that question order experiments have demonstrated few systematic and replicable effects [28]. While some notable studies have shown significant effects of context on responding to questions [51], other parametric analyses of these effects have yielded results that are not clear. Schuman and Kalton suggest the need for more research on the topic [28].

In creating the instrument for the NSBA nearly two years were spent in developing question domains, constructing individual items that were comprehensible and meaningful to the respondents, and ascertaining the best location of items within the questionnaire. Additionally, in order to increase the meaningfulness and saliency of the questions, we initially used modified cross-cultural procedures [1, 3, 16, 38, 40] in an attempt to validate the concepts and questions for blacks. For example, months were spent in black communities talking to and tape recording the open-ended responses of small groups of black Americans from all walks of life and from major regions of the country. These tape recorded sessions were transcribed and questions written reflecting their content.

In several cases we found that many concepts defied the use of closed-ended response formats. Although closed-ended formats are preferable for several reasons (economy of time, ease of coding) [28], we found that approximately one-third of the questionnaire content had to be open-ended. This is consistent with the literature that demonstrates that open-ended questions may be superior when little is known about the topic, particularly in studies of minority aged [1]. In the study of the black elderly, we have found that the use of open-ended questions is highly appropriate. Herzog and Rodgers, however, report that older adults may respond in less productive manners to open-ended questions [13]. Whether this decreased production reflects lowered quality or whether there were differential effects by race was not available from their report.

In our own work we have discovered that older blacks were less talkative in response to specific probes but that it seemed not to affect the quality of the responses. This is, however, an open question in need of further investigation. For example, Bishop, Tuchfarber and Oldendick reported in a recent study that blacks may be more susceptible than whites to question wording, as shown by their greater willingness to respond to fictitious topics [86].

The available research findings clearly indicate that question wording, order and context, mode of administration and open versus closed questions produce the largest task effects. The small amount of research on this topic with clder populations seems to suggest that the open–closed dimension is the most important in terms of differential responding, although some effects for the greater use of " don't know " response categories and stereotypic responding also appears to exist. The lack of research attention to issues of race by age interaction in prior studies leaves issues of response errors in black adults and the elderly in question. If the use of tasks (topics and questions) of little intrinsic interest result in a lack of motivation in older people generally, then this is a problem that is truly confounded among black and other ethnic and racial minority Americans. Our work suggests that careful attention to the development of a meaningful instrument, extensive pre-testing and the use of modified cross-cultural procedures [1, 28, 40] can contribute a great deal to the development of survey instruments that are responsive to many of the task problems that have been identified in the literature.

One final dimension of the survey task, community resistance, has not been the object of systematic study. It is a problem, however, that is well known to researchers who have worked in ethnic racial minority populations [3, 4, 16, 30, 39, 46, 83]. Based upon available reports this resistance to surveys research appears to be appreciably greater in ethnic racial minority communities than in white communities [83]. There are several reasons for this apparent greater resistance. Among these are the poor reputations that previous researchers have in conducting work in racial ethnic communities [1], and beliefs that such surveys can have negative and damaging effects on the community through changes in public policies. At a more personal level there may be a greater tendency to mistrust the basic intent of the survey and to believe that it is directed to ascertaining personal information about the household or individual that will have deleterious consequences (e.g. social security office checking on household composition and employment).

In our own work we have addressed this problem directly through the quality of the survey instrument, formal (newspapers and mass media) and informal (churches, ministers, barbershops) community advertising and awareness campaigns, extensive work on appropriate times to interview and most importantly on interviewer selection criteria. We have found as have others [1, 3, 4, 16, 46, 83] that the interviewer has the major responsibility of representing the credibility and presenting the positive objectives of the survey. In the NSBA we also judiciously used photographs in an advertising brochure carried by all interviewers to indicate that the principal researchers were black. We also found (as have others) that training indigenous interviewers, as part of the survey team, to be sensitive to these community issues was the most effective way to address these problems.

## INTERVIEWER AND RESPONDENT CHARACTERISTICS IN SURVEYS OF OLDER MINORITY ADULTS

### INTERVIEWER CHARACTERISTICS

Bradburn [51] concluded in his review that interviewer variables are only a small source of error in the total survey situation [81]. Research results have been non-definitive regarding the effects of interviewer characteristics on survey responding. Bradburn suggested that the definitive studies are yet to be done [51]. The most consistent effects have been found for sex and race of interviewers and their degree of experience and training. Recent research on interviewer expectations and behavior reveals few if any effects on the content of responses [28]. Cannel, et al. and his associates have consistently demonstrated that positive, contingent reinforcement during the course of the interview by the interviewer can positively affect the quantity and quality of responding [85].

The major finding, however, is that race and, to a less certain degree, sex of the interviewer, can affect responding, particularly for those questions related to topics of race or sex. The majority of the work has been conducted on race of interviewer effects [51]. In a striking example of these effects, Hatchett studied respondents' perceptions of race of interviewers within the NBES telephone survey [15]. She found for items related to racial attitudes that reported perceptions of interviewers as black resulted in greater endorsement of pro-black items than when the interviewer was perceived to be white. She also reported similar systematic biases in other domains unrelated to racial topics. These findings are consistent with reports in the literature on face-to-face interviewing. They suggest, however, that subtle cues in telephone interactions may influence perceptions of race and subsequent responding, regardless of the actual race of the interviewer. The identification of these cues are crucial since telephone interviewing has become the predominant mode of data collection in survey research.

Race of interviewer effects can be controlled through interviewer assignment in face-to-face surveys. On the telephone, however, this is not possible since it is the perception of race and not the actual race of the interviewer that is important [65]. We have even experimented with providing actual cues as to race in our three generation telephone study. In this case the interviewer indicated early in the interview through a standardized identification statement that she was of the same race as the respondent (black). Obviously one can envision situations where this manner of informing the respondent may have boomerang effects. The findings of a recent study on race of interviewer effects are particularly disquieting [88]. Their analysis of National Election Survey data over the last twenty years indicated substantial race of interviewer effects for black respondents on non-race related content areas—including actual voting behavior. Specifically, their results revealed that blacks interviewed by blacks in the pre-election surveys were significantly more likely than blacks interviewed by whites to vote in subsequent elections.

In our work we have been very concerned with clearly defining the tasks of the interviewers. Extensive training has been conducted with all black, indigenous community interviewers and they have been included as much as possible as integral members of the research team [30, 83]. These procedures dealt directly with factors identified in the literature that affect response errors—interviewer motivation, race characteristics and training [1, 28, 51]. We have been particularly sensitive to interviewer issues, since Herzog and Rodgers reported that older adults seem to be affected by interviewer characteristics and behaviors more than younger adults [13]. In our studies we have attempted to match sex and age between interviewers and respondents whenever possible. Again, extensive training, race matching, and close supervision all tend to reduce interviewer bias effects [51, 87].

## RESPONDENT CHARACTERISTICS

The major topic investigated under the rubric of respondent errors has been response sets (e.g. acquiescence or social desirability). The literature is somewhat equivocal; some findings support effects of response sets on survey responding [51] and others have rejected them [28]. Herzog and Rodgers reported the greater use of response sets among older respondents [13]. But whether this was different by race or not was not indicated. For example, some work suggests that response sets may be important sources of variability among older black Americans. Bachman and O'Malley found that younger blacks tend to use self-esteem response scales differently than whites, preferring extreme styles of responding to Likert-like items [89, 90]. Their work suggests that it is this responding variation, as much as anything else, that has contributed to mean population differences found on self-esteem scales over the years.

While Bachman and O'Malley attribute their findings to the nature of group level differences in response styles [90], an equally likely explanation may be culturally determined group differences in perceptions and responses to the nature of the questions [46, 91, 92]. It may be that the Bachman and O'Malley findings would be even more strongly supported in an examination of older blacks [89, 90], although these differences may be offset by increased similarity among aged individuals more generally [29]. In conducting the NSBA, TGFS and NBES surveys these issues were addressed through extensive pre-tests as described earlier. It was our belief that many of the questions, response scales and basic concepts were not appropriate or meaningful for black respondents. Thus, a combination of approaches were employed including random probes [94] to assess the meaning of closed-ended responses. For example, one set of findings indicated that in the case of older black respondents the use of "satisfaction with health" scales [95] may be inappropriate. In examining the random probes for this item from the NSBA, it seemed clear that respondents were not using the scales in the same comparative (self at different ages or others of a similar age) sense that its designers envisioned. Our results indicated that a more religious and transcendental interpretation should be given to the individual responses. Black satisfaction with health seemed much more dependent upon beliefs that health was the result of divine intervention.

Finally, some research has noted the existence of respondent motivation and memory factors in respondent behavior [28, 51, 62]. Herzog and Rodgers, however, report no essential differences among age groups in their work [13]. Similarly, they do not report any differences by race. Just as in other areas we feel that respondent motivation and memory problems are best addressed in survey studies of racial minorities by well designed tasks and well trained, highly motivated interviewers.

## SUMMARY AND CONCLUSIONS

Survey research methodology provides a unique and powerful set of tools for conducting social science research on aging black and other minority populations. The scope of possible topics to be covered, the use of precise statistical methods for defining and sampling from known populations, and sets of well worked procedures for eliciting relevant information make it an ideal vehicle for studying a broad range of important social science phenomena. This does not mean that other methods are less valuable, for example, anthropological approaches [6, 7]. It only suggests that survey research methodology is an encompassing, flexible and scientifically precise technology for research purposes in black and other minority populations [1, 3].

Unfortunately, much of what has transpired as survey research on black elderly in the past does not have the level of precision associated with genuine sample surveys. Most of the literature is based upon poorly designed and drawn convenience samples and questionnaire and other procedures that are not attendant to the types of task, interviewer and respondent problems reviewed here and in the major sources on this topic [28, 51, 52, 55, 56, 62]. The recent shift to telephone procedures as the predominant mode of data collection in survey research

[50] makes it even more imperative that scientifically acceptable approaches for conducting telephone surveys on blacks and other ethnic and racial groups be developed [67, 68, 86]. In addition, large numbers of black Americans and other racial ethnic minority group members in all age cohorts also suffer from some of the same types of educational and income deficiencies shown to be correlated with survey errors in older Americans generally [13]. Thus, it is probable that the types of problems leading to lack of reliability and validity in survey research on black and other racial ethnic elderly might continue to be a problem in the next few decades.

Our own survey work has been predicated upon the belief that salient questions, meaningful response scales, well trained indigenous local interviewers, carefully designed questionnaires and opportunities for respondent self-expression during the course of the interview would contribute the most to reducing interviewer and respondent errors. Just as Schuman and Kalton indicated about the general state of knowledge on errors in surveys, more research is needed among adult and aging black and other ethnic racial minority populations [28].

In sum, sensitivity to the cross-cultural aspects of research on ethnic and racial minority adults in the area of aging and human development can contribute positively to the development of superior survey research products [7, 40]. In our work, for example, we have directed attention to issues of sampling errors through the development of novel screening procedures in face to face area and telephone surveys. These procedures were designed to give *all* black Americans a known probability of inclusion in properly drawn samples. In this manner we have attempted to contribute to the better definition of the populations of interest as well as to the development of better samples of those populations [68, 70, 78]. To address non-sampling errors we have attempted, through the introduction of novel cross-cultural techniques, to develop relevant and salient sets of instruments for black elderly that are sensitive to their lifestyles and concerns. The use of black indigenous interviewers, extensive training and an emphasis on the motivation of both interviewers and respondents have been effective in improving the nature of the research product. Attention to these neglected areas of research design and methodology has resulted in: 1) better conceptualization of research questions; 2) better and more sensitive, elaborated coding schemes; and, 3) analyses and interpretations that are more responsive to the realities of adult development and aging in ethnic and racial minority groups.

## REFERENCES

1. R. M. Becerra and D. Shaw, *The Hispanic Elderly: A Research Reference Guide*, University Press of America, New York, 1984.
2. S. J. Cutler, Survey Research in the Study of Aging and Adult Development: A Commentary, *The Gerontologist, 19*, pp. 217–219, 1979.,

3. J. S. Jackson, M. B. Tucker, and P. B. Bowman, Conceptual and Methodological Problems in Survey Research on Black Americans, in *Methodological Problems in Minority Research*, W. T. Liu (ed.), Pacific/Asian American Mental Health Center, Chicago, 1982.
4. D. Montero, Research Among Racial and Cultural Minorities: An Overview, *Journal of Social Issues, 33,* pp. 1–10, 1977.
5. S. Presser, The Use of Survey Data in Basic Research in the Social Sciences, in *Surveying Subjective Phenomena*, Vol. 2, C. F. Turner and E. Margin (eds.), Russell Sage, New York, 1984.
6. J. K. Eckert, Anthropological Community Studies in Aging Research, *Research on Aging, 5,* pp. 455–472, 1983.
7. C. L. Fry and J. Keith (eds.), *New Methods for Old Age Research,* Center for Urban Policy, Loyola University of Chicago, Chicago, 1980.
8. E. Martin, Cultural Indicators and the Analysis of Public Opinion, in *Surveying Subjective Phenomena*, C. F. Turner and E. Martin (eds.), Russell Sage, New York, 1984.
9. W. K. Schaie, S. Orchowsky, and I. A. Parham, Measuring Age and Social Change: The Case of Race and Life Satisfaction, in *Minority Aging: Sociological and Social Psychologial Issues*, R C. Manuel (ed.), Greenwood Press, Westport, CT, 1982.
10. J. J. Jackson, Race, National Origin, Ethnicity, and Aging, in *Handbook of Aging and the Social Sciences*, Second edition, R. H. Binstock and E. Shanas (eds.), Van Nostrand Reinhold Company, New York, 1985.
11. C. T. Pihlblad, H. A. Rosencranz, and T. E. McNevin, An Examination of the Effects of Perceptual Frames of Reference in Interviewing Older Respondents, *The Gerontologist, 7,* pp. 125–127, 1967.
12. K. W. Schaie, *Methodological Issues in Aging Research: An Introduction*, Paper presented at the Methodological Issues in Aging Research Workshop, National Institute on Aging, Washington, DC, 1984.
13. A. R. Herzog and W. L. Rodgers, *Surveys of Older Americans: Some Methodological Investigations*, Final report to the National Institute on Aging, Institute for Social Research, The University of Michigan, Ann Arbor, MI, 1982.
14. J. S. Jackson and S. J. Hatchett, *Finding Black Respondents in Low Density Areas: The Wide Area Screening Procedure*, Unpublished manuscript, Institute for Social Research, The University of Michigan, Ann Arbor, MI, 1983.
15. J. S. Jackson, P. Gurin, and S. J. Hatchett, *The National Black Election Study*, Unpublished manuscript, Institute for Social Research, The University of Michigan, Ann Arbor, MI, 1984.
16. W. T. Liu, *Methodological Problems in Minority Research*, Pacific/Asian American Mental Health Research Center, Chicago, 1982.
17. V. Myers, Survey Methods for Minority Populations, *Journal of Social Issues, 33,* pp. 11–19, 1977.
18. A. W. Smith, *Beyond the Race Comparative Paradigm: Toward More Sensible Empiricism in Survey Research*, Unpublished manuscript, Department of Sociology, Arizona State University, Tempe, AZ, 1985.
19. G. Cardenas and C. H. Arce, The National Chicano Survey: Recruiting Bilingual Interviewers, in *Methodological Problems in Minority Research*, W. T. Liu (ed.), Pacific/Asian American Mental Health Research Center, Chicago, 1982.

20. J. B. Cuellar, *Ethnographic Methods: Studying Aging in an Urban Mexican-American Community*, Paper presented at the Western Gerontological Association, Portland, Oregon, October 1974.
21. K. S. Markides, H. D. Dickson, and C. Pappas, Characteristics of Dropouts in Longitudinal Research on Aging: A Study of Mexican Americans and Anglos, *Experimental Aging Research, 8*, pp. 163–167, 1982.
22. P. K. Nandi, Surveying Asian Minorities in the Middle-Sized City, in *Methodological Problems in Minority Research*, W. T. Liu (ed.), Pacific/Asian American Mental Health Research Center, Chicago, 1982.
23. E. Yu, Problems in Pacific/Asian American Community Research, in *Methodological Problems in Minority Research*, W. T. Liu (ed.), Pacific/Asian American Mental Health Research Center, Chicago, 1982.
24. W. M. Hurh and K. C. Kim, Methodological Problems in the Study of Korean Immigrants: Conceptual, Interactional, Sampling and Interviewer Training Difficulties, in *Methodological Problems in Minority Research*, W. T. Liu (ed.), Pacific/Asian American Mental Health Research Center, Chicago, 1982.
25. C. M. Loo, Vulnerable Populations: Case Studies in Crowing Research, in *The Ethics of Social Research*, J. E. Sieber (ed.), Springer-Verlag, New York, 1982.
26. E. B. Palmore, Cross-Cultural Research: State of the Art, *Research on Aging, 5*, pp. 45–57, 1983.
27. J. Sokolovsky (ed.), *Growing Old in Different Societies*, Wadsworth, Belmont, CA, 1983.
28. H. Schuman and G. Kalton, Survey Methods, in *Handbook of Social Psychology*, Vol. III, G. Lindzey and E. Aronson (eds.), Wiley, New York, 1985.
29. V. L. Bengtson and L. A. Morgan, Ethnicity and Aging: A Comparison of Three Ethnic Groups, in *Growing Old in Different Societies,* J. Sokolvsky (ed.), Wadsworth, Belmont, CA, 1983.
30. L. M. Burton and V. L. Bengtson, Research in Elderly Minority Communities: Problems and Potentials, in *Minority Aging: Sociological and Social Psychological Issues*, R. C. Manual (ed.), Greenwood Press, Westport, CT, 1982.
31. J. S. Jackson, The Program for Research on Black Americans, in *Advances in Black Psychology*, R. L. Jones (ed.), University of California at Berkeley, Berkeley, CA, 1986.
32. E. K. Levine, Old People are Not Alike: Social Class, Ethnicity/Race, and Sex are Bases for Important Differences, in *The Ethics of Social Research*, J. E. Sieber (ed.), Springer-Verlag, New York, 1982.
33. M. B. Spencer, G. R. Brookens, and W. R. Allen (eds.), *Beginnings: The Social and Affective Development of Black Children*, Lawrence Erlbaum Associates, Hillsdale, NJ, 1985.
34. R. W. Brislin, W. J. Lonner, and R. M. Thorndike, *Cross-Cultural Research Methods*, John Wiley & Sons, New York 1973.
35. B. M. Finifter, The Robustness of Cross-Cultural Findings, *Annals of the New York Academy of Sciences, 285*, pp. 151–184, 1977.
36. H. C. Triandis, Some Dimensions of Intercultural Variation and Their Implications for Community Psychology, *Journal of Community Psychology, 11*, pp. 285–302, 1983.
37. I. K. Kraus, Between- and Within-Group Comparisons in Aging Research, in *Aging*

*in the 1980's*, L. W. Poon (ed.), American Psychological Association, Washington, DC, 1980.

38. C. O. Word, Cross-Cultural Methods of Survey Research in Black Urban Areas, *The Journal of Black Psychology, 3*, pp. 72–87, 1977.
39. R. Valle and L. Mendoza, *The Elder Latino*, Campanile Press, San Diego, CA, 1978.
40. T. B. Rodgers, Some Thoughts on the 'Culture Fairness' of Personality Inventories, *The Canadian Psychologist, 13*, pp. 116–120, 1972.
41. M. E. Zusman and A. O. Olson, Gathering Complete Responses from Mexican-Americans by Personal Interview, *Journal of Social Issues, 33*, pp. 46–55, 1977.
42. E. W. Labouvie, Identity versus Equivalence of Psychological Measures and Constructs, in *Aging in the 1980's*, L. W. Poon (Ed.), American Psychological Association, Washington, DC, 1980.
43. W. Labov, *Sociolinguistic Patterns*, University of Pennsylvania Press, Philadelphia, 1972.
44. M. D. Gynther, White Norms and Black MMPI's: A Prescription for Discrimination, *Psychological Bulletin, 78*, pp. 386–402, 1972.
45. T. Kochman, *Black and White: Styles in Conflict*, The University of Chicago Press, Chicago, 1981.
46. J. S. Jackson, *Science, Values and Research on Ethnic and Racial Groups*, Unpublished manuscript, Institute for Social Research, The University of Michigan, 1986.
47. D. P. Warwick and C. A. Lininger, *The Sample Survey: Theory and Practice*, McGraw-Hill, New York, 1975.
48. R. Ferber, P. Sheatsley, A. Turner, and J. Waksberg, *What Is a Survey*, American Statistical Association, Washington, DC, 1980.
49. L. Kish, *Survey Sampling*, Wiley, New York, 1965.
50. P. H. Rossi, J. D. Wright, and A. B. Anderson (Eds.), *Handbook of Survey Research*, Academic Press, New York, 1983.
51. N. Bradburn, Response Effects, in *Handbook of Survey Research*, P. H. Rossi, J. D. Wright, and A. D. Anderson (Eds.), Academic Press, New York, 1983.
52. S. Sudman and N. Bradburn, *Response Effects in Surveys*, Aldine, Chicago, 1974.
53. C. F. Turner and E. Martin (Eds.), *Surveying Subjective Phenomena*, Vol. 1, Russell Sage, New York, 1984.
54. D. F. Alwin, Making Errors in Surveys: An Overview, in *Survey Design and Analysis*, D. F. Alwin (Ed.), Sage Publications, Beverly Hills, CA, 1977.
55. C. A. O'Muircheartaigh, Response Errors, in *The Analysis of Survey Data*, C. A. O'Muircheartaigh and C. Payne (Eds.), John Wiley & Sons, New York, 1977.
56. R. A. Berk, An Introduction to Sample Selection Bias in Sociological Research, *American Sociological Review, 48*, pp. 386–398, 1983.
57. R. A. Berk and S. C. Ray, Selection Biases in Sociological Data, *Social Science Research, 11*, pp. 301–340, 1982.
58. D. F. Alwin and D. J. Jackson, Measurement Models for Response Errors in Surveys: Issues and Applications, in *Sociological Methodology*, K. F. Schuessler (Ed.), Jossey-Bass, San Francisco, 1980.
59. D. F. Hawkins, *Non-Response in Detroit Area Study Surveys: A Ten Year Analysis*, Working Papers in Methodology, Institute for Research in Social Science, University of North Carolina at Chapel Hill, Chapel Hill, NC, 1977.
60. D. F. Hawkins, *The Reluctant Respondent: Two Views*, Discussion Paper Series,

Institute for Research in Social Science, University of North Carolina at Chapel Hill, Chapel Hill, NC, 1977.

61. J. R. Landis, J. M. Lepkowski, S. A. Eklund, and Stehouwer, *A Statistical Methodology for Analyzing Data from a Complex Survey: The First Naitonal Health and Nutrition Examination Survey*, DHHS Publication No. (PHS) 82-1366, US. Department of Health and Human Services, Office of Health Research, Statistics and Technology, Washington, DC, 1982.
62. J. M. Tanur, Methods for Large Scale Surveys and Experiments, in *Sociological Methodology 1983–1984*, S. Leinhardt (Ed.), Jossey-Bass, San Francisco, 1983.
63. J. R. Nesselroade, *Sampling and Generalizability: Adult Development and Aging Research Issues Examined Within the General Methodological Framework of Selection*, Paper presented at the Methodological Issues in Aging Research Workshop, National Institute of Aging, Washington, DC, 1984.
64. R. C. Gibson and A. R. Herzog, Rare Element Telephone Screening (RETS): A Procedure for Augmenting the Number of Black Elderly in National Samples, *The Gerontologist, 24*, pp. 477–482, 1984.
65. J. S. Jackson and S. J. Hatchett, Intergenerational Research: Methodological Considerations, in *Intergenerational Relations*, N. Datan, A. L. Greene, and H. W. Reese (Eds.), Erlbaum, Hillsdale, NJ, 1986.
66. M. G. Sirkin, *Discussion: Survey Methods for Rare Populations*, Proceedings of the Fourth Conference on Health Survey Research Methods, U.S. Department of Health and Human Services, Washington, DC, 1982.
67. J. Blair and R. Czaja, Locating a Special Population Using Random Digit Dialing, *Public Opinion Quarterly, 46*, pp. 585-590, 1982.
68. K. M. Inglis, R. M. Groves, and S. G. Heeringa, *Telephone Sample Designs for the Black Household Population*, Proceedings of the Survey Section, American Statistical Association, Washington, DC, August, 1985.
69. G. S. Rothbart, M. Fine, and S. Sudman, On Finding and Interviewing the Needles in the Haystack: The Use of Multiplicity Sampling, *Public Opinion Quarterly, 46*, pp. 408–421, 1982.
70. R. Tourangeau and A. W. Smith, Finding Subgroups for Surveys, *Public Opinion Quarterly, 49*, pp. 351-365, 1985.
71. D. P. Rice, T. F. Drury, and R. H. Mugge, Household Health Interviews and Minority Health: The NCHS Perspective, *Medical Care, 28*, pp. 327–335, 1980.
72. E. J. Salber and A. G. Beza, The Health Interview Survey and Minority Health, *Medical Care, 28*, pp. 319-326, 1980.
73. E. P. Ericksen, Sampling a Rare Population: A Case Study, *Journal of the American Statistical Association, 71*, pp. 816–822, 1976.
74. E. Shanas, *National Survey of the Elderly*, Report to the Administration of Aging, Department of Health and Human Services, Washington, DC, 1979.
75. National Council on the Aging, *The Myth and Reality of Aging in America*, The National Council on the Aging, Inc., Washington, DC, 1976.
76. A. R. Herzog, W. L. Rodgers, and R. A. Kulka, Interviewing Older Adults: A Comparison of Telephone and Face to Face Modalities, *Public Opinion Quarterly, 47*, pp. 405–418, 1983.
77. O. T. Thornberry and J. T. Massey, *Correcting for Undercoverage Bias in Random* Digit Dialed Naitonal Health Surveys, Proceedings of the Survey Research Section of the American Statistical Association, 1978.

78. I. Hess, *Sampling for Social Research Surveys: 1947–1980*, Institute for Social Research, The University of Michigan, Ann Arbor, MI, 1985.

79. J. A. Momeni, *Demography of the Black Population in the United States*, Greenwood Press, Westport, CT, 1983.

80. R. Gibson and J. S. Jackson, The Black Aged, in *Currents of Health Policy and Impact on Black Americans*, R. Willis (Ed.), *The Millbank Quarterly (Supplement), 65*, 1987.

81. J. S. House, *Productivity, Stress, and Health in Middle and Late Life*, Unpublished Program Project Grant Application to the National Institute on Aging, Institute for Social Research, The University of Michigan, Ann Arbor, MI, 1984.

82. F. M. Andrews, *The Construct Validity and Error Components of Survey Measures: Estimates from a Structural Modeling Approach*, Proceedings of the Fourth Conference on Health Survey Methods, U.S. Department of Health and Human Services, Washington, DC, 1982.

83. V. L. Bengtson, E. Grigsby, E. M. Corry, and M. Hruby, Relating Academic Research to Community Concerns: A Case Study in Collabortive Effort, *Journal of Social Issues, 33*, pp. 75–92, 1977.

84. C. H. Weiss, Survey Researchers and Minority Communities, *Journal of Social Issues, 33*, pp. 20–35, 1977.

85. C. F. Cannell, P. V. Miller, and L. Oksenberg, Research on Interviewing Techniques, in *Sociological Methodology*, S. Leinhardt (Ed.), Jossey-Bass, San Francisco, 1981.

86. G. F. Bishop, A. J. Tuchfarber, and R. W. Oldendick, Opinions on Fictitious Issues: The Pressure to Answer Questions, *Public Opinion Quarterly, 50*, pp. 240–250, 1986.

87. P. D. Cleary, D. Mechanic, and N. Weiss, The Effect of Interviewer Characteristics on Responses to a Mental Health Interview, *Journal of Health and Social Behavior, 22*, pp. 183–193, 1981.

88. B. A. Anderson, B. D. Silver, and P. R. Abramson, *The Effects of Race of Interviewer in SRC National Election Studies*, Paper presented at the Annual Meeting of the Americna Political Science Association, Washingotn, DC, August, 1986.

89. J. G. Bachman and P. M. O'Malley, Black-White Differences in Self-Esteem: Are They Affected by Response Style, *American Journal of Sociology, 90*, pp. 624–639, 1984.

90. J. G. Bachman and P. M. O'Malley, Yea-Saying, Nay-Saying, and Going to Extremes: Black-White Differences in Response Styles, *Public Opinion Quarterly, 48*, pp. 491–509, 1984.

91. W. W. Nobles, Psychological, Research and the Black Self-Concept: A Critical Review, *Journal of Social Issues, 29*, pp. 11–32, 1973.

92. L. T. Semaj, Afrikanity, Cognition and Extended Self-Identity, in *Beginnings: The Social and Affective Development of Black Children*, M. B. Spencer, G. R. Brookens and W. R. Allen (Eds.), Lawrence Erlbaum Associates, Hillsdale, NJ, 1985.

93. H. Schuman, The Random Probe: A Technique for Evaluating the Validity of Closed Questions, *American Sociological Review, 41*, pp. 224–235, 1966.

94. L. C. Chatters, *Health Satisfaction or Satisfaction with God: Results of a Random Probe in the National Survey of Black Americans*, Unpublished manuscript, Brandeiss University, Boston, 1986.

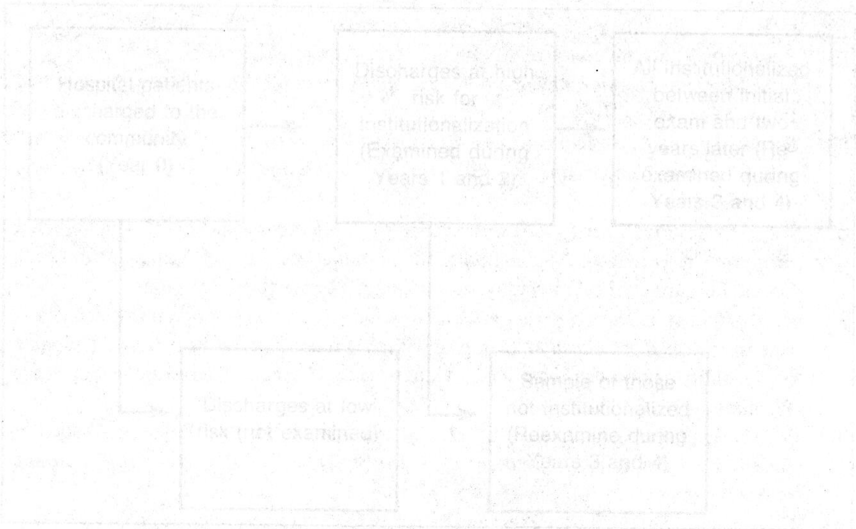

Figure 1. Model of effects of institutionalization study.

information. For example, the hospital records that we have been examining usually contain the age, sex, race, marital status, living arrangements, and education of the patients. They also usually contain the admission and discharge dates, diagnoses, mobility status, mobility aids required, activities of daily living, percent disability, mental status, competence to handle own affairs, and treatments prescribed. Of course, like real gold mines, there is a lot of ore that must be sifted and it may take some digging to find the desired piece of information, but it is usually there. Other medical records, such as health insurance association or private physician records, may be less informative, but nearly all contain much useful information for many research purposes.

If one is interested in medical care received, medical records are usually the most accurate source. Various studies have shown that most patients do not remember accurately what treatments they got from whom and when. Medical records are by far the most complete and accurate source for such detailed information. Numerous studies have used medical records as the primary source for such medical information.

## THE USE OF GOVERNMENT HEALTH SERVICES RECORDS

The Manitoba Longitudinal study is an outstanding example of the use of health service claims records to measure the amounts and kinds of health services received in a longitudinal study. [illegible] health services (including nursing home care [illegible]

CHAPTER

# 7

# Recruitment Practices for Psychological Research in Gerontology

*Cameron J. Camp*
*Robin L. West*
*Leonard W. Poon*

This chapter addresses the possibility of bias in the subject selection and recruitment methods currently employed in psychological research on aging. It will examine problems associated with studies in cognition and aging because this area subsumes the largest number of recently published studies in the psychology of aging [1, 2].

The literature shows that most research in cognition and aging utilizes cross-sectional designs which are "quasi-experimental," since experimenters cannot randomly assign subjects to different levels of age. As a result, matching with respect to various background characteristics is often used as a means of obtaining comparable groups of different ages. For example, educational level or verbal intelligence is often matched between younger and older groups recruited from college campuses and community organizations, respectively. Performance differences between matched age groups are then assumed to be due to aging.

There are two central problems with this approach to aging research. The first deals with internal validity, i.e., the ability to state unequivocally that the treatment effect produced the outcome in an experiment. Unmatched variables may be represented unequally in various groups, and they may also covary with the dependent measures. Thus, issues involving subject selection and matching procedures are fundamental to the ability to draw unambiguous conclusions.

A second problem deals with external validity, i.e., the ability to generalize results. The need to create homogeneous subject groups to control variation in extraneous factors prevents generalization to representative populations. This problem is also seen in longitudinal studies which use homogeneous samples. Recruitment practices therefore are capable of determining the generalizability (and perhaps the relevance) of the research.

Our central question is this: Having been aware of these problems for over twenty years [3], have research practices begun to deal with them, and if so, how? To answer this question, we first review the literature on research practices in cognitive gerontology. Second, we report on a survey that was designed to provide additional information not found currently in the literature. Finally, we review alternative research methodologies that have been adopted to deal with the problems in more traditional experimental methods.

## A REVIEW OF THE LITERATURE

### SUBJECT CHARACTERISTICS

Subtle biases in the selection of younger, middle-aged, and older adult samples could strongly influence researchers' conclusions. Differences in distribution among samples in level of education, verbal intelligence, gender, and health may make it difficult to draw firm conclusions about the magnitude of age effects. Most of these factors, along with the potential problems they might produce, were reviewed by Poon et al. [2]. A brief discussion of these factors will be presented.

*Education* — Poon et al. surveyed forty-one studies dealing with cognition and aging in the 1979 and 1980 issues of two journals publishing research on aging [2]. Thirty-four percent of the studies did not report a measure of educational level of the samples. They noted that there is no standard for determining educational equivalences across different patterns of education. Older age groups had less education on the average than did younger cohorts. Qualitative differences in educational experiences among different cohorts also exist. Matching different age groups on level of education may provide underestimates of population age differences if education and the dependent measure are related. That is, it is possible that an older group with the same educational level as a younger group would represent an older subpopulation that was significantly more privileged, perhaps better equipped intellectually, than the younger group exposed to today's educational milieu.

*Verbal intelligence* — Poon et al. found that 54 percent of the surveyed studies did not report a measure of verbal intelligence [2]. Poon et al. stated that verbal ability seems to have a bimodal distribution in older samples, older adults with high verbal ability performing as well as younger adults on many tasks, and older adults with low verbal ability performing worse than younger adults. Again, the verbal ability of a sample of older adults appears to be strongly related to the conclusions drawn when the performance of older samples is compared with that of younger samples.

*Gender* — Poon et al. found that 27 percent of the studies surveyed did not report gender characteristics of their samples, while 46 percent reported using unequal numbers of males and females [2]. For purposes of internal validity, it would seem best to have an equal number of males and females in a sample. However, the proportion of males to females in the general population decreases as a function of advancing age. The researcher is thus faced with a choice of using equal numbers of males and females to obtain the most powerful test of gender differences or instead to use proportional numbers of males and females (the same proportions as in the general population) in order to maximize the generalizability of results.

*Health* — Poon et al. found that 54 percent of the studies surveyed did not report health status of individuals [2]. Twenty- seven percent simply indicated that subjects seemed to be healthy. Only 2 percent screened samples on the basis of detailed health records. If we assume that the general level of health within the overall population decreases as a function of advancing age, then the use of random sampling of older adults and younger adults may overestimate the effects of aging on performance, confounding the age effect with the effect of poor health. On the other hand, using only healthy older samples will not create a true picture of ability levels within older populations in general. Poon et al. cite several studies in which outcomes were critically influenced by healthy levels of participants [2]. Similarly Hoyer et al. [1] surveyed psychological research published in the *Journal of Gerontology* from 1975 to 1982. They found that over 35 percent of the published studies failed to report the health of the subjects, while only about 12 percent had a direct measure of health or treated health as a descriptor variable. Given the potential impact that health has on performance, describing the health status of participants (especially older ones) is important if researchers wish to generate unambiguous, reliable results.

## RECRUITING PRACTICES

Poon et al. have amply demonstrated how subject matching on concomitant variables can lead to over- or underestimation of aging effects [2]. At the same time, recruitment settings and inducements offered for participation may be important factors that influence outcome either independently, or in interaction with, specific subject characteristics. For instance, Salthouse raises concerns about internal and external validity that derive from recruiting volunteers from convenient locations (campuses for younger adults and social organizations for older adults), and from maintaining subject pools of middle-aged and older adults who are tested repeatedly [4]. Similar concerns about recruitment sites and inducements have been addresed in the studies described below.

*Recruitment site* — Camp, Markely, and Danielson selected active, independently living adults of different ages in a study involving the reversing Necker cube illusion [5]. An earlier study had reported that only 19 percent of older adults could perceive this illusion [6]. In the initial sample of this study [5], age was not related to the ability to perceive the illusion — 100 percent of the older sample perceived it. Two additional samples of older adults were tested later. Within a sample of older adults from a low rent housing complex, 47 percent perceived the illusion, whereas 21 percent of nursing home residents perceived it. Though living arrangement doubtless covaries with other variables (such as health or socioeconomic status) that may actually cause such outcomes, the location of recruiting dramatically influenced the results.

Similarly, subjects recruited from nursing homes may be in poorer health than noninstitutionalized older adults, but also tend to live in a restricted environment with less opportunity for social interaction or intellectual challenge than community dwelling older adults. Such environmental differences could affect performance. Numerous studies have demonstrated that nursing home and community-dwelling elderly individuals vary in their cognitive abilities [7], and individuals from these two settings should not be included in the same subject samples for experimental research.

Five recent years of published psychological research in the *Journal of Gerontology* and *Experimental Aging Research* were examined by the authors of this chapter to uncover subject recruitment information. In spite of the potential importance of recruiting sites, only 62 percent of the studies indicated the recruiting source of their subjects. The remaining studies described a subject pool or longitudinal sample without identifying the original recruitment sites for the subject (8%), simply specified that the subjects lived in the community (18%), or provided no information about their recruitment methods (12%). Patients (inpatients and outpatients of hospitals or clinics as well as nursing home residents) either were mixed with community volunteers or were the only subjects in 17 percent of the published investigations. Less than 15 percent of the studies recruited young people from non-college sources (about half of these involved large-scale sampling techniques). In contrast, the most common sources for the older adults were senior centers and social organizations (29% of the published studies). In addition, the recruitment sites used for older adult samples vary more than those used for sampling young adults. This in turn might create increased variability or exaggerate variability within older samples compared to younger samples.

*Monetary inducements* — Are volunteers different from nonvolunteers? Schaie suggested that middle-aged people are more likely to volunteer than older individuals [8], and this finding has been confirmed by others [9, 10]. Our subject pools, then, may reflect the lower end of the age ranges we sample.

In an investigation of the effects of recruiting by offering a monetary payment, Gribbin and Schaie found no difference in volunteer rates between persons offered money or no money [9], suggesting that volunteers are not a special population. More importantly, they found "On tests of intellectual functioning and cognitive style, employment of monetary incentive had no effect on the characteristics of the sample" [9, p. 467].

There is other evidence that volunteers and nonvolunteers may not differ in performance [11]. In this study, younger and older schoolteachers were recruited and tested on a wide variety of cognitive tasks. Volunteers and nonvolunteers (later induced to participate through payment of a large honorarium) showed comparable performance on all measures for both age groups. The authors concluded, "We are confident that, given samples from as homogeneous and well educated a population as our teachers, data from volunteer subjects are representative data. ...Quite possibly volunteer effects may still undermine generalizations to heterogenous, poorly educated, or low-ability populations" [11, p. 297].

*Verbal inducements* — Schleser, West, and Boatwright used different recruiting approaches in three comparable, but separate, high-rise apartment buildings [12]. Subjects were recruited to participate in memory training using a positive ("increase your memory power!"), more neutral ("improve skills"), or negative ("avoid memory failures") approach presented first on a poster, then flyers, and finally at a group meeting. Subsequent assessments indicated that subjects who responded to the negative approach had the greatest expectation of age-related memory loss. Those who responded to the initial poster (especially the positive approach) were more anxious than those who signed up at other points in the recruitment drive. The greatest compliance with the six-session training program occurred for those who responded to the initial poster or to the negative content (no interaction). Therefore, the recruitment method had an influence on the kind of subjects that were identified.

# A NATIONAL SURVEY

## NEED FOR THE SURVEY

To further understand the impact of recruiting and subject selection practices, researchers in cognitive aging were contacted directly. This survey seemed necessary for two reasons. First of all, existing areas of consensus for appropriate selection procedures are informal and generally undocumented. Poon et al. concluded that there was no standard editorial policy on subject selection practices and statements of generalizability of results in any journals they examined [2]. They also discussed positive and negative arguments concerning the adoption of minimal editorial standards. Since recruiting decisions may critically influence research outcomes, the lack of a formal consensus continues to be problematic. One goal of the survey was to use the results as one step toward establishing such a consensus.

A second reason for the survey is that previous surveys of research practices have revealed information gaps. For example, Hoyer et al. noted that only a small number of published studies described how subject samples were obtained [1]. To demonstrate that this problem is not idiosyncratic to cognitive aging research, Gentry and Shulman sampled *Psychological Abstracts* and *Sociological Abstracts* from 1973 to 1983 for research dealing with widowhood and found that 33 percent of the studies failed to report either the resource of subjects or the sampling procedure, and 17 percent failed to report both [13].

Examinations of the published work in cognitive aging research indicate that subject characteristics are described more often than where or how subjects were recruited, but even when subject variables are reported, researchers rarely assess their impact on performance. Procedural factors—such as payment rates, participation ratios, and the number of studies completed by the same subjects—could affect research outcomes and should perhaps receive fuller treatment in published research [1]. (See a partial bibliography on pp. 185–189 of studies which deal with the influence of recruiting methods and concomitant variables on outcomes in aging research.)

## THE SAMPLE OF RESEARCHERS

The survey was designed to measure the prevalence of a variety of subject selection and research practices, and to solicit the opinions of researchers directly (see Appendix I). The questionnaire was mailed to 1100 persons, including members of Division 20 (Adult Development and Aging) of the American Psychological Association, and cognitive psychologists associated with research networks of the Mental Performance and Aging Laboratory at the Boston VA Hospital. There were 250 returned questionnaires, a 23 percent response rate. Some of these questionnaires (45) were returned uncompleted by psychologists interested in the results who were not actively conducting research at the time. The return rate was reasonably good, considering that a large number (probably fewer than one half) of the Division 20 members were actively conducting research. The majority of the respondents were associated with a university or medical center and 60 percent were from metropolitan areas larger than 300,000 persons.

The survey questions covered the demographic characteristics of research subjects, measurement of concomitant variables, inducements offered to potential subjects, recruitment sites, treatment of subjects, and researchers' opinions about standardization of recruitment methodology.

## SURVEY RESULTS

*Defining terms* — Throughout the discussion of results, "respondents" will refer to the gerontologists who completed the questionnaires and "subjects" will refer to the persons whom the respondents recruit for research. Analyses of variance and chi-square analyses were based on three data points (young, middle-aged, and old) for each respondent, reflecting the age of the subjects who were described by the respondents. Thus, in all cases the term "age differences" indicates that respondents reported differential treatment of subjects from different age groups. For the chi-square analyses, data from a 5- point scale were collapsed into three categories: 1 = "all" or "most" studies used a particular procedure; 2 = "half" or "some" studies; 3 = "none." In summarizing the data, a distinction will be made between the responses to the open-ended questions and the responses to objective questions.

*Missing data* — There were missing responses to the questionnaire, varying in number from item to item. In most cases, the percentages for each category of response indicate the percentage of all respondents who gave a particular answer. This was done in all cases where a nonresponse reflected a response of "0." For example, the respondents were asked to circle a word indicating how many of their studies used particular recruiting methods. "None" was one of the alternatives, but some respondents left the question blank. We assumed in such cases that their response was "None" and calculated percentages accordingly. However, if respondents left blank a different type of question, e.g., "Do you pay subjects from different age groups the same amount...?" (Q (question) #8E), the meaning of a nonresponse could not be inferred. In this latter case, nonrespondents were excluded from calculations, and the total N was provided in the text summary of the results. The means for the particular items were based only on the responses given.

*Demographic characteristics* — Overall, the geropsychologists surveyed had involved more older adults in their research during the course of a year than middle-aged and younger adults (Q# 1), $F$ (2,339) = 3.69, $p < .05$ (young $\overline{X}$ = 100.8, $N$ = 122; middle-aged $\overline{X}$ = 89.0, $N$ = 112; older $\overline{X}$ = 184.1, $N$ = 168).

Age ranges overlap for the three age groups sampled (Q# 3). The lower age limit reportedly used for "middle-aged" subjects was as young as thirty or as old as sixty. The mean lower and upper age limits for the recruited age groups were 18.4 and 30.1 years (young), 39.1 and 57.7 years (middle-aged), and 61.6 and 90.3 years (older). The mean age ranges were 12.7 years ($N$ = 124), 19.6 years ($N$ = 129), and 29.7 years ($N$ = 176), for the young, middle-aged, and older research samples, respectively, with significantly larger ranges for the older adult samples, $F$ (2,426) = 158.6, $p < .001$.

The range of years of education also varied as a function of age group (Q #4). For the most part, the respondents did not use education-matched samples. Only 13 percent reported that they used younger adult subjects with less than a high school education, whereas 46 percent used middle-aged subjects and 57 percent used older subjects with less than a high school education. The values reported for the minimun educational level of subjects were examined in an analysis of variance, using the age groups of the subjects as the independent variable, $F$ (2,367) = 18.8, $p < .001$ (young $\overline{X}$ = 11.5, $N$ = 112; middle-aged

$\overline{X} = 10.5$, $N = 111$; older $\overline{X} = 9.2$, $N = 147$). However, at the upper end (the maximum number of years of education of subject groups), no significant differences occurred as a function of age group recruited. The education ranges showed significantly more heterogeneity for older adults, $F$ (2,365) = 11.9, $p < .001$. The mean educational ranges were 6.0 ($N = 112$), 7.8 ($N = 110$), and 8.4 ($N = 146$) for the young, middle-aged, and older subjects, respectively.

These results emphasize the greater variability of older samples. These group differences in variability may or may not result in samples that are representative for these age groups. Many researchers have emphasized greater interindividual variability among older persons [14], but there is little empirical evidence for it [15]. Lachman et al. surveyed the sources of subjects for 113 studies dealing with cognition and aging published from 1975 to 1979 [11]. Their results also highlighted greater variability for older subject groups but they concluded that increased variability in older samples may be an artifact of sampling homogenous young subgroups and heterogenous older subgroups.

*Concomitant variables* — The respondents were asked to report the measurement of concomitant background variables in studies using random or nonrandom subject selection procedures (Q# 10). Education was the most commonly reported concomitant measure (46%). After education, the other most frequent concomitant variables used to identify subjects included health (38%), verbal intelligence (20%), and socio-economic status or occupation (28%). In their comments, many researchers wrote that more study of particular concomitant variables should be conducted, with health as the one most often mentioned.

*Inducement* — Researchers were asked to identify whether or not subjects were volunteers or were paid for research participation (Q# 8). Interestingly, in research journals, the term "volunteers" is not reserved for unpaid subjects, as authors have often given subject descriptions such as "volunteer community dwelling adults ... [were] paid $ 10 for their participation." Therefore, the survey question was designed to make a clear distinction between volunteers and paid participants.

There was considerable disparity observed in the inducement offered to potential subject groups varying in age; 46 percent of the respondents reported that payment for participation was not the same for the subjects from different age groups. The distribution of volunteers in the respondents' studies was related to the age of the subjects, $\chi^2$ (4 d.f., $N = 305$) = 10.1, $p < .05$. The young generally were unpaid (32%) or were "paid" course credit for participation (34%). Compared to the young (32%) and middle-aged (31%), more older adults were recruited as unpaid volunteers (37%).

With young subjects, 26 percent of the respondents offered monetary payment in all or most of their studies $\overline{X}$ = \$5.47 per study, $N = 62$). With middle-aged subjects, 27 percent of the respondents offered money $\overline{X}$ = \$5.34, $N = 58$), and with older adults, 39 percent of the respondents offered money in all or most of their studies ($\overline{X}$ = \$6.00, $N$ = 87). The rate of pay, for those who were offered money, did not vary with the age of the subjects (Q# 8). Age of subject was associated, however, with whether or not the subjects were reimbursed for transportation costs, $\chi^2$ (4 d.f., $N = 243$) = 10.1, $p < .05$. Such costs were paid more often for older subjects.

*Recruitment site* — The most frequent sites for recruiting young subjects (Q #6) were psychology classes (25%) and college campuses in general (10%). Middle-aged and older adults were most often recruited from health centers and hospitals (10% middle-aged and 13% older) or community centers (9% middle-aged and 19% older). Table 1 indicates the recruitment sites used by the respondents.

Table 1. Frequency of Usage for the Top Three Recruiting Locations for Each Age Group

| | Frequency of Usage | | |
|---|---|---|---|
| Location | All or Most Studies | Half or Some Studies | No Studies/ No Response |
| Young | | | |
| Psychology classes | 49 | 26 | 122 |
| Clubs and community centers | 9 | 37 | 165 |
| Other College students | 21 | 61 | 127 |
| Middle-Aged | | | |
| Hospitals and health centers | 21 | 24 | 169 |
| Clubs and community centers | 18 | 64 | 126 |
| Friends, referrals, staff at centers or universities | 11 | 48 | 162 |
| Older | | | |
| Clubs and community centers | 39 | 90 | 86 |
| Hospitals, nursing and health centers | 34 | 58 | 113 |
| Friends, referrals, staff at centers and universities | 13 | 60 | 150 |

As expected, college students were used most often for young samples, $\chi^2$ (4 d.f., $N = 273$) = 37.4, $p < .001$. Clubs and community centers were used more often for recruiting older adults than either young or middle-aged samples, $\chi^2$ (4 d.f., $N = 321$) = 68.5, $p < .001$. Age of participant was not related to recruiting in newspapers or recruiting by using friends, hospitals and university staff members, or referrals.

Participants were asked to rank order settings with respect to refusal rate (Q #9). The preferred setting (lowest refusal rates) for recruiting younger adults were introductory psychology classes, psychology students, and other college students. For the middle-aged, the preferred method was to use clubs or community centers. Next in line were alumni, friends and relatives, and hospitals, with those three categories ranked about the same. For older adults, the ranking for clubs and community centers was the highest, with hospitals and nursing homes ranked next. Although the lack of older adults in college classrooms prevents researchers from obtaining older adult students, there is no reason why adults could not be recruited from clubs and community centers, to make recruiting more uniform across age groups.

*Subject treatment* — The mean number of studies carried out annually per respondent was 3.15 (Q# 5). The respondents were asked to indicate whether or not subjects were used in multiple studies (Q# 7), and 17 percent reported that subjects were used in multiple studies on the same day. The mean number of hours for participation in one study in one day was 1.79 ($N = 164$), and the mean for multiple studies in one day was 2.65 ($N = 20$). Those respondents who gather data for multiple studies in one day ($N = 34$) use this procedure in about one-fourth of their studies. When the literature was examined for five recent years, however, only two of the published studies in *Journal of Gerontology* or *Experimental Aging Research* reported that subjects were used in multiple studies. This may be an important aspect of recruitment, but it is not generally reported.

*Standardization* — When asked whether or not recruiting practices should be standardized (Q# 11), 70 percent of the respondents said "No," 10 percent said "Yes," and the remainder of the respondents gave unclassifiable responses or no response. The main reasons given for opposition to standardization included: 1) There is too much variety in geographic areas and research settings: it would be impractical to require standardization as it might lead to reductions in research productivity in some parts of the country (31%); and 2) There is too much variability in research needs and goals (27%). The respondents went on to say, however, that journals should encourage or require specific reporting about recruitment methods, and that reviewers should take this information into account (29%).

## SUMMARY

What do these results imply about future research practices in cognition and aging? An important finding is that researchers share a growing concern that current sampling procedures will produce results that are contradictory and/or idiosyncratic to samples used in specific studies. In spite of this concern, our respondents also showed a reluctance to adopt a single, discipline-wide convention for sampling practices. The chief reasons for this dealt with the variability of research settings, needs, and goals found in gerontological research. Researchers in cognitive aging thus are faced with the task of developing a stable data base in spite of the use of a diversity of sampling methods, a diversity which seems destined to continue. The need to demonstrate both the reliability and generalizability of findings has led to the use of a variety of research methodologies. We will discuss some of these general trends next.

# RESEARCH METHODOLOGIES

Given the logistical ease of cross-sectional studies compared to other techniques, it seems safe to assume that cross-sectional research will continue to be the primary research design used by cognitive aging researchers. However, a variety of competitors seems likely to appear. Even within cross-sectional research, increasing sophistication probably will be seen both in terms of dealing with sampling issues and the problems faced with drawing causal inferences from such research (see Kausler [16], for an extensive review of the use of cross-sectional methodology in gerontological research).

## CROSS—SECTIONAL RESEARCH

Three tactics are being used with increasing frequency in cross-sectional studies: 1) attempts to use more rigorous sampling methods, generally through more restrictive sampling of older and younger research participants; 2) the use of multiple tasks with the same set of participants; and 3) an increased search for interaction effects. Two cross-sectional studies illustrate these points.

*Restrictive sampling* — Lachman et al. tested the effects of financial inducement on recruitment rate across a variety of experimental tasks [11]. Their sample included only white, female school-teachers of different age levels. For recruiting, they first used mailings and then telephone solicitation. Rejection rates for each type of recruitment method were reported. Level of monetary incentive offered was used as an independent variable. The performance of individuals at each age level who agreed to participate for a nominal honorarium ("volunteers") was compared with the performance of individuals who only agreed to participate after being offered a large honorarium ("nonvolunteers"). Lachman et al. compared the performance of different age groups in tasks measuring episodic memory, everyday memory, metamemory, etc [11]. They found that their younger adults outperformed older adults in episodic memory tasks, while in these same participants older adults outperformed younger adults in answering questions about everyday information. No age effects were found for metamemory measures. Most important, no effects for level of volunteerism were found for any measure, nor were there any significant Age x Volunteerism interaction effects.

Niederehe also tested adults of different ages using a battery of episodic, everyday memory, and metamemory tasks [17]. He was interested in studying the effects of depression on cognition in different age groups. Depressed individuals were generally recruited after admission to an outpatient clinic, while controls were recruited by a variety of tactics (among those listed were newpaper stories and ads, posters, appeals to senior organization, and word of mouth). Medical histories were taken and used to exclude individuals with indications of psychopathology, alcohol or drug abuse, neurological disorder, mental retardation, etc. Clinical interviews as well as rating scales were used to classify level of depression. All participants were screened for adequate sight and hearing. They were also given a physical exam, a battery of neuropsychological tests, a self-rating of health level, and finally a vocabulary test. Interestingly, Niederehe's outcomes paralleled those of Lachman et al. [11]. Older adults generally performed more poorly than younger adults in episodic memory tasks, performed at a higher level than the young in everyday memory tasks, and were equivalent for metamemory measures. Depression was generally unrelated to performance on these memory dimensions, nor did age interact with depression level. Thus, both the Lachman et al. and Niederehe studies employed multiple tasks with the same set of participants. Interaction effects also were a prime interest in both studies.

Lachman et al. and Niederehe paid careful attention to matching age groups as closely as possible [11,17]. The price for such restrictive sampling, however, is a loss of generalizability of research outcomes. An alternative approach to restrictive sampling in cross-sectional research is the use of representative samples.

*Representative sampling* — Botwinick emphasized the need to use representative sampling among different age groups [18]. The problem with representative samples involves the confounding of age levels with levels of other covariates (such as health or education) which might influence dependent measures. Botwinick stated that this problem can be partially overcome. After representatively sampling from different age groups, he recommended comparing age groups without reference to confounding variables by way of analysis of variance. Next, the relative contributions and interrelationships of age and confounding variables could be examined through the use of the analysis of covariance. He stated, "By this procedure a representative sampling is available, permitting generalization. The contributions of all the presumed variables are known, and this should permit more meaningful generalization" [18, p. 409]. This approach is similar to the traditional cross-sectional method described above in that age effects are measured by comparing groups means, with age used as a nominal variable. It differs in that statistical techniques are used to partial out the effects of confounding variables, and sampling is used to insure generalizability of results.

Botwinick further noted that analyses of variance and covariance analyses are special cases of regression analysis [18]. Compared to analyses of variance and covariance, "Hierarchical multiple regression analysis is mathematically comparable and preferred" [18, p. 409]. A prime reason for this is that age can be used as a continuous variable in regression analyses, thus increasing accuracy of measurement compared to using it as a nominal variable in ANOVA or ANCOVA. Other problems are sometimes introduced by this approach, however, such as the frequent violation of assumptions regarding homogeneity of variance and covariance across samples of subjects.

*Causal modeling* — A logical extension of this line of reasoning is seen in the increased use of confirmatory factor analyses and causal modeling within the gerontological research literature (see Chapters 11 by Mutran and 12 by Herzog). These approaches reflect an attempt to move away from laboratory techniques which attempt to isolate or hold constant all but one variable. Instead, increasing numbers of researchers are attempting to simulate *in vivo* conditions, in which factors impinging on the behaviors of older adults are studied within the context of a multitude of agents which interact simultaneously. Here the emphasis often involves sampling a variety of measures presumed to be representative of underlying "latent variables," i.e., theoretical constructs. Age can also be used as a dependent measure, an approach which allows the creation of regression models for the calculation of an individual's "functional" age. So much causal modeling research is appearing in the literature that the journal *Experimental Aging Research* issued a call for papers on the issues to discuss whether or not the emphasis on causal modeling has been overdone.

*Sample size* — Cross-sectional research involves between group comparisons and treats individual differences as "error variance." Using homogenous samples provides increased power in such designs, while using representative samples requires larger samples to maintain adequate levels of power. Causal modeling also requires relatively large sample sizes. Thus, the types of research recommended by Botwinick and those investigators using causal modeling may require sample sizes that are difficult or uneconomical to obtain. While some researchers do not use these newer approaches due to considerations of power or logistics, others reject the use of large samples on philosophical and theoretical grounds, which will be described next.

## IDIOGRAPHIC RESEARCH

Perhaps the most direct assault on traditional, large sample research is seen in idiographic research. In cognitive aging research, this approach is seen in the field of problems solving. Giambra and Arenberg reviewed research in problem solving and aging [19]. They were greatly discouraged by a lack of systematic findings, and blamed much of the contradiction in the research literature on a "group-mean mentality" and experimental procedures that "produce informationally sparse output" [19, p. 259]. Giambra and Arenberg advocated the adoption of the "thinking-aloud" procedure [20] to the exclusion of more traditional approaches. They wrote "One of the ideas implicit in using the thinking-aloud procedure is that a successful theory must be able to predict what *an individual* (not group) will do (or can do) *at any point* in a problem" [20, p. 258]. It should be noted that this approach yields a huge amount of data for a small number of individuals, the mirror image of traditional large sample research.

Interestingly, Giambra and Arenberg also advocated studying each individual over many problems. In this respect, they are similar in thinking to the approach taken by Lachman et al. [11] and Niederehe [17]. A similar parallel is seen in the method that Giambra and Arenberg advocated for dealing with generalization of results, which would " ... be determined by replication by other experimenters studying the problem on their small number of individuals" [19, p. 258].

## THE P-TECHNIQUE

Nesselroade discusses a possible compromise between the focus on the individual and the use of multivariate statistics, the P-technique [21–23]. The P-technique is a replicated, multivariate single-subject design. It involves assessment with multiple variables at each of many times of measurement. Nesselroade states that this technique "emphasizes the individual and the thorough study of intraindividual change as a preliminary step to the development of nomothetic relationships"[22, pp. 274–275]. As is the case with other single-subject designs, generalization of results is accomplished through replication of results across other single-subject studies [21].

While this type of design initially involved a factor analysis of data generated by the P-technique, such data can also be analyzed using multivariate time series analysis. Either exploratory or confirmatory factor analysis can be used with such data, and these analyses can also incorporate temporal lag relationships of varying intervals [23].

It might be argued that the same sampling problems face these lines of research as in more traditional studies. How representative are the small-*N* samples being used in idiographic or P-technique research? How are such samples recruited? Still, small-*N* designs (especially idiographic research) represent a shift in belief, a shift which assumes that it is best to sample a large number of behaviors from a small number of individuals rather than the reverse. Rather than being competing approaches to research, perhaps it would be best to view small-*N* techniques as complementary to large-*N* research. In this regard, hypotheses generated by large-*N* research can be verified at the level of the individual across time and settings using small-*N* designs. Hypotheses generated by small-*N* research can be tested for generalizability across individuals and for "normativeness" by the use of large-*N* techniques.

## CONCLUSION

This chapter has documented the sampling and recruiting procedures that researchers in cognitive aging are using. We also have discussed some of the ways that sampling and recruiting practices might affect research outcomes and conclusions. A variety of sampling/recruiting methods are used by gerontological researchers. Though this is a cause of concern if our discipline wishes to establish a reliable data base, there is little support among researchers for standardizing procedures when recruiting subjects in cognitive aging research. Given both the need to deal with sampling issues and the perceived need to allow for diversity in sampling and recruitment practices, researchers are attempting to address these problems with new methodologies that focus on greater knowledge of individual difference variables or broader task interrelationships in specific population subgroups. Along with traditional designs, these new approaches should glean more evidence about the impact of aging, *per se,* on cognition.

## APPENDIX I
## The National Survey Form

### SURVEY: RECRUITMENT/SAMPLING TECHNIQUES IN GERONTOLOGICAL RESEARCH

from the MENTAL PERFORMANCE AND AGING LABORATORY, VA OUTPATIENT CLINIC, BOSTON

In filling out this survey, please be accurate and thorough. It should take about 15–20 minutes to complete the survey. Many questions ask you to indicate the proportion of your studies that use particular recruiting practices. In each case, we have asked you to circle *ALL MOST HALF SOME NONE* to indicate how many of your aging studies have used these methods. If you have not conducted any research in the last few years, but you would like to obtain the survey results, record your name and address on the last page, and return the survey to Cameron Camp. If any specific question does not apply to you (e.g., some questions regarding recruiting practices with middle-aged persons will not apply if you never recruit middle-aged persons), just write "NOT APPLICABLE" next to the question and go on to the next question.

Thank you very much

1. Approximately *how many subjects* are involved in your aging studies in the course of one year? (Please write in the numbers)

   Young ____________________
   Middle-aged ____________________
   Old ____________________

2. In how many of your aging studies do you use the following *groups*? (Circle one response on each line)

| | NUMBER OF STUDIES | | | | |
|---|---|---|---|---|---|
| Young, Middle-Aged, Old | ALL | MOST | HALF | SOME | NONE |
| Young & Old Only | ALL | MOST | HALF | SOME | NONE |
| Middle-Aged & Old Only | ALL | MOST | HALF | SOME | NONE |
| Old Only | ALL | MOST | HALF | SOME | NONE |

3. Define the typical *age range* that you use for research on aging. (Please write in the numbers)

   Young typical age range is ____________________
   Middle-Aged typical age range is ____________________
   Old typical age range is ____________________

4. Define the typical *education range* that you use for research on aging. (Please write in the numbers)

   Young typical education range is ____________________
   Middle-Aged typical education range is ____________________
   Old typical education range is ____________________

5. Approximately how many *different studies* do you conduct each year?

   Indicate the number ____________________

6. A) Where do you recruit your *young* subjects? (Circle one response on each line)

| | NUMBER OF STUDIES | | | | |
|---|---|---|---|---|---|
| Psychology Introductory Classes | ALL | MOST | HALF | SOME | NONE |
| Psychology Students | ALL | MOST | HALF | SOME | NONE |
| General College Students | ALL | MOST | HALF | SOME | NONE |
| Newspaper, Announcements | ALL | MOST | HALF | SOME | NONE |
| Clubs, Churches, Community Centers | ALL | MOST | HALF | SOME | NONE |
| Friends, Relatives | ALL | MOST | HALF | SOME | NONE |
| Other: (1) ____________ | ALL | MOST | HALF | SOME | NONE |
| (2) ____________ | ALL | MOST | HALF | SOME | NONE |

B) Where do you recruit your *middle-aged* subjects? (Circle one response on each line)

| | NUMBER OF STUDIES | | | | |
|---|---|---|---|---|---|
| Hospitals | ALL | MOST | HALF | SOME | NONE |
| College Students Recruit Them | ALL | MOST | HALF | SOME | NONE |
| Newspaper, Announcements | ALL | MOST | HALF | SOME | NONE |
| Clubs, Churches, Community Centers | ALL | MOST | HALF | SOME | NONE |
| Friends, Relatives | ALL | MOST | HALF | SOME | NONE |
| University Alumni | ALL | MOST | HALF | SOME | NONE |
| Other: (1) __________ | ALL | MOST | HALF | SOME | NONE |
| (2) __________ | ALL | MOST | HALF | SOME | NONE |

C) Where do you recruit your *old* subjects? (Circle one response on each line)

| | NUMBER OF STUDIES | | | | |
|---|---|---|---|---|---|
| Nursing Homes | ALL | MOST | HALF | SOME | NONE |
| Hospitals | ALL | MOST | HALF | SOME | NONE |
| College Students Recruit Them | ALL | MOST | HALF | SOME | NONE |
| Newspaper, Announcements | ALL | MOST | HALF | SOME | NONE |
| Clubs, Churches, Community Centers | ALL | MOST | HALF | SOME | NONE |
| Friends, Relatives | ALL | MOST | HALF | SOME | NONE |
| University Alumni | ALL | MOST | HALF | SOME | NONE |
| Apartment Buildings For Older Adults | ALL | MOST | HALF | SOME | NONE |
| Other: (1) __________ | ALL | MOST | HALF | SOME | NONE |
| (2) __________ | ALL | MOST | HALF | SOME | NONE |

7. A) Approximately what percentage of your subjects take part in *more than one study* in a single day?

   Indicate the percentage ________________

   B) *How many hours* do you typically employ your subjects in a single day? (Please write in the number of hours)

   Number of hours in a single study in one day ____________
   Number of hours in multiple studies in one day ____________

8. A) Please indicate the number of your studies in which you *pay subjects*. (Circle one response)

| | | | | | |
|---|---|---|---|---|---|
| Number of studies with paid subjects | ALL | MOST | HALF | SOME | NONE |

B) How much do you typically pay your *young* subjects? (Circle one response on each line)

| | NUMBER OF STUDIES | | | | |
|---|---|---|---|---|---|
| Course Credit Only | ALL | MOST | HALF | SOME | NONE |
| Money (Typically $____/hr) | ALL | MOST | HALF | SOME | NONE |
| Transportation Costs | ALL | MOST | HALF | SOME | NONE |
| No Payment, All Volunteers | ALL | MOST | HALF | SOME | NONE |
| Other Inducement: ________ ______________ | ALL | MOST | HALF | SOME | NONE |

C) How much do you typically pay your *middle-aged* subjects? (Circle one response on each line)

| | NUMBER OF STUDIES | | | | |
|---|---|---|---|---|---|
| Money (Typically $____/hr) | ALL | MOST | HALF | SOME | NONE |
| Transportation Costs | ALL | MOST | HALF | SOME | NONE |
| No Payment, All Volunteers | ALL | MOST | HALF | SOME | NONE |
| Other Inducement: ________ ______________ | ALL | MOST | HALF | SOME | NONE |

D) How much do you typically pay your *old* subjects? (Circle one response on each line)

| | NUMBER OF STUDIES | | | | |
|---|---|---|---|---|---|
| Money (Typically $____/hr) | ALL | MOST | HALF | SOME | NONE |
| Transportation Costs | ALL | MOST | HALF | SOME | NONE |
| No Payment, All Volunteers | ALL | MOST | HALF | SOME | NONE |
| Other Inducement: ________ ______________ | ALL | MOST | HALF | SOME | NONE |

E) Do you pay subjects from *different age groups* the same amount for participating in the same study? (Circle one response)

YES NO

9. Rank order the following recruitment methods based on refusal rates (that is, the number of refusals to participate divided by the number of persons contacted). A *rank of "1"* should be given to the recruiting method which leads to the *highest* rate of refusal. Rank only those methods which you have used in at least some studies. (Please rank the recruiting methods—*"1" is for a high refusal rate*)

A) Rank these recruiting methods according to refusal rates for *young* subjects:

Psychology Introductory Classes ________
Psychology Students ________
General College Students ________
Newspaper, Announcements ________
Clubs, Churches, Community Centers ________
Friends, Relatives ________
Other (1) ____________________ ________
Other (2) ____________________ ________

B) Rank these recruiting methods according to refusal rates for *middle-aged* subjects:

Hospitals ________
College Students Recruit Them ________
Newspaper, Announcements ________
Clubs, Churches, Community Centers ________
Friends, Relatives ________
University Alumni ________
Other (1) ____________________ ________
Other (2) ____________________ ________

C) Rank these recruiting methods according to refusal rates for *old* subjects:

Nursing Homes ________
Hospitals ________
College Students Recruit Them ________
Apartment Buildings For Older Adults ________
Newspaper, Announcements ________
Clubs, Churches, Community Centers ________
Friends, Relatives ________
University Alumni ________
Other (1) ____________________ ________
Other (2) ____________________ ________

10. A) If you *randomly select* subjects from some population group, what concomitant variables (e.g., education, verbal IQ, health, etc.) do you typically measure in your subjects?

PLEASE WRITE YOUR ANSWER BELOW, IF ADDITIONAL SPACE IS NEEDED USE THE BACK

B) If you do not sample randomly for subjects, what concomitant variables do you use to select your subjects?

PLEASE WRITE YOUR ANSWER BELOW, IF ADDITIONAL SPACE IS NEEDED USE THE BACK

11. Do you think that there should be some *standardized* recruitment/sampling practices required for journal publications? Why or why not?

PLEASE WRITE YOUR ANSWER BELOW, IF ADDITIONAL SPACE IS NEEDED USE THE BACK

12. It is our intent *to collect and to share* with our respondents both published and unpublished data on the effects of recruitment practices (paid subjects vs. volunteers, refusal rates, etc.) or the effects of concomitant variables (sex distribution, verbal IQ, health, education, etc.) on cognitive performances and aging. We would appreciate it if you could share with us any published or unpublished data and theoretical papers *you know* in this domain. We wish to identify papers that focus on these issues as well as papers that have incidental references to recruitment-related subject differences. *The references below are examples.*

| *Evidence Provided by the Article* | *Reference* |
|---|---|
| Volunteers vs. paid subjects | Lachman, R., Lachman, J. L., & Taylor, D. W. Reallocation of mental resources over the productive life span: Assumptions and task analyses. In F. I. M. Craik & S. Trehub (Eds.) *Aging and cognitive processes*, NY: Plenum Press, 1982 |
| WAIS vocabulary scores and memory performance | Bowles, N. W. & Poon, L. W. An analysis of the effects of aging on recognition memory. *Journal of Gerontology*, 1982, *37*, 212-219. |
| Theoretical paper | Browning, G. B. & Spilich, G. J. Some important methodological issues in the study of aging and cognition. *Experimental Aging Research*, 1981, *7*, 175-188. |

PLEASE WRITE YOUR REFERENCES HERE. IF ADDITIONAL SPACE IS NEEDED USE THE BACK OR ENCLOSE A SEPARATE PAGE

Please provide the following information so that we may share the data with you.

Name ____________________________________________

Address __________________________________________

Telephone Number __________________________________

Please describe any of your other concerns about the samping/recruiting practices of gerontologists:

*Thank you very much* for this information. It should help us understand more clearly the consequences of our sampling/recruiting practices as gerontologists. If any data concerning recruiting practices in your laboratory can be obtained from someone other than yourself, please make an additional copy of this questionnaire for that individual to complete. Please *send this survey* WITHIN ONE WEEK to the address below:

Dr. Cameron J. Camp
Dept. of Psychology
Fort Hayes State University
Hays, Kansas 67601

If you have any *unpublished data* that are not readily available, that are relevant to the information we are requesting, please send this at your earliest convenience to this address:

Dr. Robin L. West
Dept. of Psychology
Memphis State University
Memphis, TN 38152

## REFERENCES

1. W. J. Hoyer, C. L. Raskind, and J. P. Abrams, Research Practices in the Psychology of Aging: A Survey of Research Published in the *Journal of Gerontology*, 1975–1982, *Journal of Gerontology 39,* pp. 44–48, 1984.
2. L. W. Poon, I. K. Krauss, and N. J. Bowles, On Subject Selection in Cognitive Research, *Experimental Aging Research, 10*, pp. 43-50, 1984.
3. K. W. Schaie, A General Model for the Study of Developmental Problems, *Psychological Bulletin, 64*, pp. 92–107, 1965.
4. T. A. Salthouse, *Adult Cognition*, Springer-Verlag, New York, 1982.
5. C. J. Camp, R. P. Markley, and J. Danielson, Necker Cube Reversals in Young, Middle-Aged, and Elderly Females, *Perceptual and Motor Skills, 54*, 1215–1218, 1982.
6. H. A. Heath and J. Orbach, Reversibility of the Necker Cube: IV. Responses of Elderly People, *Perceptual and Motor Skills, 17,* pp. 625–626, 1963.
7. G. Winocur and M. Moscovitch, Paired-Associate Learning in Institutionalized Old People: An Analysis of Interference and Context Effects, *Journal of Gerontology, 38*, 455–464, 1983.
8. K. W. Schaie, Cross-Sectional Methods in the Study of Psychological Aspects of Aging, *Journal of Gerontology, 14*, pp. 208–215, 1959.
9. K. Gribbin and K. W. Schaie, Monetary Incentive, Age, and Cognition, *Experimental Aging Research, 2*, pp. 461–468, 1976.
10. M. Todd, K. E. Davis, and T. P. Cafferty, Who Volunteers for Adult Development Research?: Research Findings and Practical Steps to Reach Low Volunteering Groups, *International Journal of Aging and Human Development, 18*, pp. 177–184, 1984.
11. R. Lachman, J. L. Lachman, and D. W. Taylor, Reallocation of Mental Resources Over the Productive Lifespan, in *Aging and Cognitive Processes*, F. I. M. Craik and S. Trehum (Eds.), Plenum Press, New York, NY, 1982.
12. R. Schleser, R. L. West, and L. K. Boatwright, A Comparison of Recruiting Strategies for Increasing Older Adults' Initial Entry and Compliance in a Memory Training Program, *International Journal of Aging and Human Development, 24*, pp. 55–66, 1986–87.
13. M. Gentry and A. D. Shulman, Survey of Sampling Techniques in Widowhood Research, 1973–1983, *Journal of Gerontology, 40*, pp. 641–643, 1985.
14. P. B. Baltes, Life-Span Developmental Psychology: Some Converging Observations on History and Theory, in *Life-Span Development and Behavior*, P. B. Baltes and O. G. Brim (Eds.), Academic Press, New York, Vol. 2, pp. 256–279, 1979.
15. R. Bornstein and M. T. Smircina, The Status of the Empirical Support for the Hypothesis of Increased Variability in Aging Populations, *The Gerontologist, 22*, pp. 258–260, 1982.
16. D. H. Kausler, *Experimental Psychology and Human Aging*, Wiley, New York, NY, 1982.
17. G. Niederehe, Depression and Memory Impairment in the Aged, in *Clinical Memory Assessment in the Aged,* L. Poon (Ed.), American Psychological Assoc., Washington, DC, 1987.
18. J. Botwinick, *Aging and Behavior*, 3rd Ed., Springer, New York, NY, 1984.
19. L. M. Giambra and D. Arenberg, Problem Solving, Concept Learning, and Aging, in *Aging in the 1980's*, L. Poon (Ed.), APA, Washington, DC, 1980.

20. H. A. Simon, Information-Processing Models of Cognition, *Annual Review of Psychology, 30*, 363-396, 1979.
21. M. A. Lebo and J. R. Nesselroade, Intraindividual Differences in Dimensions of Mood Change During Pregnancy Identified in Five P-Technique Factor Analyses, *Journal of Research in Personality, 12*, pp. 205–224, 1978.
22. J. R. Nesselroade, Concepts of Intraindividual Variability and Change: Impressions of Cattell's Influence on Lifespan Development Psychology, *Multivariate Behavioral Research, 19*, pp. 269-286, 1984.
23. J. R. Nesselroade and D. H. Ford, P-Technique Comes of Age, *Research on Aging, 7*, pp. 46–80, 1985.

## BIBLIOGRAPHY

## (Research Dealing with Recruitment Practices)

Abrahams, J. P., Health Status as a Variable in Aging Research, *Experimental Aging Research, 2*, pp. 63–71, 1976.

__________ Psychological Correlates of Cardiovascular Diseases, in Special Review of *Experimental Aging Research: Progress in Biology*, M. F. Elias, B. E. Eleftheriou, and P. K. Elias (Eds.), EAR, Inc., Bar Harbor, ME, pp. 330-350, 1976.

Abrahams, J. P., Hoyer, W. J., Elias, M. F., and Bradigan, B., Gerontological Research in Psychology Published in the *Journal of Gerontology* 1963–74: Perspectives and Progress, *Journal of Gerontology, 30*, pp. 668-673, 1975.

Alpaugh, P. K., and Birren, J. E., Are There Sex Differences in Creativity Across the Adult Life Span? *Human Development, 18*, pp. 461–465, 1975.

__________ Variables Affecting Creative Contributions Across the Adult Life Span, *Human Development, 20*, pp. 240–248, 1977.

Amster, L. E., and Krauss, H. H., The Relationship Between Life Crises and Mental Deterioration in Old Age, *International Journal of Aging and Human Development, 5*, pp. 51–55, 1974.

Anderson, J. W., Activities and Interests of Participants in the Scripps College Adult Development Project 1979–1980 (Tech. Rep. No. ADP82-01), Scripps College Adult Development Project, Claremont, CA, 1982.

Arbit, J., and Zagar, R., The Effects of Age and Sex on the Factor Structure of the Wechsler Memory Scale, *Journal of Psychology, 102*, pp. 185–190, 1979.

P. B. Baltes, Longitudinal and Cross-Sectional Sequences in the Study of Age and Generation Effect, *Human Development, 11*, pp. 145–171, 1968.

Botwinick, J., and Storandt, M., Speed Functions, Vocabulary Ability, and Age, *Perceptual and Motor Skills, 36*, pp. 1123–1128, 1973.

Botwinick, J., and Storandt, M., Recall and Recognition of Old Information in Relation to Age and Sex, *Journal of Gerontology, 35*, pp. 70–76, 1980.

Bowles, N. W., and Poon, L. W., An Analysis of the Effects of Aging on Recognition Memory, *Journal of Gerontology, 37*, pp. 212–219, 1982.

Browning, G. B., and Spilich, G. J., Some Important Methodological Issues in the Study of Aging and Cognition, *Experimental Aging Research, 7*, pp. 175–187, 1981.

Cavanaugh, J. C., Comprehension and Retention of Television Programs by 20- and 60-Year Olds, *Journal of Gerontology, 38*, 190–196, 1983.

Cohen, D., Schaie, K. W., and Gribbin, K., The Organization of Spatial Abilities in Older Men and Women, *Journal of Gerontology, 32*, pp. 578-585, 1977.

Dean, L. L., Teresi, J. A., and Wilder, D. E., The Human Element in Survey Research, *International Journal of Aging and Human Development, 8*, pp. 83-92, 1977.

Denney, N. W., Pearce, K. A., and Palmer, A. M., A Developmental Study of Adults' Performance on Traditional and Practical Problem-Solving Tasks, *Experimental Aging Research, 8*, pp. 115-118, 1982.

Elias, J. W., Winn, F. J., Jr., and Wright, L. L., Age, Sex, and Hemisphere Asymmetry Differences Induced by a Concurrent Memory Processing Task, *Experimental Aging Research, 5*, pp. 217-237, 1979.

Elias, M. F., and Kinsbourne, M., Age and Sex Differences in the Process of Verbal and Nonverbal Stimuli, *Journal of Gerontology, 29*, pp. 162-171, 1974.

Elsayed, M., Ismail, A. H., and Young, R. J., Intellectual Differences of Adult Men Related to Age and Physical Fitness Before and After an Exercise Program, *Journal of Gerontology, 35*, pp. 383-387, 1980.

Fullerton, A. M., Age Differences in the Use of Imagery in Integrating New and Old Information in Memory, *Journal of Gerontology, 38*, pp. 326-332, 1983.

Gardner, E. F., and Monge, R. H., Adult Age Differences in Cognitive Abilities and Educational Background, *Experimental Aging Research, 3*, pp. 337-338, 1977.

Gonda, J., Quayhagen, M., and Schaie, K. W., Education, Task Meaningfulness, and Cognitive Performance in Young-Old and Old-Old Adults, *Educational Gerontology, 7*, pp. 151-158, 1981.

Gordon, S. K., and Clark, W. C., Application of Signal Detection Theory to Prose Recall and Recognition in Elderly and Young Adults, *Journal of Gerontology, 29*, pp. 64-72, 1974.

Gribbin, K., Schaie, K. W., and Parham, J. A., Complexity of Lifestyle and Maintenance of Intellectual Abilities, *Journal of Social Issues, 36*, pp. 47-61, 1980.

Hamsher, K. S., and Benton, A. L., Interactive Effects of Age and Cerebral Disease on Cognitive Performances, *Journal of Neurology, 217*, pp. 195-200, 1978.

Hartley, J. T., Harker, J. O., and Walsh, D. A., Contemporary Issues and New Directions in Adult Development of Learning and Memory, in *Aging in the 1980s*, L. W. Poon (Ed.), American Psychological Association, Washington, DC, 1980.

Hayslip, B., Jr., and Sterns, H. L., Age Differences in Relationships Between Crystallized and Fluid Intelligences and Problem Solving, *Journal of Gerontology, 34*, pp. 404-414, 1979.

Herman, J. F., and Bruce, P. R., Adults' Mental Rotation of Spatial Information: Effects of Age, Sex and Cerebral Laterality, *Experimental Aging Research, 9*, pp. 83-85, 1983.

Hertzog, C., Schaie, K. W., and Gribbin, K., Cardiovascular Disease and Changes in Intellectual Functioning from Middle to Old Age, *Journal of Gerontology, 33*, pp. 872-883, 1978.

Heyn, J. E., Barry, J. R., and Pollack, R. H., Problem-Solving as a Function of Age, Sex, and the Role Apprupriateness of the Problem Content, *Experimental Aging Research, 5*, pp. 505-519, 1978.

Hultsch, D. F., Adult Age Differences in the Organization of Free Recall, *Developmental Psychology, 1*, pp. 673-678, 1969.

Hultsch, D. F., and Dixon, R. A., Memory for Text Materials in Adulthood, in *Life-*

*Span Development and Behavior*, P. B. Baltes and O. G. Brim (Eds.), Academic Press, New York, Vol. 6, pp. 77–108, 1984.

Hultsch, D. F., Nesselroade, J. R., and Plemons, J. K., Learning-Ability Relations in Adulthood, *Human Development, 19*, pp. 234–247, 1976.

Jansen, D. G., and Hoffmann, H., The Influence of Age, Intelligence and Educational Level on Shipley-Hartford Conceptual Quotients of State Hospital Alcoholics, *Journal of Clinical Psychology, 29*, pp. 468–470, 1973.

Kline, D. W., Culler, M. P., and Sucec, J., Difference in Unconspicuous Word Identification as a Function of Age and Reversible-Figure Training, *Experimental Aging Research, 3*, pp. 203–213, 1977.

Kline, D. W., Schieber, F., Abusamra, L. C., and Coyne, A. C., Age, the Eye, and the Visual Channels: Contrast Sensitivity and Response Speed, *Journal of Gerontology, 38*, pp. 211–216, 1983.

Kogan, N., Categorizing and Conceptualizing Styles in Younger and Older Adults, *Human Development, 17*, pp. 218–230, 1974.

Krauss, I., Poon, L. W., Gilewski, M., and Schaie, K. W., Effects of Biased Sampling on Cognitive Performances, Paper presented at the Meeting of the Gerontological Society of America, Boston, November 1982.

Labouvie-Vief, G., and Gonda, J. N., Cognitive Strategy Training and Intellectual Performance in the Elderly, *Journal of Gerontology, 31*, pp. 327–332, 1976.

Mackie, J. B., and Beck, E. C., Relations Among Age, Intelligence, and Critical Flicker Fusion, *Perceptual and Motor Skills, 21*, pp. 875–878, 1965.

Meyer, B. J. F., and Rice, G. E., Information Recalled from Prose by Young, Middle, and Old Adult Readers, *Experimental Aging Research, 7*, pp. 253–268, 1981.

Mohs, R. C., Davis, K. L., and Darley, C., Cholinergic Drug Effects on Memory and Cognition in Humans, in *Aging in the 1980s*, L. W. Poon (Ed.), American Psychological Association, Washington, DC, pp. 181–190, 1980.

Nehrke, M. F., Age and Sex Differences in Discrimination Learning and Transfer of Training, *Journal of Gerontology, 28*, pp. 320–327, 1973.

Obler, L. K., "Sex" Differences in Aging: The Experimental Literature in Psychology, *Resources for Feminist Research/Documentations sur la Recherche Feministe, 11*, pp. 209–211, 1982.

Pelham, A. O., and Clark, W. F., Close Encounters of the Word Kind: Interviewing Challenges of the California Senior Survey, Paper presented at the Meeting of the Western Gerontological Society, Albuquerque, April 1983.

Pentz III, C. A., Elias, M. F., Wood, W. G., Schultz, N. A., and Dineen, J., Relationship of Age and Hypertension to Neuropsychological Test Performance, *Experimental Aging Research, 5*, pp. 351–372, 1979.

Perlmutter, M., Metzger, R., Miller, K., and Nezworski, T., Memory of Historical Events, *Experimental Aging Research, 6*, 47–60, 1980.

Poitrenaud, J., Hazemann, P., and Lillie, F., Spontaneous Variations in Level of Arousal Among Aged Individuals. Correlations with Functional Abilities and Mental Performances, *Gerontology, 24*, pp. 241–249, 1978.

Poon, L. W., Differences in Human Memory with Aging: Nature, Causes and Clinical Implications, in *Handbook of the Psychology of Aging*, J. E. Birren and K. W. Schaie (Eds.), Van Nostrand, New York, 2nd Ed., pp. 427–462, 1985.

Poon, L. W., and Fozard, J. L., Speed of Retrieval from Long-Term Memory in Relation to Age, Familiarity and Datedness of Information, *Journal of Gerontology, 33*, pp. 711–717, 1978.

Poon, L. W., and Fozard, J. L., Age and Word Frequency Effects in Continuous Recognition Memory, *Journal of Gerontology, 35,* pp. 77–86, 1980.

Poon, L. W., and Schaffer, G., Prospective Memory in Young and Elderly Adults, Paper presented at the Meeting of the American Psychological Association, Washington, DC, September, 1982.

Poon, L. W., and Walsh-Sweeney, L., Effects of Bizarre and Interacting Imagery on Learning and Retrieval of the Aged, *Experimental Aging Research, 7*, pp. 65–70, 1981.

Poon, L. W., Walsh-Sweeney, L., and Fozard, J. L., Memory Skill Training for the Elderly: Salient Issues on the Use of Imagery Mnemonics, in *New Directions in Memory and Aging: Proceedings of the George A. Talland Memorial Conference*, L. W. Poon, J. L. Fozad, L. S. Cermak, D. Arenberg, and L. W. Thompson (Eds.), Erlbaum, Hillsdale, NJ, 1980.

Powell, R. R., and Pohndorf, R. H., Comparison of Adult Exercisers and Nonexercisers on Fluid Intelligence and Selected Physiological Variables, *Research Quarterly of the American Association of Health and Physical Education, 42*, pp. 70–77, 1971.

Rice, G. E., and Meyer, B. J. F., Prose Recall: Effects of Aging, Verbal Ability and Reading Behavior, Paper presented at the Meeting of the American Psychological Association, Anaheim, CA, August 1983.

Robertson-Tchabo, E. A., Hausman, C. P., and Arenberg, D., A Classical Mnemonic for Older Learners: A Trip That Works, *Educational Gerontology, 1*, pp. 215–226, 1976.

Rosenthal, R., and Rosnow, R. L., *The Volunteer Subject*, John Wiley, New York, 1975.

Schaffer, G., and Poon, L. W., The Individual Variability in Memory Training with the Elderly, *Journal of Gerontology, 8*, pp. 217–229, 1982.

Schaie, K. W., Methodological Problems in Descriptive Developmental Research on Adulthood and Aging, in *Life-Span Developmental Psychology: Methodological Issues*, J. R. Nesselroade and H. W. Reese (Eds.), Academic Press, New York, pp. 253–280, 1973.

__________, External Validity in the Assessment of Intellectual Development in Adulthood, *Journal of Gerontology, 33*, pp. 695–701, 1978.

__________, The Primary Mental Abilities in Adulthood: An Exploration in the Development of Psychometric Intelligence. in *Life-Span Development and Behavior*, P. B. Baltes and O. G. Brim (Eds.), Academic Press, New York, Vol. 2, pp. 68–115, 1979.

Schultz, N. R., Dineen, J. T., Elias, M. F., Pentz III, C. A., and Wood, W. G., WAIS Performance for Different Age Groups of Hypertensive and Control Subjects During the Administration of a Diuretic, *Journal of Gerontology, 34*, pp. 246–253, 1979.

Simonson, E., Performance as a Function of Age and Cardiovascular Disease, in *Behavior, Aging, and the Nervous System*, A. T. Welford and J. E. Birren (Eds.), Charles C. Thomas, Springfield, IL, 1965.

Stern, J. A., and Baldinger, A. C., Hemispheric Differences in Preferred Modes of Information Processing and the Aging Process, *International Journal of Neuroscience, 18*, pp. 97–105, 1983.

Storandt, M., Grant, E. A., and Gordon, B. C., Remote Memory as a Function of Age and Sex, *Experimental Aging Research, 4,* pp. 365–375, 1978.

Taub, H. A., and Baker, M. T., The Effect of Repeated Testing Upon Comprehension of Informed Consent Materials by Elderly Volunteers, *Experimental Aging Research, 9,* pp. 135–138, 1983.

Thompson, L. W., Testing and Mnemonic Strategies, in *New Directions in Memory and Aging: Proceedings of the George A. Talland Memorial Conference*, L. W. Poon, J. L. Fozad, L. S. Cermak, D. Arenberg, and L. W. Thompson (Eds.), Erlbaum, Hillsdale, NJ, 1980.

Vitaliano, P. P., Breen, A. R., Albert, M. S., Russo, J., and Prinz P. N., Memory, Attention, and Functional Status in Community-Residing Alzheimer Type Dementia Patients and Optimally Healthy Aged Individuals, *Journal of Gerontology, 39*, pp. 58–64, 1984.

Wilkie, FL. L., Eisdorfer, C., and Nowlin, J. B., Memory and Blood Pressure in the Aged, *Experimental Aging Research, 2*, pp. 3–16, 1976.

Zarit, S. H., Cole, K. D., and Guider, R. L., Memory Training Strategies and Subjective Complaints of Memory in the Aged, *The Gerontologist, 21*, pp. 158–164, 1981.

# PART TWO
# Longitudinal Research

The second part of this book turns to the primary research method that is indigenous to human development, the longitudinal study. It has elicited major attention among researchers in lifespan development as well as those in gerontology. Major conceptual and statistical advances have been achieved and are still being made (see, for example, the collection of invaluable methodological papers featuring new statistical methods edited by Schaie [1]).

The chapters in Part Two are intended to complement such work by assisting the researcher in the actual planning and managing of longitudinal research. Once more, the utility and the "how-to" approach are featured. As the chapters in Part Two are read, it is worthwhile to recall that other comments on longitudinal research issues have been made by some of the authors in Part One. It will be recalled that Liang and Lawrence, for example, addressed attention to the existence of excellent longitudinal data bases. They also made the excellent suggestion that an existing data base may form the baseline for designing a longitudinal followup. Carp offered a number of very practical suggestions for keeping in touch with and maximizing the cooperation of subjects who are to be studied longitudinally. Palmore noted that some health records are by their nature longitudinal and may under some conditions substitute effectively for much more painstaking face-to-face longitudinal data gathering.

## REFERENCE

1. K. W. Schaie, *Methodological Issues in Aging Research*, Springer Publishing Company, New York, in press.

# SECTION 1
# Longitudinal Panel Maintenance and Subject Attrition

This theme is continued in Section 1 of Part Two. First is an extended case history of the successful nurturing of a panel of extremely difficult-to-recruit subject families by Reisberg, Ferris, Steinberg, Shulman, de Leon and Sinaiko. The past decade has seen the emergence of the study of Alzheimers disease as one of the major research priorities. Both in the past and presently such people have been much more easily recruited and studied in institutions than those still living in the community. Thus, our knowledge has been biased by its source in subjects who exhibit all the consequences of institutional care, such as being in a later stage of the disease than community residents and their overrepresentation of the background characteristics associated with a propensity toward institutionalization, such as very old age, physical illness, and especially socially isolating characteristics like widowhood, absence of children, and so on. By the best epidemiological knowledge now available, it is likely that no more than half of all dementia diagnosed people live in institutions. It is of great interest to know more about the characteristics and the lives of those who still live in the community and about the people giving care to Alzheimers patients. Especially important is the fact that the early stages of the development of Alzheimers disease and other organic conditions can be examined best by studying people in normal communities who are only just beginning to experience problems in their lives.

Reisberg and his research team have established a research center for dementia among community residents that has been successful in maintaining the cooperation of both impaired person and family members. This documentation of the efforts of a single such endeavor is full of specifics whose generality is well worth testing. Perhaps the most important overall conclusion is that there must be some reward for the entire family to motivate them to volunteer their time and energy for research. With most Alzheimer patients' participation depending on family assistance, Reisberg and his associates have shown that family members are hungry for information, not only regarding caregiving, but about the state of scientific knowledge regarding dementia, and that providing such information motivates them to remain in the study. Their motivation was even increased by diversifying the scientific goals of the research. While feedback to impaired participants is difficult to design, providing some means for making them more comfortable seems to enhance that willingness to participate. Impaired participants' experience of the research process may well be another area for future attention.

The long period over which Reisberg's subjects were studied necessitated providing more than information and feedback regarding the research. His project may be unique in organizing a set of supportive services for caregivers as an adjunct to the maintenance of the sample, but it is very likely that such efforts will be necessary for many future projects. Recalling Carp's chapter earlier, it is of interest to note how the Berkeley developmental research projects designed analogous programs for different aged groups many decades ago.

The Reisberg research group reports the outcomes of its follow-up attempts in enough detail to be very helpful to other research workers. It is not possible to always be so affirmative about recruitment attempts. A very useful report on the yield to efforts to recruit subjects for a first occasion study of pharmacological intervention is provided by Levy, Mohs, Rosen, and Davis (1); for each successfully completed subject, twelve had to be screened. While sobering in terms of its discouragingly low overall yield, the information from Levy's research is essential for the prospective researcher to have in mind as investigations of different types are planned.

One final thought on sample maintenance is related to Liang and Lawrence's point about longitudinal research as an unanticipated later stage of an originally conceived one occasion study. Such an opportunity may present itself as an afterthought to any investigator. Yet an address and phone list made at the time of original study can rapidly go out of date. At the very least, the investigator who has even a dim notion that a follow-up study might be of scientific interest should expend an additional, but very small, amount of energy in obtaining backup information that might be helpful should the researcher wish to contact the family later. The simplest type of information is the name and address of another person (not necessarily a local person) who might be most likely to be aware of the whereabouts of the subject. Preferably this should be a person judged likely to maintain a stable residence, or several such names might be requested.

The second chapter in this section by Sharma, Tobin, and Brant, deals with attrition issues in longitudinal research. This chapter presents a review of some of the earlier research on this question. Attrition has clearly received considerable earlier attention, but the focus in much of that research has been methodological or substantive. That is, much attention has been given to understanding how selective attribution modifies the conclusions that one may draw from data obtained from survivors only. (Further discussion of some substantive issues in attrition is provided by Lebowitz in Chapter 13.) The present chapter, by contrast, is concerned with factors that help or hinder the retention of the expensively recruited subjects for later longitudinal investigations. They contribute totally new knowledge in demonstrating that two neglected factors are likely to be associated with a subject's dropping out of a study: Greater distance from the research site and, for those recruited by another study subject, the dropping out of the target subject's recruiter. In addition, certain other background characteristics were associated with dropping out while others were not.

The net result is that with this knowledge in hand, researchers will be better equipped to devote special effort to maintaining the cooperation and sense of involvement of people who are at risk of dropping out, for example, those whose health is notably impaired at the first occasion. It is an unquestionable fact that the most disabled are those likely to be missed in the original sample and selectively lost in follow-up waves, a systematic bias that may have major impact on the conclusions we draw. The mode of changing this potentially biasing effect is not, of course, to develop stronger modes of persuading sick people to comply. Rather, we need more work in developing a hierarchical series of techniques for getting as much information as possible without stretching the limits of the person's capacity to give information. Some possible techniques might include a nested set of questions or tests, where the most critical are done first and the others foregone if necessary. Much recent research is being given to the validity of proxy responses, including very ambitious pilot studies now under way by the National Center for Health Statistics in preparation for the planned 1988 National Health and Nutrition Examination Survey. While proxy responses are certain to introduce some error, the net gain as compared to the total loss of data may be substantial. Very little attention has been given to the pros and cons of choosing content areas for inquiry and modes of response that might allow a family member to elicit some responses from the impaired person.

The final chapter in this section consists of still another case study, this time on the Longitudinal Retirement History Survey (RHS) conducted by the Social Security Administration. This survey may well have been the largest multiple occasion research ever fielded, being approached only by the National Longitudinal Survey [2] and the Panel Study of Income Dynamics [3]. In their chapter Fox and Irelan focus on the concrete tasks that were required to organize, store, and make ready for analysis the enormous amounts of data generated by this five occasion study. Some of their experiences will be useful in the planning of new studies, for example, their discussion of the gains and losses associated with the decision to repeat a question verbatim at follow-up, versus improving the information gained by asking a better question. Furthermore, much of the discussion of data organization, coding, and decision tracking is applicable to the single occasion study. For example their way of documenting complex coding decisions is relevant to any interview based research. In general, their chapter contains many recommendations that should be extremely useful to the experienced researcher and result in savings of precious research effort.

## REFERENCES


1. M. I. Levy, R. C. Mohs, W. G. Rosen, and K. L. Davis, Research Subject Recruitment for Gerontological Studies of Pharmacological Agents, *Neurobiology of Aging, 3*, pp. 77–79, 1982.
2. H. S. Parnes, From the Middle to the Later Years, *Research on Aging, 3*, pp. 387–402, 1981.
3. J. N. Morgan, *Five Thousand American Families*, Vols. 1–9, Institute for Social Research, Ann Arbor, 1968–1983.

CHAPTER

# 8

# Longitudinal Study of Dementia Patients and Aged Controls: An Approach To Methodologic Issues[1]

*Barry Reisberg*
*Steven H. Ferris*
*Gertrude Steinberg*
*Emma Shulman*
*Mony J. de Leon*
*Elia Sinaiko*

## BACKGROUND

The Aging and Dementia Research Program (formerly the Geriatric Study and Treatment Program) of New York University Medical Center evaluates and treats geriatric patients with mild to severe symptoms of age-associated cognitive decline and degenerative dementia due to Alzheimer's disease and related conditions. The primary objective is to increase scientific and medical knowledge of Alzheimer's disease, normal aging, and related cognitive disorders of the aged.

For approximately ten years, obtaining subjects for this comprehensive, university-based research program was a continuous and expensive struggle. Advertisements were placed in the *New York Times* in order to obtain both initial and on-going patient populations for pharmacologic treatment trials. In the early years of the program there was little contact with the patients or their families once an eight- to sixteen-week pharmacologic treatment trial had been completed. If other pharmacologic treatments for which the subject might be a suitable

[1]This work has been supported in part by Grants AG03051 and AG01344 from the National Institute on Aging, and by Grants MH29590 and MH35976 from the National Institute of Mental Health.

candidate were being investigated, then the subject would be offered the opportunity to participate in such investigations. If not, then contact with subjects and their families was discontinued until such time as an appropriate pharmacologic program was available, making renewed participation possible.

Initially, a major complaint of patients and their family members was an absence of feedback regarding the results of our investigations. This dissatisfaction applied to feedback concerning the individual patient results, the overall study results, and the results of our investigations in general. There were many good reasons for our initial difficulty in satisfying our patients and their family members' needs. In the early years, we were uncertain as to what would constitute a meaningful response in an individual patient, and hence it was difficult to provide definitive information regarding drug response. Similarly, study results were frequently not available for one to three years after a subject had completed a drug trial. Mechanisms for communicating the results of our investigations had to be developed. Similarly, until relatively recently, there was little information on the boundaries between normal aging and degenerative dementia and on the course of Alzheimer's disease (AD). Consequently, it was difficult to share useful information with the patient.

Over the course of the first decade (1973-1983), our program evolved to the point where, although we evaluate approximately 300 new patients per year, we no longer have to advertise for patients. Furthermore, we have a three-month waiting list for our evaluation services and we refer literally hundreds of patients each year from all over the nation to local physicians and investigators for treatment and study. An outline of the mechanisms by which this remarkable transformation has envolved might be worthwhile before proceeding to an examination of the specific issues with regard to longitudinal subject follow-up procedures.

## 1. HUMAN SERVICES WHICH SUPPORTED THE EMOTIONAL NEEDS OF OUR PATIENTS AND THEIR FAMILIES HAD TO BE DEVELOPED

These human services are an absolute corollary to high quality pharmacologic research. One cannot simply give patients a drug and follow them at specified intervals for therapeutic effects and/or side effects. An active, successful research program must also offer, in a structured form, auxiliary emotional supportive services to mitigate the burden of the illness. These needs led us to develop three such auxiliary services for our patients and their families. None of these supportive services are funded through any mechanism. Nevertheless, we maintain them because it is clear that they are a corollary to humanistically based, top quality, medical research. In keeping with the humanistic goals of our entire effort, these services are all provided to the general community regardless of an individual's participation in any of our other programs.

*Counseling Services* — Our social workers and gerontologists provide information regarding such important aspects of the care of the Alzheimer's patient as: homemaking and home health aide services; strategies for patient management: third party reimbursement; decisions to institutionalize; decisions regarding handling the financial burden of AD; coping with the enormous emotional burden of the illness; and the medical and psychiatric issues directly and indirectly resulting from AD.

*Support Groups* — We provide supportive group services for both the spouses and the children of AD victims. As with all of our services, these are provided without charge to the patients or their families. The groups are open to family members irrespective of their participatory status in our program. The support groups are *continuous*. Hence, they provide an ongoing means of emotional support for family members as the patient's degenerative condition continues to evolve. We currently have six continuous support groups operating in our program. Many members have been participating for seven or more years. In many instances, members have chosen to participate even some years after the demise of their spouse.

The groups are directed by qualified gerontologists. Students and staff physicians also participate on an irregular basis.

*Cognitive Training* — In addition to participation in pharmacologic treatment trials, our patients and often their spouses as well have been offered the opportunity to participate in cognitive training programs under a psychologist's supervision. Interestingly, for the most part, we found our patients and their family members more oriented toward pharmacologic remediation than toward this form of psychologic treatment. Accordingly, this program was ultimately discontinued.

## 2. EDUCATIONAL SERVICES REGARDING THE ILLNESS AND OUR ROLE IN ITS DIAGNOSIS, TREATMENT AND CURE HAD TO BE DEVELOPED

When we began our research, Alzheimer's disease was a rare illness, obscure to physicians and unknown to the lay public. The latter did not always distinguish senile dementia from the general process of aging. Now, Alzheimer's disease has become a household word and the efforts of programs such as ours in learning about the illness have become well known. An enormous educational effort in which we have played a significant role lies between these two extremes.

A book was necessary which would describe the illness and what was known about the illness for both laymen and physicians alike. Since no such publication existed, one of us wrote and published such a volume [1]. The latter became a valuable resource for physicians and concerned family members. So rapidly did the field evolve that this text, which was initially described as "an outstanding and major neurologic text . . . that should be on the bookshelf of every clinician interested in geriatric medicine" [2] within two years was also available in paperback form as a resource primarily for laymen [3]. By this time (i.e. 1983), a much more weighty tome was necessary to satisfy physicians' appetite for increased knowledge regarding Alzheimer's disease [4]. The remarkable transformation in public and professional awareness between 1981 and 1983 had numerous facets and is worth examining in greater detail.

In 1981, an informational booklet became available from the National Institute on Aging describing Alzheimer's disease [5]. Also about the same time a guide was published describing the management of the Alzheimer's patient for laymen [6]. Concurrently national Alzheimer's societies were coalescing from a number of grass roots organizations of family members which had developed around research efforts in New York, Seattle, Minnesota, Montreal, Toronto, and elsewhere. Members of our program have supported these community groups with educational seminars. These seminars have been conducted by our professional staff for family groups in New York, Queens, Brooklyn, and Westchester counties in New York State, as well as for support groups in such diverse geographic areas as Stroudsburg, Pennsylvania; Los Angeles, California; and Venlo, in the Netherlands.

The national Alzheimer's society, (Alzheimers Disease and Related Disorders Association, ADRDA) was successful in having a week beginning in November 1982, declared National Alzheimer's Disease Awareness Week. This week represented a turning point in the study of Alzheimer's disease in that laymen became aware of the condition; for the first time they heard the name "Alzheimer's Disease." A ceremony was held at City Hall in New York, in 1982, on the occasion of a city declaration proclaiming "Alzheimer's Disease Awareness Week." The Aging and Dementia Research Program participated in this ceremony. Each of the local and network TV outlets had programs on the occasion of this week calling attention to the disease. Again the Aging and Dementia Research Program hosted several of these programs. In November 1982, the *New York Times* ran a brief story describing our work with the illness—the story was syndicated and appeared in numerous publications in North America and Europe [7].

The lay public was beginning to hear of Alzheimer's disease. We were approaching the point where we no longer had to advertise for patients in the local newspapers. However, laymen still did not understand the true nature and impact of the illness. That understanding came about through an article published in the *New York Times* by Marion Roach in January 1983 [8]. Marion and her sister have both been participants in our support groups. Their mother, the Alzheimer's victim, had been a patient in our programs.

Recognition of the illness has continued to proceed rapidly. Having learned the word Alzheimer's disease in November 1982—and the symptoms of the "incurable illness" in January 1983—laymen were ready in March 1983 to learn that efforts were underway to help remediate the disorder. The Secretary of Health and Human Services, Margaret Heckler, used the occasion of her first news conference to congratulate us on our work and to create a National Task Force on Alzheimer's Disease. In May 1983, we were called to testify before the United States Senate Subcommittee on Labor and Human Resources on the nature and magnitude of the problem and scientific advances in the understanding and treatment of the illness [9]. Simultaneously, New York State hearings on the topic were scheduled and a mayoral conference on the illness was planned. Alzheimer's disease had come out of the closet. We no longer had to advertise for patients. Our longitudinal subjects were more cooperative than ever before because they understood we were doing our part to solve their problem.

It is worth noting, in placing the above discussion in proper context, that other major longitudinal studies such as the Framingham Study and the Duke Study have received well deserved national attention. Such attention is undoubtedly positive in serving the study goals in that it emphasizes for participants the worthiness and importance of their ongoing cooperation.

The discussion above has focused on general educational efforts of our program. We have also developed specific educational tools for our study participants. An important example of these is our periodic "Study Participant Letter" describing our research gains and goals.

## 3. ASSESSMENT TECHNOLOGY HAD TO BE DEVELOPED AND REFINED

These procedures could then be wedded to prognostic and management counseling on the part of our physicians so as to improve informational transfer and hence increase satisfaction for our patients and their families.

Initially, a schema for portraying the global staging of the pathology of age-associated cognitive decline and progressive dementia of the Alzheimer's type was developed [10]. At the time we embarked upon our investigations, efforts dating back to the work of Prichard in the mid-nineteenth century had divided senile dementia into three broad clinical phases [11]. These efforts culminated in the descriptions of the 1980 *Diagnostic and Statistical Manual of the American Psychiatric Association*, known as the DSM III [12]. The manual described primary degenerative dementia (synonymous with Alzheimer's disease) as characterized by early stages in which "memory impairment may be the only apparent cognitive deficit. There may also be personality changes, such as the development of apathy, lack of spontaneity, and a quiet withdrawal from social interactions. Individuals usually remain neat and well-groomed and, aside from an occasional irritable outburst, are cooperative and behave in a socially appropriate way." The DSM III describes a middle stage of the disease in which "various cognitive disturbances become quite apparent, and behavior and personality are more obviously affected." It notes that "by the late stage, the individual may be completely mute and inattentive. At this point he or she is totally incapable of caring for himself or herself."

A measure was needed to describe the continuum of change in normal aging as well as primary degenerative dementia (Alzheimer's disease). The stages of Alzheimer's disease also had to be described in greater detail. We initially described three clinical phases of aging and dementia of the Alzheimer's type in somewhat greater detail than previously [13]. This work culminated in our development of the seven-stage Global Deterioration Scale (GDS) for age-associated cognitive decline and Alzheimer's disease which was published together with validating data in 1982 and which can be found in Table 1.

Table 1. Global Deterioration Scale (GDS) for Age-Associated Cognitive Decline and Primary Degenerative Dementia

| *GDS Stage* | *Clinical Phase* | *Clinical Characteristics* |
|---|---|---|
| 1. No cognitive decline | Normal | No subjective complaints of memory deficit evident. No memory deficit on clinical interview. |
| 2. Very mild cognitive decline | Forgetfulness | Subjective complaints of memory deficit, most frequently in following areas: (a) forgetting where one has placed familiar objects; (b) forgetting names one formerly knew well. No objective evidence of memory deficit on clinical interview. No objective deficits in employment or social situations. Appropriate concern with respect to symptomatology. |
| 3. Mild cognitive decline | Early confusional | Earliest clear-cut deficits. Manifestations in more than one of the following areas: (a) patient may have gotten lost when traveling to an unfamiliar location; (b) coworkers become aware of patient's relatively poor performance; (c) word and name finding deficit become evident to intimates; (d) patient may read a passage or a book and retain relatively little material; (e) patient may demonstrate decreased facility in remembering names upon introduction to new people (f) patient may have lost or misplaced an object of value; |

Table 1. (continued)

| GDS Stage | Clinical Phase | Clinical Characteristics |
|---|---|---|
| | | (g) concentration deficit may be evident on clinical testing.<br>Objective evidence of memory deficit obtained only with an intensive interview. Decreased performance in demanding employment and social settings. Denial begins to become manifest in patient. Mild to moderate anxiety accompanies symptoms. |
| 4. Moderate cognitive decline | Late confusional | Clear-cut deficit on careful clinical interview. Deficit manifest in following areas: (a) decreased knowledge of current and recent events; (b) may exhibit some deficit in memory of one's personal history; (c) concentration deficit elicited on serial subtractions; (d) decreased ability to travel, handle finances, etc.<br>Frequently no deficit in following areas: (a) orientation to time and person; (b) recognition of familiar persons and faces; (c) ability to travel to familiar locations.<br>Inability to perform complex tasks. Denial is dominant defense mechanism. Flattening of affect and withdrawal from challenging situations occur. |
| 5. Moderately severe decline | Early dementia | Patient can no longer survive without some assistance. Patient is unable during interview to recall a major relevant aspect of their current lives: e.g., their address or telephone number of many years, the names of close members of their family (such as grandchildren), the names of the high school or college from which they graduated. |

Table 1. (continued)

| GDS Stage | Clinical Phase | Clinical Characteristics |
|---|---|---|
| | | Frequently some disorientation to time (date, day of week, season, etc.) or to place. An educated person may have difficulty counting back from 40 by 4s or from 20 by 2s.<br><br>Persons at this stage retain knowledge of many major facts regarding themselves and others. They invariably know their own names and generally know their spouses and children's names.<br><br>They require no assistance with toileting or eating, but may have some difficulty choosing the proper clothing to wear. |
| 6. Severe cognitive decline | Middle dementia | May occasionally forget the name of the spouse upon whom they are entirely dependent for survival. Will be largely unaware of all recent events and experiences in their lives. Retain some knowledge of their past lives but this is very sketchy. Generally unaware of their surroundings, the year, the season, etc. May have difficulty counting from 10, both backward and sometimes, forward. Will require some assistance with activities of daily living, e.g., may become incontinent, will require travel assistance but occasionally will display ability to trave to familiar locations. Diurnal rhythm frequently disturbed. Almost always recall their own name. Frequently continue to be able to distinguish familiar from unfamiliar persons in their environment. |

Table 1. (continued)

| *GDS Stage* | *Clinical Phase* | *Clinical Characteristics* |
|---|---|---|
| | | Personality and emotional changes occur. These are quite variable and include: (a) delusional behavior, e.g., patients may accuse their spouse of being an imposter; may talk to imaginary figures in the environment, or to their own reflection in the mirror; (b) obsessive symptoms, e.g., person may continually repeat simple cleaning activities; (c) anxiety symptoms, agitation, and even previously nonexistent violent behavior may occur; (d) cognitive abulia, i.e., loss of willpower because an individual cannot carry a thought long enough to determine a purposeful course of action. |
| 7. Very severe cognitive decline | Late dementia | All verbal abilities are lost. Frequently there is no speech at all—only grunting. Incontinent of urine; requires assistance toileting and feeding. Lose basic psychomotor skills, e.g., ability to walk. The brain appears to no longer be able to tell the body what to do. |
| | | Generalized and cortical neurologic signs and symptoms are frequently present. |

The 1982 publication contained data describing strong, significant relationships between the global clinical stages of the GDS and psychometric, mental status and *in vivo* assessments of brain change and brain function, utilizing computerized tomographic and neurometabolic (positron emission tomographic) assessments of brain change, respectively. Much more extensive information on the relationships between these modalities and progressive global clinical changes on the GDS scale is presently available and is summarized in Table 2. As can be seen from Table 2, strong significant relationships can be demonstrated between the GDS global assessments of progressive cognitive impairment and all behavioral

Table 2. Relationship Between Global Deterioration Scale (GDS) Score Assignments and Other Behavioral and *In Vivo* Assessments of Brain Change in Subjects with Normal Aging and Alzheimer's Disease

| *Assessment Measure* | *N* | *Pearson Correlation Coefficient with GDS Assignment* |
|---|---|---|
| MENTAL STATUS ASSESSMENTS | | |
| Mini Mental State Examination (Folstein et al., 1975) [14] | 170 | 0.89*** |
| Mental Status Questionnaire (Kahn et al., 1960)[18] | 273 | 0.83*** |
| RATING SCALE ASSESSMENTS (Blessed et al., 1968) [27] | | |
| Dementia Scale | 122 | 0.67*** |
| Information Test | 121 | 0.75*** |
| Memory Test | 121 | 0.79*** |
| Concentration Test | 120 | 0.68*** |
| COGNITIVE TESTS | | |
| A. *Memory* | | |
| Memory for Paragraphs (Gilbert et al., 1968) [15] | | |
| Initial Recall | 260 | 0.79*** |
| Delayed Recall | 260 | 0.78*** |
| Paired-Associate Word Recall (Gilbert et al., 1968) [15] | | |
| Initial Recall | 260 | 0.65*** |
| Delayed Recall | 260 | 0.63*** |
| Designs Recall (Gilbert et al., 1968) [15] | 258 | 0.75*** |
| Digit Recall (Wechsler, 1958) (17) | | |
| Forward | 261 | 0.66*** |
| Backward | 261 | 0.71*** |
| Buschke Selective Reminding Test | | |
| Recall (Mean Score: Trials 1 to 5) | 202 | 0.79*** |

Table 2. (continued)

| *Assessment Measure* | *N* | *Pearson Correlation Coefficient with GDS Assignment* |
|---|---|---|
| B. *Composite Psychometric Variable* | | |
| Psychometric Deterioration Score (PDS)[a] | 251 | 0.86*** |
| C. *Language Function* | | |
| WAIS Vocabulary Score (Wechsler, 1958) [17] | 261 | 0.67*** |
| D. *Perceptual Motor Skills* | | |
| Digit Symbol Substitution Test (Wechsler, 1958) [17] | 256 | 0.78*** |
| E. *Motor Skills* | | |
| Finger Tapping (Average Score: Right and Left Hands) | 213 | 0.49*** |
| COMPUTERIZED TOMOGRAPHIC ASSESSMENTS OF BRAIN CHANGE | | |
| Cortical Sulcal Widening (de Leon et al., 1980) [21] | 213 | 0.33*** |
| Cerebral Ventricular Dilatation (de Leon et al., 1980) [21] | 213 | 0.31*** |

[a]See text for description.
***$p < .001$.

assessments examined. It is notable that the strongest relationships can be observed between the GDS measures and the most comprehensive behavioral assessment measures. Specifically, the strongest correlation (.89) was observed between GDS assessments and Mini-Mental State Scores [14]. The latter incorporates measures of initial and delayed recall, orientation, concentration and calculation, language and vocabulary, comprehension, and praxis. Consequently, it is not surprising that this excellent and widely utilized tool relates strongly to global assessments of progressive change in aging and Alzheimer's disease.

Similarly, the next most robust relationship was observed between the global GDS assessments and the combination psychometric variable, i.e., the Psychometric Deterioration Score (PDS). The PDS represents a combined score derived from an equal weighting of six tests. Tests 1-3 are taken from the Guild Memory Test [15, 16] and tests 4-6 are taken from the Wechsler Adult Intelligence Scale (WAIS) [17]. The PDS is calculated by taking the sum of the percent correct performances for 1) immediate recall and delayed recall of paragraphs; 2) immediate recall and delayed recall of paired associates; 3) recall of designs; 4) WAIS vocabulary; 5) the digit symbol substitution test, and 6) digits forward and backward; the obtained sum is then divided by the total number of tests. This score is then converted into a continuous scale with low absolute scores representing relatively little deterioration and high scores denoting very deteriorated psychometric test performance. The combined psychometric measure correlates with the GDS very robustly ($r = .86$, $N = 251$).

Not surprisingly, less comprehensive assessments of mental status such as the ten-item Mental Status Questionnaire of Kahn et al. [18], and tests of specific memory and cognition modalities relate strongly ($r$'s = .6 to .8), but somewhat less robustly to the GDS global assessments of deterioration in aging and Alzheimer's disease. Interestingly, vocabulary decline seems to relate quite robustly to the progressive dementia of Alzheimer's disease ($r = 0.67$, $N = 261$, for WAIS vocabulary scores). Similarly, even a relatively, "pure" motor task, i.e, finger tapping, shows a significant and moderately strong relationship to progressive global deterioration in aging and dementia ($r = .49$, $N = 213$).

It is also not surprising that weaker relationships can be seen between structural measures of brain change and global deterioration in aging and dementia ($r$'s = 0.33 and 0.31, respectively, for computerized tomographic assessments of progressive sulcal widening and progressive ventricular dilatation; $N$s = 213). That these structural measures relate significantly to global changes in aging and Alzheimer's disease is noteworthy, and has been reported previously [19-23].

Since the GDS assessments relate particularly strongly to the widely utilized Mini-Mental State (MMS) measures, a more detailed examination of these relationships may be instructive and can be seen in Table 3. As can be seen from

Table 3. Relationship Between Global Deterioration Score (GDS) Assignments and Mini Mental State (MMS) Scores in Community Residing Subjects with Normal Aging and Alzheimer's Disease ($N = 170$, $r = 0.89^{***}$)

| *GDS Level* | *N* | *MMS (Mean Score ± SD)* |
|---|---|---|
| 1 | 14 | 29.07 ± 2.13 |
| 2 | 41 | 28.85 ± 1.67 |
| 3 | 22 | 24.55 ± 4.14 |
| 4 | 36 | 19.58 ± 3.86 |
| 5 | 36 | 14.39 ± 4.09 |
| 6 | 19 | 8.74 ± 3.89 |
| 7 | 2 | 4.50 ± 6.36 |

$^{***}p < .001$.

Table 3, the MMS scores do not distinguish between subjects with and without subjective complaints of cognitive impairment (i.e., GDS categories 1 and 2). Similarly, some subjects with cognitive impairment sufficient to interfere with complex occupational or social functioning (i.e., at the third GDS level) continue to achieve perfect or near-perfect MMS scores and the mean score of these subjects remains within the so called "normal range." Hence, the MMS alone does not effectively distinguish a subject with cognitive deterioration of this general magnitude from a subject with, for example, a poor educational background [24]. In the range from GDS levels 3 to 6 the MMS is an excellent tool for discriminating various levels of cognitive impairment in subjects with Alzheimer's disease. However, unlike the GDS, which describes the progression of this dementing disorder in detail, the MMS, of course, provides no information about the source of cognitive disability. As we shall see, the MMS also bottoms out at a relatively early point in the evolution of Alzheimer's disease.

An interrater and test/retest reliability study was recently completed in thirty-eight patients in our program. The thirty-eight subjects consisted of normal aged individuals ($n = 3$), individuals with normal aging and evidence of cerebrovascular disease ($n = 2$), and individuals with dementia without evidence of cerebrovascular disease ($n = 27$), and individuals with dementia and evidence of notable cerebrovascular disease ($n = 6$). The mean age was $69.3 \pm 7.9$ years (age range = 54 to 82 years). The subjects consisted of sixteen men and twenty-two women. The reliability coefficient of the GDS was 0.92. An identical reliability coefficient was obtained for the MMS (i.e., 0.92). For the Mental Status Questionnaire [18], the coefficient was 0.54. For WAIS vocabulary scores, the coefficient was 0.91. The reliability coefficients of the above measures, in comparison with some of the test measures previously described and some additional measures which will be described below, in subjects with age-associated memory impairment or Alzheimer's disease, can be found in Table 4.

In addition to global measures, detailed assessments of progressive clinical changes in aging and Alzheimer's disease needed to be developed which would be capable of documenting change in various cognitive, functional, language, motoric, mood, praxic, and other parameters. This led to our development of the Brief Cognitive Rating Scale measures [25,26]. These measures are divided into "axes," each of which assesses a particular modality. Each axis is designed to be optimally congruent with the corresponding global deterioration stage. Presently, eleven such axes have been developed assessing progressive changes in (I) concentration, (II) recent memory, (III) past memory, (IV) orientation, (V) functioning and self-care, (VI) language ability, (VII) motor functioning, (VIII) mood, (IX) praxis ability, (X) calculation ability, and (XI) feeding behavior and abilities.

An additional major problem for longitudinal investigations of aging and Alzheimer's disease was that virtually all psychometric, mental status, and other behavioral assessment modalities bottom out at a relatively early point in the

Table 4. Reliability Study
Pearson Correlations of Baseline and Follow-up Measures
Aging and Dementia Subjects ($N = 38$)

| Assessment Measure | Pearson Correlation of Baseline and Follow-up |
|---|---|
| A. Clinical Assessments | |
| 1. Global Deterioration Scale (GDS) | 0.92*** |
| 2. Brief Cognitive Rating Scale (BCRS) | |
| a. Axis 1: Concentration | 0.82*** |
| b. Axis 2: Recent Memory | 0.85*** |
| c. Axis 3: Past Memory | 0.83*** |
| d. Axis 4: Orientation | 0.86*** |
| e. Axis 5: Functioning | 0.83*** |
| f. Axis 6: Language | 0.61*** |
| g. Axis 7: Motor | 0.69*** |
| h. Axis 8: Mood | 0.64*** |
| i. Axis 9: Praxis | 0.87*** |
| j. Axis 10: Calculation | 0.83*** |
| k. Axis 1-5: Total Score | 0.96*** |
| 3. Hamilton Depression Scale (Total Score) | 0.21 |
| 4. Hachinski Score (Modified Version - Rosen et al.) | 0.78*** |
| B. Mental Status | |
| 1. Mental Status Questionnaire (MSQ, total scores) | 0.54** |
| 2. Mini Mental State (MM, total scores) | 0.92*** |
| C. Cognitive Tests | |
| 1. Memory for Paragraphs: Initial Recall | 0.82*** |
| 2. Memory for Paragraphs: Delayed Recall | 0.87*** |
| 3. Paired Associates Word Recall: Initial Recall | 0.74*** |
| 4. Paired Associates Word Recall: Delayed Recall | 0.72*** |
| 5. Designs Recall | 0.55*** |
| 6. Digit Recall (Forward) | 0.47** |
| 7. Digit Recall (Backward) | 0.67*** |
| D. Composite Psychometric Variable | |
| Psychometric Deterioration Score (PDS) | 0.94*** |
| E. Language Function | |
| WAIS Vocabulary Score | 0.91*** |
| F. Perceptual Motor Skills | |
| Digit Symbol Substitution Test | 0.93*** |

**$p < .01$.
***$p < .001$.

progresssion of the illness process. The illness, as it evolves beyond this point needs to be described if longitudinal investigations are to produce meaningful results. We estimate on the basis of current knowledge that 25 to 50 percent of the potential time course of Alzheimer's disease is entirely uncharted utilizing the MMS or other mental status [18, 27–29], or psychometric assessments. For this reason (as well as others), we have developed a staging modality known as Functional Assessment Staging (or FAST staging) of normal aging and Alzheimer's disease [30, 31]. Utilizing this staging procedure, we can adumbrate sixteen successive stages from normal aging to most severe Alzheimer's disease (see Table 5). Specifically, we can now describe approximately eight successive functional stages after the point at which mental status assessments are generally not of utility. Our ability to do this is crucial to the success of longitudinal studies of aging and dementia.

In a recent investigation, we systematically examined the extent to which Alzheimer's patients followed the proposed ordinal pattern of functional deterioration [32]. Fifty-six patients, mean age 77.1 ± 8.3 years, consisting of fourteen men and forty-two women with Alzheimer's disease [33], were studied. Information was obtained as to the presence of all functional impairments on the 16-point scale. Fifty patients manifested the ordinal pattern predicted. The six exceptions were of a magnitude of one to two points on this 16-point scale. A Guttman analysis was performed to determine the likelihood that the results observed were not due to chance and to evaluate the statistical utility and validity of the FAST scale [34]. The coefficient of reproducibility—a measure of the extent to which a respondent's scale score is a predictor of one's response pattern varying between 0 and 1—was 0.9933. A general guideline to the interpretation of this measure is that a coefficient of reproducibility higher than 0.9 is considered to indicate a valid scale. The minimal marginal reproducibility (the minimum coefficient of reproducibility that could have occurred for the scale given the cutting points used and the proportion of respondents passing and failing each of the items) was 0.6138. The difference between the coefficient of reproducibility and the minimum marginal reproducibility indicates the extent to which the former is due to response patterns rather than the inherent cumulative interrelation of the variables used. The difference, the percent improvement, was 37.95. The coefficient of a scalability was 0.9827. The coefficient of scalability also varies from 0 to 1 and should be well above 0.6 if the scale is truly unidimensional and cumulative. The FAST scale appears to eminently fulfill this criterion in this analysis.

The above assessments relate primarily to the cognitive and functional changes which occur with the progression of Alzheimer's disease. Many of these changes are inevitable as the disease progresses. Hence all Alzheimer's patients who survive experience progressive changes in concentration and calculation abilities, recent and remote memory, orientation, praxis, feeding abilities and functioning as outlined in the Brief Cognitive Rating Scale and the FAST. Other behavioral changes such as agitation, paranoia, delusions, hallucinations, activity disturb-

Table 5. Functional Assessment Staging (FAST) in Normal Aging and Alzheimer's Disease (Primary Degenerative Dementia)

| *Stage* | *Clinical Phase* | *FAST Characteristics* |
|---|---|---|
| 1. No cognitive decline | Normal | No functional decrement, either subjectively or objectively, manifest. |
| 2. Very mild cognitive decline | Forgetfulness | Complains of forgetting location of objects; subject work difficulties. |
| 3. Mild cognitive decline | Early confusional | Decreased functioning in demanding employment setting evident to co-workers; difficulty in traveling to new locations. |
| 4. Moderate cognitive | Late confusional | Decreased ability to perform complex tasks such as planning dinner for guests, handling finances, and marketing. |
| 5. Moderately severe cognitive decline | Early dementia | Requires assistance in choosing proper clothing; may require coaxing to bath properly. |
| 6. Severe cognitive decline | Middle dementia | a. Difficulty putting on clothing properly<br>b. Requires assistance bathing; difficulty adjusting bathwater temperature<br>c. Inability to handle mechanics of toileting<br>d. Urinary incontinence<br>e. Fecal incontinence |
| 7. Very severe cognitive decline | Late dementia | a. Ability to speak limited to about a half-dozen intelligible words<br>b. Intelligible vocabulary limited to a single word<br>c. Ambulatory ability lost<br>d. Ability to sit up independently lost<br>e. Ability to smile lost<br>f. Ability to hold up head lost |

ances, anxieties, and phobias also appear to occur in a particular pattern with the progression of Alzheimer's disease. Unlike the cognitive and functional changes, however, these behavioral changes are not inevitable or as invariable. Our research indicates that these changes are potentially treatable [35]. They also appear to be a major concern raised by spouses of Alzheimer's patients in support group settings and a major reason cited by spouses for placing their husbands and wives in institutional settings [36]. We have outlined these potentially remediable behavioral changes which frequently occur in the Alzheimer's patient in a format useful for clinicians [37]. We have also developed a rating scale, the BEHAVE-AD, which is designed to systematically assess the incidence of these symptoms as the disease progresses [35, 38]. We are presently utilizing this important new scale in our longitudinal investigations.

As prognostic information has become available from our studies [39], we have shared this with caregivers. Management strategies at each stage of the illness were also developed [37]. Hence, we are able to provide our patients and their families with much more specific information than formerly.

### 4. A BROADER INVESTIGATIVE FOCUS FOR THE PROGRAM HAD TO BE DEVELOPED

Isolated focus on pharmacologic remediation was insufficiently rewarding for both our study population and the program investigators. Therefore investigations have been wedded to inquiries with respect to the basic nature of the illness process. These included neuroanatomic studies [20, 21], neurometabolic studies [40–42], cytogenetic studies [43], neuroimmunologic studies [44], electrophysiologic investigations [45], biochemical investigations [46], and other basic studies—all of which related directly to diagnosis and treatment. To this list has more recently been added pathologic investigations and a follow-up and tracking system has been interdigitated with our long term follow-up prospective studies.

## AGING AND DEMENTIA: LONGITUDINAL COURSE OF SUBGROUPS

When the longitudinal study was initiated, we examined the negatives of our previous, less formal, follow-up program and devised different methods to contact and maintain communication with former participants in our studies.

### OBJECTIVES

The primary objective was to examine the course of outpatient subgroups with normal aging and progressive Alzheimer's disease. A secondary goal was to determine the influence of cerebrovascular and other risk factors on the stage specific course of progressive dementia.

## SUBJECTS AND CONTROLS

Individuals of either sex, at least sixty years of age who had participated in previous extensive pharmacologic and other investigative programs in our clinic were selected for the initial longitudinal study. The number of subjects was 176. All selected subjects were to be followed with the objective of obtaining 100 percent follow-up data. The subjects come from diverse geographic, ethnic, and economic backgrounds. All lived within a 200 mile radius of New York City.

## PROCEDURES

All subjects were to be followed consecutively approximately three-and-a-half years following their initial (baseline) assessments. They were to be assessed to the fullest possible extent on as many of the initial assessment criteria as possible. We found that it would take four to six visits to complete all of the study evaluations.

The coordinators of this study are gerontologists who had previously initiated a family counseling service as part of our program. They had already accumulated years of exposure to the problems encountered by the patient and the family through personal contact in family groups, and meeting and speaking with the individuals who participate in our studies. Because of this experience, they had developed a keen sensitivity and an abundance of knowledge about the cognitive, functional, and behavioral changes brought about by the degenerative process of Alzheimer's disease.

An index card system was established, which contains the following information: name, address and phone number of participant; name and phone number of responsible caregiver (usually spouse or child); initial baseline date; past cognitive status classification (GDS), and past program participation. Large index cards were utilized, so room was available for remarks and notes when the initial contact was made.

Individual file books were set up for each subject, containing copies of the initial baseline tests administered, neurological exams, CT scan reports, EKG results, and a clinical evaluation. Included in this book is a copy of the longitudinal study protocol, with space to enter the date of each test, copies of the new tests to be given, the new clinical, neurological, EKG and CT scan reports.

Included in the record keeping are flow sheets, one listing the various tests in the initial baseline. The dates of transferring this information to the data analysis facility are inserted.

## FOLLOW-UP REPORTS

At the conclusion of each baseline and follow-up evaluation sequence, a family meeting is scheduled with the study clinician, who conveys the results at that meeting. Information is shared regarding the patient's diagnosis, stage and prognosis and management advice is offered for both the patient and the caregivers. Follow-up reports recording the results of the study are made up by the doctor assigned to the subject, who if appropriate, also recommends participation in an applicable new drug research program. A copy of this report is sent to the subject. The name is given to the study coordinator who then contacts this individual, if appropriate. Thus, the list makes up a nucleus of subjects for new research studies, cementing our ongoing relationship with the study subjects.

The importance of keeping clear and accurate records cannot be overemphasized. Setting up these books and files was time consuming initially, but it takes only a few minutes to pull this material when the subject comes in for a subsequent appointment. This saves considerable time for the tester.

## METHODS FOR CONTACT

Our experience demonstrated that only personal contact would succeed in getting our subjects to return to the program. The protocol involves a minimum of four visits. For people who are ill and elderly, who mainly use public transportation, it is difficult to make the trip to our facility. Our past experience with an annual recall program indicated that an impersonal letter would probably be discarded. We decided on the basis of our past experience that initial telephone contact would be most productive and proceeded accordingly.

Communicators were selected and trained by our two counselors. Graduate students doing field work were carefully screened and three were chosen who showed sensitivity, empathy, and maturity.

The training stressed the following:

1. an understanding of the purpose of the study, so that questions pertaining to the study could be answered adequately;
2. conveying a sense of personal caring for the subjects and caretakers—this is accomplished through an unhurried attitude, showing interest in the problems of subjects and their families, listening and offering to help resolve these problems;
3. acknowledgment of any negatives brought up by the subject or a family member;
4. directing the respondent back to the original purpose of the call;
5. treating respondents with respect and dignity, utilizing surnames and any titles the respondents may have;
6. stressing the importance of the subject's participation;
7. sensitivity to subject's and respondent's needs—not only to the needs of the project;
8. ensuring, before the call is over, that a definitive appointment has been made—we don't ask what time is convenient—we give the participant a specific date and time. If this appointment is not feasible, we have an

alternate date and time available to offer at once. We try not to accept a final refusal, but leave the door open for a future call;

9. if any information is requested during the course of the conversation that is not readily available to our communicator, a further phone call is made with the information as soon as possible;
10. if a subject adamantly refuses an appointment the first time called, we call back when we have information about new research developments and new programs available for his/her participation;
11. after the appointment is made, another call is made to the subject the day before as a reminder—this reminder call is made for each appointment necessary to complete the protocol. Here again, the importance of good record keeping is clear. An accurate calendar is kept for all appointments made, and this calendar is checked on a daily basis;
12. an interdisciplinary approach to the simultaneous treatment of subject and the family is utilized—for example, we use our updated resource material, (legal, home-making, community resources), for family counseling.

After each call is made, the interview is reviewed. Negatives and positives are discussed and corrected, if necessary. If a follow-up call has to be made, this is noted on the card, and entered on the calendar. If a delicate issue arises, or if the subject is abusive or confused, one of the counselors takes over.

## FINDINGS

In the course of calling our subjects, we encounter specific situations that require individualized procedures. If a subject lives alone who cannot travel, and they have children, the latter are generally very cooperative. Therefore, when we call the subject, we find out if they have children and how we can contact them, if we have not previously recorded this information. In instances, where there are no children, we often find a willing relative or friend to accompany the subject to our program.

If the subject has an aide, we arrange the appointments with the aide. Sometimes, it is necessary to pay for transportation if the subject implies that he or she cannot afford this cost.

## PROBLEM SITUATIONS

*Tracking Subjects* — When calling some subjects, we find that phone numbers have been discontinued, or were unlisted. Also, some individuals have moved and left no forwarding address. We were fortunate to have two undergraduate students who served as detectives. They went to the last known address of the subject, spoke with neighbors and/or local storekeepers, and they were able to locate new addresses for ten of twelve individuals.

Where people had lived in a small community, we contact the town hall to check their records, the local senior centers and have even enlisted the aide of the local police department for assistance. We located individuals who had moved to another city or state, or had moved in with their children.

*Escorted Visits* — Occasionally we find individuals who cannot travel alone due to physical difficulties, or are afraid to travel, and have no one to bring them in. If they are capable of escorted travel, we send someone for them, and then return them to their home escorted.

*Home Visits* — When the subject is physically unable to travel, visits are made to the home by a team to assess the individual.

*Out of Town Subjects* — Contact is made with these subjects and/or his/her family so as to obtain as much information regarding the patient's current status as possible. For example, a current medical history, IADL and FAST, as well as other basic behavioral assessments can be obtained by a thorough telephone interview.

*Confused Subjects* — We find some very confused individuals who still live alone. It is initially difficult to comprehend how they manage. However, someone eventually shows up to care for them. One interesting case was Mrs. B. We initially made several appointments, none of which were remembered, even though we reminded Mrs. B the same day. With the patient's consent, we sent an escort for her (one of our communicators). However, when the young woman came for her, Mrs. B refused to leave. Our escort sat with her, tried to convince her to come, changed the subject, tried in every way to overcome her resistance. By accident, a friend of Mrs. B's arrived, and because the friend was a familiar person, the patient consented to come to the clinic. Subsequently, the patient's friend brought her for all appointments. If the friend had not arrived on the scene, it would have been necessary to send the same escort repeatedly to the home of Mrs. B, so that the subject could overcome her fear of the unfamiliar person (an understandable Alzheimer's patient behavior pattern) and feel secure with her. Then, perhaps, the patient would have kept her appointments with our escort.

Another incident worthy of mention was the case of Mrs A., who lived with her spouse, but he was physically disabled and deaf. Her husband could not travel, and the patient was afraid to travel alone. We made contact with a community agency which provided the patient with an escort to bring the patient and return her home after each appointment. The escort was paid for by the subject's family.

## NURSING HOME RESIDENTS AND DECEDENTS

When a subject has died, we interview the spouse, or an adult child, using the Brief Cognitive Rating Scale (BCRS) and the FAST to obtain relevant clinical information regarding the subject's cognitive and functional status prior to death.

If the patient is institutionalized and not available for personal contact, this procedure is also utilized to obtain current information with respect to the subject's status. Every effort is made, however, to examine the patient personally. Where possible, nursing home team visits are arranged.

## ADDITIONAL PROBLEMS

1. Many calls have to be made at night, because the subject or a family member are working and not available during the day. Therefore, we require a willing staff to give this time.
2. Interdepartmental calls have to be made to make appointments for the CT and/or MRI scans. Since the time allotted is limited, we have to make sure the subject is punctual. If a subject has to cancel an appointment or if we have to cancel an appointment with the subject (e.g., if the equipment malfunctions), a new series of phone calls are necessary.
3. Our CT scan time is frequently on Saturdays only. Some subjects are averse to Saturday appointments, so they require particular encouragement.
4. There may be a span of a month or more during the protocol visit series when subjects take vacations or become ill. This necessitates keeping our records and calendar very accurately.
5. Some subjects are still working, and we have initiated provisions for night or weekend testing.
6. We have had occasional (approximately 5%) outright refusals. No amount of cajoling worked, despite the spouses' assistance.
7. Some subjects become very agitated during the course of their follow-up visits and cannot be tested. In these cases appointments have to be rescheduled. In the interim, valuable time is consumed during the visit, time during which the tester tries very patiently to make the subject cooperate.

## FIRST APPOINTMENT

Some longitudinal study subjects have not participated in our program for three or more years at the time of follow-up. During this time there may have been some changes in staff and the physical set up. These changes combined with degenerative changes in the subject can engender confusion, disorientation and agitation in the subject. In addition, the subjects and their family members are anxious about the results of the tests. They don't want to hear that the subject is worse, even though they have been living with these changes and certainly have some awareness of the decline.

Since an interdisciplinary team is involved in the assessment of the subject and the family, we instituted meetings involving every team member to stress the importance of creating a consistent, serene, caring atmosphere from time of arrival to time of departure.

While the patient is being tested, the counselors engage the caregivers in conversation about their problems. Many times we hear "This is the first time anyone asked about me." Simultaneously, the family is offered support groups, and any resource information they may require.

The caregiver, is generally the person who is responsible for making the decision involving the subject's future participation in research projects. The more help they receive, the greater the magnitude of cooperation. We try to convey, to both the subject and the caregiver, a sense of caring and support.

## RESULTS

As noted previously, we attempted to follow 176 subjects. Of these, 144 subjects had age-associated complaints of memory impairment (the current proposed terminology for this condition is Age-associated Memory Impairment or, "AAMI" [47]) or Alzheimer's disease (AD). Since the boundaries between AAMI and AD had not been well established and one of the goals of the study was to provide further information on these boundaries, the 144 subjects in this continuum formed a single study cohort, stratified by GDS severity level. We also attempted to follow thirty-two subjects with cerebrovascular disease complicating the course of central nervous system aging and dementia.

From the AAMI and AD cohort, we succeeded in following 136 of the 144 subjects. Of the eight subjects on whom we were not successful in obtaining follow-up clinical information, six refused follow-up and two could not be located. These eight individuals all came from the less severe GDS categories from which the total *N*'s were relatively substantial. Specifically, of fifty-nine GDS = 2s at baseline, fifty-four (92%) were successfully followed; of thirty-eight GDS = 3s at baseline, thirty-six (95%) were successfully followed; of thirty-two GDS = 4s at baseline, thirty-one (96%) were successfully followed, and 100 percent of the fifteen patients from more severe (GDS = 5 and GDS = 6) categories at baseline were successfully followed. Overall, follow-up data were obtained on 94.4 percent of subjects studied at baseline in the aging and AD groups. The characteristics of these subjects at baseline are described in Table 6.

From the cohort of subjects with cerebrovascular concomitants of central nervous system aging and progressive dementia, we succeeded in obtaining follow-up information on twenty-eight of thirty-two subjects initially followed (87.5%). As was the case with the AAMI and AD cohort, all of the subjects lost to follow-up came from the relatively less impaired subject groups. Some baseline characteristics of the subjects successfully followed can be seen in Table 7.

### METHODOLOGY

At follow-up some subjects were deceased. Other subjects were residing in nursing homes. Many subjects who survived had sufficient impairment such that

Table 6. Sample Size and Age of Geriatric Patients with Baseline Diagnoses Compatible with Normal Aging or Alzheimer's Disease: Baseline Characteristics for Subjects Successfully Followed[a] (Age range = 60–84 years)

| | Males | | Females | | Total | |
|---|---|---|---|---|---|---|
| *Severity Levels* | *N* | *Mean Age ± SD (Yrs.)* | *N* | *Mean Age ± SD (Yrs.)* | *N* | *Mean Age ± SD (Yrs.)* |
| GDS = 2 | 33 | 68.0 ± 6.0 | 21 | 70.8 ± 4.7 | 54 | 69.1 ± 5.7 |
| GDS = 3 | 17 | 73.0 ± 7.1 | 19 | 72.3 ± 5.9 | 36 | 72.6 ± 6.4 |
| GDS = 4 | 10 | 73.5 ± 6.3 | 21 | 72.1 ± 5.5 | 31 | 72.5 ± 5.7 |
| GDS = 5 | 6 | 74.7 ± 4.3 | 2 | 71.5 ± 13.4 | 8 | 73.9 ± 6.4 |
| GDS = 6 | 4 | 73.0 ± 3.4 | 3 | 73.0 ± 5.2 | 7 | 73.0 ± 3.8 |
| | 70 | 70.8 ± 6.6 | 66 | 71.7 ± 5.4 | 136 | 71.3 ± 6.0 |

[a]A total of 136 of 144 subjects. Of the eight subjects lost to follow-up, five had a baseline severity level of GDS = 2; two had a baseline severity level of GDS = 3, and one a baseline severity level of GDS = 4. Successful follow-up is defined as ability to obtain information with respect to the following parameters and/or more extensive information: follow-up medical status and diagnosis; follow-up residential status (institutionalized, deceased, or community-residing); and follow-up global cognitive abilities and GDS scores.

Table 7. Sample Size and Age of Geriatric Patients with Cerebrovascular Factors at Baseline Compatible with Diagnoses of Normal Aging, Multi-Infarct Dementia, or Mixed Degenerative (Alzheimer's) and Infarct Dementia: Baseline Characteristics for Subjects Successfully Followed[a] $N = 28$

| | *Male* | *Female* | *Total* |
|---|---|---|---|
| GDS = 2 | 7 | 2 | 9 |
| GDS = 3 | 4 | 4 | 8 |
| GDS = 4 | 1 | 5 | 6 |
| GDS = 5 | 1 | 2 | 3 |
| GDS = 6 | 1 | 1 | 2 |
| | 14 | 14 | 28 |
| Mean age | 71.86 years | 73.43 years | 72.64 years |
| SD | 6.93 years | 5.19 years | 6.05 years |

[a]Successful follow-up is defined as ability to obtain information with respect to the following parameters and/or more extensive information: follow-up medical status and diagnosis; follow-up residential status (institutionalized, deceased or community-residing); and follow-up global cognitive abilities and GDS.

they could not be tested using psychometric and other procedures. As noted previously, many patients from the early to mid GDS = 6 stage become untestable. All GDS = 7 subjects are essentially untestable. Some less severely impaired subjects became untestable because of agitation or the fears engendered by, what is for them, the very painful exposure of their disability. As noted earlier, because of these methodologic problems in follow-up we have over the course of this study been developing a variety of new assessment procedures which help to overcome these problems. Among these useful new procedures are the clinician rated Brief Cognitive Rating Scale (BCRS) and Functional Assessment Staging (FAST). However, these measures were developed from approximately 1982 to 1985 and hence were not available at baseline.

Because of these methodologic problems, virtually all dementia studies which have been conducted until this time have used mortality as the sole outcome measure. Most of these studies have been of persons institutionalized with dementia of diverse etiology, who have long been known to suffer an increase in mortality in comparison with cohort and control populations [48–55]. More recent studies have demonstrated an increased mortality in persons institutionalized with AD [56–58]. More recently, a decrease in survival has also been demonstrated in outpatients with specifically diagnosed AD. Barclay et al. followed (by caregiver telephone interviews) 199 patients with dementia of the Alzheimer type, sixty-four with multi-infarct dementia (MID), and forty-three with mixed dementia (MX) [59]. All demented subjects scored 7 or fewer correct on the 10-item Mental Status Questionnaire (MSQ) [18]. They noted that AD patients (mean age at baseline = 73 years, mean MSQ at baseline = 3.0 correct) had a 50 percent survival rate of 3.4 years. Survival rates were even less for their subjects with vascular dementia. Specifically, 50 percent survival was 2.6 years for MID subjects and 2.5 years for their MX group with baseline ages of seventy-six and seventy-seven years and baseline MSQ mean scores of 3. They concluded that "vascular dementias are associated with higher mortality than DAT (AD), presumably because of the associated morbidity of vascular disease." Reding et al. also followed outpatients with AD and vascular dementias "for as long as forty-eight months" [60]. They found three-year mortality rates of 37 percent, 83 percent and 57 percent for their patients with AD, MID, and MX dementias, respectively (*N*s= 34, 6, and 7; means ages = 72, 79, and 77 years, degree of dementia unspecified; "follow-up evaluation was by telephone or repeat clinic visit"). Consequently, the findings of Reding et al. are consistent with those of Barclay et al. in suggesting an increase in mortality for outpatients with AD and perhaps an even greater increase in mortality for vascular dementias although the small *N*s for the latter groups in the Reding study and the absence of severity data make any comparisons speculative. Further support for the findings of an increased mortality in initially community residing samples with AD, in comparison with age matched cohorts, and for a still greater mortality in subjects with MID comes from a very recent study of Mosla et al. [61]. They studied survival and causes of death in 218 patients with AD and 115 patients with MID initially identified in the community (mean ages 78 and 79 years). They found the six-year survival rate for AD subjects to be 21 percent and that for MID to be 12 percent. They also concluded that MID carries a less favorable survival prognosis than AD. The excess mortality in both AD and MID in their sample was independent of age.

The conclusion by Reding et al. that "intellectual failure—or even anxiety about intellectual performance—may be an important indication of illness in general in older people, analogous to "fever of an unknown origin" in a child . . . and requiring as meticulous and thoughtful a clinical evaluation" rings true. However, neither their study nor those of Barclay et al. or Mosla et al. address the question of the point at which such "failure" or "anxiety" becomes associated with morbidity. Other studies have examined prognosis for survival in community residing elderly persons who did not have diagnoses of AD [48-51]. Jarvik and Falek noted a positive relationship between survival and original scores on a series of psychological tests and a positive relationship between the five-year survival and stability of scores on these tests [50]. Subsequently, Jarvik and Blum suggested that the relationship between rate of cognitive decline and morbidity needed to be validated by prospectively designed studies [51].

Between the extremes of morbidity, relatively little is known about the differential course of cognitive symptoms in community residing elderly persons with mild, moderate, and severe cognitive impairment in comparison with unimpaired elderly cohorts. As Bergmann stated [62]: "The natural history of the early development of senile dementia remains unexplored." One study—apart from our own investigations reported in preliminary form previously [39, 63], and described in greater detail herein—has recently appeared in which the course of persons with mild AD was examined [64]. In the Berg et al. study, forty-three subjects with mild AD (mean age = 72 years), diagnosed and staged by clinical research criteria were studied with clinical, psychometric, electrophysiologic, and CT measures over a one-year interval [64]. At that time twenty-one subjects had worsened clinically, an equal number had not worsened, and one subject was lost to follow-up. Many of the clinical and psychometric measures of impairment were predictive of clinical worsening. Electrophysiologic and CT measures were not. They concluded that "longer periods of study will be necessary to determine rates of change and variables that predict those rates. Further quantitative studies of persons with SDAT (AD) are needed to document the natural history and predictive features in order to assist with patient management, family counseling, and evaluation of future therapeutic efforts." Recently, Cohen et al. noted that "although the patient with Alzheimer's disease undergoes a series of behavioral changes and losses, empirical data are still not available to describe the course of the illness [65]. More information is also needed regarding the clinical diagnostic criteria for AD in elderly persons with cognitive decline, and regarding the precise prognostic implication of that diagnosis. The paucity of information and absence of agreement with respect to diagnostic criteria for AD was recently illustrated by a study from the Section on Brain Aging and Dementia, Laboratory of

Neurosciences, National Institute on Aging, which defined a "mild DAT" subject group as having Mini-Mental State scores [14] of 22 to 29 (perfect score = 30) [66]. In contrast Folstein [24] and Crook et al. [47] have suggested cutoff scores of 23 for malignant dementias of diverse etiology.

As described earlier in this chapter, the GDS embodies a more detailed than previously available description of the clinical course of normal aging and AD, based upon cross-sectional observations. Subsequent to its publication, the GDS had been utilized to stage patients for a variety of pharmacologic investigations designed to develop improved and effective treatments for AD conducted in North America, Europe, Japan, and elsewhere. The component elements of the GDS have been studied cross-sectionally [25, 26]. Additional cross-sectional behavioral [67], and *in vivo* neuroanatomic and neurometabolic [22, 68–70], data on the relationship of progressive changes in aging and AD, assessed utilizing the GDS, in comparison to other measures, have also been published subsequent to the initial 1982 descriptions. The contribution of the GDS toward an improved description of the stages and symptomatology of age-associated cognitive decline and AD has been acknowledged by the Secretary's Task Force on AD [5]. This document also outlined some important questions regarding the course of AD which remained to be addressed and which formed the basis for our current and previous longitudinal investigations. Specifically, the report notes that although the GDS observations "provide a useful starting point for further research, nevertheless many important issues relating to clinical course remain unexamined. . . . there is still great difficulty recognizing the disease in the early stages. Little attention has been paid in the research literature to the enormous variablity in rate of deterioration and the vast differences in duration of disease—from two to twenty years." We therefore have been conducting this prospective study of aging and dementia in community residing persons with varying degrees of cognitive impairment. Our goal was to provide at least preliminary answers to some of these major questions. Specifically, we have sought to determine: 1) What are the borders between normal aging and AD?; 2) What is the "natural history," of clinical symptoms in AD?; 3) What factors, if any, can be associated with a relatively benign, or a relatively malignant course?; 4) Within a given clinical deterioration category, do prognostic subgroups exist?; 5) Is there a consistent pattern to the course of AD?; 6) To what extent do age and sex influence prognosis?; 7) Does performance on mental status and/or psychometric test variables influence outcome over and above the variance accounted for by global deterioration level?; 8) Do *in vivo* assessments of brain change, e.g., CT measures of the magnitude of ventricular dilatation or cortical atrophy, influence outcome over and above the variance accounted for by global deterioration level?; 9) What is the influence of cerebrovascular disease and cerebrovascular risk factors on outcome?

At least preliminary answers to all of the above issues and questions have been suggested by our observations and data over the course of our initial study for which follow-up was initiated in 1982 on subjects initially seen beginning in 1978. All of these preliminary answers, which are described in detail below, need to be confirmed over longer follow-up periods and with larger samples. New questions are now amenable to investigation.

## OUTCOME

A summary of the outcomes in the AAMI and AD subjects, grouped by GDS category, can be found in Table 8. These subjects were followed over a mean interval of $3.5 \pm 0.6$ years. In this summary, we utilized the change criterion of $\geq 2$ GDS levels in order to eliminate border effects and to assist in making any judgment of change a conservative one. These results help to define the general subject group borders between normal aging and AD. Specifically, if we assume that significant decline during our mean follow-up period of 3.5 years substantiated the diagnosis of AD, we can operationally define the earliest clinical severity stage of AD as that from which a majority of individuals evidence a notable negative outcome. Thus the results indicate that the fourth GDS stage, corresponding to that at which deficits are readily manifest in the course of a clinical interview, but at which individuals are still capable of surviving independently in the community (particularly if assistance with the handling of major finances is provided), appears to be most compatible (at three- to four-year follow-up) with the earliest stage of AD. More than 60 percent of these subjects were institutionalized, deceased, or notably worse clinically at follow-up, whereas 83 percent of subjects in the preceding GDS category (i.e., those with subtle deficit in the course of a clinical interview sufficient to interfere with complex occupational functioning) were not. Individuals in the fourth GDS stage were significantly more likely than individuals in the preceding GDS = 3 stage to display a negative outcome as defined above at follow-up ($p < .001$, chi square = 14.18). The magnitude of this differential outcome is even greater if one compares the subjects in the fourth GDS stage with GDS 2 subjects (who, by definition) did not display functional impairments but who did have subjective complaints at baseline of sufficient magnitude to have caused the subjects to journey to our research program on a repeated basis and to seek treatment for their memory problems. Differences between the GDS = 2 subjects and the GDS = 3 subjects with respect to negative outcome were not significant ($p > .05$; chi square = 2.96).

Similar longitudinal data from other studies of community residing subjects with progressive degrees of cognitive impairment are not yet available for the purposes of comparing our observations regarding the clinical boundaries between aging and AD. However, Folstein and co-authors have reported that sixty-three residents whom they surveyed at a retirement complex in Westchester County, New York (assumed, without examination, to be healthy) scored at least 24 points on their Mini-Mental State (MMS) examination [14,24]. Subsequently, De Paulo

Table 8. Outcome Summary
Geriatric Subjects with AAMI or AD at Baseline

| Baseline GDS | N | Follow-Up Interval (Yrs.) Mean ± SD | Neutral Outcome[a] | Negative Outcomes[b] Total | Deceased | Nursing Home | Community Residing Δ GDS ≥ 2 | Percent Negative Outcome |
|---|---|---|---|---|---|---|---|---|
| 2 | 54 | 3.42 ± 0.48 | 51 | 3 | 1 | 0 | 2 | 5.6 |
| 3 | 36 | 3.47 ± 0.67 | 30 | 6 | 2 | 2 | 2 | 16.7 |
| 4 | 31 | 3.56 ± 0.62 | 12 | 19 | 6 | 7 | 4 | 61.3 |
| 5 | 8 | 3.60 ± 0.57 | 3 | 5 | 2 | 2 | 1 | 62.5 |
| 6 | 7 | 3.71 ± 0.76 | 2 | 5 | 2 | 3 | 0 | 71.4 |
| 2–6 | 136 | 3.49 ± 0.60 | 100 | 38 | 13 | 14 | 9 | 27.9 |

[a]Community-residing and increase in GDS of less than 2 points.
[b]Deceased, in nursing home, or community-residing with change in GDS of 2 rating points or greater.
**Note:** Follow-up interval range: 0.73 to 5.12 years. Follow-up interval = time to death or time to follow-up in survivors. Follow-up interval range in survivors = 2.13 to 5.12 years.

and Folstein reported that diverse neurological patients with MMS scores of 24 or greater did not have cerebral disturbance [71].

As can be seen in Table 3, we note a strong interrelationship between MMS and GDS scores ($N = 170$, MMS range = 0–30; $r = 0.9$, $p < .001$). In this study the mean MMS of GDS = 4 subjects is 19.6 ± 3.86, and the mean MMS of GDS = 3 subjects is 24.6 ± 4.14.

Hence, Folstein's conclusion that neurologically impaired subjects with "cerebral disturbance" have MMS scores of ≤ 23 appears compatible with our observations regarding differential outcomes in GDS 2 and 3 subjects versus GDS = 4 subjects and has possible implications for the clinical borders of aging and AD. Further information regarding these borders and the influence of demographic, behavioral and neuroradiologic variables is suggested by our multiple-regression analysis.

In a multiple-regression analysis, we examined the relationship between clinical status at follow-up, in terms of global severity of illness (GDS) and baseline assessments. The latter included baseline clinical assessments (GDS scores), demographic variables (age and sex), memory measures (short- and long-term), an assessment of language function (WAIS vocabulary score), assessments of motor skills and perceptual motor skills (finger tapping and a digit symbol substitution test), a mental status assessment (the Mental Status Questionnaire), and *in vivo* assessment of brain change (CT rankings of the magnitude of cerebral cortical atrophy and cerebral ventricular dilatation [21]). In this analysis, we entered four initial "forced" variables and subsequent variables were entered in a stepwise fashion. Data with respect to the above assessments were available on 100 percent of the 136 subjects for follow-up clinical status and global severity, all of the forced variables and most (six) of the remaining variables. Of the remaining four variables, data were available on more than 98 percent of cases for MSQ, and CT scans could be rank ordered for magnitude of cortical and ventricular change in more than 92 percent of cases. Finger tapping (right and left hands, combined) data were available in 69 percent of the subjects. For these latter four variables, a mean substitution procedure was utilized in conducting the multiple regression analysis.

The major findings from the multiple regression analysis include the following: 1) As predicted in our initial hypothesis, global clinical severity at baseline correlated significantly with GDS at follow-up ($r = 0.79$, $p < .001$) and accounts for more than 60 percent of the variance in clinical severity (GDS) at follow-up. 2) Even after controlling for follow-up interval, age, and sex, a few brief psychometric tests (paragraph recall mean score of initial and delayed recall and the digit symbol substitution test) can add an additional 14 percent to the variance in clinical severity at follow-up. 3) Over and above these measures the ten-item mental status questionnaire can predict a significant additional 1 percent of outcome variance in GDS. 4) Neuroimaging measurements utilizing CT scans, and other test procedures, did not add significantly to the outcome variance in GDS score assignment, after the aforementioned variables have been taken into consideration.

Partial correlations, controlling only for baseline clinical severity, follow-up interval variance, subject age and sex examined the relationship to outcome of psychometric assessments of memory and vocabulary; motor and perceptual skills; mental status asessment; and computerized tomographic assessments of cerebral ventricular dilatation and cerebral cortical atrophy. The results of such an analysis reveal that all psychometric assessments of memory studied, except digit recall, correlated significantly with outcome clinical severity even after controlling for baseline clinical severity, follow-up interval, age and sex ($r$'s = 0.30 to 0.57, $p$'s $<.001$). Similarly, language function as measured by WAIS Vocabulary Scores also related strongly to outcome ($r = 0.36$, $p < .001$). Even a "pure" motor task, finger tapping, also correlated significantly ($r = 0.29, p < .01$) with deterioration at outcome. Relationships to a perceptual motor task ($r = 0.40$–$0.44$, $p < .001$), and a brief mental status questionnaire ($r = 0.37, p < .001$) were also observed. The partial correlations also revealed a relationship between an independently derived CT assessment of brain change, namely ventricular dilatation, and clinical worsening at outcome ($r = 0.17$, $p = .05$). Hence, *in vivo* assessments of brain change may contribute measurably to outcome changes, over and above global clinical and age-related factors.

A surprising result of our study was the absence of an effect of age on outcome. In the absence of objective data clinical speculations have been forwarded that: a) patients with an earlier onset of illness deteriorate more rapidly because their condition is "more malignant," and, paradoxically b) older patients deteriorate more rapidly because they are more frail. Our data do not lend support for either hypothesis in the twenty-five-year age range which we examined.

An absence of a strong relationship between outcome and follow-up interval in our study was due to the small variability in follow-up interval (mean follow-up interval = 3.5 years; SD = 0.6 years). Subsequent follow-up would be expected to strongly evoke this relationship.

As mentioned above, a separate cohort of twenty-eight subjects with vascular concomitants at baseline was also followed (see Table 7). Because of limitations of sample size very few subgroup comparisons can be made between this cohort and the larger study cohort. Statistically significant differences in outcome were not observed, although a tendency for these subjects to decline more rapidly than the non-vascular cohorts is present (Table 9).

## CONCLUSION

In summary, the major findings from our study to date include the following: 1) Our primary hypothesis that the magnitude of impairment in our outpatients with varying degrees of cognitive dysfunction consistent with aging and /or AD

Table 9. Outcome Summary
Geriatric Subjects with Cerebrovascular Factors Associated with CNS Aging or Dementia at Baseline

| *GDS* | *Follow-up N* | *Follow-up Interval (Yrs.) Mean ± SD* | *Neutral*[a] | *Negative*[b] | *Negative Outcome (%)* |
|---|---|---|---|---|---|
| 2 | 9 | 3.52 ± 0.64 | 7 | 2 | 22.2 |
| 3 | 8 | 3.61 ± 0.44 | 5 | 3 | 37.5 |
| 4 | 6 | 4.00 ± 0.55 | — | 6 | 100.0 |
| 5 | 3 | 4.33 ± 0.49 | 1 | 2 | 66.7 |
| 6 | 2 | 4.09 ± 0.74 | — | 2 | 100.0 |
| 2–6 | 28 | 3.78 ± 0.59 | 13 | 15 | 53.6 |

[a]Community-residing and increase in GDS of less than two rating points.
[b]Deceased, in nursing home or community-residing with change in GDS of two rating points or greater.
**Note:** Follow-up interval range = 2.97 to 4.73 years.

would predict longitudinal course, has been strongly supported; 2) A global clinical variable (GDS), appears to have been useful in predicting course; 3) Diverse psychometric variables including memory measures, vocabulary, and pure psychomotor measures, appear to have been useful in predicting course, independently of the clinical grouping variables; 4) Brief mental status measures appear to be useful predictors of course, independently of our major clinical grouping variables; 5) Non-behavioral *in vivo* structural assessments of brain change appear to have been useful predictors of course, independent of previously established age and cross-sectional severity relationships; 6) Surprisingly, age does not appear to have notably influenced outcome in our study limited to subjects sixty to eighty-five years at baseline; and 7) Although our relatively small vascular cohort does not permit a detailed examination of the effect of complicating vascular illness on outcome, the qualitative suggestion of a possibly more rapid course, which must be confirmed with larger samples and longer follow-up intervals, appears compatible with the present data.

Several questions emerge from the data at this point. The most salient of these include: 1) Do our tentative definitions of the borders between aging and AD hold for longer time intervals?; 2) Are the GDS = 2 subjects with subjective deficit at baseline different from "normal" aged controls?; 3) Are the GDS = 3 subjects truly a "border" group, the majority of whom do not deteriorate, or was the study duration insufficient to determine deterioration?; 4) Will all GDS = 4 and GDS = 5 subjects ultimately decline?; 5) Can more recently developed clinical, mental status, and neuroimaging modalities, which describe behavior, brain structure and brain metabolism in much finer detail add to our findings described above?; 6) What is the relationship between course and neuropathology?; and 7) Can further subgroupings within global grouping variables be identified with larger samples and longer follow-up times (e.g., generalizations from the 3 of 54 GDS = 2 subjects with negative outcomes at this stage would be exceedingly hazardous).

Improvements in clinical assessment methodology now permit us to assess our severe patients in considerably greater detail. Improved clinical assessments and mental status assessments may also enable us to describe even more accurately the borders between normality and AD, as well as the precise course of each stage of AD, using instruments such as the Brief Cognitive Rating Scale and Mini Mental State, as well as many of the other methodologies which have been alluded to above.

## REFERENCES

1. B. Reisberg (Ed.), *Brain Failure: An Introduction to Current Concepts of Senility*, Free Press/Macmillan, New York, 1981.
2. R. M. Gladstone, Book Review, Journal of the American Geriatrics Society, 30, pp. 789–790, 1982.
3. B. Reisberg, *A Guide to Alzheimer's Disease*, Free Press/Macmillan, New York, 1983.
4. B. Reisberg (Ed.), *Alzheimer's Disease*, Free Press/Macmillan, New York, 1983.
5. U.S. Department of Health and Human Services, *Alzheimer's Disease: Report of the Secretary's Task Force on Alzheimer's Disease*, pp. 29–33, 1984.
6. N. Mace and P V. Rabins, *The 36-Hour Day*, Johns Hopkins University Press, Baltimore, 1981.
7. N. Brozan, Coping with Travail of Alzheimer's Disease, *New York Times*, Nov. 29, 1982.
8. M. Roach, Another Name for Madness, *New York Times Magazine*, pp. 22–31, Jan. 16, 1983.
9. B. Reisberg, Testimony for Hearing: "Progress Made in the Treatment of Alzheimer's Disease," Subcommittee on Aging, *U.S. Senate Committee on Labor & Human Resources*, May 16, 1983.
10. B. Reisberg, S. H. Ferris, M. J. de Leon, and T. Crook, The Global Deterioration Scale for Assessment of Primary degenerative Dementia, *American Journal of Psychiatry, 139*, pp. 1136–1139, 1982.
11. J. C. Prichard, *A Treatise on Insanity and Other Disorders Affecting the Mind*, Haswell, Barnington, and Haswell, pp. 69–80, 1837.
12. American Psychiatric Association, *Diagnostic and Statistical Manual of Mental Disorders*, 3rd. ed., American Psychiatric Association, Washington, DC, 1980.
13. M. K. Schneck, B. Reisberg, and S. H. Ferris, An Overview of Current Concepts of Alzheimer's Disease, *American Journal of Psychiatry, 139*, pp. 165–173, 1982.

14. M. F. Folstein, S. E. Folstein, and P. R. McHugh, Mini-Mental State: A Practical Method for Grading the Cognitive State of Patients for the Clinician, *Journal of Psychiatric Research, 12*, pp. 189–198, 1975.
15. J. G. Gilbert, R. F. Levee, and F. L. Catalano, A Prelminary Report on a New Memory Scale, *Perceptual and Motor Skills, 27*, pp. 277–278, 1968.
16. T. Crook, J. G. Gilbert, and S. H. Ferris, Operationalizing Memory Impairment in Elderly Persons: The Guild Memory Test, *Psychological Reports, 47*, pp. 1315–1318, 1980.
17. D. A. Wechsler, *The Measurement and Appraisal of Adult Intelligence,* Williams and Wilkins, Baltimore, 1958.
18. R. L. Kahn, A. I. Goldfarb, M. Pollack, and A. Peck, Brief Objective Measures for the Determination of Mental Status in the Aged, *American Journal of Psychiatry, 117*, pp. 326–328, 1960.
19. J. H. Fox, J. L. Topel, and M. S. Huckman, Use of Computerized Tomography in Senile Dementia, *Journal of Neurology, Neurosurgery, and Psychiatry, 38*, pp. 948-953, 1975.
20. M. J. deLeon, S. H. Ferris, I. Blau, A. E. George, B. Reisberg, I. I Kricheff, and S. Gershon, Correlations between CT Changes and Behavioral Deficits in Senile Dementia, *Lancet*, pp. 859–860, Oct. 20, 1979.
21. M. J. deLeon, S. H. Ferris, A. E. George, B. Reisberg, I. I. Kricheff, and S. Gershon, Computed Tomography Evaluations of Brain-Behavior Relationships in Senile Dementia of the Alzheimer's Type, *Neurobiology of Aging, 1*, pp. 60–69, 1980.
22. M. J. deLeon, A. E. George, and S. H. Ferris, Computed Tomography and Positron Emission Tomography Correlates of Cognitive Delcine in Aging and Senile Dementia, in *Handbook for Clinical Memory Assessment of Older Adults*, L. W. Poon (Ed.), American Psychological Association, Washington, DC, pp. 367–382, 1986.
23. S. D. Brinkman, J. W. Largen, L. Cushman, and M. Sarwar, Anatomical Validators: Progressive Changes in Dementia, in *Handbook for Clinical Memory Assessment of Older Adults*, L. W. Poon (Ed.), American Psychological Association, Washington, DC, pp. 359–366, 1986.
24. M. Folstein, The Mini-Mental State Examination, in *Assessment in Geriatric Psychopharmacology*, T. Crook, S. H. Ferris, and R. Bartus (Eds.), Mark Powley Associates, New Canaan, pp. 47–51, 1983.
25. B. Reisberg, M. K. Schneck, S. H. Ferris, G. E. Schwartz, and M. J. de Leon, The Brief Cognitive Rating Scale (BCRS): Findings in Primary Degenerative Dementia (PDD), *Psychopharmacology Bulletin, 19*, pp. 47–50, 1983.
26. B. Reisberg, E. London, S. H. Ferris, J. Borenstein, L. Scheier, and M. J. de Leon, The Brief Cognitive Rating Scale: Language, Motoric, and Mood Concomitants in Primary Degenerative Dementia, *Psychopharmacology Bulletin, 19*, pp. 702–708, 1983.
27. G. Blessed, B. E. Tomlinson, and M. Roth, The Association Between Quantitative Measures of Dementia and Senile Change in the Cerebral Gray Matter of Elderly Subjects, *British Journal of Psychiatry, 114*, pp. 797–811, 1968.
28. E. A. Pfeiffer, Short Portable Mental Status Questionnaire for the Assessment of Organic Brain Deficit in the Elderly, *Journal of the American Geriatrics Society, 23*, pp. 433–441, 1975.

29. J. W. Jacobs, M. R. Bernhard, A. Delgado, and J. F. Strain, Screening for Organic Mental Syndromes in the Mentally Ill, *Annals of Internal Medicine, 80*, pp. 40–46, 1977.
30. B. Reisberg, S. H. Ferris, R. Anand, M. J. de Leon, M. K. Schneck, C. Buttinger, and J. Borenstein, Functional Staging of Dementia of the Alzheimer's Type, *Annals of the New York Academy of Sciences, 435*, pp. 481–483, 1984.
31. B. Reisberg, S. H. Ferris, and E. Franssen, An Ordinal Functional Assessment Tool for Alzheimer's-Type Dementia, *Hospital and Community Psychiatry, 36*, pp. 593–595, 1985.
32. J. Borenstein and B. Reisberg, Functional Deficits in Alzheimer's Disease, *American Psychiatric Association, 140th Annual Meeting, New Research Abstracts,* p. 56, (Abstract), 1987.
33. G. McKhann, D. Drachman, M. Folstein, R. Katzman, D. Price, and E. M. Stadlan, Clinical Diagnosis of Alzheimer's Disease: Report of the NINCDS-ADRDA Work Group Under the Auspices of Department of Health and Human Services Task Force on Alzheimer's Disease, *Neurology, 34*, pp. 939–944, 1984.
34. N. H. Nie, C. H. Hull, J. G. Jenkins, K. Steinbrenner, and D. H. Bent, *Statistical Package for the Social Sciences*, 2nd edition, McGraw-Hill, New York, pp. 531–533, 1975.
35. B. Reisberg, J. Borenstein, S. P. Salob, S. H. Ferris, E. Franssen, and A. Georgotos, Behavioral Symptoms in Alzheimer's Disease: Phenomenology and Treatment, *Journal of Clinical Psychiatry, 48 (Suppl),* pp 9–15, 1987.
36. S. H. Ferris, G. Steinberg, E. Shulman, R. Kahn, and B. Reisberg, Institutionalization of Alzheimer's Disease Patients: Reducing Precipitating Factors through Family Counseling, *Home Health Care Services Quarterly, 8*, pp. 23–51, 1987.
37. B. Reisberg, E. Shulman, G. Steinberg, E. Rabinowitz, R. Kahn, and S. H. Ferris, Symposium on Alzheimer's Disease: Patient and Caregiver Management, *Drug Therapy, 16*, pp. 65–93, 1986.
38. B. Reisberg, J. Borenstein, E. Franssen, S. Salob, G. Steinberg, E. Shulman, S. H. Ferris, and A. Georgotas, BEHAVE-AD: A Clinical Rating Scale for the Assessment of Pharmacologically Remediable Behavioral Symptomatology in Alzheimer's Disease, in *Alzheimer's Disease: Problems, Prospects, and Perspectives*, H. Altman (Ed.), Plenum Press, New York, pp. 1–16, 1987.
39. B. Reisberg, S. H. Ferris, E. Shulman, G. Steinberg, C. Buttinger, E. Sinaiko, J. Borenstein, M. J. de Leon, and J. Cohen, Longitudinal Course of Normal Aging and Progressive Dementia of the Alzheimer's Type: A Prospective Study of 106 Subjects Over a 3.6 Year Mean Interval, *Progress in Neuro-Psychopharmacology and Biological Psychiatry, 10*, pp. 571–578, 1986.
40. S. H. Ferris, M. J. de Leon, A. P. Wolf, T. Farkas, D. R. Christman, B. Reisberg, J. S. Fowler, R. MacGregor, A. Goldman, A. E. George, and S. Rampal, Positron Emission Tomography in the Study of Aging and Senile Dementia, *Neurobiology of Aging, 1*, pp. 127–131, 1980.
41. S. H. Ferris, M. J. de Leon, D. Christman, B. Reisberg, J. Fowler, A. George, M. Emmerich, C. Gentes, and A. P. Wolf, Positron Emission Tomograpy (PET) Studies of Regional Brain Metabolism in Elderly Patients, in *Biological Psychiatry 1981*, C. Perris, G. Struwe, and B. Jansson (Eds.), Elsevier Science Publishing Co., Amsterdam, pp. 280–283, 1981.

42. S. H. Ferris, M. J. de Leon, A. P. Wolf, A. E. George, B. Reisberg, J. Brodie, C. Gentes, D. R. Christman, and J. S. Fowler, Regional Metabolism and Cognitive Deficits in Aging and Senile Demntia, in *Aging of the Brain*, D. Samuel et al. (Eds.), Raven Press, New York, pp. 133–142, 1983.
43. H. K. Fischman, B. Reisberg, P. Albu, S. H. Ferris, and J. D. Rainer, Sister Chromatid Exchanges and Cell Cycle Kinetics in Alzheimer's Disease, *Biological Psychiatry, 19*, pp. 319–327, 1984.
44. H. Fillit, V. N. Luine, B. Reisberg, R. Amador, B. McEwen, and J. B. Zabriskie, Studies of the Specificity of Antibrain Antibodies in Alzheimer's Disease, in *Senile Dementia of the Alzheimer Type, Neurology & Neurobiology, Vol. 18*, J. T. Hutton and A. D. Kenny (Eds.), Alan R. Liss, New York, pp. 307–318, 1985.
45. L. Prichep, F. Gomez Mont, E. R. John, and S. H. Ferris, Neurometric Electroencephalographic Characteristics of Dementia, in *Alzheimer's Disease*, B. Reisberg (Ed.), Free Press/Macmillan, New York, pp. 252–257, 1983.
46. E. Friedman, K. A. Sherman, S. H. Ferris, B. Reisberg, R. T. Bartus, and M. K. Schneck, Clinical Response to Choline Plus Piracetam in Senile Dementia: Relation to Red-Cell Choline Levels, *New England Journal of Medicine, 304*, pp. 1490–1491, 1981.
47. T. Crook, R. T. Bartus, S. H. Ferris, P. Whitehouse, G. D. Cohen, and S. Gershon, Age-Associated Memory Impairment: Proposed Diagnostic Criteria and Measures of Clinical Change—Report of a National Institute of Mental Health Work Group, *Developmental Neuropsychology, 2*, pp. 261–276, 1986.
48. J. A. Wang and A. Whanger, Brain Impairment and Longevity, in *Prediction of Life Span*, E. Palmore and F. C. Jeffers (Eds.), D. C. Heath, Lexington, MA, 1971.
49. F. Wilkie and C. Eisdorfer, Terminal Changes in Intelligence, in *Normal Aging II*, E. Palmore (Ed.), Duke University Press, Durham, pp. 103–115, 1974.
50. L. F. Jarvik and A. Falek, Intellectual Stability and Survival in the Aged, *Journal of Gerontology, 18*, pp. 173–176, 1963.
51. L. F. Jarvik and J. E. Blum, Cognitive Decline as Predictors of Mortality in Twin Pairs: A Twenty-Year Longitudinal Study of Aging, in *Prediction of Life Span*, E. Palmore and F. C. Jeffers (Eds.), D. C. Heath, Lexington, MA, pp. 199–211, 1971.
52. M. Roth, The Natural History of Mental Disorders Arising in the Senium, *Journal of Mental Sciences, 101*, p. 218, 1955.
53. A. Goldfarb, Predicting Mortality in the Institutionalized Aged, *Archives of General Psychiatry, 21*, pp. 172–176, 1969.
54. V. A. Kral, Senescent Forgetfulness: Benign and Malignant, *Canadian Medical Association Journal, 86*, pp. 257–260, 1962.
55. R. B. Cahan and C. L. Yeager, Admission EEG as a Predictor of Mortality and Discharge for Aged State Hospital Patients, *Journal of Gerontology 21*, pp. 248–256, 1966.
56. A. W. Kaszniak, J. Fox, D. L. Gandell, D. C. Garron, M. S. Huckman, and R. G. Ramsey, Predictors of Mortality in Presenile and Senile Dementia, *Annals of Neurology, 3*, pp. 246–252, 1978.
57. R. C. P. Go, A. B. Todorov, R. C. Elston, and J. Constantinidis, The Malignancy of Dementias, *Annals of Neurology, 3*, pp. 559–561, 1978.
58. E. G. Thompson, M. R. Eastwood, Survivorship and Senile Dementia, *Age and Aging, 10*, pp. 29–32, 1981.

59. L. L. Barclay, A. Zemcov, J. P. Blass, and J. Sansone, Survival in Alzheimer's Disease and Vascular Dementias, *Neurology, 35*, pp. 834–840, 1985.
60. A. J. Reding, J. Haycox, K. Wigforss, D. Brush, and J. P. Blass, Follow-Up of Patients Referred to a Dementia Service, *Journal of the American Geriatrics Society, 32*, pp. 265–268, 1984.
61. P. K. Mosla, R. J. Marttila, and U. K. Rinnc, Survival and Cause of Death in Alzheimer's Disease and Multi-Infarct Dementia, *Acta Neurologica Scandinavia, 74*, pp. 103–107, 1986.
62. K. Bergmann, Chronic Brian Failure—Epidemiological Aspects, *Age and Aging, (Supplement) 4,* pp. 4–8, 1977.
63. B. Reisberg, E. Shulman, S. H. Ferris, M. J. de Leon, and V. Geibel, Clinical Assessments of Age-Associated Cognitive Decline and Primary Degenerative Dementia: Prognostic Concomitants, *Psychopharmacology Bulletin, 19*, pp. 734–739, 1983.
64. L. Berg, W. L. Danziger, M. Storandt, L. A. Coben, M. Gado, C. P. Hughes, J. W. Knesevich, and J. Botwinick, Predictive Features in Mild Senile Dementia of the Alzheimer Type, *Neurology 34*, pp. 563–569, 1984.
65. D. Cohen, G. Kennedy, and C. Eisdorfer, Phases of Change in the Patient with Alzheimer's Dementia: A Conceptual Dimension for Defining Health Care Management, *Journal of the American Geriatrics Society, 32,* pp. 11–15, 1984.
66. J. V. Haxby, C. L. Grady, R. Duara, N. Schlageter, G. Berg, and S. I. Rapoport, Neocortical Metabolic Abnormalities Precede Nonmemory Cognitive Deficits in Early Alzheimer's Type Dementia, *Archives of Neurology, 43*, pp. 882–85, 1986.
67. B. Reisberg, S. H. Ferris, M. J. de Leon, and T. Crook, Age-Associated Cognitive Decline and Alzheimer's Disease: Implications for Assessment and treatment, in *Thresholds in Aging*, M. Bergener, M. Ermini, and H. B. Stahelin (Eds.), Academic Press, London, pp. 255–292, 1985.
68. M. J. de Leon, S. H. Ferris, A. George, B. Reisberg, D. R. Christman, I. I. Kricheff, and A. P. Wolf, Computed Tomography and Positron Emission Transaxial Tomography Evaluations of Normal Aging and Alzheimer's Disease, *Journal of Cerebral Blood Flow and Metabolism, 3*, pp. 391–394, 1983.
69. M. J. de Leon, S. H. Ferris, A. E. George, D. R. Christman, J. S. Fowler, C. Gentes, B. Resiberg, B. Gee, M. Emmerich, Y. Yonekura, J. Brodie, I. I. Kricheff, and A. P. Wolf, Positron Emission Tomography Studies of Aging and Alzheimer's Disase, *American Journal of Neuroradiology, 4*, pp. 568–571, 1983.
70. M. J. de Leon, A. E. George, S. H. Ferris, D. R. Christman, J. S. Fowler, C. Gentes, J. Brodie, B. Reisberg, and A. P. Wolf, Positron Emission Tomography and Computed Tomography Assessments of the Aging Human Brain, *Journal of Computer Assisted Tomography, 8*, pp. 88–94, 1984.
71. J. R. De Paulo and M. F. Folstein, Psychiatric Disturbances in Neurological Patients: Detection, Recognition, and Hospital Course, *Annals of Neurology, 4*, pp. 225–228, 1978.

CHAPTER

# 9

# Attrition in the Baltimore Longitudinal Study of Aging During the First Twenty Years

*Sushil K. Sharma*
*Jordan D. Tobin*
*Larry J. Brant*

## INTRODUCTION

The desirability of longitudinal research to study the aging process is well documented in the literature [1–7]. However, there are a number of identifiable administrative and methodological problems inherent in the longitudinal method of research. These include the uncertainty of long-term funding to support the cost of such research, the need to obtain the required interest and commitment of participating scientists, and the special methodological requirements of longitudinal research [1, 8–11].

Longitudinal research on human subjects is dependent upon the availability of individuals at regular intervals for repeat examinations. Thus, to a large extent, the success of any longitudinal study depends upon the subjects making an ongoing commitment to cooperate and remain in the study, since longitudinal analyses depend on repeat data on the same individual as he ages. However, despite the fervent desire to maintain one hundred percent cooperation from the subjects, attrition over time is one of the major problems in longitudinal studies [1, 10, 12–15]. Attrition in longitudinal research can occur not only by reason of death, but by refusals due to diminution of motivation or interest, change in circumstances (e.g. health and economics), or a loss of contact resulting from change of residence. Different rates of attrition in longitudinal studies have been reported in the literature [16–21]. A comparison of rates is difficult since each study has used different criteria for defining a drop-out. For example, in the Boston V.A. study of aging, if a subject maintains a telephone contact only, he is considered to be an active subject (Borkan, G., personal communication); whereas in the Baltimore Longitudinal Study of Aging (BLSA), a subject is considered active only if he returns to the study center.

An important administrative function in longitudinal research is to keep the attrition rate to a minimum. Of course, one can do nothing about death since death is an inevitable end point in longitudinal research on aging. However, knowledge about the factors which lead to high or low attrition for reasons other than death allows one to adopt strategies aimed at minimizing the attrition of subjects. These strategies could be applied either at the time of recruitment of study subjects (i.e. selecting those subjects who have a higher possibility of staying) or during the course of study. It is highly important, therefore, for planners and administrators of long-term investigations to be aware of those characteristics of individuals that are likely to result in higher or lower rates of attrition. In this chapter, a multivariate logistic regression model is used to examine the effect of a few selected characteristics of subjects on their subsequent active/drop-out status.

## LITERATURE REVIEW

A review of the findings from cross-sectional studies that have compared subjects (generally college students) who agreed to cooperate with those subjects who refused are not conclusive [22]. Because longitudinal studies require the same individuals to return at regular intervals for repeat examinations, findings from only those longitudinal studies that have reported some information on drop-outs will be reviewed here. Factors that have previously been examined can be classified as 1) demographic characteristics, 2) psychological attributes, and 3) physical health. It must be pointed out that even in these longitudinal studies many of the conclusions made about drop-out subjects are not clearcut. In this chapter, only findings pertaining to demographic variables are reviewed. The major findings were that, in general, subjects who drop out are likely to be 1) older [19–21, 23]; 2) less likely to be married [24]; 3) less educated [21, 25–27]; 4) in stressful or high-demand occupations [27, 28]; 5) financially less well-off [23, 27]; and 6) in poor health [19, 21, 23, 24, 27], as compared to subjects who remain active in the study.

With regard to age, Rusin and Siegler point out that the reasons for the finding that the average drop-out is older than the average participant is the high number of deaths among older subjects [29]. Although not clearly stated, they pointed out an important methodological distinction between 1) dropping out because of death, and 2) voluntary dropping out. In essence, they recognized death as a competing risk with dropping out, warranting special attention in the analysis. The analysis presented here addresses this problem by comparing results either using or ignoring all deceased subjects data; as well as using only those who died while still considered active participants in the study. In addition to those study variables just mentioned, we have also examined the effect on attrition of 1) distance between subject's residence and study center and 2) method of recruitment. In long-term studies, one can argue that the longer a subject has been in the study preceding the occasion being analyzed the more likely he is to remain in the study provided death does not occur. We have, therefore, controlled for duration in study by entering it as an independent variable in our analysis.

## DESCRIPTION OF THE BALTIMORE LONGITUDINAL STUDY OF AGING

The BLSA was initiated in 1958 to study the physiological, biochemical, sociological and psychological changes that occur with advancing age [30]. The recruitment of study subjects in the BLSA is an ongoing one, and is entirely on a volunteer basis. There are three major modes of subject recruitment. First, most subjects are recruited by relatives and friends who are already subjects in the study. Second, some subjects are self recruits who learned of this study by reading articles in local newspapers or professional journals. Lastly, a few subjects are recruited by the BLSA staff. (Distribution of subjects by method of recruitment follows later on p. 238).

The subjects are expected to return to the study center (the Gerontology Research Center—GRC) at regularly scheduled intervals for two and a half days of intensive physiological, biochemical, psychological, and sociological examinations and tests. Subjects reside in different parts of the United States. They visit on their own time and at their own expense and provide their own transportation. No medical care is provided. However, all subjects are expected to have a family physician to whom medical reports are sent.

## THE STUDY POPULATION

The study population used in the present study is limited to those 1088 subjects who joined the study between February 1958 (the inception of the study) and June 30, 1977 (Table 1). As of the latter date, six hundred and fifty-eight subjects were actively participating in the study, two hundred and ninety-nine subjects had dropped out from the BLSA (forty-six of these first dropped out but died later on) while one hundred and thirty-one subjects died while on active status in the study. A drop-out is defined as a person who formally notifies the BLSA staff in writing or verbally, in person or by phone, his wish to withdraw himself from future participation in the study; or a subject who has not returned to BLSA within three years since his last visit and who has not responded to attempts made by the appointment clerk to reschedule him for the next visit.

The study subjects were all males who ranged in age from eighteen to ninety-six years at first visit (mean age 49 years). Most subjects were Caucasian. Most

Table 1. Distribution of Subjects by Status in the Study as of June 30, 1977

| | | | |
|---|---|---|---|
| | Total Number of Subjects | 1088 | |
| | Total Number of Active Subjects | 658 | |
| Groups | | | |
| A. | Number of subjects who died while on active status in the study. | 131 | |
| | | | Total 177 Deaths |
| B. | Number of subjects who first dropped out and then died at a later point. | 46 | |
| | | | Total 299 Drop-outs |
| C. | Number of subjects who dropped out and were known to be alive as of June 30, 1977 | 253 | |

were married (86.7%), highly educated (44.1% have a Master, Ph.D. or M.D. degree) (Table 2). In general, they represented a mostly healthy segment of the population.

## METHODS

In order to identify risk factors for dropping out from the BLSA, a multivariate logistic risk function analysis as developed by Walker and Duncan was used [31]. The independent variables or factors in the logistic model included: 1) age 2) marital status 3) education 4) occupation 5) distance between subject's residence and BLSA 6) self health assessment 7) self financial assessment 8) method of recruitment (all measured at first visit), and 9) recruiter's status. After obtaining estimates of the parameters in the logistic model each factor was subdivided and partitioned so that each class contained a meaningful number of subjects. The logistic model with its corresponding estimates was then used to calculate adjusted rates of attrition for these classes. Next, these adjusted rates were used to calculate standardized attrition ratios. These ratios measured the risk of being in a particular class of a given factor, while the effects of all other specified factors were held constant. The standardized attrition ratio (SAR) for a given factor and class was defined as the percentage of corresponding adjusted rate to the overall adjusted rate. The overall adjusted rate is the rate obtained by setting each factor at its average value, thus providing a measure of overall average risk. Further, an additional control variable 'duration of stay in BLSA' was introduced in the logistic model to account for any variability which may have been present because of subjects entering and leaving the BLSA at different times.

Table 2. Distribution of All 1088 Subjects by Status in the BLSA and Various Risk Factors at First Visit

| | Study Population | | Status in Study: Active + (Group A)[a] | | Status in Study: Group B & C | | $\chi^2$ |
|---|---|---|---|---|---|---|---|
| | N | Percent | N | Percent | N | Percent | |
| FACTORS | 1088 | 100 | 789 (131) | | 299 | | |
| Age (yrs) | | | | | | | |
| < 30 | 134 | 12 | 110 (1) | 14 | 24 | 8 | |
| 30–39.9 | 215 | 20 | 164 (1) | 21 | 51 | 15 | |
| 40–49.9 | 236 | 22 | 178 (16) | 23 | 58 | 19 | |
| 50–59.9 | 188 | 17 | 132 (27) | 17 | 56 | 19 | |
| 60–69.9 | 150 | 14 | 98 (32) | 12 | 52 | 17 | 17.9 |
| ≥ 70 | 165 | 15 | 107 (54) | 14 | 58 | 19 | ($p < .005$) |
| Marital status | | | | | | | |
| Never married | 77 | 7 | 60 (4) | 8 | 17 | 6 | |
| Married | 943 | 87 | 682 (112) | 86 | 261 | 87 | 1.5 |
| Other (S.W.D.) | 68 | 6 | 47 (15) | 6 | 21 | 7 | (N.S.) |
| Education | | | | | | | |
| < BA | 273 | 25 | 175 (31) | 22 | 98 | 33 | |
| BA | 335 | 31 | 252 (29) | 32 | 83 | 28 | 12.9 |
| > BA | 480 | 44 | 362 (71) | 46 | 118 | 40 | ($p < .005$) |
| Occupation | | | | | | | |
| Professional, Technical, Managerial | 912 | 84 | 667 (117) | 84 | 245 | 82 | |
| Manual, Blue Collar | 85 | 8 | 62 (7) | 8 | 23 | 8 | 2.1 |
| Clerical and Sales | 91 | 8 | 60 (7) | 8 | 31 | 10 | (N.S.) |

*(continued)*

Table 2. (continued)

| | Study Population | | Status in Study | | | | |
|---|---|---|---|---|---|---|---|
| | | | Active + (Group A)[a] | | Group B & C | | |
| | *N* | *Percent* | *N* | *Percent* | *N* | *Percent* | $\chi^2$ |
| Distance (miles) | | | | | | | |
| < 50 | 670 | 62 | 503 (86) | 64 | 167 | 56 | |
| 50–99 | 290 | 27 | 207 (34) | 26 | 83 | 28 | |
| 100–199 | 48 | 4 | 30 (5) | 4 | 18 | 6 | |
| 200–499 | 49 | 4 | 30 (4) | 4 | 19 | 6 | 9.9 |
| ≥ 500 | 31 | 3 | 19 (2) | 2 | 12 | 4 | ($p < .05$) |
| Self health assessment | | | | | | | |
| Average or below | 74 | 7 | 48 (17) | 7 | 26 | 10 | 2.5 |
| Above average | 925 | 93 | 680 (107) | 93 | 245 | 90 | (N.S.) |
| Self financial assessment | | | | | | | |
| Less than comfortable | 178 | 18 | 122 (16) | 17 | 56 | 21 | |
| Comfortable | 696 | 71 | 519 (93) | 73 | 177 | 66 | 4.1 |
| More than comfortable | 105 | 11 | 71 (16) | 10 | 34 | 13 | (N.S.) |
| Method of recruitment | | | | | | | |
| Staff recruitment | 32 | 3 | 21 (6) | 3 | 11 | 4 | |
| Self recruitment | 123 | 11 | 89 (13) | 11 | 34 | 11 | .79 |
| Chain recruitment | 933 | 86 | 679 (112) | 86 | 254 | 85 | (N.S.) |
| Recruiter's status in study[b] | | | | | | | |
| Recruiter dropped out | 160 | 18 | 75 (12) | 11 | 85 | 34 | 65.4 |
| Recruiter active | 773 | 82 | 604 (100) | 89 | 169 | 66 | ($p < .005$) |

[a]Number in parentheses represents number of subjects in Group A.
[b]Recruiter's status in study was determined subsequent to the first visit of his recruit.

## RESULTS

First, a univariate analysis of the crude data on all 1088 subjects resulted in four of the nine risk factors tested being significantly associated with attrition as indicated by a chi-square test (Table 2). Age, education, distance between a subject's residence and study center (all measured at first visit), and recruiter's status in study were found to be significantly associated with attrition.

Second, a multiple logistic risk function analysis on all 1088 subjects was used to identify significant risk factors for dropping out from the BLSA. In this analysis, subjects in Group A ($N = 131$, Table 1) who died within three years of their last visit were considered as active subjects in the program with a duration in study up to the time of death; and subjects in Group B and Group C ($N = 299$) were considered as drop-outs.

Since subjects are obviously at risk of dying before having an opportunity to drop out of the study, death is, as a matter of fact, a competing factor with dropping out. To control for any possible effect of death on dropping out, two separate additional logistic analyses were performed. In a second analysis, subjects who died while on active status (Group A, $N = 131$) were excluded from the analysis, while in the third analysis, all deceased subjects (Group A and Group B, $N = 177$) were excluded from the analysis. Table 2 shows the distributions of these groups with regard to the nine risk factors selected for this study.

Table 3 shows the overall adjusted attrition rates (OAAR), and for each class of factors the adjusted attrition rates (AAR) and the standardized attrition ratios (SAR) for each of the three analyses. The OAAR represents the average risk of dropping out, i.e. the risk calculated with each variable set at its average. The AAR obtained from multiple regression analysis was used to derive the SAR for each class. The SAR represents an estimate of the percentage of overall risk that we would expect if every subject in our study were removed.

In this section, we report in detail the results of the first analysis with all 1088 subjects. The results of the other two analyses shown in Table 2 can be interpreted in the same manner and all three analyses will be discussed in the Discussion Section. The multiple logistic risk function analysis revealed the following factors as demonstrating a statistically significant influence on attrition (see Table 3, analysis 1).

1. *Age*. Age at first visit was found to be a significant factor ($p < .01$). The standardized attrition ratio (SAR) ranged from seventy-eight for subjects who entered the study before age thirty to 131 for subjects who entered at age seventy or over. These values indicate a 22 percent reduction in the overall (average) adjusted attrition rate (OAAR = 24.9) for subjects under thirty years of age and a 31 percent increase in the OAAR for subjects seventy years of age or older.

Table 3. Adjusted Rates of Attrition per 100 Persons and Corresponding Standardized Attrition Ratios for Various Risk Factors

| | *Adjusted Attrition Rate* | *Standardized Attrition Ratios*[a] | | |
|---|---|---|---|---|
| | *N = 1088* | *Analysis 1 N = 1088* | *Analysis 2 N = 957* | *Analysis 3 N = 911* |
| Overall adjusted attrition rate[b] | | 24.9 | 26.9 | 24.1 |
| FACTORS | | | | |
| Age (yrs)* | | | | |
| < 30 | 19.6 | 78 | 59** | 70 |
| 30–39.9 | 21.7 | 88 | 76 | 84 |
| 40–49.9 | 23.6 | 96 | 94 | 96 |
| 50–59.9 | 25.7 | 105 | 115 | 112 |
| 60–69.9 | 27.9 | 113 | 139 | 129 |
| ≤ 70 | 32.3 | 131 | 185 | 162 |
| Marital status | | | | |
| Never married | 22.2 | 90 | 85 | 86 |
| Married | 24.6 | 100 | 100 | 100 |
| Other (S.W.D.) | 27.2 | 111 | 117 | 117 |
| Education* | | | | |
| < BA | 32.0 | 130 | 129 | 137 |
| BA | 24.7 | 100 | 100 | 100 |
| > BA | 19.8 | 81 | 80 | 79 |
| Occupation | | | | |
| Professional, Technical, Managerial | 24.0 | 98 | 96 | 96 |
| Manual, Blue Collar | 26.7 | 109 | 113 | 112 |
| Clerical and Sales | 29.6 | 120 | 132 | 131 |

| | | | | |
|---|---|---|---|---|
| Distance (miles)* | | | | |
| < 50 | 23.0 | 94 | 90 | 89 |
| 50–99 | 25.7 | 105 | 106 | 107 |
| 100–199 | 28.6 | 116 | 124 | 127 |
| 200–499 | 31.6 | 129 | 144 | 149 |
| ≥ 500 | 34.8 | 142 | 164 | 172 |
| Self health assessment* | | | | |
| Average or below | 41.4 | 168 | 192** | 196** |
| Above average | 22.0 | 89 | 89 | 89 |
| Self financial assessment | | | | |
| Less than comfortable | 34.9 | 142 | 152* | 144 |
| Comfortable | 22.7 | 92 | 92 | 92 |
| More than comfortable | 41.4 | 168 | 154 | 160 |
| Method of recruitment | | | | |
| Staff recruitment | 31.7 | 129 | 133 | 150 |
| Self recruitment | 28.2 | 115 | 116 | 123 |
| Chain recruitment | 24.8 | 101 | 99 | 99 |
| Recruiter's status in study*** | | | | |
| Recruiter dropped out | 47.6 | 194 | 184 | 199 |
| Recruiter active | 20.1 | 82 | 82 | 81 |

*$p < .01$ **$p < .001$ ***$p < .0001$

[a]Standardized Attrition Ratio = Adjusted Attrition Rate/Overall Adjusted Attrition Rate.

[b]Calculated with each variable set at its average.

2. *Education.* Level of education at first visit was found to be significantly associated with dropping out ($p < .01$). The SAR ranged from 81 for subjects with more than a bachelors degree to 130 for subjects with less than a bachelors degree. These values indicate a 19 percent reduction in the OAAR for subjects with more than a bachelors degree and a 30 percent increase in the OAAR for subjects with less than a bachelors degree.
3. *Distance.* Distance between subject's residence and GRC was found to be a significant factor ($p < .01$). The SAR increases with increasing distance from 94 for subjects living less than fifty miles away from GRC to 142 for subjects living more than 500 miles away from GRC. These values indicate a 6 percent reduction in the OAAR for subjects living less than fifty miles away from GRC and a 42 percent increase in the OAAR for subjects living 500 miles or more away from GRC.
4. *Self-health assessment.* Self health assessment was found to be a significant factor ($p < .01$). For subjects who rated their health as above average the SAR ranged from 89 to 168 for subjects who rated their health as average or below. These values indicated an 11 percent reduction in the OAAR for subjects rating their health as above average and a 68 percent increase in the OAAR for subjects rating their health as average or below.
5. *Recruiter's status in study.* Recruiter's status in study was found to have the strongest association with dropping out ($p < .0001$). The SAR ranges from 82 for subjects recruited by a fellow recruit who remained active in the study to 194 for those whose recruiters dropped out from the study. These values indicate an 18 percent reduction in the OAAR for subjects recruited by a fellow recruit who remained active in the study and a 94 percent increase in the OAAR for those whose recruiter dropped out from the study.

## DISCUSSION

For simplicity of computation and interpretation, a multiple-logistic model without interaction variables was used to study the effects of selected variables on attrition. An examination of the calculated correlations among the independent variables revealed some correlation (a condition of approximately 0.4) between the variable of education and occupation, but among the others it was very low. The correlations existing in these data are not believed to be of serious concern to the point of affecting the conclusions of the study, since univariate logistic analyses on each of the independent variables produces associations consistent with those found in the multivariate analysis [32].

The results of the univariate analysis, using a chi-square test, indicate that age, education, distance between a subject's residence and study center (measured at first visit), and recruiter's status in study, are significantly associated with attrition. The multivariate logistic analysis on the same data shows that in addition to these four factors, self health assessment at first visit is also significantly associated with attrition. In studies where multiple factors influence outcome it is highly important to use a statistical model that can weight the relative importance of a number of factors and adjust for the influence of these other factors in data presentation. The multiple logistic model used in this study offers adjustment of any given independent variable for the effect of all other independent variables. Since duration in the study is obviously related to retention, its effect has been controlled for by entering it as an independent variable in the model. However, interpretation of this variable would be inappropriate because of its tautological relationship with the outcome variable attrition.

The multiple logistic model analysis indicates that subjects who enter the study at age seventy or over with an education of less than bachelors degree, live 500 or more miles from BLSA, consider themselves as having average or lesser health, and are recruited by another subject who in turn has dropped out, have the greatest risk of dropping out from the study. The increased risk for such a subject in comparison with a subject with an average risk was 243 percent (Figure 1). Further, the analyses also indicate that subjects who enter the study before age thirty with an education of more than a bachelors degree, live less than fifty miles from BLSA, consider themselves as having above average health, and whose recruiter remains active in the study have the smallest risk of dropping out. The decreased risk for such a subject in comparison with a subject with an average risk was 54 percent (Figure 1).

In the literature a distinction has been maintained between voluntary and involuntary attrition. Attrition is considered to be involuntary when death is the reason for dropping out. For all other reasons the term voluntary attrition is used. It has been consistently reported in the literature that older subjects are more likely to drop out [13, 26]. Old age is also highly correlated with attrition due to death [20, 21, 23, 29]. Therefore we would expect death to act as a competing factor with voluntary attrition. Our data strongly support this finding. When subjects who died while on active status (Group A) were excluded from the analysis (analysis 2, Table 3), age became an even more significant factor ($p < .001$). The increased risk of dropping out for a subject seventy years of age and over at first visit increased from 31 percent to 85 percent whereas the risk for a subject under thirty years of age at first visit decreased from 22 percent to 41 percent.

Further, it has been reported that subjects who perceive their health as poor are more likely to be older, and older subjects are more likely to drop out [19, 21, 23, 24, 27]. Older people are also more likely to have physical illnesses and old people are more likely to drop out due to death. Therefore, if we exclude deceased subjects from the analysis, we should not expect self health assessment to be a significant factor. In fact, in our study, we observed an interesting departure from prediction. When we excluded deceased subjects from the analysis, (analyses 2 & 3), the standardized attrition ratio indicated an increase in the average

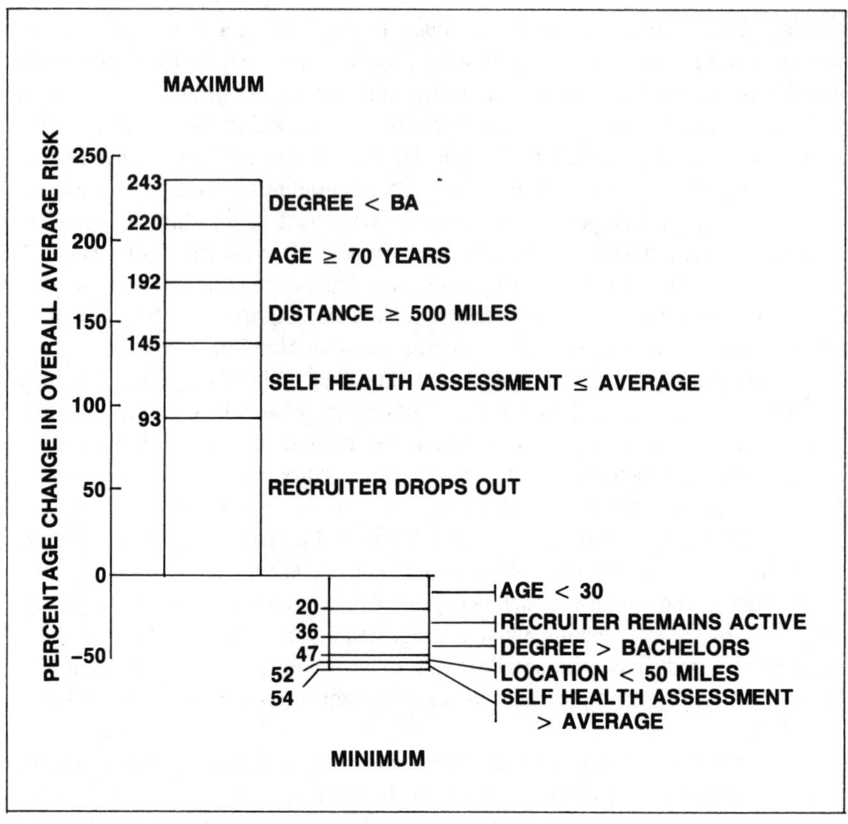


Figure 1. Relative contribution of each risk factor for dropping out.

risk of 92 percent and 96 percent respectively among subjects who rated their health as average or below, while there was no change in the risk of those who rated their health as above average ($p < .001$). We believe that these differences in the analyses are due to the fact that people who are assessing their health as only average or less and in turn do not die during the course of the study are possibly conceiving their health as much worse than it actually is.

Rose and Bell suggested that subjects for long-term studies should be recruited from the same locality as the study center [26]. Their rationale was that the closer the distance, the better the participation on the part of the study subjects. Our study supports this hypothesis. The risk of dropping out increased with distance.

Methods of recruitment and its effect on subjects' stability in long-term studies have not been given the attention that they deserve. This study categorized subjects as being recruited by staff, self, or chain methods of recruitment, and thus allowed us to examine the relative effectiveness of these three methods. Although the risk for dropping out under these three methods of recruitment was not found to be statistically significant, the standardized attrition ratio indicated the chain method of recruitment as having a lower risk than staff and self methods of recruitment. However, subjects recruited by the chain method can be further characterized by their recruiter's status in the study, which may have a differential effect on attrition. By combining these categories, their significance may become dissipated since the 24.8 AAR represents an average of these two categories thereby making it necessary to examine their effects separately.

When the chain method of recruitment was further examined in terms of the effect of recruiter's status on attrition, the recruiter's status was found to have the strongest association with attrition. The standardized attrition ratio indicated a reduction in average risk of 18 percent among subjects recruited by a fellow subject who remains active, while there was a 94 percent increase in the average risk of dropping out among those whose recruiter drops out. This finding suggests that the social relationships among subjects have an important influence on subject stability or subject loss. This supports the notion that human beings are highly social and that, in general, people tend to join long term studies with others whom they like. Other studies that do not so designate methods of recruitment still may have active interpersonal relationships among subjects and potential for the same "infectious" risk.

## REFERENCES


1. R. Andres, The Study of Aging in Man: Practical and Theoretical Problems, in *Theoretical Aspects of Aging*, M. Rockstein (Ed.), Academic Press, New York, 1974.
2. J. E. Birren, Principles of Research on Aging, in *Handbook of Aging and the Individual*, J. E. Birren (Ed.), University of Chicago Press, Chicago, 1959.
3. R. N. Butler, Aspects of Survival and Adaptation in Human Aging, *Journal of Psychiatry, 123*, pp. 1233–1243, 1967.
4. E. Palmore, *Normal Aging*, Duke University Press, Durham, NC, 1970.
5. M. W. Riley and A. Foner, Aging and Society: An Inventory of Research Findings, Russell Sage Foundation, New York, 1968.
6. M. B. Sussman, Use of Longitudinal Design in Studies of Long Term Illness: Some Advantages and Limitations, *Gerontologist, 4*, pp. 25–29, 1964.
7. W.H.O. Public Health Aspects of the Population, Regional Office for Europe, Copenhagen, Denmark, 1959.
8. J. Botwnick, Research Problems and Concepts in the Study of Aging, *Gerontologist, 4*, pp. 121–129, 1964.
9. E. W. Busse, Administration of the Interdisciplinary Research Team, in *Normal Aging*, E. Palmore (Ed.), Duke University Press, Durham, NC, 1970.
10. H. E. Jones, Problems of Method in Longitudinal Research, *Vita Humana, 1*, pp. 93–99, 1958.

11. S. Shapiro, E. Weinblatt, and P. Densen, Longitudinal vs. Cross-Sectional Approaches in Studying Prognostic Factors in Coronary Heart Disease, *Journal of Chronic Diseases, 19,* pp. 935–945, 1969.
12. N. Goldfarb, *An Introduction of Longitudinal Statistical Analysis: The Method of Repeated Observations from a Fixed Sample,* Free Press, Glencoe, IL, 1960.
13. C. L. Rose, R. Bosse, and W. T. Szretter, The Relationship of Scientific Objectives to Population Selection and Attrition in Longitudinal Studies, *Gerontologist, 16,* pp. 508–516, 1976.
14. D. C. Spear and A. Zold, An Example of Self Selection Bias in Follow-Up Research, *Journal of Clinical Psychology, 27,* pp. 64–68, 1971.
15. H. S. Parnes, Longitudinal Surveys: Prospects and Problems, *Monthly Labor Review,* pp. 11–15, 1972.
16. B. Bell, C. L. Rose, and A. Damon, The Normative Aging Study: An Interdisciplinary and Longitudinal Study of Health and Aging, *Aging and Human Development, 3,* pp. 5–17, 1972.
17. S. Granick and R. D. Patterson (Eds.), An 11-Year Follow-Up Biomedical and Behavioral Study, *Human Aging, II,* Publication No. (H.S.M.) 71-90371, U.S. Dept. of H.E.W., Washington, DC, 1971.
18. M. F. Lowenthal and D. Boler, Voluntary vs. Involuntary Social Withdrawal, *Journal of Gerontology, 20,* pp. 363–371, 1965.
19. E. A. Powers and G. L. Bultena, Characteristics of Deceased Drop-Outs in Longitudinal Research, *Journal of Gerontology, 27,* pp. 530–535, 1972.
20. K. F. Riegel, R. M. Riegel, and G. Meyer, A Study of the Drop-Out Rates in Longitudinal Research on Aging and the Prediction of Death, *Journal of Personality and Social Psychology, 5,* pp. 342–348, 1967.
21. A. J. E. Wilson and I. L. Webber, Attrition in Longitudinal Study of an Aged Population, *Experimental Aging Research, 2,* pp. 367–387, 1976.
22. R. Rosenthal and R. Rosnow, *The Volunteer Subject,* John Wiley and Sons, New York, 1975.
23. R. C. Atchley, Respondents vs. Refusers in an Interview Study of Retired Women. An Analysis of Selected Characteristics, *Journal of Gerontology, 24,* pp. 42–47, 1969.
24. G. Maddox, A Longitudinal Multidisciplinary Study of Human Aging—Selected Methodological Issues, Proceedings of the Social Statistics Section of the American Statistical Association, 1962.
25. G. R. Berelson, P. F. Lazarsfeld, and W. N. McPhee, *Voting,* University of Chicago Press, Chicago, 1954.
26. C. L. Rose and B. Bell, Selection of Geographically Stable Subjects in Longitudinal Studies of Aging, *Journal of American Geriatrics Society,* pp. 143–151, 1965.
27. G. F. Streib, Participants and Drop-Outs in a Longitudinal Study, *Journal of Gerontology, 21,* pp. 200–209, 1966.
28. W. T. Szretter, Attrition in the Normative Aging Study, Paper presented at the 28th Gerontological Society Meeting in Louisville, KY, 1975.
29. M. J. Rusin and I. C. Siegler, Personality Differences Between Participants and Dropouts in a Longitudinal Aging Study, Paper presented at the annual meetings of the Gerontological Society, Louisville, KY, November 1975.

30. J. Stone and A. H. Norris, Activities and Attitudes of Participants in the Baltimore Longitudinal Study, *Journal of Gerontology, 21*, pp. 575–580, 1966.
31. S. H. Walker and D. B. Duncan, Estimation of the Probability of an Event as a Function of Several Independent Variables, *Biometrika, 54*, pp. 167–179, 1967.
32. T. Gordon, Hazards in the Use of the Logistic Function with Special Reference to Data from Prospective Cardiovascular Studies, *Journal of Chronic Diseases, 27*, pp. 97–102, 1974.

CHAPTER

10

# Managing a Longitudinal Study: Lessons from the Social Security Administration's Retirement History Study[1]

*Alan Fox and Lola M. Irelan*

Longitudinal studies provide much information not available with cross-sectional studies, but at considerable cost. Apart from the obvious cost of repeatedly interviewing a panel of respondents, managing the data can require considerable outlays of staff time and data processing resources. The latter costs may not always be recognized at the inception of a longitudinal study, but unless budgeted, can considerably degrade the usefulness of the resulting data. Any improperly managed data file is difficult to work with; a longitudinal file improperly managed is even more so. Analysis of the research questions that prompted the study can be delayed considerably, made inaccurate, or abandoned entirely, if the file is not constructed properly.

With the Social Security Administration's Longitudinal Retirement History Study (RHS) now complete, we at SSA are acutely aware of both the opportunities provided by longitudinal research and the associated costs and problems. The opportunities are obvious from the rapidly increasing number of research reports being written nationwide using RHS data. This chapter concentrates on the costs and problems of managing this file and is written with the hope that those currently undertaking or planning longitudinal studies will be able to avoid some of the problems we have had.

[1]This chapter was written while the authors were with the Division of Retirement and Survivor Studies, Office of Research and Statistics, Office of Policy, Social Security Administration. The opinions expressed in this chapter are those of the authors and do not represent policies of either past or present employers.

The chapter first describes the RHS's survey design, sample attrition and weighting are then discussed followed by the question comparability over time. Editing, longitudinal variable construction, and income nonresponse are discussed followed by consideration of the management of the ensuing data set. While many of these comments are applicable to any data set, the sheer magnitude of the RHS makes them especially important. The first focus is on file documentation, preparation of extracted ("work") files, the merging of data files, and the presence of alphabetic codes.

## THE LONGITUDINAL RETIREMENT HISTORY SURVEY

The Retirement History Study is the country's largest, longest-running study of the process of American retirement.[2] Fielded initially in the Spring of 1969, its goal is the analysis of the aspects of American work life and retirement of most concern to social insurance policy makers: labor force participation, sources and amounts of income, health and health care, basic expenditures, and the planning and carrying-out of retirement. For additional information on the RHS design and some of its results, see Irelan et al. [1] and Schwab and Irelan [2].

The sample was nationally-representative, comprising 11,153 persons aged fifty-eight through sixty-three at the time of the first interview. Blacks were included proportionally to their representation in the population. Married women were not sampled, although wives of men in the sample were interviewed. The widows and widowers of sample members who died during the course of the study were interviewed as members of a "surviving spouse" category. In 1979, after six biennial interviews, the expected attrition from death and refusal left over 6,000 original sample members and more than 1,000 surviving spouses. Information from the death certificates of deceased respondents was also collected.

In addition to the data from the six waves of interviews, data from Social Security's administrative records on earnings and benefits are included in the file. Benefit records are extracted every two years; they now cover the years 1969 to 1980. The interview records have all been released to the public, and the benefit records soon will be released.[3] However, the complete earnings records will never be released because of confidentiality restrictions on tax data.

### SAMPLE ATTRITION AND WEIGHTING

If researchers are particularly concerned with generalization to population values, weighting can be a problem. In reporting our 1969 data [1], we represented a picture of the country's preretirement population. These descriptive statistics were all weighted. Of course, attrition is not likely to be random, and to the

[2]The University of Michigan's Panel Study of Income Dynamics and Ohio State's National Longitudinal Study also include persons entering retirement. Those samples are, however, not directed specifically at this age group.

[3]The data files can be obtained from the National Archives, Washington, DC.

extent that it is not, the original weights are perturbed. For longitudinal analysis, however, being primarily interested in studying relationships among variables, and not in describing a population, we have "solved" the weighting problem by essentially ignoring it. We believe, however, that RHS users need not be overly worried about results of attrition, at least in the earlier RHS waves. No stratum had a much greater probability of being sampled than any other, so weights do not vary a great deal. Using the first four waves, 1969-75, Goudy examined the effects of attrition from causes other than death, and concluded that sample's representativeness was not seriously impaired [3]. Another team of researchers, comparing the first and third (1969-73) waves, came to similar conclusions [4]. We do not know how sample attrition through the sixth wave will have affected the representatives of the final surviving sample.

## QUESTION COMPARABILITY

We have now had direct experience with some of the maxims we learned in our first research courses—like "When you're doing a longitudinal study, you should ask the same questions, verbatim, every time." This ideal condition may be unachievable for many reasons, sometimes justifiably. It may be necessary to change an item because it was considerably less than perfect the first time. Or historical factors may intervene. For example, after Supplemental Security Income (SSI) became available it made no sense to ignore this source of income in the interest of question comparability. Such practical matters as limits on research money can eliminate items or item sets; in large part for that reason the 1973 instrument was considerably shorter than all the others. The closest RHS came to total questionnaire replication was with the last one, in 1979, which, with one minor exception, repeated the 1977 instrument. The lesson to be learned is "Try to repeat items, but be prepared to cope with the lack of complete replication."

A recent study reported some adaptations to question non-comparability. Under an SSA grant, researchers at Portland State University constructed fifty-four indices of well-being for the first three waves of RHS. Using whatever data were available, in each wave, indices were constructed for health, social integration, finances, and attitudes. Of the twenty-seven indices constructed for all three waves, nearly half were identical across waves and could be used in a wide variety of statistical procedures. The remaining indices included items to some extent different from wave to wave. Although not usable in some of the more demanding statistical techniques, these measures do appear to satisfy the requirements of such common tools as linear regression [4].

## EDITING, LONGITUDINAL VARIABLES, AND INCOME NONRESPONSE

Each response variable was subjected to a computer edit that tested for responses that were impossible on logical grounds and either identified them as such or corrected them. The editing procedures often made logical inferences and imputations about missing or consistent responses by analyzing whole sequences of related responses. Probabilistic imputation techniques, commonly used in editing cross-sectional surveys, could not be used, in order to avoid generating spurious changes in characteristics for individuals from one survey to the next. For the same reason it was also necessary to keep the editing methodology consistent from one survey to the next.

All editing procedures were developed, specified, and documented by means of decision logic tables. Not only are decision logic tables technically powerful in problem solving and programing specification, but they provide excellent documentation of the editing procedures [5]. The tables for editing one wave's responses serve as the point of departure for developing editing procedures for the following wave.

The decision-logic procedure is worth illustrating in detail. A simple example of a decision-logic table as applied to one question, 37a, is shown in Figure 1. Question 37a, and the series of questions in which it was embedded, is displayed. As can be seen, costs for food eaten at home were developed in questions 34 and 35. Respondents who worked were then asked question 37a, "About how much do you spend in a typical week for meals eaten at work?" The decision-logic table used to edit this question is shown in Figure 2. ERWHC is a variable developed in a previous decision-logic table describing a combination of employment status characteristics of the respondents. The decision process begins by distinguishing between ERWHC responses that are 5 or more and those less than 5. Responses of persons who were not working and were incorrectly asked the question were set to zero. If the respondent had been working and should have been asked the question, his or her response was then accepted. This decision-logic table also shows the coding for the single-digit completion code (ER37A1CC) to the item which describes essential characteristics of the money amount field and points to two computer subroutines which combined responses to this question with an earlier question on expenditures for food at home.

Use of these tables made it possible to bring consistency and completeness to a procedure ususally characterized as *ad hoc* and "messy." It produced more consistency between variables since all the variables which should have been considered if the editing of one variable were taken into account. And the procedure gave assurance of completeness since all relevant skip patterns and prior exclusions could be considered systematically.

Computer programmers then programmed directly from the decision-logic tables to produce edited data files. This allowed communication of precise instructions from analysts to programmers.

The advantages of decision-logic tables for data editing can be summarized as follows:

1. They provide an instrument for the identification and organization of the elements and combinations of elements required for editing each variable.

| Section IV – HOUSEHOLD ACTIVITIES | | |
|---|---|---|
| ☐ Respondent pays for rooms and meals or has no cooking facilities – *SKIP to 37a* | 250 | 1 ☐ |
| 34. We would like to get some idea of your household's food costs – | | |
| a. How much was spent in grocery stores and general food stores last week? | 251 | a $ |
| *If entry in 34a is "0" SKIP to 34c* | | |
| b. About how much of that was for non-food items like soap, paper napkins, household supplies, tobacco, pet food, and things like that? | 252 | b $ |
| c. Was anything spent on food items from other places, like bakeries, fruit stands, roadside markets, dairy stores, or from individuals last week? | 253 | 1 ☐ Yes – How much?<br>2 ☐ No |
| | 254 | c $ |
| d. Were any food items such as eggs, bakery items, milk, or dairy products, delivered to your home last week? | 255 | 1 ☐ Yes – How much?<br>2 ☐ No |
| | 256 | d $ |
| Add a, c, and d . . . . . . . . . . . . . . . . | 257 | $ |
| Subtract b . . . . . . . . . . . . . . . . . . . . | 258 | $ |
| TOTAL FOOD COSTS<br>*(Enter this amount in 35a)* . . . . . . . . | 259 | $ |
| 35a. This means you spent about $______ for food last week. Is this about what you usually spend for food from grocery stores, general food stores, and these other places, or for food delivered to your home? | 260 | 1 ☐ Yes – *SKIP to 36*<br>2 ☐ No |
| b. Do you usually spend more or less? | 261 | 1 ☐ More<br>2 ☐ Less |
| c. How much do you usually spend? | 262<br>263 | $_________ per<br>1 ☐ Week 3 ☐ Month<br>1 ☐ Biweekly 4 ☐ Year |
| 36. How many people usually eat from this food supply at least four days a week? | 264 | ___________ |
| ☐ Respondent does not work – *SKIP to 37b* | 265 | 1 ☐ |
| 37a. About how much do you spend in a typical week for meals eaten at work? | 266 | $ ___________ |
| ☐ Respondent has no spouse in household – *SKIP to 38a* | 267 | $ ___________ |
| b. About how much does your spouse spend in a typical week for meals eaten at work? | 268 | 1 ☐ Spouse does not work |
| 38a. About how much do you (and your spouse) spend in a typical month for dinners eaten away from home? | 269 | $ ___________ |
| b. For other meals and snacks eaten away from home? | 270 | $ ___________ |

Figure 1.

DECISION LOGIC TABLE NO. *37A1* (*1971 49A1*) Revision Date: ______

Social Security Administration, Officer of Research Statistics

1973 Retirement History Survey Edit

| | | 1 | 2 | 3 | 4 | 5 | 6 | 7 | 8 | 9 | 10 | 11 | 12 | 13 | 14 | 15 | 16 |
|---|---|---|---|---|---|---|---|---|---|---|---|---|---|---|---|---|---|
| *1* | VERIFICATION | *4* | *1* | *1* | *1* | *1* | | | | | | | | | | | |
| *2* | 1 *ERWHC:* | *≥5* | *<5* | *<5* | *<5* | *<5* | | | | | | | | | | | |
| *4* | 2 *SC266:* | — | *>00000* | *= 0* | *= DK* | *other* | | | | | | | | | | | |
| | 3 | | *≤99999* | | | | | | | | | | | | | | |
| | 4 | | | | | | | | | | | | | | | | |
| | 5 | | | | | | | | | | | | | | | | |
| | 6 | | | | | | | | | | | | | | | | |
| | 7 | | | | | | | | | | | | | | | | |
| | 8 | | | | | | | | | | | | | | | | |
| | 1 *ER37A1=SC266* | | *X* | | | | | | | | | | | | | | |
| | 2 *=ZERO* | *X* | | *X* | | | | | | | | | | | | | |
| | 3 *=BLANK* | | | | *X* | *X* | | | | | | | | | | | |
| | 4 *ER37A1CC=* | *3* | *1* | *3* | *4* | *5* | | | | | | | | | | | |
| | 5 *COMPUTE ER37A2=* | | | | | | | | | | | | | | | | |
| | 6 *ER36A2+ER37A1* [1] | *X* | *X* | *X* | *X* | *X* | | | | | | | | | | | |
| | 7 *SET ER37A2CC* [1] | *X* | *X* | *X* | *X* | *X* | | | | | | | | | | | |
| | 8 *GO TO 37B1* | *X* | *X* | *X* | *X* | *X* | | | | | | | | | | | |
| | 9 | | | | | | | | | | | | | | | | |
| | 10 | | | | | | | | | | | | | | | | |
| | 11 | | | | | | | | | | | | | | | | |
| | 12 | | | | | | | | | | | | | | | | |

NOTES:

[1] *By CC subroutine*

| | BY | DATE |
|---|---|---|
| Coded: | *DFR* | *9/25/74* |
| Checked: | *BCR* | *10/2/74* |
| Approved: | | |

Prepared by CAMBRIDGE COMPUTER ASSOCIATES, INC.

Figure 2.

The decision-logic table is self-verifiying so that the user can be assured that all possible sets of conditions have been included.
2. They provide precise, complete instructions to computer programmers.
3. They provide complete documentation of the editing procedures in a form comprehensible to computer programmers and nonprogrammers.
4. They provide a vehicle for the direction and control of data editing procedures. Without these it would have been difficult for the study's analysts to oversee the decisions used in the editing.
5. For use in a longitudinal study the tables provide assurance that editing concepts and methodology were consistent from one wave to another. As a consequence comparability of information was not jeopardized by methodological variation.

This system for editing responses started with the 1971 wave, and has been highly successful. However, the effort has not been trivial. For the 1971 survey, for example, about 750 decision logic tables were required to produce about 1,700 fields of response data.

One feature peculiar to longitudinal data, requiring its own characteristic handling, is the development of time-defined variables. In a one-time survey, one would learn about the initial date of Social Security benefit receipt by asking "When did you/do you expect to start receiving Social Security benefits?" In a biennial panel interview one asks, in each wave, "Are you receiving Social Security benefits? Did you receive any last year?" The practical result is that this information may appear in any one of six different places (in a-6 wave study), sometimes with different category codes. Before analysis can proceed, extra time must be spent in compiling and summarizing such information into variables, which can be a very tedious task.

An example is the code we have developed for the timing of Social Security benefit receipt, using data in five separate extracts from SSA's Master Benefit Record (MBR). This requires checking all five extracts for a date of entitlement to benefits and deciding which one to choose in case of conflict. Then the search branches to the applicable MBR extract, picking up information on type of benefit (retired worker, disabled worker, dependent spouse), payment status (payable, postponed because of the earnings test), and whether disability payments had ever been received. For those with benefits postponed because of high earnings, we search subsequent MBRs for the first one in which cash benefits are recorded, signalling actual "retirement." This is an involved process, requiring over three pages of FORTRAN coding. Analyses keyed to the year of retirement must then search RHS survey records before and after that date and be adjusted to a common metric if necessary. For example, income amounts received in different years must be adjusted to the same year (the year of retirement or some fixed year) using an index of prices or wages.

Longitudinal variables derived from the survey records themselves can be even more involved, as nonresponse to any wave of data collection or to specific survey questions must always be anticipated. (Nonresponse is not such a problem with administrative records such as the MBR). Furthermore, inconsistent category coding must be dealt with.

Nonresponse becomes particularly serious for composite items such as total income, where nonresponse can occur in any one of many components. Over all waves of the RHS the average nonresponse rate was about 25 percent. Nonresponse between pairs or triplets was uncomfortably high. However, having longitudinal income data presents some unique opportunities for inter-year editing. A re-edit of income data from all six waves of the RHS was performed, using various techniques, including the following:

- For sources from which income is expected to be received continually once begun (asset income and private pensions, for example), responses in adjacent surveys were used in an interpolation procedure.
- For some sources, additional information was available from administrative records. Thus, earnings were filled in using data from the Summary Earnings Record.
- For rare sources, zeros were imputed if there was no indication of receipt in other years.
- Checks were built into the system to prevent imputations of amounts of substantially larger or smaller than those in preceding or succeeding years.

These relatively simple imputation procedures reduced the average "non-response" rate for total income from about 25 percent to 7 percent in a single survey. Multi-year income comparisons are now possible, with acceptable nonresponse rates. Distributions of both aggregates and individual income sources before and after longitudinal edit are remarkably similar. This operation was applied only to the 6,243 cases in which the sample person was interviewed in all six waves.

## DATA MANAGEMENT

As mentioned earlier, the RHS is a large, unwieldy data set. Each sample record contains over 13,000 variables, and spans 40,000 character positions. At 6,250 bits per inch (BPI), the densest packing currently available, the data fill three tapes. With records of such magnitude, all the basic principles of economic, efficient data management come to be extremely important.

The following comments relate especially to those who function as survey managers and analysts, and emphasize the use of certain program packages. More and more analysts are doing their own programming, and with good reason: except for the simplest analysis it is difficult to specify *a priori* everything that must be done. A learning process is involved, which is best carried out by an analyst interacting with a computer, with occasional help from a professional programmer.

Many packaged programs cannot handle a data set as large as the RHS at all. Regardless of the program, no IBM computer can handle such a large record without it being split up, and those computer programs that can deal with multipart records usually require extra coding to do so.

With this background, some suggestions for dealing with this sort of data set follow. First we discuss the advantages of computerized documentation and the uses of small working files. An example of how one program package makes working files demonstrates how easy it can be, provided some time is previously spent making the file usable by such a package. We then give reasons to avoid such irritants as alphabetic coding, and speak about record keeping and file security.

## ADVANTAGES OF SMALL FILES

We recently did a benchmark time-and-cost comparison of processing large and small files. A simple cross-tabulation, using eleven variables, cost $130 to run on the full RHS file. Turnaround time, on a computer with excess capacity and excellent service, was one to two hours. We then extracted the same variables, using a packaged program, and wrote them into disk storage; this cost $155, and took one to two hours. Then, using the disk file as input to the same tabulation program, the run came back in less than one minute and cost $5.

The implications are obvious. One almost never sees a tabulation or other analysis run correctly on the first try; often, with the complexity that is the hallmark of any longitudinal survey, it takes five to ten attempts before getting the correct results. The extraction step is well worthwhile under these circumstances, particularly if it is easy to do or redo (if, for instance, the analyst discovers that a variable was missing from the original extract).

At some installations the turnaround comparisons are even more striking. For example, a run of this magnitude on a heavily-used computer such as our own Univac might take four hours or longer if three tapes must be mounted, even at the highest possible priority. Most often such an analysis can only be run overnight, raising turnaround to close to twenty-four hours. By putting such data on mass-storage the turnaround time could be reduced to minutes. (Unfortunately the latest version of OSIRIS, which is the only package we know of that can handle the full RHS file, has not been adapted to the Univac.)

## COMPUTERIZED DICTIONARIES

There are few cases nowadays where file documentation should not be computerized. This does not mean simply that the documentation should be typed on a word processor; the error correction advantages of a word processor over a regular typewriter are obvious. Computerized documentation implies much more than this: it implies the ability for program packages to use the documentation directly and thus to manipulate data in ways totally infeasible otherwise. To be absolutely clear, we use the term "dictionary" to refer to computerized documentation. A data dictionary, operating within some program system (OSIRIS, SPSS, SAS, for example) shows at least the following for each variable: variable name or number, brief variable description, starting location, and field width. Our remarks emphasize the University of Michigan's OSIRIS package, which we have recently implemented for the RHS file [6]. Other packages are available, but none seems capable of handling such a large with easy (example are SPSS, SAS, and BMDP). Advantages of computerized dictionaries include the following:

## EASY MANIPULATION OF FILES

In a file as large as ours, this is of utmost importance. Using OSIRIS, extracting a working file is almost trivial; a program to do that reads like this:

```
            //DICTIN ...  JCL: Description of the complete file dictionary, on disk
            //DATAIN ...  JCL: Description of the full RHS file, on 3 tapes
           //DICTOUT ...  JCL: output dictionary, written on disk storage
           //DATAOUT ...  JCL: output data, on tape or disk storage
               ..... ...  3 other setup cards
              &TRANS ...  Begin routine to extract fields
          PRINT-OUTD ...  Print output dictionary, with updated field locations
VARS = 1, 16, 25-112 ...  Variables to be written out
                &END
```

That is all that is required. This program produces a new file containing only the variables specified (and note the ability to specify contiguous variables easily, without listing each one, something not all such programs can do). The output dictionary contains the variable names and numbers, along with updated field locations. The output file can be used by OSIRIS or most other dictionary-oriented packages, specifying variables by their original names or numbers, or by other packages or languages (CROSSTABS, FORTRAN, PL-I), which specify variables by field location.

Cresting an extracted version of the RHS without OSIRIS took us several months the last time it was attempted, and a great deal of clerical time was spent updating field locations. Because it was such an elaborate process we were especially hesitant about leaving out variables we might possibly want, which partially negated the real value of extraction, namely, the ability to make files compact enough to keep in mass storage. Because of this we almost never made work files.

*Easy File Merging* — A longitudinal file is by its very nature a growing organism. Adding new variables to the file is a 20-line OSIRIS program that does not require a professional programmer to write.

*Easy Variable Naming for Future Runs* — If operating within the system which created the dictionary, usually the analyst need only specify the name or number of the variable, not its location.

*Easy Dissemination* — The dictionary of the entire RHS file (13,000 variables and growing) can be listed on a standard high-speed printer and photocopied, or can be listed with quality suitable for publication, very compactly, on a laser printer. Errors can be corrected and updates entered easily, and the complete document, or portions of it, can easily be disseminated to users.

## FULL DOCUMENTATION

With certain packages the entire file documentation can be put in machine readable form. What OSIRIS calls a "codebook" includes the dictionary, described above, along with full-text description of the question and any notes desired, plus descriptions of each code category. This enables one to obtain complete documentation of all or part of the file without referring to multiple volumes of loose-leaf paper (the RHS documentation now occupies over a foot of shelf space). Frequency distributions of the specified codes can be obtained with OSIRIS, and listed alongside the codes.

We have not taken this step because to do so would involve a great deal of typing, at a skill level that of most secretaries. Besides, we already have typewritten documentation, and it seems wasteful at this point to abandon all that work.

## ALPHABETIC CODES

Whenever possible, alphabetic codes should be avoided. By these we mean anything other than zero to nine, and minus signs. Other symbols, including blanks, can cause great trouble, depending on the program being used. For instance, no version of FORTRAN that we are familiar with (including Univac ASCII-FORTRAN, IBM FORTRAN-G, and IBM WATFIV) will accept an alphabetic code where a number is expected. Similarly, most statistical packages do not handle alphabetic codes easily. To perform arithmetic operations on a field that might contain some alphabetic code requires reading the field in alphabetic ("A") format, converting all expected alphabetic codes to some number, and then converting remaining numeric codes into numeric ("I" or "F") format. This is very cumbersome, both in programming and machine time.

Alphabetic codes are most common where they seem, on the surface, to make the most sense. It is tempting to code "Don't know" as "DK." Where space is at a premium, an alphabetic field can represent far more categories than a similar sized numeric field. But most analysts find such codes nothing but a bother.

Another difficulty may emerge in the coding of multi-response questions. It is tempting to construct a variable that left-justifies whatever answers are given, in numerical order. For instance, if six answers are possible, one might have a single six-position variable, with answers left (or right) justified and space filled. For example, if answers '2', '3', and '6' were given, the variable would read '236bbb'. This is extremely difficult to deal with later, both because of the variables length and because of the blanks. Better to waste a bit of documentation space and have six binary (0, 1) variables, one for each possible response.

The possibilities are almost endless, as are the opportunities for real problems. It is better yet to resolve to fill every field (with zeroes, if necessary), and set DK's and NA's to some positive "nonsense" number like 99, 98, 999999, or 99998. The programmer will be grateful for the foresight.

## RECORD-KEEPING

In addition to keeping a full set of data documentation it is necessary to maintain complete records of how variables and indices were constructed. In any survey, especially one as complex as the RHS, decisions are made all the time regarding variable specification. These decisions must be written down and kept in a central location, accessible to all who use the file, for many years. Relying on the memory of those who made the decision is not good enough: people move around, but data sets remain.

A corollary is that all documents must be dated. An undated document invites trouble years later, when two conflicting versions show up.

With the most careful specifications it is inevitable that some variables will not be coded as the analyst might desire. This is particularly true where variable specifications must be developed before the data have been collected. Problems often appear only when a subject-matter analyst actually tries to use a variable, sometimes many years later. This situation reinforces the advisability of maintaining complete, dated records of how variables were specified, and maintaining the capability of altering and updating an incorrect variable.

## FILE SECURITY

The impossible can and does happen: files get destroyed, lost, or written over. It is imperative that at least one set of basic data tapes be archived in a place other than the principal computer installation.

## CODING COMPATIBILITY

As we have already stated, unless absolutely necessary, questions should be worded identically from one wave to the next. Perhaps less often remembered is that the variables should be coded the same as well. Dealing with six survey waves where there are three or four different coding schemes can be very time-consuming.

In conclusion, this chapter has emphasized that problems of data quality do not end with data collection. Each small step of data and file management represents a potential hazard to the overall quality of research. The problems discussed in this chapter only sample a larger number. Sensitivity to some of the generic problems discussed here should alert the researcher to take active steps to foresee and deal preventively with others.

## REFERENCES


1. L. M. Irelan, D. K. Motley, K. Schwab, S. R. Sherman, J. Murray, and K. Bond, *Almost 65: Baseline Data from the Retirement History Study*, Office of Research and Statistics, Social Security Administration, Washington, DC, Research Report No. 49, 1976.
2. K. Schwab and L. M. Irelan, The Social Security Administration's Retirement History Study, in *Aging and Retirement: Prospects, Planning, and Policy*, G. McCluskey F. Borgatta (Eds.), Sage Publications, Beverly Hills, CA, 1981.
3. W. J. Goudy, The Retirement History Study: Two Methodological Examinations of the Data, Sociology Report 1511, Department of Sociology & Anthropology, Iowa State University, Ames, IA, 1982.
4. B. Stewart (Ed.), Methods of Assessing Well-Being and Change in the Retirement History Study, Final Report, Social Security Administration Grant 10-P-98078-10-02, Portland State University, Portland, OR, 1982.
5. K. R. London, *Decision Tables*, Van Nostrand, New York, 1972.
6. *OSIRIS-IV*, Survey Research Center, University of Michigan, Ann Arbor, 1981.

# SECTION 2
# Examples of Structural Equation Modeling and Confirmatory Factor Analysis

Once again, a series of several chapters would be required to deal adequately with the statistical tools essential for longitudinal data analysis. This task, has, in fact, been performed in the Schaie book previously cited [1]. For the present book, two *illustrations* of a method, rather than a treatise on structural modeling, are presented in the chapter by Elizabeth Mutran and Christopher Hertzog. Structural modeling is a generic approach to test the degree of fit of one's data to a set of observations involving multiple measurements and multiple constructs, whose hypothesized causal relationships are part of the model specifications. One sees increasingly in the literature the use of particular statistical programs to analyze such structural relationships. The two in most frequent use are LISREL [2] and EQS [3]. They are new enough and complex enough to have engendered a substantial mystique regarding their use. One facet of the mystique is that they are inaccessible to most users. While formal instruction may be required for most investigators, Mutran's chapter, by stating the conceptual basis for the technique first and following with a worked-out example, shows the naive reader that the logic of structural modeling is straightforward and that the imposing results from applying the method can be interpreted in a very understandable manner.

Specifically, Mutran chooses two important generic types of longitudinal-analytic questions as illustrations. It should be noted first that Campbell and Mutran have previously discussed the use of LISREL for measuring processes of change over time [4], a task for which three occasions of measurement are required. In the present chapter, Mutran asks first whether the measurement properties of a latent construct remain the same over time, a question too frequently ignored when studying people longitudinally. Mutran notes the several conditions that might disturb the ability of indicators to measure the same construct in the same people across time. She then illustrates the pursuit of such a question with a model that gives the reader a basis for applying the method to a variety of similar questions.

The second question is an even more familiar one: Do the causal paths for one group of subjects differ significantly from the causal paths for another? All of us have probably seen correlation coefficients compared between two groups, or regressions or path analyses performed separately for such groups. LISREL provides a means to test the equality of a specific causal path within a specified model across subgroups and thus permits much firmer conclusions about subgroup differences within a causal model. Once more, her empirical example should give the reader some confidence in applying the method to a new problem.

Hertzog's chapter also provides an illustration of the uses of LISREL, but his chapter, "Using confirmatory factor analysis for scale development and validation" goes into some depth in a single content area of research. This content area is what is broadly labeled "subjective well-being," a construct that has been used to include a large number of more specific indicators of psychological state variously referred to as life satisfaction, morale, perceived well-being, mental health, positive affect, negative affect and many others. Research in this topic area has been one of the most frequent types of investigation in gerontology. Thus it is most appropriate to use a highly used (and misused) construct like subjective well-being as a fit topic for the application of a new method.

Hertzog includes in his chapter a critical review of some of the recent literature in which LISREL has been applied to understanding subjective well-being. His intent is to make the prospective user acutely aware of how important it is to understand the assumptions one makes in proceeding to apply confirmatory factor-analytic techniques. In the process his chapter succeeds better than any previously published work in showing how the classical theory of psychometrics underlies the use of such techniques. One emerges with a much enhanced appreciation of the pitfalls of confirmatory analysis while at the same time gaining some assurance that this technology can be brought within range of the ordinary statistical user.

Together the two chapters display the versatility of LISREL in handling two everyday types of analytic problems. The reader may thus be motivated to search the present and future literature for new applications.

## REFERENCES

1. K. W. Schaie, *Methodological Issues in Aging Research*, Springer Publishing Company, New York, in press.
2. K. G. Jöreskog and D. Sörbom, *LISREL, Analysis of Linear Structural Relationships by the Method of Maximum Likelihood*, International Educational Resources, Chicago, 1978.
3. P. M. Bentler, *EQS, BMDP*, Statistical Software Inc., Los Angeles, 1985.
4. R. Campbell and E. Mutran, Analyzing Panel Data in Studies of Aging, *Research on Aging, 4*, pp. 3–41, 1982.

CHAPTER

# 11

# An Example of Structural Modeling in Multiple-Occasion Research

*Elizabeth Mutran*

Research on aging has begun to test theories involving a causal process using the linear structural relations (LISREL) model [1–5]. The popularity of LISREL as a research tool rests in its flexibility for testing many different types of hypotheses. The range of hypotheses appears to be limited only by the researcher's imagination and includes hypotheses about measurement issues as well as structural equations.

In terms of measurement issues, the researcher begins with a set of items that he or she may speculate are multidimensional and actually specify a model which states that the items indicate *Z* number of underlying constructs. The items define the constructs. The LISREL analysis determines whether the specified model adequately reproduces the observed variances and covariances in the items. This is known as an "all *y* model" and is a basic confirmatory factor analysis approach.

LISREL can also be used to correct for measurement error, a feature of the program which is particularly helpful when one has a number of constructs that vary in the accuracy with which they are measured. Thus for each construct, the variance in an item is divided between true or shared variance and error variance, that part of the variance unique to a given item. The measurement error in one item may also be correlated with the measurement error in other items and the LISREL program will estimate the amount of correlated error.

While all of this is useful for cross-sectional analysis, this set of relationships produces a new series of testable hypotheses in longitudinal data and forms an essential first step in the analytic procedure. From the outset, the researcher is faced with a set of decisions to make. First, should the researcher allow the effect of each indicator on the underlying construct to change at different time points or should these estimates be constrained to be equal? Does the amount of measurement error remain stable over time or does it change? If the estimates of the construct are allowed to vary between time one and time two, is the same phenomenon being studied? If you constrain the estimates to be stable for the purpose of insuring constancy in the meaning of the construct, will the empirical model adequately reproduce the variances and covariances?

The above hypotheses deal with issues related to the measurement portion of the model; however, for most researchers the primary goal is the analysis of the structural equations that compose the causal model, that is, the hypothesized influences of one variable on another. In cross-sectional data, a researcher must theoretically make a case for the causal ordering of the variables. This is also true in longitudinal studies as well but the time ordering of events makes this somewhat less problematic. In cross-sectional data, the causal ordering of variables may be impossible to determine or the theory may actually specify feedback effects. One solution is to test for reciprocal effects between variables in which there is theoretical justification for either variable being a determinant of the other. The LISREL program facilitates this type of analysis. Where longitudinal data are available, the researcher is able to hypothesize cross lagged effects, for example, type of job in time one influences health in time two controlling for health at time one. Concurrently, health at time one influences type of job in time two controlling for type of job at time one.

## SOME USES OF LISREL IN LONGITUDINAL RESEARCH

Campbell and Mutran demonstrated the use of LISREL in analyzing panel data [1]. The present chapter will extend that discussion to show other features of the LISREL model, features that are particularly important in analyses of longitudinal data and yet are less often used. The focus of the analyses in this chapter is on equality constraints, and on tests of hypotheses that effects are *equal across time* and that effects are *equal across groups*. Both of these constraints are applicable to the estimates of effects in the structural equation. The researcher analyzing longitudinal data may want to know if the effect of a given independent variable on an outcome measure changes in magnitude from mid to late adulthood. A regression analysis of time two may show the effect to be of somewhat different size then it was at time one, but how does one determine whether the effects are significantly different from one another? It may even be that the effect of the variable is significant at one time period, but not in the other period; however this only tells the researcher that the path is significantly different from zero at one point while not different from zero at another point. It does not inform the researcher whether the paths are significantly different from each other or across the time periods. This question can be addressed by first constraining the paths to be equal and then allowing the paths to differ. A comparison of the two chi squares for the two models with the loss of one degree of freedom can be made.

It can then be determined whether there has been a significant improvement in the fit of the model by allowing the paths to vary.

The importance of the LISREL approach to be discussed and illustrated here lies in the ability to provide the researcher with greater precision and flexibility in specifying and evaluating empirical hypotheses. In the measurement model, one asks, for example, do the indicators of construct *Z* have consistent reliabilities over time or across panels, or do different indicators gain or lose reliability as other important changes occur over time? In the causal model, hypotheses which involve constraints over time allow the researcher to ask questions involving the strength and stability of a relationship, e.g., is that relationship constant over time, does its strength increase, decrease, or is the relationship erratic over time? In adition to being able to ask if the relationship between variable A and variable B is the same between waves two and three of a panel model as it is between waves one and two, one can also apply these constraints to subgroups of subjects.

The ability to constrain parameters across subgroups in a sample allows the researcher to evaluate interaction hypotheses with a great deal of precision. In the standard regression model one can specify multiplicative interaction terms which, if statistically significant net of the other variables in the equation, indicate the presence of a group based interaction. However, if it is theoretically necessary to investigate a large number of potential interactions, such terms will quickly create insoluble multicollinearity problems which will not only make interactions difficult to detect but may obfuscate main effects as well. The LISREL approach to investigating such hypotheses allows for precise and general tests of interaction to be conducted free of the threat of multicollinearity. Hypotheses are evaluated in terms of whether or not the effect of a variable can be constrained to be equal across two (or more) groups; if so, the hypothesis of interaction can be rejected; if not, the relative size, significance, and direction of the divergent effects reveals the substantive impact of the interaction.

This type of analysis helps the researcher to address a variety of questions related to aging. The basic question is whether the aging process is the same for different groups of people. Specifically, the researcher might be asking, does retirement affect the mental health of men to the same degree as for women in the early years of retirement as in later years? Is the relationship between marital status and labor force participation the same for men and women over time? Do the factors that influence health vary in their impact on blacks as compared to whites at various time periods in their lives?

## AN EXAMPLE USING LISREL IN LONGITUDINAL RESEARCH

To demonstrate the use of equality constraints a three-wave model predicting annual hours worked is presented and the appropriateness of the model for men with different job characteristics is assessed. The model has two unmeasured constructs: health and job demands. Each construct has multiple indicators and is measured at two points in time. The first hypothesis is whether or not the relationships of these two constructs with their indicators is the same in time two as it is in time one. If the indicators demonstrate radically different relationships with a construct over time, the assumption that the construct has the same meaning over time may be questioned; the researcher may wish to constrain the parameters from construct to indicators to be equal across waves so as to test this hypothesis before proceeding to estimate the structural parameters in the model.

A second type of equality constraint may be imposed. One might hypothesize that the relationship between job demands and health is quite strong for those whose jobs are extremely taxing, particularly because of physical demands. The relationship between job demands and health may be much weaker or nonexistent where the job is not very strenuous. This is a test for interaction, one that asks whether the relationships between any set of variables is the same across a number of groups for example, men and women; elderly, middle-aged and young adult; Blacks and Whites. In this case the model is analyzed for two groups of men, those whose jobs are above average in physical demands and those whose jobs fall bellow average in physical demands. The data are from the National Longitudinal Study of Mature Men, 1971, 1976 and 1981. The men in the study were ages fifty–fifty-four in 1971.

## THREE-WAVE MODEL OF LABOR FORCE PARTICIPATION

*Model* — The hypotheses to be investigated are shown in path diagrammatic form in Figure 1 and involve relationships among job demands, health, and annual hours worked arranged in a three-wave panel design. First, job demands and health in 1971 are hypothesized to affect job demands in 1976 and health in 1976. In addition, job demands in 1976 is thought to affect health in 1976. In the next wave, job demands in 1976 is hypothesized to affect health in 1981 as well as labor market experience, as measured by annual hours worked in 1981. Health in 1976 is thought to affect labor market experience in 1981 in addition to health in 1981; the latter is hypothesized to affect hours worked in 1981 as well.

A few additional comments should be made about the model in Figure 1. Between waves one and two, job demands are expected to show a good deal of stability, and this should be reflected by a large, positive path coefficient between job demands in 1971 and 1976; the coefficient is referred to as the 'stability' parameter in models of this type. There are also two 'stability' parameters which measure the impact of health in an earlier panel on health in a later panel; as job demands are hypothesized to affect health, however, a lower level of consistency could be expected. This is an empirical hypothesis and the results may suggest that health is relatively stable and unaffected by job demands. On the other hand, the health of the worker is expected to influence the type of job the worker can hold five years later. Essentially, the model in Figure 1 suggests two alternative hypotheses:

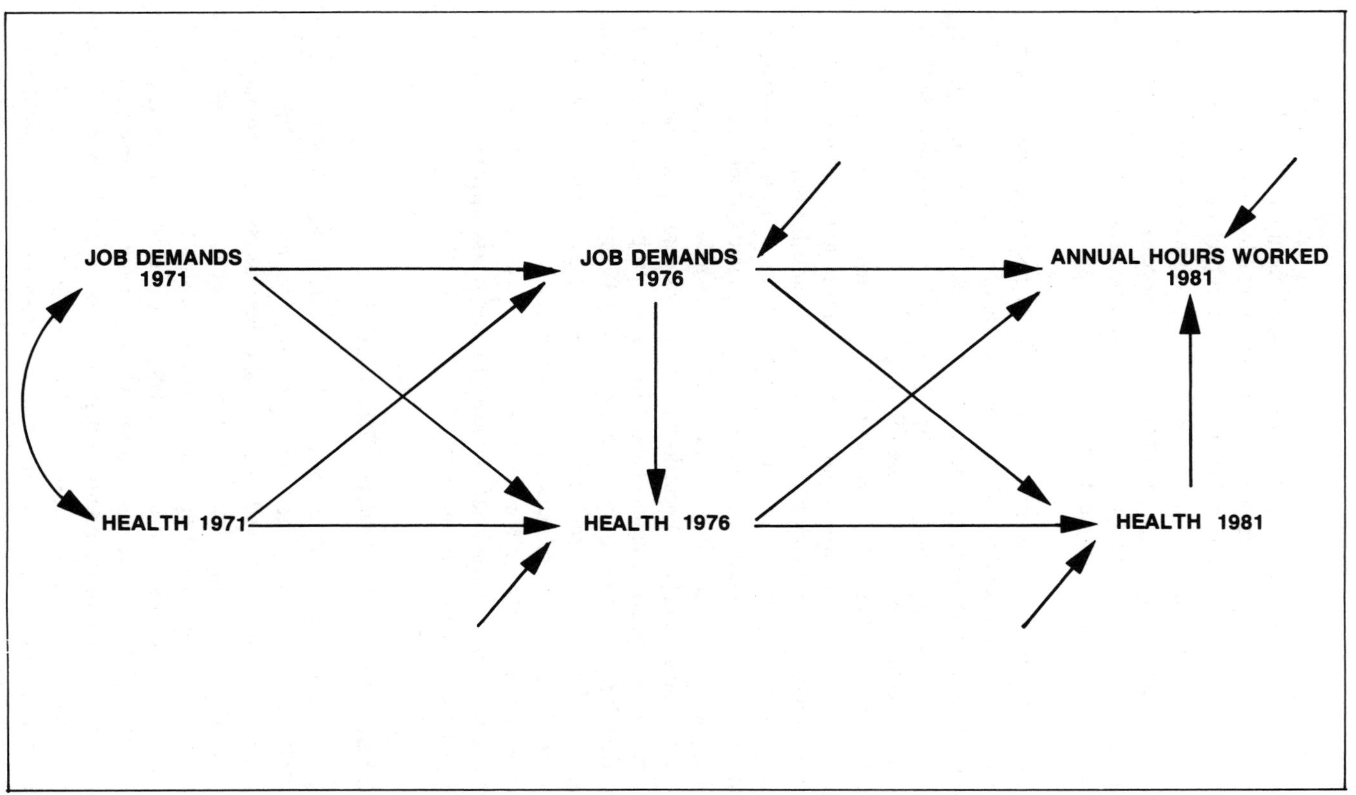


Figure 1. Structural equation model relating job demands, health, and annual hours worked.

1) over time there is an intertwinement of the relationship between health and job demands, such that labor force participation is eventually affected; or 2) health and job demands are relatively stable and do not affect each other, and that labor force participation in the final wave is affected by long term, stable patterns of job demands and health. These hypotheses are not necessarily competing ones, but are suggestive of different underlying causal processes; it may be the case that both are operating to some degree.

*Measurement* — Job demands are defined in terms of the physical demands made of the workers. In this analysis, the physical nature of the job is represented by a construct with three indicators: strength (lifting, carrying, pulling, pushing) scored 1 to 5; climbing (climbing, balancing) scored 0 or 1; stooping (stooping, kneeling, crouching, crawling) scored 0 or 1.

Health is measured in 1971, 1976, and 1981. The items selected for inclusion in this analysis are those which most closely parallel job demands. In 1971, respondents were asked if they had any health problems that limited the kind or amount of work they did, or limited their other activities. If they answered yes to either of the above questions, they were asked detailed questions about their health including three questions that are used here as indicators of health: does health allow using stairs or inclines; does health allow stooping; does health allow lifting or carrying heavy weights. These three health problem items were asked in identical form in the three waves, except that in 1976 and 1981 these items appeared on the questionnaires without the screening questions. The items are scored one if the health problem exists, zero otherwise.

The remaining variable in the model is the hours worked in 1981 which was computed by multiplying the usual number of hours worked per week times the number of weeks worked in the year.

## ANALYSIS OF THE MEASUREMENT MODEL

The analysis begins with an evaluation of the measurement models for health and job demands at each of the three waves. In order to estimate the stability parameters for these unobserved constructs and the impacts that each may have on the other, as well as their impact on labor force participation, it is necessary to establish the measurement properties of each construct at each time period. Can indicators be seen as measuring each construct in exactly the same manner across time? In addition, we can also ask whether or not each construct can be measured in the same manner across subgroups in the analysis. Beginning with the job demands constructs, measured at two time points, 1971 and 1976, the first hypothesis would take the form: is the construct for physical job demands in 1976 determined by strength, climbing, and stooping to the same degree as these three characteristics defined job demands in 1971? This hypothesis is presented in either panel of Figure 2, and would imply that the coefficient labeled

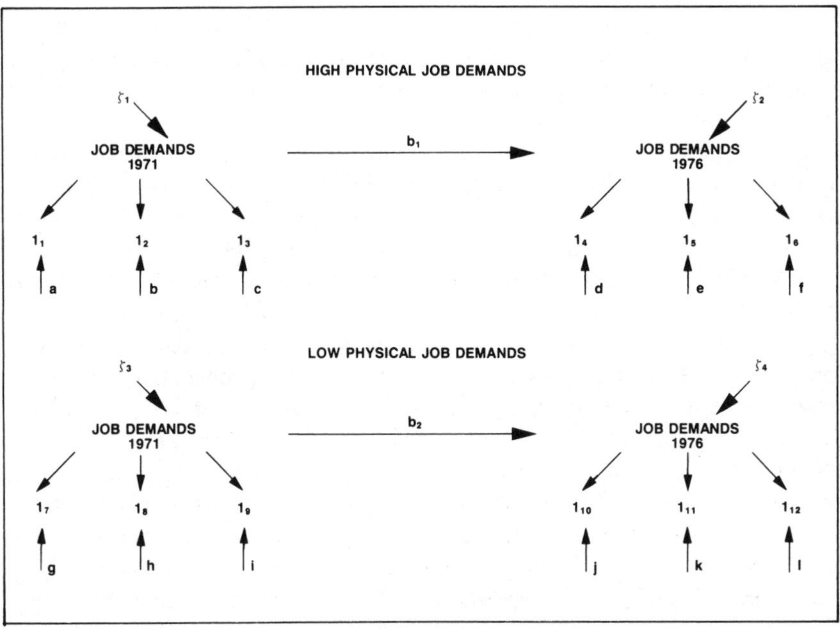


Figure 2. Measurement model for job demands from 1971 to 1976 across two groups.

$1_1$ would be equal to that labeled $1_4$; $1_2$ would equal $1_5$; and $1_3$ would be constrained to equal $1_6$. The second hypothesis essentially extends these equalities to the measurement of job demands in the second subgroup; in this case, the groups are defined on the degree of physical demands placed on the respondents in their jobs, highly physical job occupants in one group and lower physical job occupants in the second group. In Figure 2, this would mean that $1_1 = 1_4 = 1_7 = 1_{10}$, $1_2 = 1_5 = 1_8 = 1_{11}$, $1_3 = 1_6 = 1_9 = 1_{12}$. It does *not* mean that $1_1 = 1_2 = 1_3$, or $1_4 = 1_5 = 1_6$. Substantively, this model indicates that, for example, if strength primarily determines job demands in 1971, it also does so in 1976, and this same variable would have the strongest effect in both subgroups of physically demanding jobs.

The variance in each of the observed indicators is divided into two parts. One part of the variance in each variable is explained by the same underlying factor, the unmeasured construct, or in this case the physical demands of work. The second part of the variance is that which is unique to each observed measure and is the measurement error. In Figure 2 , the measurement error in the observables is represented by $e_1$ to $e_{12}$. In the model, an equality constraint is not placed on the error terms so that $e_1$ to $e_{12}$ are *not* constrained to be equal. Included in the analysis is the causal path from job demands in 1971 to job demands in 1976.

This effect is labelled $b_1$ in the first group (men with highly demanding jobs) and $b_2$ in the second group (men with less demanding jobs). The errors in equations are also estimated. In the initial analysis, $b_1$ equals $b_2$, and the errors in equations are equal across groups, that is $\zeta_1 = \zeta_3$, $\zeta_2 = \zeta_4$.

Models like those in Figure 2 are evaluated in two general ways: overall goodness of fit, or the degree to which the estimated parameters can be used to derive the observed variances and covariances, and in terms of more traditional measures of fit such as significance tests on estimated parameters and explained variances in dependent variables. As it is the purpose of this section of the analysis to evaluate the general measurement strategy, the discussion will focus on overall goodness of fit, as indicated by two indices: $\chi^2$ and the goodness of fit index provided in the LISREL program. The $\chi^2$ is evaluated primarily in terms of its relative size compared to the degrees of freedom associated with it, the latter being an indication of how much of the available information in the model, i.e., the observed variances and covariances among the variables, has been used up statistically to estimate the parameters in the specified model: the larger the $\chi^2$ is relative to the degrees of freedom, the worse the fit of the overall model and the poorer the ability of the model to reproduce the observed relationships in the data. The value of $\chi^2$ also depends on the number of observations being analyzed, such that in a large sample analysis such as that presented here, it is difficult to achieve a $\chi^2$ value that is nonsignificant. The second indicator of overall fit, the goodness of fit index, is provided to address this problem: it is in some sense a standardized measure of fit which is independent of the sample size. The goodness of fit index varies between 0 and 1, and Jöreskog and Sörbom suggest that it should approach or exceed .95 before a model can be considered acceptable. It should be noted that in some models, e.g., those with a number of perfectly measured constructs, $\chi^2$ and the goodness of fit index may never reach the ideal levels discussed here, and in such cases overall fit should be evaluated in terms of the relative improvement in fit of a final, less restrictive model to the initial, more restrictive model (see ref. [6], for a discussion of strategies for model comparisons).

The results of the analysis of the model given in Figure 2 produced a $\chi^2$ of 4544.68 with 25 degrees of freedom, and though the sample size is large, 2832, this is not an acceptable fit, as further indicated by the goodness of fit index, which was equal to .728. In order to ascertain precisely where restrictions in this model could be relaxed so as to improve the overall fit, the modification indices produced by the LISREL program were examined. This feature was added to recent versions of LISREL and indicates where the model should be adjusted in order to more accurately reproduce the observed variances and covariances. In this particular model, the results indicated that the assumption made in Figure 2 that the errors of measurement for each indicator are independent is untenable, and that the overall fit of the model could be improved by relaxing this assumption. In addition to suggesting the presence of correlated measurement error, the modification indices also suggested that correlated error in the indicators for men in highly demanding jobs is not equal to the correlated error in the indicators for men with less demanding jobs.

Other equality constraints had to be lifted as well. The restriction on the stability of the job constructs across the two groups was lifted, and the errors in equations were found to be greater in one group versus the other. The implications of relaxing these restrictions are that the stability of job demands can not be considered to be equivalent in these two groups of workers; the presence of larger errors in equations in one group versus the other may reflect greater variances in constructs across groups and/or the degree to which the variables in the model, in this case, the stability parameters, explain variation in job demands in 1976 in each group. The results of the relaxation of these restrictions are given in Figure 3.

The final $\chi^2$ was 327.12 with 12 degrees of freedom. The goodness of fit index increased to .984. At this point in the analysis, the model was accepted as having an adequate fit to the data. The only remaining "improvements" that could be made would be to correlate further measurement errors, but the improvement to the overall $\chi^2$ would not be substantial in comparison to the improvement already made. Thus it can be concluded that the lambda coefficients, or the estimate of the relationship of job demands to its observed indicators, can be considered equivalent across time and across groups.

## MEASUREMENT OF HEALTH

Before moving to the analysis of the full structural model, a similar procedure is used to examine the relationship of the indicators of health to the underlying construct. The first step is to test the hypothesis that health is measured by three indicators, using stairs, able to stoop, lifting; and that each of these indicators plays the same role in defining health in 1971, 1976, and 1981. Further, the hypothesis that the entire model for men in highly demanding jobs is equal to the model for men in less demanding jobs is also evaluated. It should be noted that the implications of such a restricted model for the stability parameters are that, between each measure of health, e.g., 1971 to 1976, 1976 to 1981, stability is assumed to be equal across subgroups; stability parameters are not constrained to be equal across waves within each group, although the researcher might wish to test such an hypothesis, and could do so within the context of the models and methods used here. Although this may not be a reasonable assumption for constructs such as health and observations based on individuals, it may be more reasonable for other constructs and other units of analysis (see Greenberg et al., 1979 [7], for an example of stability constraints).

The errors in equations are also constrained to be equal. The restrictions are taken one step further in the present analysis than in the analysis of job characteristics, that is, the measurement errors in each indicator are initially constrained to be equal across groups.

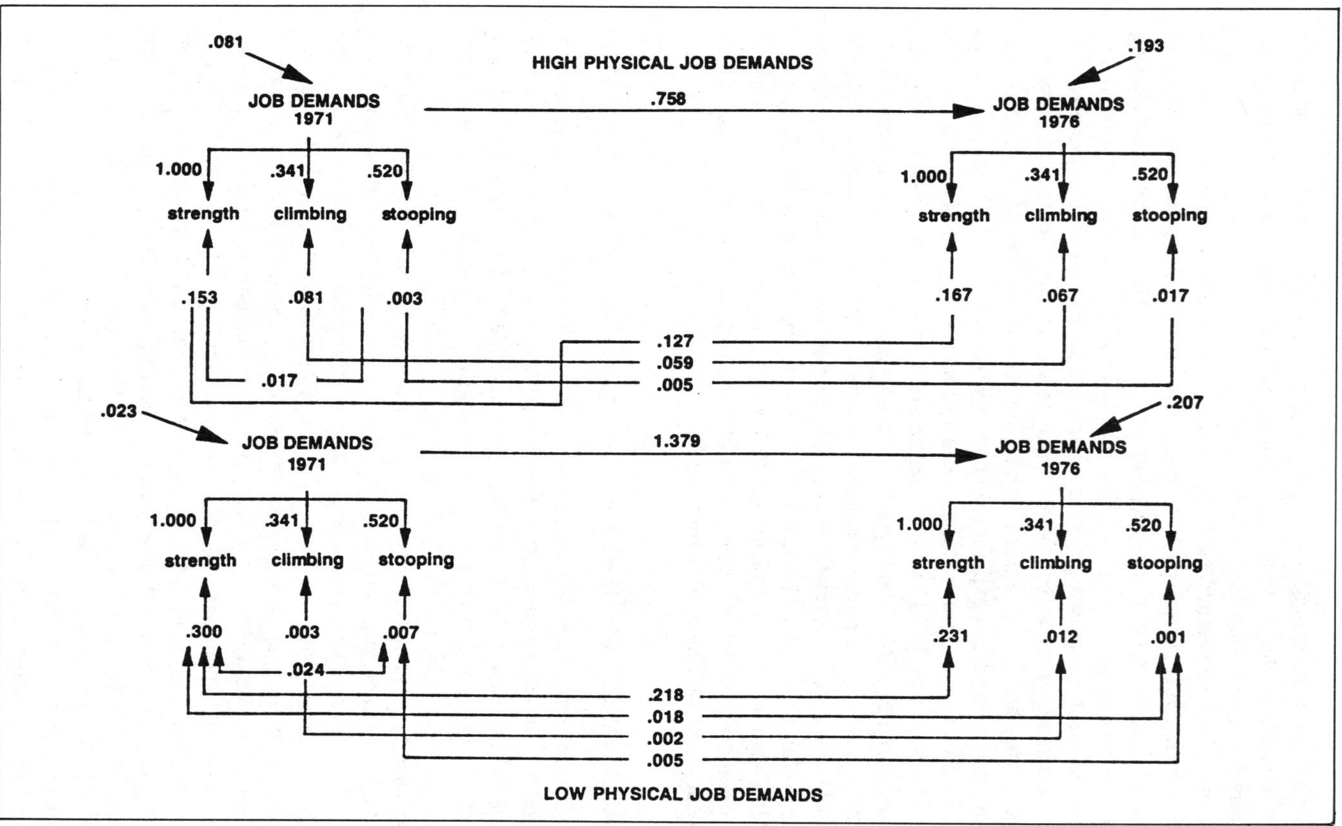


Figure 3. Results for the measurement model for job demands 1971–1976.

The results of the first analysis with all of the equality constraints were much better than the first attempt for job characteristics. The $\chi^2$ with 74 degrees of freedom is 677.71 and a goodness of fit index of .947. By freeing the measurement error, correlating a couple of error terms, and lifting the constraints on the errors in equations, the $\chi^2$ was reduced to 280.22 with 58 degrees of freedom, and the goodness of fit index was increased to .977. The difference between the $\chi^2$ statistics and associated degrees of freedoms from two 'nested' models [8] is itself considered to be distributed as a $\chi^2$; the improvements in the measurement of health obtained here are considered significant based on this $\chi^2$ difference test: 677.71–280.22 = 397.49; 74 df–58 df = 16; resulting $\chi^2$ is statistically significant, indicating improved relative fit in the model.

In both instances, the measurement of health and the measurement of job demands, it was determined that the researcher could safely use the same indicators at each point in time, and constrain the factor loadings to be equal. Thus comparisons would be made using identical constructs at each period, and the researcher would not be put in the position of making the proverbial comparison between "apples and oranges."

## STRUCTURAL MODEL

The structural model is analyzed using the information gained by the examination of the measurement model, that is the indicators of the constructs are constrained to be equal across time and across groups but the measurement error and the errors in equations are freely estimated for each group. In the first attempt to analyze the causal model, the researcher may wish to examine whether the relationships between the constructs are the same for each group, that is, is the effect of a coefficient for a given independent variable on health among men in highly demanding jobs, equal to the corresponding effect among men in less demanding jobs? In this first analysis all regression coefficients are constrained to be equal across the two groups. The results were marginally acceptable, $\chi^2$ of 1082.71 with 204 degrees of freedom and a goodness of fit index of .951; however, further analysis was conducted to explore the possible interactions between variables affecting work and health among men in highly demanding jobs versus men in less demanding jobs.

Only minimum adjustment needed to be made in the model to make it acceptable ($\chi^2$ = 833.94, df = 199, goodness of fit index = .971). One substantive hypothesis was not borne out. The stability of job demands between 1971 and 1976 is not the same for those whose work is physically demanding in comparison to those in less demanding jobs. Results are presented in Table 1.

Taking a closer look at the results, men who have a less physically demanding job in 1971 have a higher probability of remaining in that job five years later while those who are in jobs which are more physically taxing are much less

Table 1.

Lambda Estimates for Job Demands and Health for Both Goups of Men

| | *Job Demands 1971* | *Job Demands 1976* | | *Health 1971* | *Health 1976* | *Health[a] 1981* |
|---|---|---|---|---|---|---|
| Strength | 1.000 | 1.000 | Lifting | 1.000 | 1.000 | 1.000 |
| Climbing | .341 | .341 | Using stairs | .618 | .618 | .618 |
| Stooping | .519 | .519 | Able to stoop | .777 | .777 | .777 |

Parameter Estimates for Structural Model

| *Dependent Variables* | *Independent Variables* | | | | | | |
|---|---|---|---|---|---|---|---|
| | *Job Demands 1971* | *Health 1971* | *Job Demands 1976* | *Health 1976* | *Health 1981* | $R^2$ *High* | $R^2$ *Low* |
| Job Demands | | | | | | | |
| 1976 | .759*[b] (1.364*)[c] | .051* | | | | .197 | .176 |
| | .329[d] (.592) | .036 | | | | | |
| Health | | | | | | | |
| 1976 | .081 | .717*[e] | .024 | | | .356 | .337 |
| | .031 | .585 | .022 | | | | |
| Health | | | | | | | |
| 1981 | | | –.014 | .703* | | .487 | .440 |
| | | | –.012 | .681 | | | |
| Annual Hrs Worked | | | | | | | |
| 1981 | | | –.583 | –2.841* | –3.207* | .114 | .075 |
| | | | –.028 | –.150 | –.175 | | |

Correlated Errors in Measurement[f]

| *Highly Demanding Jobs* | | *Less Demanding Jobs* | |
|---|---|---|---|
| Strength 1971 and Stooping 1971 | −.017 | | .024 |
| Strength 1971 and 1976 | .127 | | .217 |
| Climbing 1971 and 1976 | .059 | | .002 |
| Stooping 1971 and 1976 | .005 | | .005 |
| Lifting 1971 and 1976 | .023 | | .038 |
| Lifting 1976 and 1981 | .064 | | .078 |
| | | Strength 1971 and Stooping 1976 | .018 |
| | | Stooping 1971 and Strength 1976 | .015 |

*Significant at .05 or less.
[a]Health is coded with those who have health problems as high on the variable.
[b]Unstandardized coefficient.
[c]Estimate for those in less demanding jobs. All other parameters are equal for both groups.
[d]Standardized coefficient.
[e]The path from health 1971 to health 1976 is not significantly different from the path from health 1976 to health 1981.
[f]Unstandardized estimates.

likely to have jobs with similar physical demands in 1976. This finding is shown in the parameter estimates where the respective stability coefficients are .759 for men in highly demanding jobs (standardized coefficient of .329) compared to 1.364 for men in less strenuous jobs (standardized coefficient of .592).

Interestingly, in the present model there appears to be no direct effect of job characteristics on changes in health at any point in time, and this is true for men regardless of whether they are in very demanding jobs or less demanding. Health is moderately stable across the ten-year period and initially looks like it might even be more stable in the latter five years than in the first five–year period. The unstandardized coefficients are .717 for 1971 to 1976 and .703 for 1976 to 1981. The standardized coefficients are .585 for the first five years and .681 for the second period, and thus it appears that health is more stable as men move from their late fifties to early sixties. One further analysis was conducted to constrain these two paths to be equal to test whether they are significantly different. The result of this analysis indicated that the difference between the two coefficients was not significant ($\chi^2$ of 834.11, 200 *df*, goodness of fit index .971). Thus, by using the ability to test for equalities in causal relationships across time in the LISREL program the researcher can avoid trying to theorize in a *post hoc* fashion or explain something that is as counterintuitive as that health becomes more stable as people age.

While the analysis revealed no effect of job characteristics on health, health does affect the amount of involvement in that job later in life. Men who have poor health in 1981 are also working fewer hours in 1981 ($b = -3.207$). In addition there is also a lagged effect of health, so that those whose health was poor in 1976 are working even fewer hours ($b = -2.841$).

There is only one other path with a *t*–value above 1.96, and that is the path from health in 1971 to the characteristics of one's job in 1976 ($b = .051$). The relationship is the opposite of what was expected and indicates those who have poorer health find themselves in more physically demanding jobs in 1976. The strength of this relationship is so small, $b = .082$ with a beta of .046, that its statistical significance is due to the large *N* and substantively little should be made of it.

## PROS AND CONS OF USING LISREL

Repeating what was said at the beginning of the chapter, LISREL offers many advantages to the researcher. One can examine the underlying factor structure in the data, one can easily correct for measurement error and eliminate the attenuation of effects that results from this error. Importantly, the researcher does not have to make the unrealistic asumption that his/her constructs are measured perfectly.

LISREL is a powerful tool for testing theoretical ideas involving reciprocal relationships, for example, feedback effects between one's self esteem and other's evaluation of the self. And finally, one can examine any number of equality relationships.

However, all of this comes at a cost. First, there is the financial cost which is not minor, and especially not minor when one is paying for it with grant dollars. LISREL is now available for microcomputers which may be one way of reducing costs.

A second type of cost is the difficulty of running the program. Error messages are practically nonexistent and even those very familiar with the program can be terribly frustrated when the program is unable to iterate. Failure to iterate is primarily due to inappropriate starting values, a problem which has been alleviated somewhat by the newer versions of LISREL. Users of the early versions had to provide starting values, a place for the program to start iterating in order to reach a solution. This is no longer necessary. However there are times when even the program generated start values are flawed, and the researcher is left looking at the maze trying to figure out where to begin tinkering.

Perhaps most dangerous is that the program can return values which are logically impossible, and the researcher must be familiar enough with the data and with the analysis procedure to know that the results are unacceptable. Workshops in the use of LISREL are particularly instructive for this purpose.

Finally, LISREL is not a solution to all problems. If one wishes to analyze the timing of an event such as retirement, event history analysis should be used [9]. If one has a dichotomous dependent variable such as in or out of the labor force, the researcher probably should use a logit analysis [10]. If one has social psychological measurements on a daily basis over several months, Box-Jenkins ARIMA models may be appropriate [11].

With all the caveats and exceptions, LISREL is a powerful and flexible tool and should be in the repertoire of those who are interested in longitudinal data analysis.

## REFERENCES

1. R. T. Campbell and E. Mutran, Analyzing Panel Data in Studies of Aging, *Research on Aging, 4*, pp. 3–41, 1982.
2. K. F. Ferraro, E. Mutran, and C. M. Barresi, Widowhood, Health, and Friendship Support in Later Life, *Journal of Health and Social Behavior, 25*, pp. 245–259, 1984.
3. J. Liang, A Structural Integration of the Affect Balance Scale and the Life Satisfaction Index A, *Journal of Gerontology, 40*, pp. 552–561, 1985.
4. J. Liang and K. A. Bollen, The Structure of the Philadelphia Geriatric Center Morale Scale: A Reinterpretation, *Journal of Gerontology, 38*, pp. 181–189, 1985.
5. E. Mutran and D. C. Reitzes, Retirement, Identity and Well-Being: Realignment of Role Relationship, *Journal of Gerontology, 36*, pp. 733–740, 1981.
6. M. E. Sobel and G. W. Bohrnstedt, Use of Null Models in Evaluating the Fit of

Covariance Structure Models, in *Sociological Methodology, 1985*, N. B. Tuma (Ed.), Jossey-Bass, San Francisco, 1985.

7. D. F. Greenberg, R. C. Kessler, and C. H. Logan, A Panel Model of Crime Rates and Arrest Rates, *American Sociological Review, 44*, pp. 843–850, 1979.
8. J. S. Long, *Covariance Structure Models: An Introduction to LISREL*, Sage Publications, Beverly Hills, CA, 1983.
9. R. T. Campbell, E. Mutran, and R. N. Parker, in *Research Methodology and Research on Aging*, E. F. Borgatta and C. Hertzog (Eds.), 1986.
10. M. D. Hayward, The Influence of Occupational Characteristics on Men's Early Retirement, *Social Forces, 64,* pp. 1032–1045, 1986.
11. R. McCleary, R. A. Hay, Jr., E. M. Meidinger, and D. McDowell, *Applied Time Series for the Social Sciences*, Sage Publications, Beverly Hills, CA, 1980.

CHAPTER

# 12

# Using Confirmatory Factor Analysis for Scale Development and Validation

*Christopher Hertzog*

The past several years have been marked by an accelerating rate of increase in sophisticated new methods for conducting valid and informative empirical research on the measurement properties of psychological scales. One of the more important approaches has involved the use of confirmatory factor analysis to test properties of individual items and whole scales, examining factorial validity, reliability, and the like [1–4]. These methods are of special interest to gerontologists, because they explicitly provide a way of testing for age group equivalence in scale properties. The methodological foundations for using confirmatory factor analysis to examine measurement properties in scales, and to test age group equivalence in measurement properties, has been discussed in some detail by Schaie and Hertzog [5], and of course, in more technical material on the topic. This review is not designed to duplicate this material, but rather, to add to it by emphasizing practical issues associated with applications of the method. I avoid a mathematical treatment of the topic, and instead attempt to keep the focus at the level of discussing existing work that has used confirmatory factor analysis for scale validation. The topic is unfortunately somewhat complex, and we will wade into deep water occasionally. My hope is that the emphasis on discussing empirical applications will help the reader keep his or her head above the water line!

There are several different types of confirmatory factor analysis designs appropriate for scale development and validation. They fall into two very broad classes: 1) those that analyze the factor structure of sets of individual items; and 2) those that analyze sets of scales (often, summative scales of items using Likert-type ratings). Schaie and Hertzog discuss in some length the analysis of scales for the purpose of evaluating reliability and validity in gerontological research applications [5]. Here I shall focus more attention to the analysis of items, although there will be a brief discussion of the analysis of scales as well.

# ITEM FACTOR ANALYSIS

## GENERAL ISSUES

Confirmatory factor analysis has been employed with increasing frequency to perform item factor analysis of psychological scales, especially measures of subjective well-being (life satisfaction, morale) in older populations [6, 7]. Reviews of the subjective well-being concept are beyond the scope of this review [7–9]. This literature can be somewhat overwhelming, in that complex models are presented with little justification or explanation. This chapter illustrates some of the basic features of confirmatory factor models for item factor structure with special reference to an analysis of a leading depression scale. With this discussion as background, I shall then review the literature analyzing scales of subjective well-being in adult populations, focusing primarily on methodological issues.

The advantage of confirmatory factor analysis for analyzing scale properties is that it is often the case that the items have been selected in advance to measure hypothesized dimensions. In some cases, it is assumed that all the items in a scale measure one latent variable. Cronbach refers to such scales as homogeneous scales, and discusses the merits and disadvantages of scale heterogeneity [10]. The assumption that all items are determined by a single latent variable (one, hopefully, that the scale is designed to measure) has been termed *unidimensionality* by McDonald [11]. It is a little appreciated fact that the calculation of Cronbach's $\alpha$, or of other internal consistency estimates of reliability, depends crucially upon the validity of the unidimensionality assumption. In fact, $\alpha$ is a lower bound estimate of the reliability, and a scale that is not unidimensional will have a reliability larger than that estimated by internal consistency methods. Thus, one reason to perform item factor analysis on a scale is to test the assumption of unidimensionality.

Related reasons for using confirmatory factor analysis for scale validation arise when a scale is hypothesized to contain multiple subscales (i.e., multidimensionality). In particular, one may be interested in whether as many factors are required to account for item correlations as were originally hypothesized, and whether, in some instances, it makes sense to collapse or combine subscales on the basis of factor analysis results in order to achieve parsimony. In this case, it is useful to specify an item factor model that tests whether the items actually factor as hypothesized by the investigator. Depending upon the results of the analysis, it may be judged necessary and/or appropriate to alter the number of scales calculated from the questionnaire. Confirmatory approaches are appropriate in this context because the focus is on validating a model for item factors that has been specified *a priori*. Thus it is possible to test the hypothesized item factor structure directly without resort to interpretation of exploratory factor analyses.

Use of exploratory factor analysis for assessing item factor structure is often appropriate and informative. It is *not* my purpose to castigate previous work on the grounds that exploratory factor analysis was used. Nevertheless, use of exploratory factor analysis can lead to unnecessary interpretive ambiguity, especially if the scales (and their corresponding item factors) correlate at moderate to high levels. Why is this a potential problem? On one extreme, most computer programs use an orthogonal rotation (usually, varimax) as a default option. Use of an orthogonal rotation when the item factors are truly correlated can distort factor pattern matrices and lead to erroneous conclusions about relations of items to factors. On the other hand, use of an oblique rotation to get correlated factors is not necessarily an adequate solution to the problem. There are, in exploratory factor analysis, an infinite number of rotational solutions. With oblique rotation, there are multiple, legitimate rotations that may vary dramatically in the degree of factor correlation permitted by the rotation algorithm. For example, the promax rotation constant controls the maximum degree of factor intercorrelation, and changes in the constant can result in dramatic changes in the estimated factor correlations. This fact should cause discomfort, for it is precisely these factor correlations that are the basis upon which one must decide whether multiple scales can be combined with minimal loss of information.

Even if the scales are expected to be orthogonal, there are distinct advantages of confirmatory factor analysis for an item set, including 1) ability to test the hypothesized configuration of item factor structure, and 2) direct testing of the hypothesis of orthogonality. Confirmatory factor analysis provides a formal basis for testing hypotheses, because it is possible to take the difference in the $\chi^2$ goodness-of-fit test for competing models as a test of the restrictions contained in the more restricted model (for gerontological examples, see refs. [12–15]). Thus, if one wanted to test the hypothesis of orthogonal scales, is is a simple matter to specify two alternative models for a set of items. One model allows the item factors to intercorrelate freely. The second model forces the factor correlations to be fixed to zero. The difference in $\chi^2$ between the two models is a test of the hypothesis that the factor correlations are, indeed, zero in the population. This sort of approach is general and quite powerful, permitting the use of clever psychometric designs to test a number of hypotheses about item and scale interrelationships.

The advantages of confirmatory factor analysis listed above relate to the *factorial validity* of a multidimensional scale. Factorial validity implies that the items form item factors as predicted by their hypothesized relation to an underlying psychological construct [10, 16]. Factorial validity is an important part of demonstrating the construct validity of a scale. The confirmatory factor analysis approach also enables the researcher to address other aspects of construct validity. With item factor analysis, this can be accomplished by modeling the relationships of the item factors to other variables. Latent variable models for *convergent validity* (do the multiple item factors interrelate, and do they converge with item factors from other scales to measure the same construct), *discriminant validity* (are converged latent variables less than perfectly correlated with cognate constructs [17]), and *predictive validity* (does a laent variable predict other variables in a manner consistent with the assumption that it is a valid measure of the construct defined by theory) can easily be formulated provided that other latent variables have been measured as part of the design [3, 17]. Use of confirmatory modeling approaches to demonstrate evidence for factorial, convergent, discriminant, and predictive validity would in principle constitute compelling evidence for the construct validity of a scale.

## AN EMPIRICAL EXAMPLE

As an illustration of item factor analysis, I use data collected by David Hultsch, Roger Dixon, and myself as part of a validation study of the Dixon and Hultsch [19] Metamemory in Adulthood questionnaire. The data were collected on two samples: 1) 437 adult volunteers, ages twenty to eighty from a family practice in Annville, Pennsylvania (hereafter, the Annville sample), and 2) 270 adult volunteers ages fifty five to seventy-seven from Victoria, B.C. (hereafter, the Victoria sample). Participants rated themselves on items from the Center for Epidemiological Studies Depression Scale (CES-D; [20]). The 20-item CES-D scale was specifically designed to measure degree of depressive symptoms in the population at large. Subjects are asked to respond how frequently during the last week a list of statements apply, using a 4-level rating scale (scored 0–3). Scores of 16 or higher are considered above the cutoff for mild depression [20]. The CES-D has become an increasingly popular measure of depression [21] and recently Gatz, Hurwicz, and Weicker reported large cross-sectional data on age and depression using the CES-D [22]. The original validation study by Radloff [20], and subsequent work by Aeneshensel [23], suggest that there may be four factors contained in the CES-D: (depressive) Affect, (lack of) Well-Being, Somatic Symptoms (also labeled Psychomotor Retardation), and Interpersonal Problems.

The analysis summarized here was designed to test the four factor model using confirmatory factor analysis. Further information on the CES-D item analysis may be found in ref [24]. Before discussing the confirmatory factor analysis, it is instructive to ask what an exploratory factor analysis tell us about the item factor structure of the CES-D. For illustrative purposes, the Annville sample data were analyzed by the principal factor method, with squared multiple correlations on the diagonal as communality estimates. The least squares solution was then rotated by varimax to an orthogonal solution, and also by promax to two different oblique solutions (one with the rotation constant set at 3, the other at 10). Table 1 reports the factor pattern weights for all three solutions, and the factor correlation matrices for the two oblique rotations. Each column labeled R contains the varimax factor loadings estimated by Radloff [20]. The columns labeled V contain the varimax rotation from the Annville data. The columns labeled P3

Table 1. Comparison of Alternative Exploratory Factor Models for the CES-D Factor Loadings[a]

| | *Factors* | | | | | | | |
|---|---|---|---|---|---|---|---|---|
| | *Affect* | | | | *Well-Being* | | | |
| *Item* | *R* | *V* | *P3* | *P10* | *R* | *V* | *P3* | *P10* |
| Bothered | 23 | 11 | −09 | −25 | −09 | *−31* | −28 | −28 |
| Appetite | 12 | 12 | −01 | −11 | 00 | −17 | −11 | −06 |
| Blues | *60* | *36* | 27 | 26 | −15 | *−35* | −23 | −20 |
| Good | 11 | −05 | 16 | *35* | *68* | *42* | *48* | *57* |
| Mind | 24 | 21 | 08 | −02 | −10 | −03 | 15 | *37* |
| Depress | *64* | *55* | *53* | *62* | −18 | *−44* | −28 | −26 |
| Effort | 15 | *30* | 17 | 10 | −07 | −18 | −01 | 14 |
| Hopeful | −10 | −21 | −06 | 03 | *68* | *59* | *66* | *82* |
| Failure | *44* | 29 | 16 | 08 | −28 | *−38* | *−31* | −29 |
| Fearful | *31* | *38* | *40* | *48* | −19 | −05 | 17 | *35* |
| Sleep | 21 | 13 | −04 | −20 | 01 | −12 | 00 | 14 |
| Happy | *−38* | −25 | 00 | 18 | *62* | *63* | *63* | *72* |
| Talk | 00 | 23 | 16 | 15 | −10 | −22 | −14 | −11 |
| Lonely | *72* | *50* | *49* | *57* | −06 | *−38* | −22 | −17 |
| Unfriendly | 15 | 11 | 01 | −08 | −07 | −22 | −20 | −18 |
| Enjoy | *−35* | −26 | −04 | 12 | *68* | *61* | *61* | *69* |
| Cry | *65* | *52* | *66* | *91* | −01 | −12 | 08 | 17 |
| Sad | *78* | *64* | *69* | *88* | −09 | *−37* | −16 | −09 |
| Dislike | 15 | 15 | −01 | −17 | −04 | −23 | −16 | −07 |
| Getgoing | 14 | 21 | 07 | −03 | −11 | −12 | 02 | 17 |

| | *Factors* | | | | | | | |
|---|---|---|---|---|---|---|---|---|
| | *Somatic* | | | | *Interpersonal* | | | |
| *Item* | *R* | *V* | *P3* | *P10* | *R* | *V* | *P3* | *P10* |
| Bothered | *51* | *51* | *52* | *75* | 10 | 01 | −14 | −27 |
| Appetite | *50* | *44* | *46* | *66* | −13 | 01 | −10 | −21 |
| Blues | *41* | *47* | *33* | *40* | 13 | 13 | −06 | −15 |
| Good | −01 | −16 | −04 | −03 | −11 | −28 | −22 | −27 |
| Mind | *59* | *48* | *48* | *66* | 11 | *33* | 27 | *31* |
| Depress | *43* | *41* | 14 | 06 | 15 | 23 | 00 | −07 |
| Effort | *64* | *63* | *61* | *83* | 06 | 14 | −01 | −11 |
| Hopeful | −06 | −15 | 08 | 18 | 01 | −17 | −02 | 00 |
| Failure | 07 | 28 | 09 | 04 | 11 | *38* | 26 | *32* |
| Fearful | 26 | *33* | 20 | 19 | 13 | 29 | 20 | 23 |
| Sleep | *55* | *49* | *51* | *72* | −07 | 24 | 16 | 16 |
| Happy | −25 | *−40* | −21 | −24 | −05 | −29 | −11 | −09 |
| Talk | *54* | *38* | *33* | *43* | 20 | −01 | −14 | −26 |
| Lonely | 18 | *34* | 08 | −03 | 09 | 29 | 10 | 09 |

Table 1. (continued)

| | *Factors* | | | | | | | |
|---|---|---|---|---|---|---|---|---|
| | *Somatic* | | | | *Interpersonal* | | | |
| *Item* | *R* | *V* | *P3* | *P10* | *R* | *V* | *P3* | *P10* |
| Unfriendly | 07 | −03 | −19 | *−34* | *84* | *47* | *48* | *67* |
| Enjoy | −14 | *−33* | −11 | −07 | 02 | *−35* | −19 | −21 |
| Cry | 15 | 22 | 01 | −12 | −04 | 09 | −07 | −13 |
| Sad | 20 | *32* | 01 | −17 | 15 | 29 | 07 | 05 |
| Dislike | 08 | 18 | 05 | 00 | *83* | *56* | *55* | *73* |
| Getgoing | *66* | *57* | *59* | *83* | 07 | 14 | 02 | −05 |

[a]Decimals omitted.

**Note:** Comparison of Radloff [20] four-factor Varimax solution (Column R) and three different four factor solutions on Annville Validation study data: Varimax rotation (V), promax rotation with constant at 3 (P3), and promax rotation with constant = 10 (P10). Loadings ≥ .3 are italicized.

and P10 contain the factor loadings for the two promax solutions for this data set. As can be seen, the varimax-rotated factor loadings for the two samples are similar. The difference in the varimax and promax solutions is predominantly in the number of nonzero loadings in the varimax solution—a pattern that would be expected if an orthogonal solution were inappropriately imposed on oblique factors.

Note the difference in the factor correlations estimated in the three solutions for the Annville sample, as reported in Table 2. In the varimax rotation the factors correlations are zero, by fiat. In the promax solution with default values of the constant set at 3, the correlations are substantial and predominantly in the .5 to .6 range. With the promax constant set at 10, the factors are highly oblique, with most of the correlations .7 or higher. The well-being items have not been reverse scored, so the negative correlation of Well-Being with the other factors is expected. Note that the semantically polar opposites, *happy* and *sad*, have very high loadings

Table 2. CES-D Item Analysis: Factor Correlations[a]

| | *Promax (constant = 3)* | | | | | *Promax (constant = 10)* | | | |
|---|---|---|---|---|---|---|---|---|---|
| Affect | 1 | | | | Affect | 1 | | | |
| Well-being | −56 | 1 | | | Well-being | −80 | 1 | | |
| Somatic | 68 | −66 | 1 | | Somatic | 88 | −83 | 1 | |
| Interpersonal | 42 | −46 | 53 | 1 | Interpersonal | 75 | −75 | 79 | 1 |

[a]Decimals omitted.

**Note:** Factor correlations for two oblique rotations on the Annville Validation Study data set.

on Well-Being and Affect, respectively, but the factor correlations are not sufficiently close to $-1.0$ to conclude that Well-Being and Affect are opposite poles of the same dimension. While this result is evident in both promax solutions, the differences in the magnitudes of the factor correlations between the two solutions presents an important interpretive problem. Which one is "right?" How should the factor correlations be treated, given that their magnitude is dependent upon the constant used in the promax rotation? Given that there are an infinite number of possible rotated solutions, under what rotational transformations would we find the correlation of Affect and Well-Being sufficiently close to $-1.0$ to alter our conclusions in favor of considering the factors bipolar opposites? In sum, the dependence of estimated factor correlations upon the selection of a particular rotation constant renders a critical research question ambiguous and arbitrarily dependent upon methodological criteria.

In the confirmatory approach, there is no ambiguity about the factor correlation matrix. It has been uniquely identified by the specification of many non-zero factor loadings. In fact, the large number of fixed zero loadings overidentifies the model, and supplies surplus degrees of freedom for evaluating the model's goodness of fit. There is still a methodological and substantive issue, of course. It is whether the relationships of items to scale factors are indeed those specified in the model. In particular, one could be concerned about the accuracy of the assumptions of *lack* of relationships between items and factors—as represented in the fixed 0 factor loadings. A different specification of item-factor relationship would lead to different scale factors and different factor correlations, with the degree of variation depending upon the differences between specifications and their relative deviation from the "correct" model. However, in confirmatory analysis the model specification is clear, and the approach allows us to assess the adequacy of the model in terms of its fit to the sample data.

Table 3 gives the LISREL estimates of the regression coefficients (factor loadings) for a model postulating the isolated configuration of item factors suggested by the Radloff analysis [20]. The solutions for both the Annville and Victoria samples are reported. The model fares well in both samples, with significant factor pattern weights for all items. The correlational patterns are similar, although of smaller magnitude in the Victoria sample.

It is critically important to replicate results in multiple samples. Given that the four factor solution proposed by Radloff fare well in both the samples studied here [20], there is reason to have greater confidence in its validity. *Replication* should not, however, be confused with *confirmation*. Our model may be consistently misspecified, and the misspecified model may be replicable, even if incorrect. Confirmation is more critically important than replication, and is attained when 1) additional predictions of a theory lead to *new* predictions about the behavior of the factors identified by Radloff [20], and 2) these predictions are upheld by new, independent data (see refs. [12, 25, 26] for further discussion of this issue). Nevertheless, the ability to replicate results is critically important.

Table 3. LISREL Model of CES-D Items for Annville (AVS) and Victoria (VIC) Samples

| | *Factor Loadings*[a] | | | | | | | |
|---|---|---|---|---|---|---|---|---|
| | *Affect* | | *Well-being* | | *Somatic* | | *Interpersonal* | |
| | *AVS* | *VIC* | *AVS* | *VIC* | *AVS* | *VIC* | *AVS* | *VIC* |
| Bothered | 0 | 0 | 0 | 0 | 56 | 54 | 0 | 0 |
| Appetite | 0 | 0 | 0 | 0 | 46 | 52 | 0 | 0 |
| Blues | 69 | 75 | 0 | 0 | 0 | 0 | 0 | 0 |
| Good | 0 | 0 | 47 | 35 | 0 | 0 | 0 | 0 |
| Mind | 0 | 0 | 0 | 0 | 56 | 63 | 0 | 0 |
| Depress | 85 | 80 | 0 | 0 | 0 | 0 | 0 | 0 |
| Effort | 0 | 0 | 0 | 0 | 76 | 82 | 0 | 0 |
| Hopeful | 0 | 0 | 64 | 54 | 0 | 0 | 0 | 0 |
| Failure | 65 | 69 | 0 | 0 | 0 | 0 | 0 | 0 |
| Fearful | 52 | 62 | 0 | 0 | 0 | 0 | 0 | 0 |
| Sleep | 0 | 0 | 0 | 0 | 55 | 46 | 0 | 0 |
| Happy | 0 | 0 | 87 | 88 | 0 | 0 | 0 | 0 |
| Talk | 0 | 0 | 0 | 0 | 48 | 43 | 0 | 0 |
| Lonely | 77 | 77 | 0 | 0 | 0 | 0 | 0 | 0 |
| Unfriendly | 0 | 0 | 0 | 0 | 0 | 0 | 52 | 55 |
| Enjoy | 0 | 0 | 85 | 77 | 0 | 0 | 0 | 0 |
| Cry | 52 | 52 | 0 | 0 | 0 | 0 | 0 | 0 |
| Sad | 83 | 85 | 0 | 0 | 0 | 0 | 0 | 0 |
| Dislike | 0 | 0 | 0 | 0 | 0 | 0 | 75 | 71 |
| Getgoing | 0 | 0 | 0 | 0 | 64 | 69 | 0 | 0 |

Factor Correlations[a]

| *AVS* | | | | | *VIC* | | | | |
|---|---|---|---|---|---|---|---|---|---|
| Affect | 1 | | | | Affect | 1 | | | |
| Well-being | –85 | 1 | | | Well-being | –76 | 1 | | |
| Somatic | 83 | –73 | 1 | | Somatic | 71 | –55 | 1 | |
| Interpersonal | 65 | –63 | 48 | 1 | Interpersonal | 54 | –41 | 47 | 1 |

Goodness of fit:

AVS: $\chi^{2\ (164)} = 343.84$ GFI = .93 AGFI = .90

VIC: $\chi^{2\ (164)} = 280.79$ GFI = .91 AGFI = .88

[a]Decimal omitted.

**Note:** Ali 0 loadings and standardized factor variances were fixed by hypothesis. All nonzero parameter estimates were significantly different from 0 beyond the .1 percent level of confidence.

Replication is also crucial for lending credence to any modifications in the model that are based upon the original model's fit to sample data. In the present analysis we modified the model for the Annville sample, using LISREL's modification indices and other diagnostics to free several parameters that were fixed to 0 in the original model. These additional parameters reduced the $\chi^2$ and increased the LISREL goodness-of-fit index. But the critical issue is deciding whether these model modifications are pointing to an improved model for the population, or alternatively, simply capitalizing upon chance to maximize fit to the particular sample. The best way to assure oneself of the broader applicability of the modified model is to cross-validate it in a separate sample. When we cross-validated these modifications in the Victoria sample, we found that the new factor loadings were not statistically different from zero. This result forced us to conclude that the modifications were merely improving fit to the Annville sample, not the general population. Given the importance of replication, it is always advisable either 1) to collect data on more than one sample, or 2) to collect enough data in a single sample to be able to randomly assign subjects to half-samples. In confirmatory factor analysis sample sizes of 200 or greater are preferred, so an overall sample size of 400 or more is optimal [27].

Another issue illustrated in the analysis of the CES-D involves the proper interpretation of a model's fit to sample data. A model can be accepted as useful even if its likelihood ratio $\chi^2$ test is statistically significant. A significant $\chi^2$ implies that we reject the model as fully adequate in accounting for the sample correlation matrix. It is often (indeed, usually) the case that this test statistic will be significant in samples of moderate size. With sample size of 250 or greater, the likelihood ratio test is very powerful and will be significant even when a model is *stable* (in the sense that parameter estimates do not change greatly if new parameters are added to the model) and when it accounts for most of the information in the correlation matrix. Given the power of the likelihood ratio test with large samples, it is a good idea to calculate an index of fit that is independent of sample size. Bentler and Bonett [28] and James, Mulaik, and Brett [29] describe some alternative fit indices. The LISREL program provides its own, alternative, relative fit indices. For the CES-D item analyses, the LISREL goodness-of-fit index in both samples is around .9, indicating a fairly satisfactory level of fit.

The fit of the CES-D model is actually quite good for an item factor analysis, for two different reasons. First, the assumptions of multivariate normality are violated in data consisting of ordinal rating scales. Huba and Harlow showed that this violation did not greatly affect the LISREL parameter estimates, but it did inflate the standard errors and the likelihood ratio $\chi^2$ fit test [30]. The second reason to be satisfied with the fit of the model concerns the nature of inter-item relationships. It is often the case in item analysis that individual items may correlate with each other to a degree not fully accounted for by the item factors. Two items may have very similar wordings, and therefore have a residual relationship with each other even if both load on the same item factor. Such specific relationships will cause lack of fit to the factor model, but such deviations may be relatively trivial, so long as the estimates of the factor loadings and factor correlations have stabilized and are replicable. In our CES-D analysis, the primary parameter estimates did not shift greatly when additional modifications were made to the model. It seems safe to conclude that Radloff's model for the CES-D is a reasonable representation of the underlying factor structure [20].

The principal pragmatic question after the confirmatory factor analysis is what it implies for calculating CES-D scale scores. Is it appropriate to combine all twenty items into a single scale score measuring depression? Is one better off estimating scale scores for each of the four factors separately? These issues can only be summarized briefly here (see ref. [21] for a fuller discussion). A decision to use the Radloff model as a basis for calculating four subscales of the CES-D is predicated upon the validity of the four factor model [20]. Clearly, it has survived the confirmation test, and can be accepted as a useful model for the item factors. This finding lends credence to the four factor representation as a possible basis for creating subscales for the CES-D. However, there may be practical problems with calculating four separate subscales. A decision to use the four scales must face two issues: 1) the scales will be highly intercorrelated, and 2) two of the four scales are based upon an unacceptably low number of items, minimizing scale reliability. The fourth factor, Interpersonal Problems, is defined by two items—too few to be considered an adequate basis for a separate subscale. The Well-Being factor is defined by four items, and similar concerns apply.

Gatz et al. used unit weighting to combine the items using the assignments implied by the Radloff model [22]. Their internal consistency estimates of reliability were relatively low for the Interpersonal Problems scale. On the other hand, Gatz et al. did find quite different mean age differences on the four subscales, with larger age differences in Well-Being than on the other CES-D subscales [23]. Their results may indicate that the Well-Being scale is measuring something different than the other CES-D subscales, a notion consistent with the factor correlations estimated in the Hertzog et al. analysis [24]. Certainly, it does not appear that Well-Being and Depressive Affect are polar opposites, even though they have a strong negative correlation. This finding is consistent with studies on psychological well-being and distress [31, 32] suggesting that Distress (a factor marked by depressive affect and other indicators) and Well-Being should be considered independent, negatively corrrelated dimensions. Apparently there is merit in separating positive and negative affect in well-being measures [8, 9]. Note also that, unlike the exploratory factor analyses, both confirmatory analyses suggest that the fourth factor, Interpersonal Problems, has lower correlations with the other three factors. The four factors are substantially correlated, with the lowest correlation beween Interpersonal Problems and the other three scales.

What case can be made for the single CES-D scale score? The relatively high intercorrelations among the scales indicate that there is justification for summing all items into a single CES-D depression scale score. More definitive justification for the single scale may be assessed by performing second-order factor analysis on the four first-order item factors [6, 33, 34]. Figure 1 shows the Liang model for a second-order factor in a measure of life-satisfaction [33] (see below). The critical concept is that the second-order factor determines the first-order factors.

Let us assume for the moment that the primary issue driving the research is whether subscale scores should be combined into a single scale (given the high

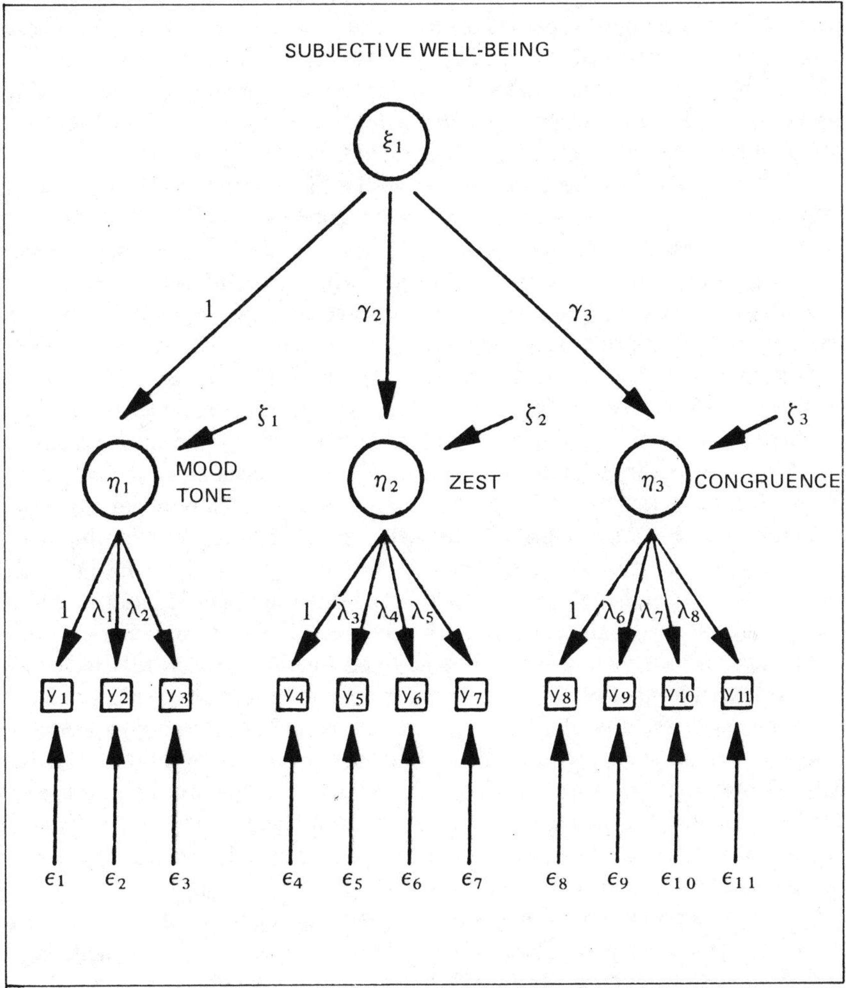


Figure 1. Second-order factor model of Liang [33] relating Subjective Well-Being to three first-order factors (Mood Tone, Zest, Congruence). Items are represented by squares, first-order and second-order factors by circles.

subscale correlations). The second-order factor analysis enables a full evaluation of this issue. There are three separate questions to be addressed. The first question is: are the first-order factors properly specified? This issue has already been addressed for the CES-D data set. The second question is: how well does the second-order factor model account for the first-order factors? There are two different aspects of this question to be considered. First, can the first-order factors be represented by some (possibly multidimensional) second-order factor model? Second, how much of the variance in each first-order factor is determined by the second-order factors? The first question is essentially asking whether it is plausible to model higher order factors, and if so, whether the second-order model specified fits the data well. This issue of *fit* is conceptually distinct from the issue of how much of the variance in the first-order factors is predicted by the second-order factors. *It is possible for a second-order factor to fit well but still account for relatively little variance in the first-order factors.*

The third question to be addressed is: do the first-order factors covary with other important constructs independent of the second-order factor? This question is, in a sense, the most critical one to be addressed in deciding whether to combine the scales, yet it is one generally neglected in the emergent literature on second-order factors. Of course, if the second-order factor accounts for all the variance in the first-order factor, the third question is moot. That outcome would indicate that there is no residual component at the first-order level left to correlate with other variables. However, if there is substantial residual variance at the first-order level, then it is possible (and perhaps likely) that some variables of interest may covary with the first-order factor independent of the second-order factor. If these variables are of specific interest in a research problem, combining the subscales into a single overall scale would mask this relationship.

Hertzog et al. ran a second-order factor analysis of the CES-D data, simultaneously estimating the first and second-order solution in LISREL [24]. The model specified a single second-order Depression factor, and restricted the residual covariance matrix to be diagonal (modeling the second-order factor as the sole determinant of covariance among the first order factors). Table 4 reports the second-order factor loadings and residual variances. The second-order loadings were substantial, and significant for all four first-order factors. In the Annville data, Depression accounted for 70 percent or more of the variance in three of the four factors. The pattern was similar in the Victoria study, although less variance was determined by Depression. In both studies, Interpersonal Problems had the weakest relationship to Depression.

How do we test whether Depression adequately accounts for the covariances among the first order factors? As is so often the case in confirmatory modeling, this question may be addressed by examining differences in fit between two alternative models. In this case, we have imposed additional restrictions on the first-order factor model by specifying the Depression factor as the sole source of the covariances among the four first-order factors. The difference in $\chi^2$ between these

Table 4. Models with a Second-Order Depression Factor for the CES-D in Annville (AVS) and Victoria (VIC) Samples (Standardized Solution)

| | *Factor Loadings*[a] | |
|---|---|---|
| | *Depression* | |
| *First-Order Factor* | *AVS* | *VIC* |
| Affect | 98 | 98 |
| Well-Being | –87 | –77 |
| Somatic | 84 | 72 |
| Interpersonal | 65 | 55 |
| | *Unique Variances*[a] | |
| | *AVS* | *VIC* |
| Affect | 03 | 05 |
| Well-Being | 25 | 40 |
| Somatic | 30 | 48 |
| Interpersonal | 58 | 69 |

Goodness of fit:

AVS: $\chi^{2\,(166)} = 350.55$ GFI = .92 AGFI = .90

Loss of fit from first order: $\chi^{2\,(2)} = 6.71$, $p < .05$; $\Delta$ AGFI = .01

VIC: $\chi^{2\,(166)} = 282.43$ GFI = .91 AGFI = .88

Loss of fit: $\chi^{2\,(2)} = 1.64$ (N.S.), $\Delta$ AGFI = .00

[a]Decimals omitted.

two models tests the loss of fit caused by adding the second-order factor to the model. In both samples, the loss of fit is small (see Table 4). So the Depression factor does a good job of accounting for the covariance among the factors. However, the goodness-of-fit test does not tell the whole story. In both samples, the covariance of Interpersonal Problems with Somatic Symptoms is *overfit* (a higher predicted than observed covariance), whereas the covariance of Affect and Well-Being is *underfit*. The consistency of this difference suggests there may be subtle, additional relationships that cannot be detected because of omitted factors. On the other hand, it is clear that the second-order factor is a very useful approximation to the relationships among the first-order factors. We can conclude that the combined scale—as reflected in the second-order factor—does have *factorial validity*.

Of course, the third question—the adequacy of predictive validity by the second-order factor—cannot be addressed merely by analysis of the CES-D. It can only be addressed by research that measures the CES-D and other constructs (and outcome measures) of theoretical interest.

These results, then, support the factorial validity of the single CES-D score. They also suggest that the four first-order factors relate differentially to the second-order factor. Thus, although one is justified in using the single (combined) CES-D depression scale, there may be research applications in which maintaining the separate factors is important and useful. Further evidence of predictive and construct validity of both the overall CES-D scale score and the four subscales is needed, however, for this information will be the critical determinant of whether (and when) one is best served by using the overall scale or the four subscales.

A few additional conclusions are warranted by the item analysis. First, if a maximally homogeneous measure of self-report depression is desired, it would be appropriate to form a 14-item scale combining only the Depressive Affect and Somatic Symptoms subscales. These two factors seem closest to a face-valid definition of depression and have strong correlations with each other. Second, the fact that Interpersonal Problems does not relate as strongly to the second-order Depression factor in the CES-D leaves open the possibility that it may be associated with other personal characteristics (e.g., introversion, neuroticism; [35]) in addition to depression. The issue of discriminant validity for this subscale needs to be addressed in further research. The same issue seems important for the Well-Being subscale, for it seems, at the level of face validity, highly related to items contained in Subjective Well-Being scales. Finally, if these latter two scales are found to have convergent and discriminant validity with respect to the domain of depression, and if they have predictive validity of important other constructs independent of the Depression factor, then these subscales would be of interest in their own right. In that event additional items measuring these dimensions should be developed and added to the scale.

## CONFIRMATORY FACTOR MODELS OF SUBJECTIVE WELL-BEING

With the preceding discussion of item factor analysis, we are now poised to discuss the burgeoning literature on the factorial validity of measures of subjective well-being in adult populations. This literature has shown a decided progression from the use of exploratory factor analysis to the use of confirmatory methods. One of the first uses of confirmatory factor models was reported by Hoyt and Creech [36]. Using LISREL models, they were unable to confirm the original model for the original Neugarten versions of the Life Satisfaction Index (LISA) [37]. Hoyt and Creech subsequently used exploratory factor analysis to arrive at a reduced three-factor model for eight of the LSIA items [36]. Liang and colleagues [6, 33, 34, 38, 39] have conducted several SEM investigations of the item factor structure of measures of subjects well-being, including the Philadelphia Geriatric Center Morale Scale (PGC) [40], the LSIA, and Bradburn's Affect Balance Scale (ABS) [41]. A central feature of the Liang work has been the simultaneous estimation of first and second-order factors. For example, Liang and Bollen reported an item factor analysis of the PGC that specified three first-order factors: Agitation, Dissatisfaction, and Attitudes Toward Aging [34]. However, they also estimated a single second-order factor (Subjective Well-Being), and found that the loadings on the second-order factor were high. They argued from these results that the multidimensionality of the PGC was at question. Subsequent analyses by Liang and Bollen [38] and Liang et al. [39] have supported the second-order factor model and indicated invariance of the first and second-order factors across age (young-old versus old-old) and sex groups. The Liang analysis of the LSIA [33] (depicted in Figure 1) posited the three first-order factors (Zest, Mood Tone, and Congruence) suggested by Neugarten et al. [37] that had been previously replicated by Hoyt and Creech [36]. This model was fit to eleven of the seventeen LSIA items using responses from a large national sample, divided into four subsamples for model replication. The model fit acceptably well and replicated across the four subsamples. As in the Liang and Bollen model for the PGC [34], Liang estimated a single second-order factor of Subjective Well-Being [33]. Subjective Well-Being was marked primarily for Zest for Life, and (Positive) Mood Tone, with a much smaller loading for Conguence.

There is much to appreciate in Liang's work. First, the rationale for item selection is clear and explicitly stated. Second, the model specification is fully delineated and relatively complete results reported. This allows the reader to evaluate the results and the models carefully and critically, a feature not present in all reported work in this domain [42]. Third, the models fit well and are parsimonious. Finally, the results are replicated on multiple subsamples, increasing confidence in their generality.

There can be substantive and methodological concerns regarding the analyses however, and these studies should not be considered definitive closure on the appropriate models for subjective well-being (a point noted by Liang and his colleagues in their own papers). What kinds of concerns can be raised? Some are minor methodological points that, in the long run, probably will not vitiate the general conclusions drawn. For example, Liang and his colleagues routinely rely on pair-wise deletion of missing data in order to create (Pearson and polychoric) correlation matrices based upon maximum sample sizes. If items are not missing at random, then this practice can lead to distortions in the solutions, although the replication across multiple subsamples eases some of the concern. A more substantial concern specific to the Liang analysis of the LSIA is that items were deleted for multiple reasons, including "cross-construct error covariances" [32]. Apparently, items with relationships not fully accounted for by the model were deleted from the analysis. This approach suggests that the utility of the model was achieved to some degree by elimination of some of the complex interrelations among items. One might well be suspicious of this approach, however, in that a good solution is achieved in part through elimination of items that do not behave according to theory. On the other hand, the Liang and Bollen model for the PGC specified multiple residual item covariances that seem to form two relatively large clusters [34]. These clusters seem to involve negative affect (anger, frustration) and perception of negative change in the last year (eg., loss of pep). There is therefore some question as to whether additional item factors could have been extracted, and what that would have implied for the adequacy of Subjective Well-Being as a second-order factor.

Third, although estimation of the second-order Subjective Well-Being factor addresses some useful questions (as illustrated above for the CES-D), one should not prematurely close on the idea that well-being can be adequately measured by a single subjective well-being scale score. Liang's results demonstrate that these scales can have well-defined, multiple dimensions, and still measure a higher-order construct. However, it is important to point out that the models estimated by Liang do *not* provide a definitive test of the single second-order factor model in one important sense. The PGC and LSIA models specify only three first-order factors. In these cases, the Subjective Well-Being factor is *just-identified.* Just-identification is a technical term I cannot fully define here. It means, in essence, that a solution for the parameter estimates may be calculated but that this solution places no restrictions on the model whatsoever. In this case, just-identification of the second-order factor loadings means that the second-order factor fits the covariances among the first-order factors perfectly (and trivially so). Thus it is not possible to use model restrictions to test the adequacy of the fit of the second-order factors (as we did in the example with the CES-D given above). It is true that Liang's estimated factor loadings are large enough to warrant the conclusion that Subjective Well-Being is a valid second-order factor. However, we cannot use the logic of $\chi^2$ to test the adequacy of the second-order factor model as a representation of the covariances among first-order factors. Moreover, the most critical issue regarding the Subjective Well-Being factor—whether it mediates relationships between first-order factors and other constructs—is not in any way addressed in the Liang analyses. The fact that the coefficients of determination for some first-order factors are about 50 percent suggests that there is at least the possibility that the first-order factors (e.g., Congruence) will relate to other constructions independent of Subjective Well-Being.

The problem of a just-identified second-order factor was avoided in Liang's study combining data from the LSIA and the ABS [6]. Liang identified four item factors (Congruence, Happingess [formerly, Mood Tone], Positive Affect, and Negative Affect) on the basis of fifteen items from the two scales [6]. The Positive Affect and Negative Affect factors derive from Bradburn's conceptualization of these two factors of well-being [40] and are marked by eight items from the ABS. In this analysis, Liang *dropped* the Zest item factor defined by the LSIA from the model. Thus, seven of the original LSIA items remain, marking the Congruence and Happiness factors. Liang found good fits to his model, which included a single second-order Subjective Well-Being factor [6]. Given that the four first-order factors overidentify the SWB factor, it is possible to test the fit of the single-factor model relative to an unconstrained first-order factor structure. Unfortunately, this was not done (directly). Instead, Liang demonstrated that the second-order model fit better than an orthogonal first-order factor model, and that adding residual covariances among first-order residuals improved the fit, but not by much [6]. Since this latter model is just-identified at the level of the second-order analysis, its fit would equal that of a model specifying only first-order factors. Therefore, we can conclude that there is a slight loss of fit for the model with Subjective Well-Being determining all first-order factors. However, Liang appears to be correct in his argument that the loss of fit is not substantial [6]. The most important contribution of the Liang [6] analysis is to show that item factors from two separate scales relate strongly to the second-order factor, justifying the argument of convergent validity for well-being.

Conclusions that appear justified for the Subjective Well-Being factor parallel those outlined above for the CES-D Depression factor. In some cases, it may be preferable to estimate a single scale. However, there is sufficient residual variance for some first-order factors to leave open the question of whether Subjective Well-Being mediates relationships to other constructs. Moreover, Liang's careful approach to item selection may have pushed the analyses in the direction of validating the single second-order factor model. Liang found a small but significant residual for the Positive and Negative affect factors, and one wonders if there might not have been positive residuals for Zest and Happiness (given the strong relationship of the two in the Liang analysis [33]) had the Zest factor been included in the analysis. The conservative approach to item selection was undoubtedly justified, given the confusion in the literature on the structure of these scales. At this point, however, the emphasis should be placed upon risking the model by adding more items and factors and testing the single second-order factor model. This may require new items rather than analysis of the remaining items in the existing scales. Nevertheless, closure on the single Subjective Well-Being factor as adequate to account for the first-order item factors may be premature.

Stock, Okun, and Benin [7] have criticized Liang's [6, 33] model for the LSIA and ABS on conceptual grounds, questioning Liang's first-order item factors. They formulated and estimated an alternative model using SEM. It is based primarily upon the Bradburn perspective, emphasizing Positive and Negative Affect, but was also influenced by Andrews and McKennell [43]. Their first-order factors were Positive Affect, Negative Affect, and Cognition (in essence, items reflecting an evaluation or appraisal of the significance and meaning of one's own life; operationally defined as items involving "social comparison, a self-to-self comparison over time or a life review" [7, p. 95]. These factors were specified to account for six ABS items (Liang used 8 [6]) and the eleven LSIA items used by Liang [33]. The model was fitted to the same data set used by Liang [6, 33]. In addition to their own model, Stock et al. fitted an SEM model based upon the Liang model for the LSIA (including Zest, Mood Tone, and Congruence as factors) [33]. They argued that their model fit as well or better as one based upon the Liang model [33], and championed their own as being more soundly based upon a theory of subjective well-being.

The Stock et al. [7] analysis obviously was conducted before the Liang [6] model was known to them, for the Liang model does include Positive and Negative Affect (see above). As such, the conceptual differences between the Stock et al. [7] model and the Liang [6] model have narrowed, relative to the Liang model [33]. As the Liang [33] model was based upon Hoyt and Creech [36], I shall attempt to avoid confusion by labeling it the Hoyt-Creech model. In any event, the Stock et al. analysis does not appear to be definitive with respect to which approach is the most appropriate basis for a model for subjective well-being [7]. Although their three factor model fits somewhat better than the Hoyt-Creech model (specifying Zest, Mood Tone, and Congruence), it does so by adding more parameters. They do achieve a small but appreciable gain in the relative fit index, but their theory specifies many factor loadings that, empirically, were either not statistically reliable or of small magnitude. Their original model encountered empirical identification problems that were solved by dropping an item from the analysis. Moreover, their model does not appear to cross-validate across two samples as well as the Hoyt-Creech model they estimate (or as well as the Liang model [6]). There is little to differentiate their Cognition factor from the Hoyt-Creech Congruence factor. The items that mark one factor saliently also mark the other, and the loadings that differ, by specification, are not large in magnitude. Moreover, the factor correlations Stock and colleagues report for their Hoyt-Creech model are somewhat more consistent across the two samples than are the correlations in their preferred model.

On the other hand, the pattern of correlations in the Stock et al. model has intuitive appeal [7]. They report a negative correlation of Negative Affect with Positive Affect and Cognition (consistent with Liang's [6] report of a negative second-order factor loading, and consistent with other work on subjective well-being; see above). Their factor correlations are also lower than those among the factors from the Hoyt-Creech model, which may have empirical advantages (e.g., independence of prediction to outcome measures).

At this point, it would appear that both Stock et al. [7] and Liang [6] have offered important alternatives to the Hoyt-Creech formulation. Liang's model can be viewed as merely an extension of the basic Hoyt-Creech model to add ABS factors, whereas the Stock et al. model is a legitimate reformulation. It is too early to tell which model will ultimately prove more useful. Since Liang [6] deleted LSIA items marking Zest, and Stock et al. [7] specified three factors instead of Liang's four, it is difficult to make direct comparisons between the models. At this time, it is not known whether a five-factor model based upon Liang's [6] extension of Hoyt-Creech, but reintroducing Zest, would fit appreciably better than the Stock et al. three factor model [7]. It is also unclear whether a single second-order Subjective Well-Being factor could account for the relationships among the five factors implied by the Liang [6] extension of the Hoyt-Creech model. What is clear, however, is that the debate so far has centered exclusively on the issue of factorial validity for alternative item models, and that it has not yet been extended to an additional focus upon the issues of discriminant and predictive validity of those factors. Additional insights will probably require moving beyond analysis of existing scales from large data archives to the creation of additional item pools formed on theoretical grounds [7]. With respect to the specific issues of selecting an optimal item model (Hoyt-Creech, Liang, Stock et al., or some as-yet-unspecified alternative), any definitive verdict will probably require 1) extension of the item factors to account for new items constructed on theoretical grounds to load on the different factors, and 2) the ability of the different factors to model relationships to other constructs (e.g., depression) and to meaningful outcome measures (e.g., social isolation, morbidity).

One methodological lesson to be learned from this literature is that use of confirmatory factor analysis—in and of itself—does not necessarily resolve disputes about the empirical behavior and proper interpretation of latent variables. Resolution is dependent upon a well chosen design that clearly establishes the alternative models and grounds them in meaningful empirical tests. Thus the discriminative power of confirmatory factor models rests primarily on the measures selected and populations studied, and not upon the statistical procedures *per se* [12]. However, the orientation to use the logic of model falsification inherent in confirmatory analysis establishes the possibility that critical tests of the alternative models can be devised and investigated empirically. Thus one can perceive that a context of discovery has been created in the domain of subjective well-being assessment, fueled largely by the introduction of confirmatory logic and method into the area. The work just reviewed appears to have set the stage for new research that offers a more definitive test of alternative conceptions of well-being scales. There is a justification for optimism that this process will ultimately lead to more valid measures of well-being in adult populations.

## MODELS FOR MEASUREMENT PROPERTIES OF SCALES

The type of item analysis just discussed is important for demonstrating that individual scale items map into a summative scale (or subscales) as predicted by the measurement theory. One can also use confirmatory methods to test a variety of hypotheses about the measurement properties of the scales themselves. For this type of analysis, what was a first-order factor in item analysis is converted into an observed variable (scale), and interest focuses on the covariances among these variables.

Schaie and Hertzog discuss in great detail the literature on using confirmatory factor analysis to estimate reliability and to assess equivalence of measurement properties across multiple populations [5]. Here I shall focus on one recent application of these methods, for it nicely illustrates two important concepts: 1) the conceptual distinction between *scale reliability* and *stability of individual differences* and 2) the use of alternate forms to reveal information about the measurement properties of scales. The data to be discussed were originally collected by Nesselroade, Mitteness, and Thompson [4], and consist of self-ratings of elderly individuals of two mood state factors: Anxiety and Fatigue. The design involves a short-term retest, so that individuals were given the mood state questionnaires twice, with approximately one month intervening between administrations. The three measures of state Anxiety included Spielberger's State Anxiety scale and Forms A and B of Curran and Cattell's Eight State Questionnaire [44]. The three measures of Fatigue were actually sets of items from the Eight State Fatigue scale. Our interest here is on the measurement properties of the Anxiety scales. In particular, Nesselroade et al. demonstrated that the Anxiety and Fatigue factors could be identified using confirmatory factor analysis, and that the stability of individual differences in Anxiety was substantial, but not perfect, over the one-month period [45]. Hertzog and Nesselroade [13] reanalyzed the Nesselroade et al. data [4], focusing on estimating the measurement properties of the Forms A and B of the Eight State Questionnaire.

The model used by Hertzog and Nesselroade is shown in Figure 2 [13]. This model specified that the three scales of state anxiety loaded on an Anxiety factor, and that there was a residual covariance for the Spielberger scale across the two measurement occasions. In a series of models, Hertzog and Nesselroade [13] tested whether the Cattell Forms A and B could be considered parallel forms [46]. Parallel forms are interchangeable, because they have equal reliabilities and equal variances. The hypothesis of parallelism was tested by constraining factor loadings and residual variances (error variances of measurement) to be equal for Forms A and B [1, 2].

Hertzog and Nesselroade also tested whether the measurement properties of Forms A and B were equivalent across the two measurement occasions [13]. The test of equivalence over time was made by constraining these parameters equal across the first and second administrations of the questionnaires. The results showed clearly that 1) Forms A and B were parallel, and 2) that the measurement properties of Forms A and B were identical over the two occasions of measurement. The estimated reliability for Forms A and B was .89. Clearly, the Cattell Eight State Anxiety scales have excellent measurement properties in older populations.

The high reliabilities for the scales contrast with the moderate (but lower) stabilities of individual differences in the latent variable, Anxiety. The stability of individual differences is an important issue in gerontological research, for a major question is whether individuals maintain their relative differences on psychological attributes as they grow older [5, 47]. In the Hertzog and Nesselroade analysis [13], the stability of individual differences is reflected in the covariance between the latent Anxiety factors over the two measurement points ($\phi_{3,1}$ in Figure 2). Using the parameter estimates from the Hertzog and Nesselroade analysis [13], an estimate of .72 is obtained for the correlation of the Anxiety factor with itself over a one-month period. The advantage of using a latent variable

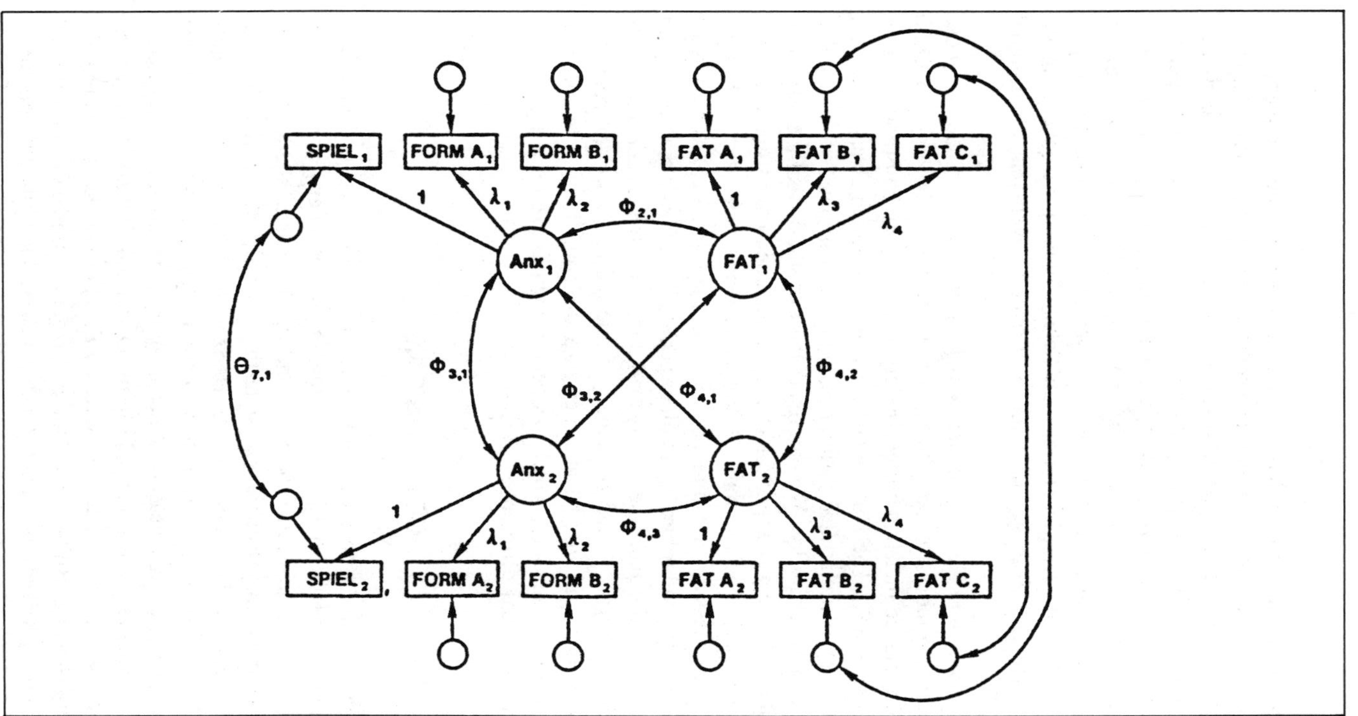


Figure 2. Model for two mood state factors, Anxiety (ANX) and Fatigue (FAT) measured at two longitudinal occasions. For Anxiety, three measures were available, Spielberger's State Anxiety Scale (SPIEL) and two alternate forms of the 8-State Anxiety scale (FORM A, FORM B). A series of models tested the measurement properties of these alternate forms and their relationship to SPIEL at the two occasions (see text). Reprinted with permission from Hertzog and Nesselroade [13].

model here is that the factor correlation is not attenuated by measurement error (as are the correlations among the scales themselves). The implication of this disattenuation is that the correlation could be as high as a perfect 1.0 if individual differences in Anxiety were perfectly consistent across the one-month period. The estimated correlation was certainly greater than zero, but less than 1.0, indicating individual differences in mood state change between the two times. It stands in marked contrast to the long-term stability of intelligence and personality constructs. For example, Hertzog and Schaie found that a general intelligence factor correlated .9 or greater with itself over a seven-year longitudinal test interval [14].

From the Hertzog and Nesselroade analysis [13], we can conclude that those who are anxious at time 1 are likely to be anxious at time 2, but only about 50 percent of the variance in self-reported anxiety at time 2 can be predicted from anxiety levels at time 1. The most important feature of the analysis, however, is that this stability of individual differences has been estimated in a way that disentangles it from reliability. We can reject the hypothesis that the less-than-perfect stability in Anxiety is a function of attenuation due to measurement error. Conversely, the analysis shows that the lability in mood states does not imply that the mood state measures are unreliable. Indeed, the Eight State Anxiety scale appears to have very good reliability in older populations. Given that one would expect mood states to fluctuate, the lability of Anxiety, and the excellent measurement properties of Forms A and B, actually argue indirectly for the construct validity of the scales, and suggest that they measure something different from the personality trait of Anxiety, which has been shown to exhibit a high degree of stability of individual differences [35].

## CONCLUSIONS

As is always the case with a complex topic, this chapter has not covered a number of additional applications that illustrate important other features of confirmatory factor analysis for scale validation. One important area, alluded to above, is the use of confirmatory techniques for testing convergent and discriminant validity of multiple scales [25]. For example, Hertzog, Hultsch, and Dixon recently reported results of a series of confirmatory factor analyses that show convergent validity of two questionnaires measuring metamemory (an individual's knowledge and beliefs about memory functioning) [24]: the Dixon and Hultsch Metamemory in Adulthood questionnaire [19] and the Memory Functioning Questionnaire [48). The analysis by Hertzog, Hultsch, and Dixon also demonstrated the discriminant validity of a memory self-efficacy beliefs factor, taken from both questionnaires, and other psychological constructs [e.g., neuroticism, internal local of control, and subject well-being) [24].

Space did not permit an extended discussion of one of the chief advantages of confirmatory factor analysis for scale validation: the use of simultaneous multiple groups analysis to test the equivalence of factor structures across multiple age groups. In a sense, this chapter provides a foundation that can be generalized to the case of multiple groups analysis. Technical (but rewarding) reading on this topic may be found in several sources [1, 4, 5, 25, 49]. Hertzog reviews a number of empirical applications of confirmatory factor analysis and structural equation models in gerontological research, including the use of multiple groups analysis [50].

There are some disadvantages to confirmatory factor analysis for scale development, but I will leave it to others to point them out in detail! Part of the rationale for doing so is the rapid technological advances that are currently underway. Techniques that avoid some of the assumptions of standard maximum likelihood estimation procedures are now generally available, both in LISREL and competing programs such as EQS [51]. Specialized methods for dealing with categorical and ordinal variables are also appearing [52]. The general principles of confirmatory factory analysis illustrated in this chapter hold for these newer techniques as well.

The thesis of this chapter has been that confirmatory factor analysis provides a powerful method for evaluating the measurement properties of psychological scales. I have sought to show that confirmatory models can be profitably used for item factor analysis and scale validation. As this technique becomes more widely understood and available, it is likely that the current literature using confirmatory approaches to scales of subjective well-being, as reviewed above, will be mirrored in other measurement domains crucial for the study of adult development and aging. This is an exciting prospect, for it suggests that, as a field, we will be making considerable progress in evaluating the reliability and validity of our measures.

## REFERENCES

1. D. F. Alwin and D. J. Jackson, Measurement Models for Response Errors in Surveys: Issues and Applications, in *Sociological Methodology 1980*, K. F. Schuessler (Ed.), Jossey-Bass, San Francisco, pp. 68–119, 1979.
2. K. G. Jöreskog, Simultaneous Factor Analysis in Several Populations, *Psychometrika, 36*, pp. 409–426, 1971.
3. K. G. Jöreskog, Analyzing Psychological Data by Structural Analysis of Covariance Matrices, in *Contemporary Developments in Mathematical Psychology*, D. H. Krautz, R. C. Atkinson, R. D. Luce, and P. Suppes (Eds.), W. H. Freeman, San Francisco, Vol. 2, pp. 1–56, 1974.
4. D. A. Rock, C. E. Werts, and R. L. Flaugher, The Use of Analysis of Covariance Structures for Comparing the Psychometric Properties of Multiple Variables Across Populations, *Multivariate Behavioral Research, 13*, pp. 403–418, 1978.

5. K. W. Schaie and C. Hertzog, Measurement in the Psychology of Adulthood and Aging, in *Handbook of the Psychology of Aging*, J. W. Birren and K. W. Schaie (Eds.), Van Nostrand Reinhold, New York, 2nd Edition, 1985.
6. J. Liang, A Structural Integration of the Affect Balance Scale and the Life Satisfaction Index A, *Journal of Gerontology, 40*, pp. 552–561, 1985.
7. W. A. Stock, M. A. Okun, and M. Benin, Structure of Subjective Well-Being Among the Elderly, *Psychology and Aging, 1*, pp. 91–102, 1986.
8. E. Diener, Subjective Well-Being, *Psychological Bulletin, 95*, pp. 542–575, 1984.
9. M. P. Lawton, The Varieties of Well-Being, *Experimental Aging Research, 9*, pp. 65–72, 1983.
10. L. J. Cronbach, *The Essential of Psychological Testing*, Harper and Row, New York, Third Edition, 1970.
11. R. P. McDonald, The Dimensionality of Tests and Items, *British Journal of Mathematical and Statistical Psychology, 34*, pp. 100–117, 1981.
12. C. Hertzog, On the Utility of Structural Regression Models for Developmental Research. Chapter to appear in *Life-Span Development and Behavior,* P. B. Baltes, D. L. Featherman and R. M. Lerner (Eds.), Lawrence Erlbaum Associates, Hillsdale, NJ, Vol. 10, in press.
13. C. Hertzog and J. R. Nesselroade, Beyond Autoregressive Models: Some Implications of the Trait State Distinction for the Structural Modeling of Developmental Change, *Child Development, 58*, pp. 93–109, 1987.
14. C. Hertzog and K. W. Schaie, Stability and Change in Adult Intelligence: 1. Analysis of Longitudinal Covariance Structures, *Psychology and Aging, 1*, pp. 159–171, 1986.
15. J. L. Horn and J. J. McArdle, Perspectives on Mathematical/Statistical Model Building (MASMOB) in Research on Aging, in *Aging in the 1980's: Psychological Issues*, L. W. Poon (Ed.), American Psychological Association, Washington, DC, pp. 503–541, 1980.
16. S. Messick, Constructs and Their Vicissitudes in Educational and Psychological Measurement, *Psychological Bulletin, 89*, pp. 575–588, 1981.
17. L. J. Cronbach and P. E. Meehl, Construct Validity in Psychological Tests, *Psychological Bulletin, 52*, pp. 281–302, 1955.
18. P. M. Bentler, The Interdependence of Theory, Methodology, and Empirical Data: Causal Modeling as an Approach to Construct Validation, in *Longitudinal Research on Drug Abuse, Empirical Findings and Methodological Issues*, D. B. Kandel (Ed.), Hemisphere, Washington, pp. 267–302, 1978.
19. R. A. Dixon and D. F. Hultsch, Structure and Development of Metamemory in Adulthood, *Journal of Gerontology, 38*, pp. 682–688, 1983.
20. L. S. Radloff, The CES-D Scale: A Self-Report Depression Scale for Research in the General Population, *Applied Psychological Measurement, 1*, pp. 385–401, 1977.
21. P. M. Lewinsohn, D. S. Fenn, A. K. Stanton, and J. Franklin, Relation of Age at Onset to Duration of Episode in Unipolar Depression, *Psychology and Aging, 1*, pp. 63–68, 1986.
22. M. Gatz, M. Hurwicz, and W. Weicker, *Are Old People More Depressed?* Cross-Sectional Data on CES-D Factors, Paper presented at the meeting of the American Psychological Association, Washington, DC, 1986.
23. C. S. Aneshensel, Race, Ethnicity and Depression: A Confirmatory Analysis, *Journal of Personality and Social Psychology, 44*, pp. 385–398, 1983.

24. C. Hertzog, D. F. Hultsch, and R. A. Dixon, What Do Metamemory Questionnaires Measure? A Construct Validation Study. Paper presented at the 95th Annual Convention of the American Psychological Association, New York, NY, 1987.
25. C. Hertzog, Applications of Confirmatory Factor Analysis to the Study of Intelligence, in *Current Topics in Human Intelligence*, D. K. Delterman (Ed.), Ablex, Norwood, NJ, pp. 59–97, 1985.
26. S. A. Mulaik, Toward a Conception of Causality Applicable to Experimentation and Causal Modeling, *Child Development, 58*, pp. 18–32, 1987.
27. A. Boomsma, The Robustness of LISREL Against Small Sample Sizes in Factor Analysis Models, in *Systems Under Indirect Observation: Causality, Structure, Prediction*, K. G. Jöreskog and H. Wold (Eds.), North Holland, Amsterdam, Volume 1, pp. 149–173, 1982.
28. P. M. Bentler and D. G. Bonett, Significance Tests and Goodness of Fit in the Analysis of Covariance Structures, *Psychological Bulletin, 88*, pp. 588–606, 1980.
29. L. R. James, S. A. Mulaik, and J. M. Brett, *Causal Analysis: Assumptions, Models, and Data*, Sage, Beverly Hills, CA, 1982.
30. G. J. Huba and L. L. Harlow, Robust Estimation for Causal Models: A Comparison of Methods in Some Developmental Data Sets, in *Life-Span Develoment and Behavior*, R. M. Lerner and D. L. Featherman (Eds.), Academic Press, New York, Vol. 6, 1986.
31. J. S. Tanaka and G. J. Huba, Confirmatory Hierarchical Factor Analysis of Psychological Distress Measures, *Journal of Personality and Social Psychology, 46*, pp. 621–635, 1984.
32. C. Veit and J. E. Ware, Jr., The Structure of Psychological Distress and Well-Being in General Populations, *Journal of Consulting and Clinical Psychology, 51*, pp. 730–742, 1983.
33. J. Liang, Dimensions of the Life Satisfaction Index A: A Structural Formulation, *Journal of Gerontology, 39*, pp. 613–622, 1984.
34. J. Liang and K. A. Bollen, The Structure of the Philadelphia Geriatric Center Morale Scale: A Reinterpretation, *Journal of Gerontology, 38*, pp. 181–189, 1983.
35. P. T. Costa, Jr. and R. R. McCrae, Influence of Extraversion and Neuroticism on Subjective Well-Being: Happy and Unhappy People, *Journal of Personality and Social Psychology, 38*, pp. 668–678, 1980.
36. D. R. Hoyt and J. C. Creech, The Life Satisfaction Index: A Methodological and Theoretical Critique, *Journal of Gerontology, 38*, pp. 111–116, 1983.
37. B. L. Neugarten, R. Havighurst, and S. Tobin, The Measurement of Life Satisfaction, *Journal of Gerontology, 16*, pp. 134–143, 1961.
38. J. Liang and K. A. Bollen, Sex Differences in the Structure of the Philadelphia Geriatric Center Morale Scale, *Journal of Gerontology, 40*, pp. 468–477, 1985.
39. J. Liang, R. H. Lawrence, and K. A. Bollen, Age Differences in the Structure of the Philadelpia Geriatric Center Morale Scale, *Psychology and Aging, 1*, pp. 27–33, 1986.
40. M. P. Lawton, the Philadelphia Geriatric Center Morale Scale: A Revision, *Journal of Gerontology, 30*, pp. 85–89, 1985.
41. N. M. Bradburn, *The Structure of Psychological Well-Being*, Aldine, Chicago, 1969.
42. G. A. Wilson, J. W. Elias, and L. J. Brownlee, Factor Invariance and the Life Satisfaction Index, *Journal of Gerontology, 40*, pp. 344–346, 1985.

43. F. M. Andrews and A. McKennell, Measures of Self-Reported Well-Being: Their Affective, Cognitive, and Other Components, *Social Indicators Research, 8*, pp. 127–155, 1980.
44. J. P. Curran and R. B. Cattell, *Handbook for the 8-State Questionnaire*, Institute for Personality and Ability Testing, Champaign, IL, 1976.
45. J. R. Nesselroade, L. S. Mitteness, and L. K. Thompson, Short-Term Changes in Anxiety, Fatigue, and Other Psychological States in Older Adulthood, *Research on Aging, 6*, pp. 3–23, 1984.
46. F. M. Lord and M. R. Novick, *Statistical Theories of Mental Test Scores*, Addison-Wesley, Reading, MA, 1968.
47. P. B. Baltes, H. W. Reese, and J. R. Nesselroade, *Life-Span Developmental Psychology: Introduction to Research Methods*, Brooks-Cole, Monterey, CA, 1977.
48. M. J. Gilewski and E. M. Zelinski, Questionnaire Assessment of Memory Complaints, in *Handbook for Clinical Memory Assessment of Older Adults,* L. W. Poon (Ed.), American Psychological Association, Washington, DC, pp. 93–107, 1986.
49. K. G. Jöreskog, Statistical Analysis of Sets of Congeneric Tests, *Psychometrika, 36*, pp. 109–133, 1971.
50. C. Hertzog, Applications of Structural Equation Models in Gerontological Research, in *Annual Review of Gerontology and Geriatrics*, K. W. Schaie (Ed.), Vol. 7, pp. 265–293, 1987.
51. P. M. Bentler, *Theory and Implementation of EQS: A Structural Equations Program*, BMDP Statistical Software, Los Angeles, 1985.
52. R. J. Mislevy, Recent Developments in the Factor Analysis of Categorical Variables, *Journal of Educational Statistics, 11*, pp. 3–31, 1986.

# SECTION 3
# Conclusion: Scientific Change and Longitudinal Research

Lebowitz's chapter is a fitting conclusion for this book on special methods, for he calls our attention to neglected issues that have a major impact on the success of all research, but issues that are particularly relevant to longitudinal research. His view is clearly meta-analytic, being concerned with processes of change that affect the way research is performed.

Lebowitz's chapter is organized to focus successively on change in subjects, changes in methods, and finally changes in the social context of research. The special significance for longitudinal research in aging of selective attrition for health-related reasons is discussed first. Particularly meaningful is his acknowledgment of the frequency with which unanticipated changes in status of types other than chronological aging occur in longitudinal research. "Crossover," for example, a "control" subject moving to the condition that characterizes a "case," happens all the time. Lebowitz's hope that enough crossover subjects might accrue to constitute a separate subgroup for analysis will not always be fulfilled. His delineation of the necessity for anticipating and accepting this phenomenon as a reality should sensitize every researcher to take care to track and report every such change in status. All too often, such instances are either silently dropped from the sample or simply counted along with subjects lost for miscellaneous reasons. At the very least, letting readers know how often the crossover occurs adds an increment to the understanding of the phenomenon under study.

Changes in the state of the social scientific art are particularly cogent to the conduct of longitudinal research. Lebowitz advances our comprehension of the significance of such changes first by noting that such changes may occur in concepts, measurement, and statistical data analysis. He notes that the longitudinal researcher who is the beneficiary of more knowledge than was available at the beginning of the study will probably have an easier time using improved data-analytic methods than introducing new theoretical constructs or new measures once a commitment has been made to those introduced at the beginning. Nonetheless, he forces us to think first about the gains and losses introduced by non-comparable follow-up measuring instruments. Even more importantly he argues for openness to the possibility of incorporating such new knowledge discussing, among other topics, the possibility that new theoretical concepts demand new measures and how these may be integrated with the earlier ones.

It may be instructive to note an instance of such readiness to change. In current research on samples that have been studied over a period of fifty years, researchers at the Berkeley Institute of Human Development have subjected very diverse subject records to a methodological advance that incorporates within it the ability to deal with changing personality constructs. Specifically, Haan, Millsap, and Hartka [1] used the later-developed California Q-sort [2] to elicit ratings from researchers, ratings capable of measuring personality traits not included for direct measurement in the early years of the studies.

Lebowitz appropriately ends his chapter, and the book, with his reminder that the conduct of research—the content of research, the methods used for the research, and especially the uses made of the research findings—is strongly affected by the changing social and political context. For longitudinal research, the possible impact of such secular environmental changes is major. The career of the researcher, a time-extended process, in itself may be subject to such changes, for example, changes in who provides financial support for the research, in how appealing the investigator's longitudinal project aims may be for legislators, or in how well latecoming longitudinal findings may convince granting agencies of the further fundability of the research.

## REFERENCES

1. N. Haan, R. Millsap, and E. Hartka, As Time Goes By: Change and Stability in Personality Over Fifty Years, *Psychology and Aging, 1*, pp. 220–232, 1986.
2. J. Block, *The Q-Sort Method in Personality Assessment and Psychiatric Research*, Charles C. Thomas, Springfield, IL, 1962.

CHAPTER

# 13

# Scientific Change and Longitudinal Research: Subjects, Methods, and Environments[1]

*Barry D. Lebowitz*

Longitudinal designs have been a part of the methodological armamentarium of gerontology for decades. As life-course concepts and models have proliferated, however, the concern with longitudinal research has moved beyond the scientific community of gerontologists to most of the major research fields involving human investigation and animal models of human phenomena. Such concern has been driven by many dynamics. Methodological and technical developments have given us the capacity to develop models of development and change in both large and small systems. The pooling of large data sets has given us the opportunity for sequential and cohort analyses in ways previously impossible to complete. Developments in public policy and large-scale social experimentation in health care, social services, mental health programs, and a variety of housing, transportation, and nutrition services for the aged have carried with them requirements for evaluation, many of which have involved short-term longitudinal studies. Public concerns with health promotion and disease prevention, and the translation of these concerns into the political arena, have, by definition, required longitudinal thinking in order to be accomplished.

Of course, not all issues lend themselves to longitudinal designs, nor can longitudinal designs necessarily provide us with definitive conclusions in many areas. Clearly, where the focus of a study is on *difference*, then a cross-sectional, single point in time study would be sufficient. As has long been acknowledged, however, the relative contribution of age, cohort, and historical period to empirically observed differences cannot be estimated in cross-sectional studies. To

[1]The analyses and interpretations presented in this chapter are personal and do not represent the policy of the United States Government.

explain difference, to depict the process of development or change, and to project future states, however, longitudinal approaches are the methodology of choice. Difference and development are the shorthand terms for capturing the benefits of the cross-sectional and longitudinal approaches. Methodological concerns around the design of cross-sectional and even short-term experimental and quasi-experimental studies have been well articulated and have entered much of the standard practice of research investigators. When a longitudinal approach is being considered, however, the investigator soon realizes that the usual canons of internal and external validity are inadequate to deal with an emergent set of methodological and substantive concerns.

This chapter is concerned with a number of these emergent issues. No attempt is made to be encyclopedically complete, but merely to illustrate a representative class of issues and problems. Three such sets of issues are discussed: changes in subjects; changes in methods; and changes in research environments.

## CHANGES IN SUBJECTS

In all the areas of development in methodology and research design, a paramount concern has been the isolation of main effect, treatment effect, or true variance from random change, error, or individual difference. Well established techinques of randomization, matching, standardization, and statistical adjustment have been developed. Design standards having to do with bias from selection or differential mortality, from regression toward the mean, and from maturation of subjects have been articulated and incorporated to some degree into most time-based research.

In the longitudinal design, however, these issues take on different meanings and have very different implications for the study. For example, *attrition* becomes a prominent design problem in longitudinal studies, for as a group is followed over time, one is increasingly studying survivors. If survivorship were a randomly distributed phenomenon or attribute, it would be no cause for concern. But, in many longitudinal studies, particularly those with a health focus, survivorship is correlated with many of the factors under investigation. In general, *the sick die young*, or at least are more likely to die younger than the well. Therefore it should not be particularly surprising to observe that a followed population gets healthier as it ages, since the sick ones are more likely to be dead.

Mortality, in the literal sense, is not merely a methodological contaminant in longitudinal studies — it is a significant outcome variable in its own right and needs to be dealt with conceptually as well as methodologically. In order to be incorporated into the design of the study however, mortality should be anticipated and appropriate provisions made for follow-up using at least the death certificate, but optimally also hospital and other records information from a surviving spouse or other informant.

Health-focused longitudinal studies raise several unique concerns. A major controversary exists around the problem of the management of treatments. For example, in following a group of cardiac patients, children with attention deficit disorders, or young adults with schizophrenia should the treatments provided to the subjects be controlled or should the subjects be allowed to seek whatever treatment they wish? Obviously, the puristic position would maintain that an uncontrolled or naturalistic treatment condition is unacceptable. A more moderate position, on other hand, would hold that treatments can be uncontrolled as long as the characteristics of the treatments are monitored and, if significant, dealt with in the analysis of the data in some appropriate manner. On the other hand, since the selection of the uncontrolled treatment is not random, the interpretation of the comparative treatment data would be difficult and imprecise.

Another issue in this area deals with the problem of the crossover of subjects from control to study population. Examples of this sort of issue are easy to identify: married controls who become widowed in the course of the study, normal controls who develop various disorders, or community dwelling controls who relocate to congregate or institutional environments. The investigator has at least two choices in dealing with crossover. First of all, the subject could be dropped from the study; one can conceive of a number of circumstances in which this would be done either for methodological or management reasons. Methodological grounds could be related to treatment, while management reasons could be related to such matters as bed space, therapy hours, or equipment access.

On the other hand, this crossover population, if sufficiently large, can provide us with significant premorbid data, especially the sort typically unavailable in most longitudinal studies. That is, in most health-related studies subjects are identified on the basis of an existing condition—the typical study is the time based comparison of a group of sick patients to a group well subjects. We may have medical records and some recall data from the patients, but neither is particularly satisfactory. It is only with the crossover subjects that the study has actual normative data on the premorbid state. Such events can therefore add significant insight to the study as long as adequate provision is made for incorporation of the issue of crossover subjects into the design of the study.

To summarize—longitudinal studies, particularly those in the health area, provide the investigator with two particular problems: mortality and crossover. Each can be seen as a nuisance, a source of error, a reason to drop subjects, or as an opportunity for analysis and further development. Though the circumstances may indicate one or another or these approaches, my obvious preference is for the last one. The value of incorporating mortality and crossover into the design is very great, for insights and propositions previously unanticipated might well emerge. Of course, the risk is that there will not be sufficient numbers of cases in either situation to merit an analysis that has any weight.

This risk must be borne, however, though the issue of case-finding that it raises is a significant one—and one without an obvious solution. Case finding, either for specific analysis or for the study in general, is not a problem unique to longitudinal studies, but the problem is certainly magnified in them. Again, examples are relatively easy to enumerate. The tremendous national decline in cardiac and stroke mortality, the enormous drop in the number of mentally ill persons committed to psychiatric hospitals, and the virtual elimination of various childhood diseases have made case finding for research in these areas enormously difficult—and thankfully so. By no means am I advocating the reinstitutionalization of hundreds of thousands of persons or the restoration of death rates to previously high levels for the sake of research. Rather, the comparative rarity of certain events or situations is a fact for inclusion in the general strategy and planning developed for the research. Some evidence must be provided that access to sufficient numbers of subjects is available and contingency planning must be developed for active case identification and follow up. Yet both scientific advancement and public policy development continually change the research environment in which we operate. Awareness of that changing environment seems to me essential for those who are embarking upon longitudinal investigation. In this aspect of longitudinal investigation, more so than in any other mode of research, the textbook model of the isolated investigator is inappropriate. The recognition of environmental factors and the development of approaches whereby such change can work to the benefit and advantage of the research is an essential part of the planning for longitudinal study. By planning and maintenance of proper openness of the design, the investigator can take advantage of fortuitous occurrences in the research environment and use them both to explore new areas of study and to support and complement ongoing work.

## CHANGES IN METHODS

Another class of changes can be handled with less facility, however, the whole set of changes having to do with scientific theory, conceptualization, and methodology. Science changes—either through revolution or through evolution—and concepts become more specialized, models become more sophisticated, measurement becomes more precise, and statistical methods become more powerful. Examples of such developments come readily to mind: changing criteria for identification and diagnosis in psychiatry has been embodied in the transition from DSMII to DSMIII; scale development in the mental health field has moved from global assessments to the precise differentiations of the Diagnostic Interview Schedule; a large-scale change in statistical data analysis stragegy has been brought about by LISREL in its various versions.

Each of these examples, and this is a truly selective list, could easily be magnified and multiplied several times over. My point is not to extend the list, but rather to illustrate the very serious and perhaps irresolvable problems that accompany such scientific development when seen from the context of longitudinal investigation.

Of the three sets of issues, developments in statistical data analysis techniques probably provide the least problem. That is, as developments in statistical analysis are made available, they can be assessed to determine their suitability to the research at hand. If they are suitable, and if the data from previous waves of the longitudinal study are available for use, then there is no problem. If previous data are no longer available or if they are not in a format appropriate to the procedure, or if the procedure requires a level of measurement unavailable in portions of the data, then there is trouble. The trouble is resolvable, but not easily. For example, an investigator might be faced with an extraordinarily difficult choice of gaining statistical power and efficacy by the laborious process of going back further in a longitudinal data set and facing the many problems involved in deriving usable data entries from pre-computer archives. Obviously, however, if the choice involves only the data analysis and does not affect the type of data collected, then there is no issue—both strategies can be pursued fruitfully.

On the other hand, if a more powerful data analytic strategy requires a different level of measurement, obtainable only through new scaling procedures or adoption of new instrumentation, then the problem not only reappears, but it is significantly magnified. This problem begs a more general question, however, regarding the development of new instrumentation in the course of a longitudinal study. More than any other single issue, this raises a question that is the critical one for longitudinal investigations.

A longitudinal investigator is confronted by perhaps the most difficult decision in the design of followup waves around the question of incorporating new instrumentation. Clearly, comparability is compromised whenever new instrumentation is adopted; therefore one position, maintained by some, would involve not doing it. This position, however, might then relegate the study to a state of irrelevance, unsophistication, or simply to a situation of being discredited by not being at the state of the art. Here there is clearly no best way, and the investigator must attempt to minimize loss rather than to maximize gain. No matter what, something is lost—either comparability or power. For a general operating strategy, I would propose maintaining some minimal comparability while aggressively pursuing state-of-the-art developments in instrumentation. This holds true for both pencil and paper types of instruments as well as the high technology tools of modern investigation known more by their acronyms: CT, PET, MRI, for example, than by their real names. Clearly, the burden is on the new instruments to demonstrate that their yield and precision is sufficiently great to warrant their incorporation. In addition, some selective use of older instruments, if feasible economically and not unduly burdensome to subjects, should probably be attempted for validation purposes.

The final concern in this section, that of conceptual development, is not a terribly difficult problem. For the most part, new concepts can be incorporated within an ongoing framework without any great trouble. In fact, if the raw data from various waves of the study are accessible then it is sometimes possible for past data to be reorganized in ways to incorporate the new concept or idea. Most times this will not be the case, however, and additional data will have to be gathered in future waves of the study. By and large, new concepts should be introduced as long as they are in keeping with the aim of the study and can provide some insight to the phenomena and relationships under investigation.

To summarize this section, longitudinal studies run the risk of the science base's moving out from under them. Whether the change is conceptual or technical, the investigator is continually faced with critical judgments assessing the yield of innovations in theory and method. The decision is a difficult one, for it typically involves considerations of the state-of-the-art and keeping pace with scientific development while, at the same time, maintaining valuable sets of data and observations which are irreplaceable and in which the investigator typically has personal investments. No matter which way the decision is made the costs are great, though it would seem that a price of outmodedness or irrelevance is too great to pay solely in order to keep a longitudinal data set intact.

## CHANGES IN RESEARCH ENVIRONMENTS

Though changes in subjects and changes in the science base can be anticipated during the course of longitudinal investigation, and sometimes can be used to the advantage of the study, there are other sources of changes that can have serious impacts. For the sake of convenience, these are summarized under the rubric of the research environment, that is, the culture and organization of scientific activity.

The culture of science is that set of rules—both explicit and implicit—around the nature of issues considered appropriate for research and around the methods considered acceptable for conduct of the study. In recent years, we have seen a major change in the nature of the culture of science and the introduction of public and even legal scrutiny of the research enterprise. This chapter is not the place to repeat the well-known examples of abuse or of questionable scientific or professional judgments that have laid the groundwork for much of the developments in this field. Let it be sufficient to enumerate several of these developments: privacy, confidentiality, voluntary informed consent, access to special population in research, access to medical and psychiatric records, the right to treatment, and the right to refuse treatment. Each of these developments has entered the culture of science and has affected both the conduct and the process of research in significant ways. Some of these developments have been relatively recent, but, nonetheless, at this point it is impossible to systematically enumerate and discuss in depth their impact on either cross-sectional studies or on short- or long-term longitudinal projects. Nonetheless, a few speculative examples can indicate the directions in which the culture of science is moving.

It appears, for example, that an increasing number of populations are being added to the list of specialized groups with which research must make special provisions. Such groups include prisoners, hospitalized psychiatric patients, and children. In general, it is now held that research can be done with these groups only if the study is relevant to the circumstance or condition that the individuals within these groups find themselves. For example, it is legitimate to do criminologic research on prisoners or psychiatric research on patients, but it is not legitimate to use either as a convenience sample or control group of adults for a study of nonspecifically relevant phenomena. Some would maintain that such provisions should be extended to the elderly, to nursing home residents, and to Alzheimer's disease patients. Should these activities result in broadening the definition of special populations then, clearly, several difficulties will emerge in longitudinal investigation.

A second area of significant change is in the confidentiality of records and restriction of access to personal information in a variety of medical, financial, and social areas. As the technological capability for linking of diverse computerized records has increased, so has the concern with privacy and confidentiality of these materials. It is likely that many of the protections used for individual medical records will be transferred to other areas as well. This move will, of course, have a serious negative impact on longitudinal studies in two ways: It will make more difficult the linking of records for multidimensional follow up and the identification of specialized subgroups for intensive or specialized study.

What is clear from just these few examples is that longitudinal research in many ways becomes more difficult as a result of these changes in the culture of science with many paying the penalty for the excesses of a few investigators who may have violated the often unspoken contract between investigator and subject. It is unlikely that any relaxation of these provisions will be forthcoming; the investigator must simply accommodate to the changes as they are introduced.

The organization of science is the final issue to raise in this discussion. Researchers can be based in a number of different settings: universities, hospitals, independent institutes, and corporations. Research can be supported through a number of mechanisms: government grants and contracts, donations, gifts, foundations, or corporations. The prototypic combination, however, is the government support of the university-based researcher, and I will restrict the discussion to this situation.

Government support of research through grants and contracts is a post-World War II invention. Prior to that, the government's interest in research was restricted to that carried out in its own laboratories. A famous series of post-war reports and commissions proposed the project grant system in pretty much the way it exists at the present time. The basic terms of this relationships between government and researcher involve the self-regulation of science through peer review and the vesting of authority in the National Science Board and the advisory councils of the Public Health Service. A second piece of the relationship involves the certification by the scientific community of the research and development paradigm, whereby basic science leads to applied research, which in turn leads to demonstration, evaluation, and finally to change. The funding agencies of government are put in the middle of this relationship by having to certify that the scientific process is producing results which, in turn, justify continuing public expenditures in the area. Through the appropriations process in the Congress, both the executives of the funding agencies and the investigators themselves, are called upon to provide input to the funding decision. There is a need for results in a short enough time to be useful in the appropriations process. Thus, the agency executive is faced with a difficult dilemma in balancing a research portfolio in such a way that results are available when needed while, at the same time, making sure that long-term follow-up can proceed. This problem, however, creates a situation in which the attractiveness of longitudinal studies—from a political standpoint—is low indeed. From this standpoint, all other things equal, it would be very useful for the design of a longitudinal study to incorporate mid-point milestones for which cross-sectional and early longitudinal findings could be made available through presentation and publication.

This procedure of developing mid-term findings is useful, as well, from another perspective, namely that of review. Either through statute, through custom, or through the tyranny of the printing press, the five-year term of a grant seems to be accepted as the maximum. Thus, the investigator is put in a position of having to show sufficient scientific progress over a roughly four-year period to justify continued support. Though many have argued that the five-year term is inadequate, it seems unlikely to change—at least in the direction of extension. Consequently, the investigator must accommodate to this periodic review requirement and make the best possible case for continuation. It would seem reasonable that the easiest way to do that is by building the types of milestones by means of which certain significant analyses could be accomplished prior to completion of the entire project.

The university base of the research poses yet an additional set of problems in longitudinal studies. Among the most significant issues is the question of tenured appointments and the granting of tenure. As in the other issues raised in this section, the question of tenure is intimately tied to the issues of scientific productivity. The primacy of "publish or perish" has been restored in academia, with the demographic contribution of the college-bound reducing even more the competing academic rule of "circulate or suffocate." Longitudinal studies, in their early years, typically do not provide the type of data upon which a great deal of publication can be based. Consequently, involvement in the early stages of a longitudinal study can be destructive to the career of the non-tenured faculty member.

Consequently, this message is both consistent and clear—for administrative, funding, and career reasons it is essential that mid-project reporting systems be incorporated into the design of longitudinal studies so that appropriate provision is made for the publication of results. As long as one does not make the methodological error of attributing longitudinal significance to cross-sectional findings, this should not cause any great difficulty. On the contrary, these findings can provide precisely that ammunition necessary to support continuation of the follow-up projects.

## CONCLUSION

In summary, in this chapter I have identified several unique challenges encountered in the design and execution of longitudinal studies. It should be clear that the recommendations I have made are neither exhaustive nor firm, for it is difficult to generate general prescriptions for specific problems or issues. The areas opened up by longitudinal research are exciting, however, and problems encountered should be seen as challenges rather than barriers or dead ends. Unique and significant possibilities are opened by longitudinal studies, and with proper attention and planning, exciting findings can emerge.